Renaissance of American Coinage 1909 – 1915

by
Roger W. Burdette

ISBN 0-9768986-2-4

P. O. Box 1423
Great Falls, Virginia 22066-1423

Printed in the USA by
Signature Book Printing
www.sbpbooks.com

Copyright 2007 by Roger W. Burdette

All rights reserved. No portion of the text or images contained in this publication, excepting short portions for critical review, may be reproduced in any form except with the written permission of the copyright holder. Certain images printed herein are the property of their respective owners and are used by permission.

No warranty or representation of any kind is made concerning the accuracy or completeness of the information presented herein, or its usefulness in numismatic sales or purchases, or its suitability for any purpose. The opinions of others may differ from those of the author and/or publisher.

Renaissance of American Coinage

1909 – 1915

by
Roger W. Burdette

Production
of

Renaissance of American Coinage 1909-1915

Was Underwritten
by

**Heritage Auctions, Inc.,
Dallas, Texas**

TABLE OF CONTENTS

Author's Preface and Acknowledgements ix
   About This Volume ix
     Sources x
     Acknowledgements x
Foreword xiii
Introduction 15
   Previous Designs 16
   Saint-Gaudens' Children 18
Chapter 1 – Connecting the Oceans 19
   New Coinage Designs 19
   Panama Canal Connection 21
   Silent Rivalry – Barber vs Brenner 24
Chapter 2 – Mr. Lincoln's Portrait 29
Chapter 3 – A Frenzy Throughout the Country 53
   Distribution... 67
   Brenner Fades Away 69
Chapter 4 – Patterns and Proofs 73
   Proof Coins 77
Chapter 5 – Novus Ordo Seclorum 81
   New Director, New Direction 81
   This Is Not A Square Deal – 1909 83
   General Washington's Nickel – 1909-1910 93
   Some Practices at the Mint 98
     The Director's Sting 100
     A Speculative Scenario 109
   Pattern Hub Destruction – An Inventory 112
Chapter 6 – A Better Metal 133
   Alloy Experiments 133
   Coinage Bill of 1912 137
     Perforated Planchets – The Mint Experiments 138
   The Treasurer's Treasure 146
Chapter 7 – Something of Real Merit 161
   The Fraser Approach 161
   MacVeagh and Company 163
   Fraser Meets the Mint 166
   Andrew Leaves the Treasury Department 175
Chapter 8 – Hobbs Goblins 179
   A Ferocious Looking Animal 185
   The Commission of Fine Arts 186
     Rostron Medal 189
   A Great Waste of Time 190
   Official Acceptance 194
   A Decision At Last 206
Chapter 9 – Most American of Coins... 211

A Tiny Memorial	211
Public Commentary	213
A Unity of Theme	216
Models for the Nickel – Obverse	218
Models for the Nickel – Reverse	222
Fraser's Coinage Legacy	225
Chapter 10 – Designs, Patterns & Proofs	**227**
Designs	229
Role of Patterns	233
Electrotype Patterns	234
U.S. Mint Patterns	241
Initial Production and Proofs	249
Chapter 11 – Design Changes	**251**
Later Hub Changes	257
Chapter 12 – Panama-Pacific International Exposition	**261**
The Exposition	262
Sculpture at the Exposition	264
Origin of the Commemorative Concept	266
Mint Bureau Preparations	267
Legislation Passed	268
Commemorative Coin Design	272
Producing the Coins	289
Missing Mintmark	290
Delivery of Dies	291
Souvenir Medal	293
Farran Zerbe – Marketing Coins and Medals	299
Mint Exhibit	300
Money of the World	302
Locking the Gates	310
Silver Half Dollar Design – Charles E. Barber	311
Gold Dollar Design – Charles Keck	313
Gold Quarter Eagle Design – Charles E. Barber	313
Gold Quintuple Eagle & Souvenir Medal Designs – Robert I. Aitken	315
Souvenir Medal Description	316
Award Medal – John F. Flanagan	317
Patterns and Proofs	319
Epilog and Ephemera	**321**
1913 Liberty Nickel	322
T. Louis Comparette – A Friend at Court	323
Appendix	**333**
Biographies	333
Bibliography	**341**
Index	**347**

Author's Preface and Acknowledgements

About This Volume

The scope of this volume differs somewhat from its companions. Volumes I (1905-1908) and III (1916-1921) stick closely to origin, design and early production of the respective circulating coins with limited exploration of other events at the Mint Bureau. This middle volume covers the cent and nickel circulation designs, but also branches out to explore events taking place at the Mint Bureau during the years between 1909 and 1915, including the Panama-Pacific International Exposition (PPIE) commemorative coins.

In this period we also find a great *terra incognito* of American numismatics: a nearly forgotten short-term mint director,[1] stories of special deals involving pattern coins, dealers buying rarities "direct" from mint employees, and a dozen other unsubstantiated "facts" clutter numismatic history. Some of these tales were cooked up by auctioneers and catalogers, others by collectors determined to establish preeminence in their specialty, yet others as sly cover for the truth. As will become evident, several events occurred which changed the course of the mint and coin collecting. Other supposed events either never occurred, or happened very differently than reported in contemporary hobby publications.

Although not regular circulating issues, the Panama-Pacific International Exposition commemorative coins carried forward the ideals encouraged by Saint-Gaudens and Roosevelt, only now the artists were from the succeeding generation. The exposition was the largest showcase of American art and industry held on the West Coast. It incorporated more than 635 acres of exhibits and amusements near San Francisco and included an extensive, highly publicized showcase for American painting and sculpture. Virtually every sculptor who had been involved in the new circulating coins, or who would later create circulating or commemorative designs during the first half of the twentieth century, exhibited

---

[1] The mint does not have an official medal of A. Piatt Andrew (November 1909–June 1910) or of his predecessor Frank A. Leach.

their talents at the exposition. The commemorative coin program was the most ambitious undertaken until the late twentieth century Olympic commemoratives. It was also, along with the redesign of subsidiary silver coins in 1916 (officially suggested by assistant secretary William P. Malburn while the PPIE coins were being designed), the last great expression of pre-war numismatic artistry on America's coinage.

For numismatists of today, this may be the most personal of the three volumes. Many a seasoned collector began his or her hobby searching pocket change for Lincoln "pennies" and Buffalo nickels; the day's finds carefully squeezed into openings of a blue and silver Whitman© coin folder. Those little folders may rest, still half completed, at the bottom of ten thousand storage trunks, holding memories as tightly as they hold their cargo. By the time most of America's circulating coinage boasted portraits of dead politicians, by the time those small, album-held treasures were nothing more than "average circ.," the gold coin had become nickel-clad copper and artists' works, monumental and prosaic, no longer inspired.

The renaissance begun by Roosevelt and Saint-Gaudens lasted as semi-official policy but twenty-five years. Some of the world's finest artists, home grown and adopted from Europe, tackled the problems of making tiny pieces of stamped metal into inspirational carriers of national pride. By 1932 political opportunism and bureaucratic caution turned our coinage away from the allegorical, toward the imitative, pseudo-realistic and commonplace.

Sources

Much of the basic research material about the Lincoln cent and Buffalo nickel comes from a microfilm collection (T620) and a document file prepared by the National Archives (now National Archives and Records Administration – NARA) staff in the early 1960s. These are the sources of most material in previously published accounts of the coins' creation. Archivists collected all the documents relating to these two coins and placed them in separate files. Regrettably, this removed most of the documents from their original context, making it more difficult to relate documents to one another. Although most relevant documents were identified and filed together, several escaped notice. These included letters in Mint Bureau press copy books, and correspondence from persons not obviously associated with the projects so far as the archivists could determine. Unfortunately, over time the physical files including some of the photos shown in Taxay's *U.S. Mint and Coinage,* have become separated from letters and telegrams.

Acknowledgements

Sincere appreciation is extended to the following individuals and organizations who have aided this project: David Alexander, Len Augsberger, Q. David Bowers, Ken Bressett, Joe Clossey, Mark Coffey, Jane Colvard, Beth Deisher, Richard Doty PhD, Henry Duffy PhD, Anne Evans, Michael S. Fey PhD, Bill Fivaz, Ann Benson Green, Nancy Green, Mark Hagan, Jim Halpern, Eleanor Harvey PhD, Mark Hooten PhD, Steve Ivy, D. Wayne ("Dick") Johnson, Robert Karrer, Douglas Mudd, James Ownby, Germana Pucci, David Plowman, Jeffrey M. Reichenberger, David Roepke, Saul Teichman, Judith Throm, Mark Van Winkle, Jane B. Waldron, Fred Weinberg, Wayne Wilcox; American Field Service, American Numismatic Association, American Numismatic Society, Ashland University Archives, Bowers & Merena Galleries, Inc., Bronx Zoo Library, California Historical Society, Commission of Fine Arts, Connecticut State Library, Heritage Auctions, Historical Society of Pennsylvania, Georgetown University, Goldberg Coins and Collectibles, Harvard University, Harry W. Bass, Jr. Foundation, Heritage Auctions, Johns Hopkins University, Library of Congress, Lockheed-Martin Corporation, Massachusetts Historical Society, Museum of San Francisco, National Cowboy & Western Heritage Museum, National Sculpture Society, Saint-Gaudens National Historic Site – National Park Service, Smithsonian Institution (Archives of American Art, Peter A. Juley & Son Collection, American Art Museum, Museum of American History, National Numismatic Collection, National Postal Museum), San Francisco Memories, Stack's of New York, Inc. (and the former American Numismatic Rarities), United States Mint, University of Chicago, University of Montana – Missoula, University of Nevada – Reno,

Special appreciation is extended to David W. Lange who generously lent the author his personal document and photo files on the Lincoln cent.

Artist Jane B. Waldron has produced yet another engaging and evocative cover design created around the central image of a Suffragette campaigning for women's voting rights. The title page image is of a young Yakima Nation woman, photographed in 1899.

Foreword

A hundred years ago, American coinage went through a true renaissance. Outside sculptors were brought into the mint, and coin designs were created that have remained unequaled since that time. The artistic impact of the coins produced during this era (1907-1921) continues to this day. The Lincoln cent has been in continuous production since 1909, Augustus Saint-Gaudens' double eagle design was resurrected in 1986 for the mint's gold bullion program, and most recently James Fraser's Buffalo nickel design was re-used for the mint's .999 gold bullion pieces in 2006. It was Roger Burdette's goal to examine as completely as possible this renaissance period of American coin designs. A noble and ambitious goal certainly, but this period had been examined by many numismatic writers in the past. How would his examination differ?

The first time I spoke with Roger was in connection with writing the book *The Coinage of Augustus Saint-Gaudens as Illustrated by the Phillip Morse Collection* (a.k.a. "The Morse Book"). Prior to the publication of Volumes I and III of his three-volume series, *Renaissance of American Coinage*, only a couple of articles had appeared in *Coin World* by this previously unknown author/researcher. From reading the *Coin World* articles, it appeared he could make a valuable contribution to the writing of our book and when I contacted him it was immediately obvious that he could. At that time, all I knew was the working title of his three-volume series and did not really comprehend the scope of what he was attempting. When I spoke to him I asked if he was familiar with Homer Saint-Gaudens' article in the June 1927 issue of *The Mentor* magazine. Yes, he replied, he was familiar with it and he would not consider it as a source for his book. His response initially surprised me. He explained that Homer's article was a secondary source, 20 years removed from events, and written by someone who was not actually involved in the process of producing the coins. It was then that I began to realize what Roger was attempting to publish: a comprehensive history of the renaissance of American coinage from its earliest inception in 1905 through the Peace dollar in 1921 based entirely on original source materials. When Volumes III and I were published in 2005 and 2006 respectively, they set a new standard for numismatic research. The reception of those two volumes was uniformly positive throughout the numismatic community, and predictably the 1916-1921 volume received the 2006 Book of the Year Award from the Numismatic Literary Guild.

Volume II (1909-1915), the present work, continues to examine the renaissance that began with Augustus Saint-Gaudens and President Theodore Roosevelt. This middle period covers three presidential administrations: the final days of Theodore Roosevelt, all of William Howard Taft, and the beginning of Woodrow Wilson's first term. Once again, splendid coins were designed in this period; coins that, for the most part, have a particularly American theme. Unlike the classically inspired Saint-Gaudens coinage, designs from this middle period feature the rail-splitter president, Abraham Lincoln, and the realistic depiction of a Native American on the Fraser-designed nickel of 1913 that is paired with an equally American bison on the reverse. The commemorative coins of the Panama-Pacific end Volume II. These coins combined the efforts of both mint engravers and outside talent. Together, these three volumes include nearly a thousand pages of detailed research using original sources.

There is some inevitable duplication of material from other works, most notably David Lange's books on the Lincoln cent and Buffalo nickel (to which Roger also was a contributor). However, most of this volume, as with Volumes I and III, presents material that is entirely new to collectors. As such, it represents a significant contribution to the numismatic knowledge of this important and extensively collected era in U.S. numismatics. Once again, Roger Burdette has raised the bar for numismatic research.

Mark Van Winkle
September 2007

Introduction

It is difficult to characterize the new gold coin designs of 1907 and 1908 as completely successful. Few ordinary citizens ever handled gold. Those who did were likely to be bank tellers and payroll clerks whose interest was in efficiency in counting and stacking the pieces. In a largely cash-based retail economy, counting house efficiency was more important than beauty. The 1907 Saint-Gaudens designs were admired by many who saw them, but there were complaints about the unnatural eagle on the reverse of the $10 coin, the somewhat "soft" detail to the Liberty portrait, and "missing" religious motto. Bela Pratt's designs were less well thought of, due in large measure to the experimental sunken relief used on the coins, and possibly the U. S. Mint's alteration of his Indian head portrait. The generally "scruffy" appearance of the coins – a result of the exposed fields being easily damaged – only added to the problem.

Augustus Saint-Gaudens died in August 1907, but his little army of former assistants had already fanned out over the artistic countryside to preach and keep the faith. These successors to America's Gilded Age worked amid rumblings of new arts and perceptions beneath post-Victorian society. By late 1908 Roosevelt's eclectic view of the world and political progressivism placed him outside the mainstream of his Republican Party. William Howard Taft had been elected president in November and Taft's agenda was managerial not imperial. The progressive and personal energy of Roosevelt's administration quickly dissipated – four years later Roosevelt would try for the White House one final time, without Republican Party backing.

Roosevelt's final numismatic acts were to "suggest" the use of Victor David Brenner's portrait of Abraham Lincoln on a circulating coin, and to then approve its use on the one-cent piece. Roosevelt played little role in the coin's design except to veto use of a Roman "V" in place of Latin "U" in the coin's inscriptions.

The collaboration of Saint-Gaudens and Roosevelt had begun a process of artistic change, however undefined and *ad hoc* it might seem. Numismatists of the twenty-first century often hold the Saint-Gaudens double eagle, particularly the extremely high relief version or its sister high relief issue, as America's most beautiful coin design. For beauty of composition and detail, it probably deserves all the accolades. The extension of William Sturgis Bigelow's technical innovation for the half eagle came as much a natural consequence, as did Bela Pratt's realistic Native American portrait. Yet, it is the humble buffalo nickel, stuff of street car rides, candy machines and soda pop, that may well be the most completely and convincingly American of any coin issued by this nation. The only anachronistic element in the entire redesign period is Brenner's weak, mediocre Lincoln standing as much an individual as emblem. During the fourteen year period between 1907 and 1921 the United States Treasury Department performed the most radical redesign of the nation's coinage ever attempted. Every denomination was redesigned, and with the exception of the $2½ and $5 gold coins, each denomination had its own unique design. Special commemorative coins were also issued – five of them gold. New technology increased productivity just when the nation's economy demanded more coin for daily commerce. In the personal economy of most wage earners, the need for coins in circulation varied with every change in local employment patterns.

Previous Designs

The introduction of steam powered presses and rolling mills in 1836 led to the complete redesign of all denominations by 1840. This effort resulted in monotonous consistency: all gold coins shared the same basic design, all silver shared its design, and the copper cent and half-cent also had their own design.

Figure 1. Cent designs from 1859 to 1909, and nickel designs from 1866 to 1912. Note omission of the motto IN GOD WE TRUST on all designs except the shield nickel. The flying eagle cents of 1857-58 were rarely seen in circulation by 1909. The cent and nickel were redesigned during the 1909-1915 period.

Occasional variety was introduced as Congress mandated new denominations, yet the overall appearance of America's circulating coins was of uniformity. The coinage system had been simplified by the Act of 1873, and again in 1890[2], which eliminated duplicative and under utilized denominations, but the designs for the remaining coins were left intact. The Longacre "Indian" cent, in circulation since 1859 and Liberty nickel design, since 1883, were engraved entirely by U.S. Mint personnel. It was among the minor denominations that greater variety of design existed, yet these, too, fell far below contemporary standards for public art. By the end of the nineteenth century they were viewed by many as tired, out of date designs. Occasional new designs were proposed by mint engravers during the early 1880s, but the only result was replacement of Longacre's simple graphics on the five-cent piece with a chubby portrait of *Liberty* by engraver Charles E. Barber in 1883.[3]

By 1890 the Treasury department sought to bring in talented artists from outside the U. S. Mint to redesign subsidiary silver coins.[4] This was commonplace done in Europe and the artistic quality of some European coinage, particularly the French, was admired by many in the treasury department. A competition was organized, abandoned, replaced, reorganized and again abandoned. The inexperience of Treasury officials in dealing with independent, professional artists resulted in the silver coins being redesigned by mint engraver Charles E. Barber. Although the mint director exercised considerable control over the work, there was little he could do about the lack of creativity and variety in the mint engraver's output. Thus were born the stuffy, graceless Liberty Head dime, quarter and half dollar – better known to hobbyists as the "Barber coins."[5]

The Barber subsidiary silver designs were widely disliked by artists and efforts began to replace them almost as soon as they were issued in 1892. Through the administrations of Presidents Cleveland and McKinley, and the tenure of six mint directors ideas for replacement designs bubbled just below the surface. The mint staff engravers were, understandably, protective of their role in designing the nation's coins, and for more than a hundred years they had successfully resisted attempts to make them share that role with others.[6] When President Theodore Roosevelt took office after McKinley's assassination in 1901, a new more vibrant attitude came to the Executive Departments of the Government. It was clearly evident from political, military, economic and social impetus that Roosevelt was not going to tolerate a "second rate America" – in anything. Although the great issues of the day did not include the nation's coinage, Roosevelt devoted an unusual amount of time to its improvement. His grand plan was for a complete redesign of the nation's coins, but after talking with the country's most prominent sculptor, Augustus Saint-Gaudens, Roosevelt settled for beginning with the eagle and double eagle gold coins. The story of the gold coin redesign is told in a companion to this volume; likewise for the silver subsidiary coinage. For the 1909 and 1913 minor coin redesign and Panama-Pacific com-

---

[2] 51st Congress, Session I, Chapter 945 – *An act to discontinue the coinage of the three-dollar and one-dollar gold pieces and three-cent nickel pieces.* Passed September 26, 1890.
[3] Barber's title was "Engraver of the United States Mint at Philadelphia" other engravers at the mint had the title of "Assistant Engraver." The familiar term "chief engraver" is a modern invention used infrequently in contemporary mint correspondence.
[4] Charles Barber and George Morgan dominated the mint's engraving staff. Both men were British natives. Barber acquired his position due to being assistant to his father who had been engraver from 1869 to 1879. Morgan was hired because of the lack of suitable American-trained artists, and mint director Linderman's doubts about William Barber's artistic and engraving skills.
[5] Ed Reiter, *Coin Design Contests: They've Given Us Some Prize Winners*, PCGS Articles, October 25, 1999. www.pcgs.com/articles/.
[6] Reiter, op cit.

memorative coinage, the momentum for change, begun with President Roosevelt and Saint-Gaudens, continued but with a wider audience.

Saint-Gaudens' Children

He was called "The Saint" by his assistants; the "greatest of American artists" by French admirers; "charming" by visitors and "utterly demanding" by those seeking his opinion. To a great extent, the post-Civil War sculptors of America looked to Augustus Saint-Gaudens as the most accomplished artist of the Gilded Age. His New York, and later Cornish, New Hampshire studios and workshop were home to a long list of artists destined for notoriety among creative Americans. Every designer of American coins from 1907 to 1921, with the exception of Victor Brenner, had been a Saint-Gaudens assistant or student, or worked under one of the Saint's assistants, and all felt his dominant influence in their early careers.

Saint-Gaudens' children were not the son, Homer, borne by his wife Augusta, or the secret son by his mistress Davida Johnson Clark, Louis nicknamed "Novy." These were biological offspring. His real children were the generation of American artists born in the 1870s and 1880s, who studied with him, worked for him, imitated his works, occasionally pawned his gold medals, and eventually found their own place in the cauldron of architects, illustrators, sculptors, painters and writers that bubbled in the New World. The Saint had a knack for picking potential genius from the midst of good artists and nurturing it to independence. His ethic was demanding and his criticism unwaveringly honest; many a wishful-thinking artist had his efforts dissected by Saint-Gaudens. He played no favorites. Reputation, political connections, wealth or influence offered no protection from inferior art or technique. Yet his critique was always balanced; the dissection was invariably followed by suggestions to reassemble the creative corpus and ultimately led to stronger, more expressive work by the supplicant.

His array of assistants and students included many of the early twentieth century's best sculptors: Philip Martiny, John Flanagan, Frederick W. MacMonnies, Mary Lawrence Tonetti, Adolph Weinman, Charles Keck, James Fraser, Bela Pratt, A. Phimister Procter, Elsie Ward, Albert Jaegers, Francis Grimes and Henry Hering.

James Earle Fraser, often called "Jim," may have been the Saint's most significant find. Talented, intelligent, astute, Fraser was already a good sculptor when Saint-Gaudens saw his work in the Paris Salon of 1898. Adopted as one of the many assistants, Jim Fraser matured quickly, establishing himself as the best of American national sculptors by the Panama-Pacific Exposition of 1915.

In turn, these artistic children of Saint-Gaudens nurtured another generation, among which was coin designer Anthony de Francisci.

Chapter 1 – Connecting the Oceans

Many numismatists think of President Theodore Roosevelt's involvement in the nation's coinage as ending with the Saint-Gaudens and Pratt gold coins. Volumes have been written describing the exhilarating artistic-political collaboration of 1905-1908; however, limited attention has been paid to redesign of the other coin included in Roosevelt's plan – the bronze cent or "penny." Few also realize there are really two themes to the origin of the Lincoln cent story: one follows Theodore Roosevelt's ideas about redesigning American coinage; the other is the quest for a waterway connection between the Atlantic and Pacific oceans. These themes diverge, then reconnect six years later with the Panama-Pacific Exposition.

New Coinage Designs

The new one-cent coinage story begins in 1904.[7] President Roosevelt, with suggestions from painter Frank Millet and wife Edith, had concluded that coins American workers carried in their pockets and received in pay envelopes were in need of artistic improvement. He wrote to secretary of the treasury Leslie Mortier Shaw:[8]

> My dear Secretary Shaw:
> I think our coinage is artistically of atrocious hideousness. Would it be possible, without asking permission of Congress, the employ a man like Saint-Gaudens to give us a coinage that would have some beauty?
> Sincerely yours,

By mid-January 1905 Roosevelt had cajoled Augustus Saint-Gaudens into creating a special Inaugural medal and agreeing to redesign the United States coinage. The presi-

---

[7] See Burdette, *Renaissance of American Coinage 1905-1908* for a detailed account of events leading to the design and production of new gold coins by Saint-Gaudens and Pratt, and for information on the abandoned cent designs.
[8] *Roosevelt Letters*, Harvard, op. cit., vol. 4, p.1088. Letter dated December 27, 1904 to Leslie Mortier Shaw from Roosevelt.

dent's plan was to have America's most renowned artist provide new designs for all coinage denominations – cent through double eagle. After checking with treasury secretary Shaw and learning that designs could not be changed more frequently than once every twenty-five years, he settled for modifying the gold coins and bronze cent. When Saint-Gaudens formally accepted the coinage commission in July 1905 for the sum of $5,000, it included only obverse and reverse designs for the gold coins (one pair of designs to be used on all four circulating denominations), and the cent.

It appears Roosevelt thought the whole process would take only a few months, but it dragged on for nearly two years. Variations on one composition or another were proposed, with the $20 double eagle gold coin receiving most of the attention. Saint-Gaudens presented a nearly completed design for this coin to Roosevelt in December 1906, and in February 1907, a design for the cent.[9] The president's personal interests led to further adjustments and addition of a Native American war bonnet to the cent obverse portrait.

Figure 2. Saint-Gaudens' 1907 designs for the bronze cent. At left is the original obverse submitted in February, at center is the revised obverse with Indian headdress requested by Roosevelt. At right is the final reverse. (Courtesy National Park Service, Saint-Gaudens National Historic Site, Cornish, NH.)

In late May 1907 Roosevelt decided to use the Liberty with Indian headdress, intended for the cent, on the $10 eagle gold coin. The small bronze cent, lacking in regal presence possessed by the large gold coins, was not important to the President and was dropped from consideration at that time.

In early 1908, with Saint-Gaudens' designs in use on the $20 and $10 coins and the great artist dead, the plan was to use the double eagle design on the half and quarter eagle coins. However, before the final versions were accepted, Roosevelt decided to follow a suggestion from his long-time friend, Dr. William Sturgis Bigelow, to use the portrait of a Native American (Indian) on the $5 gold coin. The idea included use of sunken relief rather than normal relief as Saint-Gaudens had done. Bigelow's idea and Bela Pratt's design were accepted in May 1908 and issued for circulation in November of the same year on both $5 and $2.50 gold coins.

All four gold denominations were now complete and Roosevelt turned his attention to the one-cent coin. With the centennial of Abraham Lincoln's birth approaching in February 1909, Roosevelt was intrigued with the idea of commemorating the first Republican president on a coin. Booklets, tokens, medals and memorial plaques honoring Lincoln were already commonplace and a coin seemed the obvious official recognition of Lincoln's contribution to the nation. A half dollar was frequently suggested by correspondents to the

---

[9] See Burdette, *Renaissance of American Coinage 1905-1908* for detailed information on Saint-Gaudens cent designs.

treasury department, but that would require congressional action and Roosevelt did not want congress involved. The President was already a "lame duck" and his anointed successor, Taft, had easily captured the Republican presidential nomination in June 1908.

Roosevelt had also been stung by the lack of general notice and acceptance of the new gold coins. Artistic praise came for Saint-Gaudens' designs from connoisseurs, but little except complaint from commercial interests. This should not have been a surprise, since few ordinary Americans handled large denomination gold coins. His personal secretary, William Loeb, wrote to the American Numismatic Association on September 24, 1908:[10]

> ....The president took the advance ground last year and did all he could but received very little support from public opinion. He does not know what more he can do, but he will of course do whatever he can.

Pratt's design earned limited public recognition and generated further gripes from those resistant to change. In this situation, all Roosevelt wanted was a Lincoln coin – a cent was fine since it was part of the original plan – but a five-cent coin was also acceptable since that piece was now eligible for redesign, too. Engraver of the United States Mint at Philadelphia, Charles Edward Barber, was aware of the approaching centennial and had wanted to design a Lincoln nickel, but was dissuaded from this when the President informed mint director Leach that he liked Victor Brenner's memorial medallion of Lincoln, and thought it might make a good coin. Barber then concentrated his efforts on a Washington portrait intended for use on the five-cent coin.

Unlike the 1905–07 Saint-Gaudens collaboration, neither the Pratt gold coins nor Brenner's Lincoln cent were of personal interest to President Roosevelt. Neither artist received personal notes of encouragement or letters of appreciation from the Chief Executive approaching the scale of Saint-Gaudens.[11] The President did not openly praise or promote the new coins as he had those of Saint-Gaudens, and no one encouraged collectors to obtain examples of special versions as had been done in 1907. The few pattern and experimental pieces made were systematically melted on orders from the director, with none kept for the mint's own cabinet of coins. The cynical might conclude that Roosevelt saw no political value in either Pratt or Brenner, so associating them with his administration was unimportant. He may also have recognized that no American artist had emerged to claim the stature of Saint-Gaudens.

Panama Canal Connection[12]

A canal connecting the two great oceans through the isthmus of Panama was a dream long held by European and American businessmen. Several companies were organized to build a canal, but none succeeded. The only European company to attempt construction was the French *Compagnie Universelle du Canal Interoceanique* from 1881-1889. The United States finally purchased rights and property from the French successor

---

[10] *The Numismatist.* October-November, 1908, p.315-317. Committee report delivered by Thomas Elder.

[11] Brenner received a framed and signed letter and a copy of the Panama Canal Service medal from Roosevelt in appreciation of his work. By the time the new cent was issued Roosevelt was in Africa on a wild game hunt.

[12] Background material for this section based on an article by Todd Wheatley, "The Panama Canal Service Medal – The 'Junk' Medal," *The Medal Collector*, November 1983. There are also several letters in the mint archives for 1909–1910 referring to the medal and its production.

firm for $40 million in gold with the assets accepted April 23, 1904, under authority of the Panama Canal (Spooner) Act of 1902.[13]

President Roosevelt put the United States squarely on the side of a canal and was instrumental in promoting a "revolution" in the northern part of Colombia, which then controlled the isthmus. When the smoke cleared, the U.S. had exclusive rights to build a canal, locks and infrastructure to connect the Atlantic and Pacific through the new country of Panama. In the fall of 1906 President Roosevelt visited the Canal Zone. During extemporaneous remarks in a speech at the close of his visit to the city of Cristobal he said:

> I shall see if it is not possible to provide for some little memorial, some mark, some badge, which will always distinguish the man who for a certain space of time has done his work well on this Isthmus.

In December 1906, the New York *Tribune* published the following statement released by the White House:

> ...Medals of a suitable character are to be given to all citizens of the United States who have served the government satisfactorily on the Isthmus of Panama for two years. A competent artist will be engaged and the design for a medal prepared. President Roosevelt is anxious that suitable tribute to, and recognition of service shall be shown by the government, and believes the effect will be salutary and wholesome.

It wasn't until December 23, 1907, when Roosevelt wrote to Colonel George W. Goethals, chairman of the Isthmian Canal Commission, that anything official was done. The letter "... direct[ed] that the details of the scheme be perfected by the Commission." By April 27, 1908 the commission had decided on eligibility rules and the basic design of the medal:

> (a) It shall be approximately the size of an American silver dollar and shall be of composition of bronze from old French canal scrap.
>
> (b) On one side shall be a medallion head of President Roosevelt, and on the other side the seal of the Canal Zone.
>
> (c) The medal shall be inscribed, "For Two Years Continuous Service on the Panama Canal" and "Presented by the President of the United States."
>
> (d) Each medal shall be engraved with the name of the employee, the number of the medal and the years included by his two years service.

By mid-1908 the minor uproar caused by Saint-Gaudens' eagle and double eagle designs had subsided. Nearly all the experimental and special coins of the previous year had been distributed and controversy surrounding the religious motto settled. Bela Pratt's Indian head and modified edition of Saint-Gaudens' standing eagle were complete and models approved by the president (with Dr. Bigelow's urging). Before leaving on vacation, director Leach apparently told Barber that he appreciated his efforts on the gold coinage and that he would try to convince the president to use the engraver's designs on a Lincoln coin, and possibly a Washington coin as well.

With hot summer weather came a slower pace in Philadelphia and Washington. Both cities were known for sultry summer months and in the days before air conditioning, everyone who could leave town, did so. The president traveled to Oyster Bay, Long Island

---

[13] See NARA-CP Record Group 185, *Records of the Panama Canal*.

in June, not to return until autumn.[14] Secretary Cortelyou headed to his summer house in New Hampshire. Congressmen and Senators vanished into as many rustic cabins, lodges and summer homes. Director Leach took the train to Oakland to visit his home state of California and see his son Edwin, who had worked at the San Francisco Mint the previous year.[15] Philadelphia Mint management left town too, although for more modest vacations. Superintendent Landis and family went to visit his parents' farm in Indiana, leaving operations in the hands of Dr. Albert A. Norris. Engraver Barber took his annual vacation at Cape May, New Jersey feeling reasonably assured that, unlike the previous August, no one would demand his return from holiday to fix the design work of some "high class artist."[16]

Barber enjoyed an uninterrupted rest at the Atlantic shore. On his return in September, he began cutting hubs for the new sunken relief half and quarter eagles. While these were slowly being formed by the Janvier reducing lathe, the engraver began his models of President Washington.[17] According to director Leach, Washington's portrait would be used on the cent or nickel, although no decision had been reached about which denomination.

The summer vacation season had barely concluded when Leach learned of the Panama Canal medal from Barber:[18]

> ...When I was in Philadelphia a few weeks ago Mr. Barber told me that he had heard that the Panama Canal Commission intended to issue some medals – quite a large number. Yesterday a gentleman from their office called upon me to see about getting them struck at your Mint, and in conversation I learned that when the idea of issuing the medals was first proposed, a draughtsman in the employ of the Commission submitted a design for the medals, which was subsequently given to Mr. [Frank] Millet to make the models, [and] upon his recommendation [Victor] Brenner of New York was employed to make the dies. These dies are about completed. The Commission desires the medals to be struck from bronze recovered on the isthmus from old French material that was used in the original canal enterprise....

On February 10, 1909, *The Canal Record* announced that 1,000 pounds of "French scrap" had been sent to the Philadelphia Mint by the Chief Quartermaster of the Isthmian Canal Commission. The first shipment included twenty-five pounds of staybolts, thirty pounds of excavator bearings, twenty-four pounds of bushings, another lot of twenty-eight pounds of excavator bearings, and thirty-five pounds of locomotive driver bearings, all taken from old French equipment. Director of the Mint Frank Leach had the "junk" assayed and advised the Commission that the only metal acceptable or striking the medals was contained in the staybolts. As a consequence, a total of 1,000 pounds of staybolts were shipped to Philadelphia. This was sufficient to make all the medals and service bars.

On April 14, 1909 samples of the medal were received by the Isthmian Canal Commission and production began of the first 5,000 pieces at the Philadelphia Mint. By June 23, 1909 the Commission had decided "...that Canal Medal bars be numbered consecu-

---

[14] *Roosevelt Letters*, Harvard, op. cit., vol. 8, appointment calendar.
[15] *US Mint*, NARA-CP, record group 104, entry 229, box. 256. Letter dated August 14, 1907 to Preston (as acting director) from Leach.
[16] See Burdette, *Renaissance of American Coinage 1905–1908* for additional information on Barber's role in coining Saint-Gaudens' designs. The comment was made by director Edward Leech in 1891 and aimed at Saint-Gaudens and other professional sculptors and painters.
[17] It took approximately one day to cut a single 20mm diameter hub on the Janvier lathe.
[18] *US Mint*, NARA-CP, op. cit., entry 235, vol. 368, p.827. Letter dated October 1, 1908 to Landis from Leach. See also pp.832, 916, 931 and 1005 for Canal Medal information.

tively to show the order in which each is earned, and that the years of service represented be also indicated thereon." The first production medals were delivered on September 3, 1909 with 2,264 pieces arriving on the steamship *Colon*. Distribution began immediately.

Figure 3. Panama Canal medal designed by Frank Millet and sculpted by Victor Brenner in August 1908. (Courtesy David Plowman and Robert Karrer.)

Numismatists have generally thought the medal was designed by Victor D. Brenner, however *The Canal Record* of October 29, 1913 notes that the designer was Francis (Frank) D. Millet – no stranger to collectors of American medals, especially those of the United States Army.[19] The medalist was identified as Victor M.[sic] Brenner. Additional research supports Millet's role as designer, although Brenner prepared the models and had at least two portrait sittings with President Roosevelt at Oyster Bay, New York.[20] It was during one of these sittings, in August 1908, that Brenner showed the president a bronze desk plaque he had made as a speculative venture.

Thus, Roosevelt's interest in new coinage designs, and the Panama Canal led directly to redesign of the one-cent coin, and the artist who created the composition.[21]

Silent Rivalry – Barber vs Brenner

There had been an increasing deluge of souvenirs for several years leading to the centennial of Abraham Lincoln's birth. Among these were numerous medals by artists both skilled and inept. Europeans had long ago adopted Lincoln as an iconic American symbol and medalists from many countries produced works of exceptional quality and spirit.

---

[19] Millet was a painter of international reputation and had also designed several service medals for the Army in 1904-06. He was not a sculptor and deferred to others to model his designs. It is unfortunate that Brenner placed his name in a prominent position behind Roosevelt's shoulder, but omitted the designer's name. The Army medals likewise fail to include Millet's name or initials on the pieces, although they are properly credited in Army literature.

[20] See the letter quoting Charles Barber, below.

[21] Another connection is that painter Frank Millet suggested to Roosevelt that Saint-Gaudens design the 1905 Inaugural medal, as well as being the designer of the Canal medal.

Among American medal and coin collectors there was considerable speculation about a circulating Lincoln half dollar or a series of official medals. As speculation on a coin featuring Lincoln grew, many wondered if it would be better to honor the first President, George Washington, on a coin also. Washington's own admonition not to use his portrait on a coin was contrasted with his stature as the most honored of Presidents. Engraver Chares Barber was aware of events and prepared preliminary designs for a Washington five-cent coin, but had nothing featuring Lincoln as 1908 drew to a close.

Cent documentation in the Mint Bureau files begins in January 1909 with an exchange of letters between sculptor Victor Brenner and director Frank Leach. At this point it appears events had already moved toward use of Brenner's design for the cent. It would have been logical for the director to be looking for something prepared by his mint to show the president in competition with Brenner's medallion. However, the only coin available was an 1866 pattern five-cent piece (Judd-486, Pollock-575) featuring a portrait of Lincoln prepared by mint engraver James B. Longacre. Although this was sufficient for use by numismatist Robert Hewett in a publication about the Lincoln centennial[22] it gave Leach nothing to show the President in competition with Brenner's medal.[23]

Figure 4. President Theodore Roosevelt (left) and sculptor Victor David Brenner. Both portraits date from approximately 1908 although not at the time Roosevelt was posing for the Panama Canal medal. Notice the President poses with his hand on a globe; compare with President Taft's portrait (see Chapter 2) made the following year. (Courtesy Library of Congress, and George Grantham Bain collection, right.)

Brenner obviously had the President's interest, and confirmed this on January 4, 1909 when he commented, "I was thinking of embodying the portraying of Mr. Lincoln in the cent piece, and find that it will compose very well."[24] Brenner further obviated Barber making a Lincoln design on January 6 when he wrote, "I am glad to say that the president

---

[22] *US Mint*, NARA-CP, op. cit., entry 235, vol. 376. Letter dated January 2, 1909 to Landis from Leach.
[23] *US Mint*, NARA-CP, op. cit., entry 235, vol. 376. Letter dated January 8, 1909 to Landis from Leach.
[24] *US Mint*, NARA-CP, op. cit., entry 1A 328I, folder "Coins, Lincoln Cent History." Letter dated January 4, 1909 to Leach from Brenner.

has a copy of my Lincoln medal and likes it very much. On several occasions I noticed the keen sense of art the president has."[25] Roosevelt had nothing of Barber's to hold in his hand and ponder. Even if he had, the larger bronze medal was much more impressive than a cent-sized pattern.

For his part, engraver Charles Barber had no doubt that he and assistant George Morgan were the best artists to design the nations coins and medals. In response to praise from director Leach about the Atlantic Fleet medal, a cooperative design by Barber and Morgan, the engraver wrote: [26]

> ...It is very gratifying to Mr. Morgan and myself to find that our effort to commemorate an event so important in the history of our Navy has met with such general approval, and if it has helped to establish our contention, namely that the Mint service is not compelled to call for outside talent for the execution of medallic work, either coin or historical medals, then surely this medal has served a double purpose...

Figure 5. Atlantic Fleet medal (reverse) by Barber and Morgan, struck starting in January 1909. The obverse copied Barber's portrait of President Roosevelt from the U.S. Mint's 1905 Inaugural medal. (NARA.)

Events were moving very quickly in part because Brenner already had a finished model of the Lincoln bust, which he shipped to Washington on January 18. It appears that by the first of February, Leach had decided to concentrate Barber's efforts on a Washington portrait for the five-cent coin. Although the President would make the final decision, and Leach continued to imply that either the cent or nickel were possibilities, Barber was already at work on a Washington nickel:[27]

> ...We have only two coins on which we can make a change now, the penny and the nickel. For one of these coins I had already requested Mr. Barber to submit a

---

[25] *US Mint*, NARA-CP, op. cit., entry 1A 328I. Letter dated January 6, 1909 to Leach from Brenner.
[26] *US Mint*, NARA-CP, op. cit., entry 229, box 270. Letter dated January 21, 1909 Leach from Barber. According to a postscript, two hundred thirty-seven of the medals struck to commemorate the Atlantic Fleet's departure from Hampton Roads, Virginia on an around the world cruise, had been sold as of the letter's date.
[27] *US Mint*, NARA-CP, op. cit., entry 1A 328I. Letter dated February 2, 1909 to Brenner from Leach.

design, and therefore I can only use your design, if it is accepted, on the penny or the nickel.

With a Lincoln design by Barber effectively eliminated, the engraver focused attention on his design for a Washington piece. Since Brenner seemed to prefer the one-cent coin, the outside sculptor was assigned the lowly cent, and Barber concentrated on perfecting his Washington five-cent coin.[28] Both Leach and Barber felt the five-cent piece was the most commonly used coin in the country, and Leach felt this was the superior denomination. The nickel was also larger than the cent and would give Barber more space in which to perfect his design.

---

[28] See below for more information on Barber's Washington nickels dated 1909 and 1910.

Chapter 2 – Mr. Lincoln's Portrait

The earliest available letter mentioning Victor Brenner's coin designs was written to director Frank Leach in response to a meeting held prior to January 4, 1909. It is likely the subject was discussed between them in late December, possibly much earlier:[29]

> My dear Mr. Leach:
> When I had the pleasure of being with you, I forgot to ask you what sum Mr. St Gaudens received for his models of the eagle's head and also what Mr. Pratt got for his.
> I was thinking of embodying the portraying of Mr. Lincoln in the cent piece, and find that it will compose very well.
> With the seasons best wishes,
> Very truly yours,
> V. D. Brenner

Their conversation a few days earlier apparently had covered a possible half dollar and five-cent coin design in addition to the cent. Leach replied on the 5th and Brenner wrote back on January 6:[30]

> Many thanks for your letter of yesterday. I am glad to say that the President has a copy of my Lincoln medal and likes it very much.
> On several occasions I noticed the keen sense of art the president has, and feel sure that with your appreciation and his we will arrive to have(?) a set of coins that will be a pleasure to all.

The "Lincoln medal" referred to was a desk medal produced in 1908 by Gorham Company for Brenner. It was a speculative venture from which Brenner hoped to earn a significant profit. This medal was to become the prototype for Brenner's cent obverse although it depicts Lincoln with curly rather than straight hair. Victor Brenner was possibly

---

[29] *US Mint*, NARA-CP, op. cit., entry 1A 328I. Letter dated January 4, 1909 to Leach from Brenner.
[30] *US Mint*, NARA-CP, op. cit., entry 1A 328I. Letter dated January 6, 1909 to Leach from Brenner.

the leading medalist in the United States at this time. His direct, realistic style and prodigious output suggested an artist at the top of his craft. Although not one of Saint-Gaudens' students or assistants, he was thoroughly familiar with the Saint's style and approach to portraiture.

Figure 6. Lincoln commorative desk medal produced by Gorham Co. from Victor Brenner's models. Notice the artist's signature at the rim to the left of Lincoln. Compare with the lead impression in Figure 13, below. (Courtsy Smithsonian Institution, Peter A. Juley & Son archive, photo by Johnathan Williams.)

The immediate inspiration for this medallic portrait (and a 1907 rectangular plaquette) appears to be an 1864 photograph of President Lincoln taken in Mathew Brady's

Figure 7. Photo of Abraham Lincoln taken in 1864 (left). This may have been Brenner's inspiration for his portrait used on the cent. There are, however, many differences between the photo and Brenner's rendition. The photo on the right, of the President and his son, Tad, may also have been part of the artist's inspiration (The image on the right was heavily retouched by photographer Anthony Berger.) (Courtesy Library of Congress.)

Washington, D.C. studio by assistant Anthony Berger. However, a letter written by Brenner and published on April 1, 1909 opens the possibility that the medalist also had in mind a portrait of the President reading to his son, Tad.[31]

> ...I have made Lincoln smiling. You will see it on the coin. I wanted to show the sunshine as well as the goodness of life. Indeed, I had [been] hard put to find a photograph of him in which the slightest idea of a smile appeared. At last I found one.
> Then I began to study out a situation in which Lincoln might have appeared at his brightest. I finally imagined him as talking to a child. And that is the face on the coin.
> Do you know, a man or woman is natural when speaking to a child. When I talk to you or you to me we are on our guard. It is always that way with adults.
> But when we talk to children our faces relax and we are at our best. So I tried to imagine Lincoln.

The article concludes with a comment that the photo mentioned by Brenner was owned by Eliot Norton of New York, and that the sculptor had been working on the portrait for "more than a year." If both the individual portrait and one with Tad were taken the same day in 1864, as most sources claim, it is possible the trace of a smile on the President's face was due to his son's presence.

By mid-January, Brenner's next letter indicated he was forwarding the Lincoln cent model to Washington.[32]

> By ex[press] please receive plaster models for the Lincoln cent which if it pleases you and the president as it is, or with some changes, it could be ready for a formal acceptance for the 22 of Feb. the date of Mr. Lincoln's birth.
> I am working on the other models, and improving them, and they will be finished and coming soon.
> Awaiting your favor,
> I am, very sincerely yours,

The mint director took the cent models to the White House on the morning of January 30 and showed them to President Roosevelt. Upon returning to the treasury building, Leach wrote to Brenner informing the sculptor Roosevelt was pleased with the initial designs:[33]

> I had the pleasure of showing your beautiful model of the Lincoln head and the reverse design for the one cent piece to the president this morning. The president was greatly pleased with the models and authorized me to use them if it can be done legally. This is a matter I am now taking up with the Secretary and Comptroller, and it is possible that we may have to ask Congress to pass an act authorizing their use.
> I would like to know what you will charge the government if we should finally find that we can make use of these two models.
> If the general idea of these models is adopted there will have to be some modifications in order to comply with the law. The word "liberty" would have to be

---

[31] *Christian Science Monitor*, "New Lincoln Penny Shows the Leader With Smiling Face," April 1, 1909. p.8. It is also possible Brenner used images of Saint-Gaudens' "Standing Lincoln" which was one of the best known images of Lincoln. In that sculpture, the President wears the same type of coat and a bow tie, as on the cent portrait.
[32] *US Mint*, NARA-CP, op. cit., entry 1A 328I. Letter dated January 18, 1909 to Leach from Brenner.
[33] *US Mint*, NARA-CP, op. cit., entry 235, vol. 380, pp.198-199. Letter dated January 30, 1909 to Brenner from Leach. A press release was issued the same day stating that the half dollar would probably be used for the Lincoln portrait, but that legislation might be necessary.

placed on the side carrying Lincoln's' bust. The law also required that the motto "E Pluribus Unum" should be on the reverse side, but it never has been put on the small penny, and, following precedent, it is possible we may omit it. The date of the coinage year has to be carried on the bust side instead of on the reverse. However, these are mere matters of detail.

I am pleased to say to you that the few persons to whom I have shown your models are strong in their praise of this work.

Is not this Lincoln cast from the same design as the medal of which you recently sent me a copy? If so, there may be some trouble about its adoption; and if adopted it would undoubtedly necessitate the discontinuance of the making and sale of the medals. Are many of the medals out?

Figure 8. Original obverse and reverse designs for the Lincoln cent as submitted by Victor Brenner. The obverse is nothing more than the sculptor's desk medal with the dual dates removed. The reverse is an imitation of the reverse of then-current French subsidiary silver coins. White horizontal streaks on the obverse are folds in the only known photographic print. (NARA.)

The initial pair of designs seems to reflect an approach by the artist of doing little new or original to earn the commission. For the obverse, Brenner evidently used the same mold as for his desk medal being sold by Gorham. The only change being to remove the dates 1809 and 1909.[34] Leach's letter says that the date and inscription LIBERTY will have to be on the obverse, clearly indicating that the first obverse model lacked these elements.

The reverse is also an enigma. For a well-known artist to imitate the reverse of the French franc would be very unusual. Perhaps Brenner forgot about the French silver coins and thought his design was original, or possibly he intentionally imitated a successful coin and thus copied the French prototypes. The differences between Brenner's version and the French original by Baré are so minor as to make one wonder that the sculptor thought he could get away with submitting this adaptation.[35]

Director Leach seemed genuinely pleased with Brenner's initial concepts and offered only minor suggestions for change: adding the date and LIBERTY to the obverse, and possibly E PLURIBUS UNUM to the reverse. The question of having to obtain authorization

---

[34] *US Mint*, NARA-CP, op. cit., entry 44, box 1, folder "Lincoln cent." The photo in the NARA file does not have Brenner's name on the model.
[35] *US Mint*, NARA-CP, op. cit., entry 44, box 1, folder "Lincoln cent." ND. Pencil drawing on Treasury Department letterhead with two annotations: at top, "Copied from French 2 franc piece;" at bottom, "First design suggestion by Brenner. Brenner's design, One cent Piece."

from Congress depended on whether the portrait of a real person would qualify as a depiction of Liberty. Duplication of the portrait from the medal's version was a potential problem. The mint was constantly concerned about counterfeiting and carefully guarded any reproduction of a coin design whether originally on a medal or photograph.

On February 1, Brenner replied indicating that only thirty-five of the original one hundred ten Lincoln medals had been sold:[36]

> I beg to thank you for your favor of the 30th. As already tried, there are only 35 of the medals out, 9 in silver, and the rest in bronze. I had struck of these medals with the Lincoln head 100 in bronze and 10 in silver but could not sell many of them on account of my price; and [it] appears that they will sell now as the [centennial] date approaches, in fact I have had inquiries for large quantities, and have now suspended the work. I have ex[pressed] to you four plaster casts today, one is a new Lincoln head just finished resembling the one you know only in the work [i.e.: finished medal].
>
> The model of this Eagle is inspired by the engraving you gave me, and if my last Lincoln head is adopted the Eagle could well serve for the other side. I think that a half a dollar would be more suitable for the Lincoln coin than a penny?
>
> In a day or so, I shall send out to you a helmeted head of Liberty to go for one side of the cent or nickel. The figures in the models sent, are meant for casting of the cent and Nickel, so that with this head I too send, I think that the models for the three coins would be completed, except the changing of the denominations, and final finishing of detail in faces and otherwise. I would also finish the hubs so as to get all I want in the finished size. As to my remuneration, I wish to know how to measure it. I could not ask the price Mr. St. Gaudens got for his, and I would leave it to you to consider same with the proper officials that are concerned with it. I should consider it a privilege to have the cent and nickel adopted during the President's administration whose time expires but too soon.
>
> If the Lincoln Half dollar could be adopted, I might be able to get photographs ready by the 12th. The head naturally would have to be reduced in relief so as to bring it up without pressure.
>
> Kindly advise me as to how my latest models please you and the President, also, as to what sum I may express for them.

Here, Brenner laid out his grand plan for coin designs: a Lincoln half dollar, the cent and nickel, one with a helmeted head of Liberty and the other with a walking Liberty imitative of the French two franc coin. He also discusses a reverse design depicting an eagle, apparently based on an engraving provided by Leach, as part of his plan for a Lincoln half dollar. Finally, Brenner tried to get Leach to name a fee, probably so he could begin negotiations for his work.

It is not clear if Brenner's expansive proposals including the Lincoln half dollar confused Leach, or made him skeptical of the artist's motives. All prior discussion – including initial comments by Brenner – seem to indicate they were in agreement on putting Lincoln on the cent.

Just after sending his letter, Brenner reread Leach's January 30 comment and evidently became concerned about the director's statement regarding discontinuance of sale of the Lincoln medals. He sent a telegram to the Mint Bureau stating that thirty-five medals had been struck and asked Leach to wire him if the director wanted sales of the medals

---

[36] *US Mint*, NARA-CP, op. cit., entry 1A 328I. Letter dated February 1, 1909 to Leach from Brenner.

stopped. The telegram landed on Leach's desk in slightly garbled condition and a confused mint director wrote to Brenner:[37]

> Your dispatch of today, which reads as follows:
> "Thirty five medals stolen in all. Please wire to stop sale," is not understood by me. I have been wondering if an error was not made in its transmission. I have not complied with your request for me to ask you to stop the sale of the medals because there is too much uncertainty about the adoption of the design by the government.
> I submitted the question of whether we could use the design or not on the pennies to the Comptroller of the Treasury last Saturday, and he has informed me that it is not a question for him to decide, but is a matter that should be referred to the Attorney General. I am endeavoring to see the Secretary of the Treasury to request him to submit the matter to the Attorney General, as suggested by Mr. Tracewell.

Brenner also suggested redesign of the silver subsidiary coins (something he would continue to do until mid-1916). Director Leach wrote on February 2 to correct any misunderstanding and emphasize that only the cent or nickel could be considered. He also insisted that the fees paid to Saint-Gaudens and Pratt could not be divulged, and that Brenner must tell him how much it would cost to design the coin:[38]

> Your letter of the first instant just received. It is useless at this time to make any attempt to change the designs of the subsidiary [silver] coins, as no change in these coins can be made for seven years yet without permission of Congress. We have only two coins on which we can make a change now, the penny and the nickel. For one of these coins I had already requested Mr. Barber to submit a design, and therefore I can only use your design, if it is accepted, on the penny or the nickel.
> In the matter of making a price for these designs, I cannot act as suggested by you. The Government's method of doing business makes it imperative that you should make your price, then it will be necessary for the Secretary of the Treasury to say whether it is acceptable or not. If we can settle this matter and it should be decided that we can use the design, it will be possible to complete the work before the expiration of this administration. All engraving must be done by the engravers at the Philadelphia Mint. I think we all prefer the second model of Lincoln which you sent.

The director is clear that not only were new designs limited to the cent and nickel, but engraver Barber had already been authorized to work on designs for use on one of these denominations. This left Brenner with only one coin to design, although he had submitted several preliminary models.

Brenner replied the next day:[39]

> Replying to your favor of the 2nd inst. I beg to say that I would be pleased to finish the two sets of my models or twelve hundred dollars, $1,200.00. One set for One thousand dollars $1,000.00.
> Since learning that a Lincoln coin could not be adopted, I stopped on the modeling of the head of which I spoke in my last letter.
> Awaiting your favor, I am,

---

[37] *US Mint*, NARA-CP, op. cit., entry 235, vol. 380, p.204. Letter dated February 1, 1909 to Brenner from Leach.
[38] *US Mint*, NARA-CP, op. cit., entry 235, vol. 380, p.218. Letter dated February 2, 1909 to Brenner from Leach.
[39] *US Mint*, NARA-CP, op. cit., entry 1A 328I. Letter dated February 3, 1909 to Leach from Brenner.

By "…Lincoln coin…" Brenner refers to his suggested half dollar which Leach had already rejected in concept. It is unclear why Brenner was confused between the cent and half dollar, since previous correspondence clearly referred to a Lincoln cent. It is likely that correspondence on this point is missing. The sculptor had also written to President Roosevelt who had his secretary check with director Leach to verify that only the cent was under consideration for change:[40]

> The president understands that Brenner's design is to be used for the penny. Is that correct? Please return the enclosed letter from Brenner with your reply.

Leach received Brenner's note with the cost included and replied almost immediately accepting the sculptor's offer:[41]

> Your letter of the 3rd instant received. If I understand you correctly, you offer to supply the government with one set of models to be used for the penny coin, embracing the bust of Lincoln for the obverse and the design sent here for the reverse, for the sum of one thousand dollars. If this is true, your offer is accepted, with the understanding that these models shall be altered so as to suit the requirements of the statutes and the coinage operations. I would prefer that you come down here so that I can explain what is necessary to be done. It would be very difficult to do this through correspondence. The government will pay your transportation and subsistence expenses while making this visit to Washington. I would like to have you be here next Monday forenoon.

Leach was fully aware of the original agreement with Saint-Gaudens which stipulated $5,000 for two coin designs, the final settlement with Augusta for $6,000, and the miserly $600 paid Bela Pratt for his half eagle work. He had participated in both compensation discussions, and must have felt he was getting a bargain at only $1,000 for the Lincoln cent. At this point Brenner's commission was officially narrowed to include only the one-cent coin. The mint paid Brenner's transportation and lodging expenses and on February 8 he met with director Leach to discuss the cent design.[42] Barber had been kept informed about the meeting and offered Leach a bit of technical advice:[43]

> I find upon coming to my office this morning that the one cent dies are both on radius 25 when soft. This may be of use to you when you see Mr. Brenner.

The artist and director met for nearly two hours with Leach laying out some of the practical requirements for the design and plaster models. Brenner had submitted a sample reverse design for the cent that was a close copy of the reverse of the French silver franc coins. He also submitted a second possible reverse design, this one showing a full length portrait of Liberty. Presumably, he thought Lincoln did not qualify as "emblematic of Liberty," so this composition was intended to provide the necessary figure.

---

[40] *US Mint*, NARA-CP, op. cit., entry 1A 328I. Letter dated February 4, 1909 to Leach from William Loeb, Secretary to the President.
[41] *US Mint*, NARA-CP, op. cit., entry 1A 328I. Letter dated February 5, 1909 to Brenner from Leach.
[42] *US Mint*, NARA-CP, op. cit., entry 1A 328I. Letter dated February 6, 1909 to Brenner from Leach.
[43] *US Mint*, NARA-CP, op. cit., entry 1A 328I. Letter dated February 6, 1909 to Leach from Barber.

Figure 9. Second reverse design sketch submitted February 8, 1909, left, and earlier obverse model which Brenner evidently proposed for use on a half dollar. The figure was later identified as "Columbia." The artist's name "V. D. Brenner" is at the bottom of the obverse design. Compare to the obverse of the current French silver coins featuring Roty's **The Sower (Marianne)**. *(NARA.)*

Again, Brenner had done little more than imitate the obverse style of French silver coins, but this time the mint's objection was to having a second representation of Liberty on the coin.[44] Director Leach provided a summary of the project for secretary Cortelyou on February 9:[45]

> In the matter of furnishing the designs for the proposed new one cent coinage, Mr. Victor Brenner is insistent upon introducing another design of the reverse side in place of the one first offered. It is necessary that we should have some other design than the one first submitted by him, for I have discovered that it is an exact copy of the design used by the Government of France on its two franc piece, the only difference being in the inscriptions. We should also refuse to adopt the second design offered, embracing a female figure, first, for the reason that there is a question as to its legality. This figure is supposed to symbolize Liberty, and to use it, it seems to me, would destroy our license to use the Lincoln head, so much desired, on the obverse side. The law does not provide for two impressions or figures emblematic of Liberty. Then, as this is the simplest coin we have, it seems to me it should call for the plainest and most distinct design.
>
> Another objection, which is not so serious, being only a mechanical one, is that a figure on the reverse side of the coin, unless of the lowest possible relief, would interfere in securing the best results in producing the Lincoln portrait on the obverse side.
>
> Respectfully,
> Frank A. Leach

[manuscript comment below]

> Approved, after submitting this matter to the president and requesting his approval.
> George B. Cortelyou
> Secretary of the Treasury

---

[44] *US Mint*, NARA-CP, op. cit., entry 44, box 1, folder "Lincoln cent." Photo of plaster model with "V. D. Brenner" at bottom near the rim.

[45] *US Mint*, NARA-CP, op. cit., entry 1A 328I. Memorandum dated February 9, 1909 to Cortelyou from Leach.

Little hope remained that the new design could be approved in time for the Lincoln birth centennial on February 22, 1909. Brenner's Lincoln portrait was generally satisfactory; however, his Liberty reverse design had only confused the situation and Leach wanted a third new design. We do not know if Brenner's imitations of French coins raised doubts about the artist's intentions, and there is nothing in mint letters to indicate there was general mistrust of the artist. Director Leach wrote to Brenner officially advising him of the need for a new reverse design:[46]

> The subject of the design for the reverse of the penny has been discussed by the president and the Secretary and myself, and it was decided that owing to the law permitting of only one figure emblematic of Liberty to be on the coin, and the desire that the coins should be plain and simple, your suggestion of the female figure, left with me yesterday, is rejected; and you are requested to submit another design which shall be in compliance with the memorandum furnished you yesterday.

Brenner was thus sent back to the drawing board with few suggestions except the reverse "…should be plain and simple." A letter of February 10 states Brenner's understanding of what should be on the one-cent coin, based on his meeting with Leach two days earlier:[47]

> Referring to your letter of Feb. 5th, I beg to say that my price for supplying the Government with one set of models for the Cent piece for One thousand doll. is correct.
> I beg also to acknowledge receipt of your letter dated Feb. 9th fixing the designs for the Cent piece – for the Obverse to have the portrait of Mr. Lincoln with the words Liberty and the date of the coinage, for the Reverse to have "United States of America, One Cent and E Pluribus Unum."
> I shall submit my arrangements of this design to you shortly.

The artist's letter was received at the Mint Bureau and a copy shown to engraver Barber who took time to provide additional information:[48]

> Your letter of the 10th inst., received and the contents has been discussed with the Director who I understand has given you certain instructions regarding the design.
> Mr. Leach tells me that he has explained to you that he desired the field of coin to be finished with a fixed radius or curve, therefore the model must be made with a fixed radius.
> I find in your Lincoln medal that the field in front of the face is one plane while the field at the back of the head is an entirely different plane, this you will see will never do as we have to finish the field of the dies mechanically in order to comply with the wish of the Director, namely to have the field finished smooth and one radius.
> The radius best suited for a coin must be determined by the disposition of the design and the area of the coin, in this connection I may say that the present cent dies are of 25 radius.
> In making your design you must avoid as much as possible one bold part of your design coming opposite another on the other side of the coin, as that would be fatal to the coining of the piece.

---

[46] *US Mint*, NARA-CP, op. cit., entry 1A 328I. Letter dated February 9, 1909 to Brenner from Leach.
[47] *US Mint*, NARA-CP, op. cit., entry 1A 328I. Letter dated February 10, 1909 to Leach from Brenner.
[48] *US Mint*, NARA-CP, op. cit., entry 1A 328I. Letter dated February 13, 1909 to Brenner from Barber.

> In regard to what relief you had better adopt I am sorry to say that I cannot give you any fixed instructions as so much depends upon the design of both sides and the particular metal the design is for, also the area of the coin.
>
> You can look at the cent, judge from that, and that is the extent of the relief that can be successfully used for the one cent coin, and you will also see that from the point of utility, that the design is good, as it is so arranged that no one point comes in opposition to another, and as these coins are struck by tons every year, not thousands, but millions, and if the usual average per pair of dies was not produced, the coiner would condemn the dies at once.
>
> In designing for a coin you must give due weight to the mechanical requirements of coinage and remember that great quantities of coin are demanded against time, and therefore, everything that can be done to simplify both the making of the dies and the production of the coin, must be considered.
>
> You also know that the coins drop from the press at the rate of 120 per minute and that unlike a medal there is no bronzing or finishing of any description, no chance to bring out your design by coloring, it comes from the press one color and that [is] the color of the metal whatever that may be.

Brenner worked quickly and on February 17 delivered new models of the obverse and reverse to the director.

Figure 10. Models for Lincoln cent similar to those submitted on February 17, 1909 were similar to the illustrations above. One version had the artist's name along the obverse rim. The first "wheat ears" reverse used a Roman "V" in the inscriptions to which President Roosevelt objected. This was changed to a normal Latin "U" in Brenner's' final model, as shown above. (Courtesy David W. Lange, original images from the Philadelphia Mint)

These were immediately taken to the president who liked the overall appearance of the design but would not accept use of the Roman letter *V* in place of the Latin letter *U*. This was consistent with his approach to the Saint-Gaudens' designs in 1906-07 where the Roman *V* was used in the date, but not in the inscriptions. This was also the only instance of President Roosevelt rejecting a design.[49]

> I succeeded in having an interview with the President this morning for the purpose of showing him the models you left yesterday of the new penny. He was pleased with the general appearance of the new design for the reverse, but very

---
[49] *US Mint*, NARA-CP, op. cit., entry 1A 328I. Letter dated February 18, 1909 to Brenner from Leach.

> emphatic in his objection to the use of the V in place of the letter U, consequently you will have to change your lettering in each and every instance where the V has been used for the U.
>
> Upon making the alterations in the lettering, and putting the plaques in shape for delivery to the engraver, you will send them to me. I will ship the models to you today by express.
>
> *[note below]*
>
> P.S. Since dictating the above, and after packing the models, I found that the boxes would not hold all the models. The one you prepared for the reverse side of the penny with the figure of Columbia I will hold here until some time when you visit Washington when you can take it away with you.

The next day Leach shipped the models and also advised Brenner that all models used in final production of the coin would become government property. He further commented, "For this reason I shall be unable to retain the plaster cast of Lincoln you so kindly gave me."[50] Brenner received the box of models the next day and agreed to government ownership of the final models.[51] He suggested the plaster model of Lincoln he had given the director as a personal memento be converted into a cameo without lettering:[52]

> With regards to the plaster model I presented to you, it occurs to me, were you to cut away the lettering from around the head, you could keep same. In the finished model of the cent, many changes are to come, so your keeping of the head would interfere little, but you know best.
>
> I have acknowledged receipt of your letters, and of the models in another letter to you.
>
> I shall change the "V" as suggested by the President.

On February 26 Brenner sent his "final" models to the Mint Bureau:[53]

> I have the honor to inform you that I have today Expressed to you the completed models of the Lincoln Penny, also three moulds of same. I trust you will find them satisfactory. I will appreciate the permission of examining the hubs before they are hardened, and should any retouching be necessary, to do so under the supervision of Mr. Barber.

---

[50] *US Mint*, NARA-CP, op. cit., entry 1A 328I. Letter dated February 19, 1909 to Brenner from Leach.
[51] *US Mint*, NARA-CP, op. cit., entry 1A 328I. Letter dated February 20, 1909 to Leach from Brenner.
[52] *US Mint*, NARA-CP, op. cit., entry 1A 328I. Letter dated February 20, 1909 to Leach from Brenner.
[53] *US Mint*, NARA-CP, op. cit., entry 1A 328I. Letter dated February 26, 1909 to Leach from Brenner.

Figure 11. Final Lincoln cent designs submitted February 26, 1909. These photos are of galvanos made from the models at the Philadelphia Mint. Note Brenner's name is on the reverse near the rim. It was later removed by mint engraver Barber and the initials "V.D.B." substituted. It appears that two galvanos were combined for the obverse (left) so the portrait could be lowered slightly and possibly to correct die radius irregularities. (Courtesy David W. Lange, original images from the Philadelphia Mint)

The models arrived in Washington the next day and Leach took them straight to the White House for President Roosevelt's approval. Although the Lincoln cent could not be issued before the end of Roosevelt's administration, it would at least have the distinction of being approved in the waning days of his presidency. Leach's transmittal letter to the Philadelphia Mint also mentions replacing the artist's full name with only his initials "in an unobtrusive way" on the models in prelude to events of early August:[54]

> I send you by express today the models adopted by the President of the design for the proposed new issue of the one cent piece. I notice that Mr. Brenner insists upon putting his name in full on the obverse side. I am sorry to have to disappoint him in this matter, but after consultation with the Secretary of the Treasury upon the subject it was decided that only his initials could be permitted, and that in an unobtrusive way.
> Mr. Brenner writes me that he desires to see the hub in time to have touched up any imperfections that he might notice. I wish you would advise me whether or not his request is practicable.
> As soon as the dies are ready and proof [i.e.: sample] pieces struck I shall be pleased to be advised of the fact.

Engraver Barber examined the models on March 1 and wrote to superintendent Landis discussing their suitability for coinage. By this time, it appears his Washington five-cent coin design had been placed on hold until work on the cent was complete. In his long-winded style, the engraver found much to dislike about the models and little to commend:[55]

---

[54] *US Mint,* NARA-CP, op. cit., entry 1A 328I. Letter dated February 27, 1909 to Landis from Leach.
[55] *US Mint,* NARA-CP, op. cit., entry 1A 328I. Letter dated March 1, 1909 to Landis from Barber. The engraver uses "radius" to refer to the radius of curvature of the die. "Six" means "radius of 6 inches;" "24" means a radius of 24-inches, or substantially shallower than that of Brenner's reverse model. At this time, the U. S. Mint was one of the few that used convex coinage dies. Most countries used flat-faced dies. See Barber's July 31, 1905 report on foreign mints in NARA-CP, RG-104, entry 229, box 232.

> The plaster casts for the one cent coins have arrived this morning, also a letter for the Director, but I do not find any instructions or comment regarding the models, I therefore before proceeding to make reductions must ask for some instructions and also call attention to the condition of the models.
>
> In an interview with the Director I understood him to say that he desired the dies for the one cent to be finished with the field of one curve or as we term it, finished on a basin, the same as the coins for the Philippine Island and all U. S. Coins formerly were finished.
>
> I therefore call your attention first to the obverse, which has evidently been modeled without regard to the Director's wish, as there is not one curve, the field being several different curves, and therefore, will not basin upon any fixed radius. The Director will at once understand the impossibility of using a basin as he will see before one part of the die came to the radius another part would be ground out, consequently we cannot use a basin at all, there not being one radius to the model.
>
> The field in front of the face is one radius, back of the head another, and the field above the head something entirely different from both.
>
> The next question before me is the reverse. While there appears to have been made an effort to establish a fixed radius to this side, it has the objection of being too round [i.e.: convex], as you will see. The model so far as I am able to ascertain has a radius of sixty and the reduction will be about ten or one tenth that of the model, this will bring the first reduction to a radius of six, and by the time the dies are made and tempered they will be still rounder, or something less than six.[56] Our one cent dies finish at twenty-five radius.
>
> You will see from this explanation that the model for the reverse is entirely too round.
>
> The next question is the borders, they are so narrow that by the time they are reduced ten times there will be nothing left, only a knife edge.
>
> You will understand the difficulties before me and until I receive some instructions I do not know how to proceed.
>
> I wish to explain that there is no difficulty in making the reductions and if that is all that Mr. Brenner and the Director require, then that can easily be accomplished, but if the dies are to basin and to be made with any hope of them being suitable for coinage when made, then the models must be altered to meet the requirements of the coinage department, and the models must be made of such a radius that when reduced they will approach other coins the dies of which we have proved to be adapted to coinage.
>
> As stated before the cent is of twenty-five radius, the twenty centavo Philippine coin of about the same diameter is twenty-five radius.
>
> I beg to state that in response to a letter from Mr. Brenner making certain inquiry regarding the preparation of his models and in order to carry out the Director's wish in this matter, I wrote Mr. Brenner. I enclose a copy of my letter.
>
> In conclusion, I beg to state that if the idea of having these dies to basin is abandoned, then the matter of die making is simplified and I will ask if, when the reductions are made, are they to be sent to Mr. Brenner?

Maintaining the same radius of curvature over the face of a die was necessary to ensure that all coins were of equal thickness throughout their circumference. If the radius differed from one part of the die to another, it could easily produce coins that were thicker at one part of the rim than another. This would make the coins more difficult to stack and interfere with cashiers and other money counters' ability to estimate the value of stacks of coin.

---

[56] This paragraph, and similar statement by Barber, confirm that the original models were 7.5-inches in diameter.

Leach decided it would be best for Brenner to go to the Philadelphia Mint to consult with Barber in person and resolve the radius problem.[57] The meeting took place on March 4 and ended with Brenner agreeing to make the changes Barber wanted:[58]

> I saw Mr. Barber today and have taken the plaster models with me for some alterations.
> I fully agree with you that my name on the Obverse looks intrusive, and thank you for calling my attention to it. I shall take it out, and put it in small letters on the reverse near the rim.

This is the first time Brenner suggests placing his name on the reverse of the coin although Leach had already decided to use initials. There is no record of further objection to this and it appears Barber removed the name and added the three raised initials to the reverse, cutting them by hand into the master die. Not only are the initials slightly askew, but they are off-center, and unevenly spaced. All three of Brenner's initials were used so his work was clearly differentiated from Barber's lone initial on the silver coins.[59] All subsequent reverse hubs and dies had his initials near the bottom of the reverse at the rim.

Figure 12. Galvano of cent reverse with sculptor's name at lower rim (left), and the first version of 1909 released into circulation with initials "V.D.B." (right). (Left, courtesy David W. Lange, original image from the Philadelphia Mint; right courtesy Numismatic Guarantee Corporation.)

Another meeting occurred on March 4, 1909, but in Washington, DC. It was the last official gathering of President Theodore Roosevelt's Cabinet, and the first moments of the administration of President William Howard Taft. The day dawned with a near blizzard of snow and ice. Trains were snarled, telephone and telegraph lines snapped under the weight of ice, and Capitol groundskeepers gave up trying to clear snow from the east front

---

[57] *US Mint*, NARA-CP, op. cit., entry 235, vol. 380, p.420. Letter dated March 2, 1909 to Brenner from Leach.
[58] *US Mint*, NARA-CP, op. cit., entry 1A 328I. Letter dated March 4, 1909 to Leach from Brenner. Agreement to alter the models was confirmed by a note from Landis to Leach on March 5.
[59] See: *US Mint*, NARA-CP, op. cit., entry 1A 328I. Letter dated August 4, 1909 to Norton from Landis; and memorandum of the assistant secretary dated August 17, 1909, discussed below for indications that Barber added the initials. Those who examined the hubs and pattern coins may have felt the initials were inconspicuous but in August the newspapers thought otherwise. Based on photos supplied by the mint, it appears that Barber removed the name "Brenner" from the lower reverse of the hub. He then cut V.D.B. into a master die. This would have been called the "mother die" since all subsequent master hubs were made from it, not direct from the original models.

plaza. At 11:00 o'clock Taft's Inauguration ceremony was transferred to the Senate chamber where guests scrambled for seats when they arrived. With the departure of ex-president Roosevelt on a special train that afternoon, some at the Mint Bureau may have felt they could relax. Gone was the energetic, micromanaging chief executive and his seemingly arbitrary decisions. In his place was a methodical manager, who sometimes nodded off during meetings – perfect for operating a store but devoid of imagination to lead the country.[60]

Brenner went to the Philadelphia Mint on March 15 but returned with concerns about Barber's attitude:[61]

> I saw Mr. Barber again today, and had sent him the model last week. He thinks that now there is no hurry for the execution of the cent, but I fail to see the reason except if it be his personal reason. It is my intention to avoid any friction, and I ask you therefore to kindly write to him not to delay the execution of this coin any longer
> Thanking you in advance, and hoping to see you in person, I am,

Director Leach was on his way to visit the western mints and assay offices.[62] Acting director Preston told Brenner he would forward the letter, although he probably made sure Landis and Barber were aware of the sculptor's comments.[63] Within less than a week Barber had completed reductions and asked permission to send them to Brenner for final touchup.[64] Acting director Preston immediately refused on the grounds that the material could not be allowed to leave the mint. Barber, who by now wanted as little to do with responsibility for the new coin as possible, wrote to Preston asking him to reconsider.[65]

> Mr. Landis has just shown me your letter regarding the request of Mr. Brenner to have the reductions from his models sent him for approval and any retouching that he may consider necessary for the proper representation of his work.
> I hope that you will reconsider your refusal to comply with Brenner's request as I think it only a reasonable one and most desirable as perfectly safe, as no doubt Brenner only wants to look the reductions over and sharpen some points that he may think have lost distinctness in the process of reducing, this he ought to be allowed to do, and I know of no other way of his doing this, than sending him the reductions.
> There can be no extra risk in this, as Mr. Brenner will have no advantage over the Mint that he does not already possess, as he has the model and also some medals having the Lincoln head and therefore, has all the opportunity to play crooked if he wanted to, which I do not think he has any disposition to do, his request being only natural, that before making this coin that he should be allowed to see that the reductions properly represent his work, and if not, that he should be allowed to touch up any parts that he may think ought to be improved.
> I do not want to be in the position where Brenner can say that he was not allowed to do his best.

---

[60] Taft apparently suffered from *sleep apnea* aggravated by his weight, which topped 330 pounds during his single term as President. At times, he would nod off while listening to a Cabinet member present his report. The condition improved after he left office and lost considerable weight.
[61] *US Mint*, NARA-CP, op. cit., entry 1A 328I. Letter dated March 15, 1909 to Leach from Brenner. Barber's attitude may have resulted from either Roosevelt's leaving the presidency or passage of the Lincoln birth date.
[62] *US Mint*, NARA-CP, op. cit., entry 1A 328I. Letter dated March 16, 1909 to Brenner from Preston.
[63] Robert Preston was a former mint director and career bureau employee. He and Barber were two of the longest serving mint employees and shared a common view about outside artists designing coins.
[64] *US Mint*, NARA-CP, op. cit., entry 1A 328I. Letter dated March 23, 1909 to Preston from Landis.
[65] *US Mint*, NARA-CP, op. cit., entry 1A 328I. Letter dated March 25, 1909 to Preston from Barber.

> You know the St. Gaudens' people have appeared in print asserting that the Mint would not execute St. Gaudens work as he desired, and now Mr. Bigelow in his reply to Chapman regarding the half and quarter eagle makes the statement, that the remark of Chapman "that the treatment of the head being hard and crude," refers to the retouching done at the Mint.
>
> I want to be spared this humiliation and therefore ask that Brenner be allowed to do his own retouching as he requests, and I could not think of undertaking.
>
> The reductions I have made from the Brenner models are good, but he may want to go over them in some points to satisfy himself and from the peculiar style of the modeling it would be impossible for anyone else to retouch his work in a satisfactory manner to him,
>
> I therefore can see no alternative but to let him have the reductions and return them as soon as he has passed upon them, which I am quite sure will be very soon, as he appears most anxious to have the coin brought out.

There might have been considerable justification in Barber wanting to avoid any association with Brenner's work. The Saint-Gaudens and Bigelow criticism must have been hurtful to read, particularly comments about changes to Pratt's $5 design made by Barber. Only six months before, director Leach had stated: "…This work is very satisfactory indeed, and I desire…to express my congratulations and approval to Mr. Barber for the excellent result he has given us in the new die. It is about as fine a specimen of work as could possibly be made…."[66] It may have seemed to him that designing a coin was considered a trivial matter in the eyes of any "high class artist" outside the mint, until one of them was given a commission and then had to consult the engraver for help in making the design coinable. All of his many hours of lost vacation and overtime spent in making the Saint-Gaudens designs usable on commercial coin, had resulted only in public criticism by the artist's widow and friends. The Pratt sunken-relief designs had fared little better and one can understand Barber wanting nothing to do with yet another Presidentially-ordered artist wandering about the Philadelphia Mint.

Preston must have accepted Barber's argument because only two days later, Brenner wrote to Barber enclosing the retouched hubs:[67]

> I am sending back the hubs, having retouched the reverse, the obverse has been rubbed,[68] and is too indistinct, so it will have to be recut. If it pleases you, you need not send me the die for the reverse for retouching, as there need only be a few lines rectified. Please suit yourself about that.
>
> It appears to me that something has happened to the model of the portrait side, as the whole neck looks rather fallen in.
>
> In the next reduction please use no brush over it, and send it on as it leaves the reducing machine.
>
> P.S. In case you shall finish up the die for the reverse of the cent, I would thank you to let me see an impression before its being hardened.

As had happened with the Saint-Gaudens coins (and would occur again in 1916), the mint staff were being accused of inability to make reductions and hubs of the highest quality from models by outside artists. Barber complained that relief was too high, or the

---

[66] *US Mint*, NARA-P, op. cit. Letter dated October 10, 1908 to Landis from Leach. The $5 trial pieces were made with dies aligned medal-turn so Barber could identify them if Leach or the President rejected the samples.
[67] *US Mint*, NARA-CP, op. cit., entry 1A 328I. Letter dated March 27, 1909 to Barber from Brenner.
[68] The term "rubbed" as used in this context means "polished" or "burnished" to smooth imperfections. Brenner claims the mint did too much smoothing.

field radius was incorrect, or that the artists did not understand that fine detail would be lost during the reduction process. The sculptors, all of whom had experience in creating medals, but limited understanding of making coinage reductions, saw Barber as incompetent and not up to modern standards of workmanship. From the perspective and experience of a century, we can see that problems were both technical and personal. On the mint's side of things, neither Barber nor assistant engraver Morgan had been fully trained to use the Janvier reducing lathe purchased in late 1906. Barber knew more than Morgan thanks to spending a week in early 1907 watching Henri Weil[69] from Deitsch Brothers, Co. make reductions of the first Saint-Gaudens models. Yet both were fundamentally nineteenth century artisans and had little in common with either the sculptors, or commercial die makers with whom the sculptors normally dealt. For Barber and Morgan every hub required retouching to sharpen lettering or enhance details.

For their part, the outside artists persistently failed to listen to Barber's admonitions about excessive relief. They felt the mint should be able to do whatever a private company or the Paris Mint could do, and refused to supply models with lower relief and more deeply cut detail. They also ignored requests to incorporate a suitable protective rim or to maintain some small distance between design elements and the rim of the coin. All failed to grasp the role that excessive reduction played, with the result that artists often provided models that were ten to fifteen times the size of finished coins. This meant that exquisitely detailed models, impressive in their own right, lost much of their impact as detail became reduced to barely visible scratches.

Barber wanted nothing more to do with the cent obverse and wrote a pointed letter to superintendent Landis on March 29. He also enclosed a copy of Brenner's March 27 letter:[70]

> I beg to enclose a letter from Mr. Brenner regarding the reduction made from his model of Lincoln for the one cent coin.
>
> In view of the fact that everything has been done to make this work entirely satisfactory to Mr. Brenner and we have failed, I beg to ask that Mr. Brenner be allowed to furnish a steel hub of his model, that is, that he be allowed to furnish the reduction, having it done in New York, under his supervision, the same as he is doing with his medals.
>
> I make this request as I am quite sure we cannot satisfy Mr. Brenner. He does not appear to understand that when he asks to have the relief of the model reduced mechanically, some detail must necessarily be sacrificed and, therefore, he must prepare his model accordingly, which he has not done.
>
> The model furnished is of soft impressionist character and when reduced to one-tenth of the size of the model, and especially reduced in relief, the natural result is a want of detail, which Mr. Brenner complains of. It will facilitate the matter if Mr. Brenner be allowed to do as I suggest, but, if the Director positively objects, I can think of no way out of this difficulty, except to ask that we be furnished with a bronze casting of the model from which to make the reduction.
>
> I sincerely trust that the Director will grant this request to let Mr. Brenner furnish the reduction, as it will save much time and avoid friction of a most unpleasant character.

Director Leach, still on his western tour, wrote to acting director Preston about the new Lincoln cent:[71]

---

[69] By 1909 Henri Weil and his brother Felix were operating their own business, Medallic Art Company, in New York.
[70] *US Mint*, NARA-CP, op. cit., entry 1A 328I. Letter dated March 29, 1909 to Landis from Barber.

> ...In the matter of the new pennies, I wish you would see to it that they do not undertake the regular coinage of the pieces until I have passed upon the proof or pattern pieces.
>
> I am willing, and think it is a good idea to try and have Mr. Brenner satisfied with the work before it is commenced, but it is not essential to the production of the pieces that we should depend upon Mr. Brenner, as I think it quite likely that we may finally have to do what was done finally with those of the Saint Gaudens design to make it a success....

It is clear that Leach had limited confidence in Brenner's ability to deliver suitable models for the cent. He refers to the double eagle of 1907 which Barber had to re-engrave in order to produce dies that could be used on normal single-stroke coinage presses. In a follow-up letter on April 5, the director further advised Preston:[72]

> ...I think you better communicate with Mr. Brenner and ask him if he is willing to make the hub as suggested by Mr. Barber, and get the cost of doing so beforehand. I suppose that would be required to get his claim for doing the work allowed...

Preston wrote to Brenner asking if he was willing to make the obverse hub, and if so, at what cost.[73] The sculptor replied on April 12 "...I will be pleased to supervise the reducing of the obverse side of the Lincoln penny and will supply you with the finished hub for $100.00."[74] Brenner evidently felt the problem was with the reduction from the plaster model because the next day he wrote to Barber stating, "In a day or two I shall have a hard bronze casting and with such a model it seems to me you ought to get as good a reduction as Wile [sic] can do."[75]

Engraver Barber did what he could to reinforce placing the hub making in outside hands with a letter on April 14:[76]

> The charge for making the reduction of the Lincoln model of the one Cent, is enough, but not exorbitant.
>
> Regarding the reduction for the reverse hub I beg to state, that I have made that and Mr. Brenner has expressed himself as satisfied and returned the hub, which I now have ready for making coining dies.
>
> I enclose a copy of a letter received this morning from Mr. Brenner.
>
> In this connection I think it advisable to state that there is no difficulty in our making good reductions which we are doing constantly, provided, the model is made with a proper understanding of the effect that will be obtained when the work is reduced to one tenth of the size of the model, and the evidence that our reductions are correct, is shown in this particular case, the reverse model being chiefly a design consisting of letters has given a satisfactory result, but the Lincoln being very soft and undefined in character, when reduced to one tenth of the size of the model has lost all detail, which Mr. Brenner objects to, and therefore, it is not a

---

[71] *US Mint*, NARA-CP, op. cit., entry 1A 328I. Letter (excerpt) dated April 2, 1909 to Preston from Leach. The balance of the letter deals with operational issues of the mint and includes the comment, "I was also surprised to learn that at New Orleans they could not continue work after the first of May for lack of appropriation, for Mr. Southon thought he would be able to continue until the first of July."

[72] *US Mint*, NARA-CP, op. cit., entry 1A 328I. Letter (excerpt) dated April 5, 1909 to Preston from Leach.

[73] *US Mint*, NARA-CP, op. cit., entry 1A 328I. Letter dated April 10, 1909 to Brenner from Preston.

[74] *US Mint*, NARA-CP, op. cit., entry 1A 328I. Letter dated April 12, 1909 to Preston from Brenner.

[75] *US Mint*, NARA-CP, op. cit., entry 1A 328I. Letter dated April 13, 1909 to Barber from Brenner. "Wile" was Henri Weil, now of Medallic Art Company, who had helped Barber cut the first Saint-Gaudens hubs in January 1907.

[76] *US Mint*, NARA-CP, op. cit., entry 1A 328I. Letter dated April 14, 1909 to Landis from Barber.

question of our ability to make a reduction, which we can do equally well as any one. This difficulty all rests with the model, and therefore I can see no other way than to allow Mr. Brenner to provide the reduction and then if it is satisfactory to the Director pay him. This I found Mr. Brenner not inclined to do, as when I called attention to the character of the model and pointed out that the detail would not carry and would be lost when reduced so many times smaller than the model, Mr. Brenner did not agree with me.

As Mr. Brenner has had the model returned sometime and now writes that in a day or two he will have a casting, I infer that he has been making changes in the model which may prove advantageous. I hope it may so prove to be, and to facilitate Mr. Brenner furnishing the hub that the Director may have something to pass upon.

Barber's exasperation with the situation is reasonable: he had gone through the same thing in 1907 with Saint-Gaudens and like the great artist, Brenner refused to believe him. Brenner wrote acting director Preston advising that the bronze cast, "…retouched by me, so that the reductions can be made at the mint as well as here…" was ready on the 14th and asked to whom it should be sent.[77]

Preston, not wishing to waste any more time, advised the artist on April 15:[78]

Your offer of the 12th instant to furnish a satisfactory reduction for the obverse of the Lincoln one-cent piece for the sum of $100 is accepted. I will thank you to proceed with the work and to forward a finished hub to the Mint at Philadelphia as early as practicable.

In accepting your offer it is understood that the reduction made by you will be one from which dies can be made that will produce a coin in every way satisfactory.

Telegrams confirming Preston's letter passed between the director's Office, Philadelphia Mint and Brenner's New York studio. On April 28 Barber confirmed that the hub had been received and examined at the mint:[79]

Regarding the one cent hub being prepared by Mr. Brenner I beg to say that he has made the reduction of the Lincoln bust and sent it to me to harden and make a die, and also asked to have the die sent him in the soft condition, that he might do some touching up.

As the word Liberty, also the date of the year were both very faint in hub and die I suggested that he should make both stronger before returning the die. The die was sent him yesterday and no doubt will be returned here this week, and in that case I will be able to send impressions for approval very shortly.

Barber had used the hub supplied by Brenner to impress a master die (negative). It was this die that was sent to Brenner for strengthening of the legend and date. A lead impression of this initial version exists and is catalogued as A-1907 in the 8th edition of J. H. Judd's book *United States Pattern and Experimental Pieces*.

---

[77] *US Mint*, NARA-CP, op. cit., entry 1A 328I. Letter dated April 14, 1909 to Preston from Brenner.
[78] *US Mint*, NARA-CP, op. cit., entry 1A 328I. Letter dated April 15, 1909 to Brenner from Preston.
[79] *US Mint*, NARA-CP, op. cit., entry 1A 328I. Letter dated April 28, 1909 to Preston from Barber.

Figure 13. Lead impression of the obverse of the original Lincoln cent desgn. This version appears to have been made before Brenner strengthened the lettering and date. Compare the modified galvano made at the mint to the lead impression. (Left, courtesy prvate collection; right, David W Lange from U.S. Mint.)

This version was nearly identical to the 1908 Gorham medal (see Figure 6) with the exception of moving the portrait slightly to the right and replacing the "1809" date with the word LIBERTY. Brenner agreed to pay for another master die on May 4, "Please sink another die of the Lincoln at my expense."[80] By May 12, Brenner had returned the retouched master die and Barber made five bronze impressions of the new dies. The first pattern Lincoln cents were thus made from a reverse cut by the mint and an obverse made by Medallic Art Company. These pattern pieces were sent to superintendent Landis (who was in Washington at the time) and acting director Preston:[81]

> I enclose three coins struck this day from the first pair of dies (proof) made for the one cent bronze coin, Brenner design.

Two days later Albert Norris, acting Philadelphia Mint superintendent, explained the number and distribution of the first pattern Lincoln cents:[82]

> As requested in your letter received today I beg to enclose herewith two specimens of the one-cent bronze piece, Brenner design. There were but five of these struck by the Engraver, three of which were forwarded to Mr. Landis in your case, and the two enclosed. We have sent none to Mr. Brenner, as he has not requested any and we had no authority to do so even if he had.

Between May 14 and 20 director Leach issued instructions to modify the cent and on the 20th, Landis sent samples of a second version to Washington:[83]

> I beg to enclose herewith four specimens of the new one cent piece, changed in accordance with your request, and two of those first submitted, for comparison.

---

[80] *Barber*, ANA. Telegram dated May 4, 1909 to Barber from Brenner.
[81] *US Mint*, NARA-CP, op. cit., entry 1A 328I. Letter dated May 12, 1909 to Landis from Norris. The term "proof" refers to a sample struck on a medal press and not necessarily to polished specimens made for collectors. Modern terminology often calls these "satin proofs" although they are nothing more than first impressions from fresh dies struck under hydraulic pressure.
[82] *US Mint*, NARA-CP, op. cit., entry 1A 328I. Letter dated May 14, 1909 to Preston from Norris.
[83] *US Mint*, NARA-CP, op. cit., entry 1A 328I. Letter dated May 20, 1909 to Leach from Landis.

The revised obverse design moved the portrait lower in the field and added the motto IN GOD WE TRUST above Lincoln's head. Director Leach ordered the changes because he felt moving the portrait would improve striking characteristics of the coin. To fill the extra space between top of head and rim the optional religious motto was added. Leach may also have had the 1908 law requiring the motto on gold coins in mind and acted to avoid another controversy.[84]

It wasn't long before Brenner heard of the pattern cents and sent an inquiring letter to director Leach:[85]

> I learned today that proofs of the Lincoln Cent were approved by you. I would much appreciate your sending me one if possible.
> Enclosed please find bill for models and hub for your kind approval.

Leach replied with a somewhat formal letter on May 21:[86]

> In reply to your letter of the 20th [sic] instant you are respectfully informed that it will be some time before the Lincoln one-cent pieces will be issued. When they are ready for distribution you will be duly notified.

The same day, Leach ordered the Philadelphia Mint to begin preparation of new dies for the Lincoln cent based on the revised model with motto added.[87] Also, possibly thinking the artist deserved a better explanation than his previous curt response, Leach wrote a more detailed note to Brenner:[88]

> I have to inform you that I was not satisfied with the first proof of the Lincoln cent. I found that you had not dropped the Lincoln portrait down so that the head would come nearer the center of the coin, a matter I called your attention to when we were discussing the model. This is necessary to get the best result in bringing out the details of the features in striking the coin, therefore I had Mr. Barber make me a proof of this change, and as this left so much blank space over the top we concluded that it would be better to put on the motto "In God We Trust." This change has made a marked improvement in the appearance of the coin. I cannot send you a sample but if you feel enough interest in the matter it would be better for you to go down to Philadelphia where Mr. Barber can explain and show you what has been done.
> There is such a demand from influential people for samples of this coin that we cannot comply without unjust discrimination, neither will we be able to make any distribution of the coins until enough has been struck to supply all demands.
> I acknowledge receipt of your bill, and as soon as the design has been finally approved I will file it for payment.

As had happened before and would happen again, the Mint Bureau ignored the original artist at a critical point in the design creation process. Director Leach and engraver Barber decided what was and was not "…a marked improvement…" Given limited opportunity to modify the design himself, Brenner could do little but complain to colleagues about the director's treatment.

---

[84] It was unlikely that anyone would object to adding the motto; however, its omission might have been noticed.
[85] *US Mint*, NARA-CP, op. cit., entry 1A 328I. Letter dated May 21, 1909 to Leach from Brenner.
[86] *US Mint*, NARA-CP, op. cit., entry 1A 328I. Letter dated May 21, 1909 to Brenner from Leach.
[87] *US Mint*, NARA-CP, op. cit., entry 1A 328I. Letter dated May 22, 1909 to Leach from Norris.
[88] *US Mint*, NARA-CP, op. cit., entry 1A 328I. Letter dated May 22, 1909 to Brenner from Leach.

It appears there were three pattern varieties prepared by the Engraving department: #1 from Brenner's hub with Lincoln's head nearly touching the upper rim (as on the medal); #2 based on Brenner's model but with Lincoln lower in the field, more to the right and part of the lower bust removed; #3 same as #2 but with IN GOD WE TRUST added between top of the head and rim. These three versions would likely resemble the illustrations, below.

Figure 14. Recreations of 1909 pattern Lincoln cents based on descriptions provided in official corresondence. Left, original design shown on a lead trial piece; center, version with portrait lowered on the planchet leaving a gap above the head; right, circulation variety with the gap filled with motto IN GOD WE TRUST. Compare all with the medal design, above. (Left, courtesy private collection.)

On May 26 the first (no motto) and third (with motto-added) pattern cents were shown to President Taft. The brief meeting was described to Barber by director Leach:[89]

> I am pleased to inform you that in company with Assistant Secretary of the Treasury Norton, I this day visited the President and exhibited to him the trial pieces made from the new design for the one cent coin, one of which was from the original model, and the other one, modified by my directions, placing the head of Lincoln nearer the center of the coin and adding the motto "In God We Trust" over the portrait. The President was greatly pleased with the appearance of the coin and spoke in high praise of your work. He approved the modified design, or the one bearing the motto, therefore I desire that as soon as you have the new die made you will proceed in preparing dies for the new design one cent piece.

The next day Landis and Barber sent the director a letter stating that all of the pattern Lincoln cents had been destroyed:[90]

> I beg to acknowledge receipt of your letter of the 26th instant in reference to the new one cent piece and enclosing the eleven examples which were sent to your office. I hereby certify that these eleven pieces, and two additional pieces – which include all specimen pieces of the new one cent Lincoln piece which were struck – have been totally destroyed this day in the presence of the engraver and myself.

The director may have counted himself fortunate in following the same procedure as with the Pratt gold coin patterns – destruction of all pattern pieces. On June 2 a letter arrived from the American Numismatic Society requesting examples "…from the Lincoln 'one cent' piece dies for 1909 specimens without the motto."[91] With all experimental coins

---

[89] *US Mint*, NARA-CP, op. cit., entry 1A 328I, folder "Lincoln Cent Inquiries." Letter dated May 26, 1909 to Barber from Leach.
[90] *US Mint*, NARA-CP, op. cit., entry 1A 328I. Letter dated May 27, 1909 to Leach from Landis and Barber.
[91] *US Mint*, NARA-CP, op. cit., entry 229, box 274. Letter dated June 2, 1909 to Leach from William Poillon, curator, ANS collection.

destroyed he could truthfully state that none were available and avoid being pestered by collectors and museums.[92]

Figure 15. President William Howard Taft, May 1909. The President approved the Lincoln cent design on May 26, although Leach had already ordered the Philadelphia Mint to make working dies. Unlike Roosevelt, President Taft had little involvement in either the cent or nickel designs. Taft poses with his hand on the telephone – a symbol of managerial communication. Compare with a similar portrait of Roosevelt (see Chapter 1) who has his hand on the globe. (Courtesy William Howard Taft papers Library of Congress, Manuscript Division.)

Dies for the new cent were ready for shipment to San Francisco on June 22.[93] In Philadelphia production began in June with 20,000,000 pieces struck nearly a month before the design became official.[94] On July 12, Landis advised:[95]

> In reply to your letter of the 12th instant I beg to inform you that we have on hand about $203,000 in one cent bronze pieces, of which $200,000 are of the new die. I desire to say that we have not yet received any official announcement that the Lincoln cent has been adopted as the standard cent.

---

[92] This duplicates Leach's decision in 1908 to have all patterns of the Saint-Gaudens $5 and Pratt $5 destroyed – not saving even a single piece for the mint collection.
[93] *US Mint*, NARA-CP, op. cit., entry 229, box 282. Letter dated June 22, 1909 to Leach from Norris.
[94] *US Mint*, NARA-CP, op. cit., entry 229, box 287. Letter dated January 26, 1910 to Andrew from Landis, including list of one-cent pieces struck by design by month for 1909.
[95] *US Mint*, NARA-CP, op. cit., entry 229, box 283. Letter dated July 13, 1909 to Leach from Norris.

> We will notify the employees to report for work on the 19th instant.

July 19th was a Monday and had been scheduled as a "furlough day" to save money. However, most of the staff worked a full day producing new cents. The Mint Bureau had already furloughed several skilled people from the coining departments at Denver and Philadelphia, although most were recalled within a few weeks.[96] With 20,000,000 Lincoln cents, all from the version with designer's initials on the reverse on hand, the level of confidence in adoption of the new design must have been very high. This was a huge number of coins to have stockpiled for initial release on August 2. The Philadelphia Mint would strike another 5,400,000 cents in July and 2,595,000 pieces in August (totaling 7,995,000 – $79,950 more of this version) before production was suspended on Thursday August 5.

On July 14 treasury secretary MacVeagh made the Lincoln cent official:[97]

> The design of the one-cent piece bearing the head of President Lincoln, as prepared by Mr. Victor D. Brenner, and modified by the Director of the Mint by placing the head of President Lincoln nearer the center of the coin and adding the motto "In God We Trust," is hereby approved, and the coinage of the one-cent piece of this design is hereby authorized.
> The issue of these pieces will commence August 2, 1909.

With a new coin eagerly anticipated by the public, the Mint Bureau discontinued Longacre's old design and pushed Lincoln cent production at Philadelphia. When transportation of the coins to the west coast for simultaneous release on August 2 appeared to be a problem, the San Francisco mint was authorized to produce Lincoln cents also. During June, July and a few days of August the Philadelphia Mint produced nearly twenty-eight million of the new coins; San Francisco made 484,000 before suspension of production on August 5. The first sets of dies were retired on August 12.[98]

---

[96] The mints habitually hired, then fired, then rehired workers as demand for coinage fluctuated. Correspondence files are filled with letters of dismissal, followed immediately by letters rehiring the same people at the same *per diem* rate. It appears only the most senior, skilled workmen and supervisors were immune from this capricious policy.

[97] *US Mint*, NARA-CP, op. cit., entry 1A 328I. Letter dated July 14, 1909 to Leach from MacVeagh.

[98] *US Mint*, NARA-CP, op. cit., entry 229, box 287. Letter dated January 26, 1910 to Andrew from Landis, including list of one-cent pieces struck by design by month for 1909. The San Francisco total does not match the per-die total of 486,480 cents given in a detailed list provided on January 5, 1910 by San Francisco coiner William M. Cutter (*US Mint*, NARA-CP, op. cit., entry 229, box 287. Memorandum dated January 5, 1910 to superintendent Edward Sweeney from coiner William M. Cutter.) Farran Zerbe was advised that 309,000 Indian and 484,000 Lincoln VDB cents were produced in San Francisco. (*US Mint,* NARA-CP, op. cit., entry 229, box 288. Letter dated February 3, 1910 to Zerbe from U.S. Mint.) There is also a difference for the Indian head type cents. Both differences are likely due to defective coins being included in the per-die totals.

Chapter 3 – A Frenzy Throughout the Country

Public awareness and demand for the new Lincoln cents was exceptional. A multi-year buildup to the centennial fueled by newspaper and magazine articles, commercial production of commemorative medals, plaques, buttons, pins, tokens, mementos and trinkets, and official announcement of the new coin, had collectors and the common man eager to see the Lincoln cent. Interest was further heightened by the Government's refusal to permit photos or drawings of the coin to be published. This lead to speculation, rumor and innuendo about what the portrait would look like. The curious sent letters to the mint asking about the coin. Most public inquiries were answered by attaching a short note to the original and returning everything to the sender, or sending a pre-printed post card. The mint had neither staff nor funds to prepare individual replies to everyone.[99] A letter to director Leach from coin dealer Lyman H. Low was probably typical of many received:[100]

> I desire to secure 500 Lincoln cents. The Superintendent of the Mint in Philadelphia, advises me that he is unable to furnish me with more than one or two, without instructions from your Department.
> Kindly advise me in the matter at your early convenience. I will also be obliged if you are able to state when they will be issued to the Public.
> Yours very truly,

Demand was such that director Leach, who was visiting the San Francisco Mint, telegraphed acting director Preston in Washington on July 30:[101]

---

[99] Since announcement of the Saint-Gaudens gold coins in 1907, the Mint Bureau in Washington and the Philadelphia Mint had seen a substantial increase in letters from the general public. This caused the mint to abandon its policy of writing a letter replying to each inquiry, and forced the new procedure mentioned in the text. For researchers, the result is a reduction of public comment preserved in the NARA files from approximately mid-1907 forward to approximately 1930.
[100] *US Mint*, NARA-CP, op. cit., entry 229, box 283. Letter dated July 26, 1909 to Leach from Low.
[101] *US Mint*, NARA-CP, op. cit., entry 229, box 283. Telegram dated July 30, 1909 to Preston from Leach.

> I think best for you wire superintendent here the district he is to supply with new cents and the limit to each customer.
> He has several requests from sections in Mississippi valley.
> Leach, Director

Official release of the Lincoln cent began the morning of Monday August 2, 1909 through larger banks and the sub-Treasuries. People stood in long lines to buy their limit of five, ten or twenty-five coins. Some immediately sold their coins for two cents each to curious passersby, then got back in line to buy more. Newspaper boys openly hawked Lincoln cents at two or three for a nickel.

Everything seemed to be going well until the afternoon of August 2. Late in the day assistant treasury secretary Charles D. Norton received a press inquiry from the *Washington Star*, "Did the Treasury have any comment on the initials 'V.D.B.' conspicuously placed on the reverse of each new cent; and did the Treasury permit such advertising on United States coins?"[102] The next day more questions were asked and the newspapers now had little articles quoting various anonymous officials stating the initials were illegal advertising, or were not supposed to be there. As was common at the time, reporters for large newspapers often invented "facts" to make a story more interesting and entice readers to buy papers.[103] Anyone who would speak to a reporter was likely to be quoted as an "expert" on the subject.[104]

Norton telephoned superintendent Landis on the morning of August 4 and asked about initials on the new cents. Landis replied by telephone and letter that afternoon:[105]

> ...I have investigated the matter of the designer's initials on the Lincoln cent and find they were authorized by the Director of the Mint in his letter of February 27, 1909, copy of which I enclose. The design, as completed, was approved by the Honorable Secretary of the Treasury and the Director of the Mint July 15 [sic 14], 1909, copy of which is also enclosed.
> I would say that it was proposed that the initial of Mr. Brenner's last name only be used, but as this was the same as that on the present subsidiary silver coins designed by Mr. Barber, it was not distinctive enough and the three initials had to be used.
> All United States coins, with the exception of the eagle and five-cent piece, have the initials or monogram of the designer upon them.

Assistant secretary Norton had become involved because when director Leach returned from his visit to the western mints and assay offices, he was informed that his resignation, submitted as a courtesy in March, had been accepted effective July 31, 1909.[106] Secretary MacVeagh and President Taft wanted to bring someone experienced in financial theory and central bank concepts into the administration and the mint director's spot was a

---

[102] *US Mint*, NARA-CP, op. cit., entry 1A 328I. Annotation on back of memorandum dated August 5, 1909 to Norton from MacVeagh.
[103] One of the most blatant examples of inventive numismatic journalism was a December 15, 1907 *New York Times* article, "The Women Who Served As Models for the Coins," that claimed to be a detailed interview with "young Irish lass Mary Cunningham, model for the new gold coins." The article was entirely fictitious. The nonexistent Mary Cunningham was to later feature in another article claiming she was the model for the Indian cent of 1859. Mary must have aged quite gracefully.
[104] The tradition of false and misleading "journalism" is well maintained by the modern tabloid paper industry who play to the ignorant, gullible and shallow of society.
[105] *US Mint*, NARA-CP, op. cit., entry 1A 328I. Letter dated August 4, 1909 to Norton from Landis.
[106] Leach and his family were also anxious to return to California: they hated the Washington climate both meteorological and political.

convenient "holding pen." Leach was also perceived as being too much a "Roosevelt man" for the new, more conservative party leaders. His replacement was Abram Piatt Andrew, Professor of Economics at Harvard University. Politically, Andrew was somewhat more progressive than Leach. But, he possessed a vast store of knowledge on the effort to form a central bank, and was prepared to give the Taft administration a significant boost on that important issue. A further advantage was that he was from a large state, Massachusetts, rather than the small state of California as measured by congressional representation. In discussions about Brenner's initials on the cent, assistant secretary Norton and secretary MacVeagh, with advice from Charles Barber and treasurer Charles H. Treat, handled the matter.[107]

By the August 2 release, public awareness and demand had reached extraordinary levels. In part this was in response to the esteem in which President Lincoln was held by

Figure 16. Newspaper boys, such as these in Hartford, Connecticut, not only sold papers but traded in new Lincoln cents until public interest waned. According to the photo's original caption, "Boy in middle, Joseph DeLucco, has been selling for 8 years. Was arrested for stealing papers a while ago." (Courtesy Library of Congress, photo by Lewis Wickes Hine, March 1909.)

most of the population. It was also fueled by the novelty of being the first circulating coin to depict an historical person rather than an allegory. Although somewhat lengthy, the following newspaper article seems to present a reasonably accurate overall assessment of events.[108]

---

[107] *US Mint*, NARA-CP, op. cit. Memorandum dated August 5, 1909 to Preston from Norton. This includes a handwritten annotation: "Do not send to Andrew" suggesting the new director was intentionally excluded from any discussions.
[108] *The Washington Post*, "New Cents Will Stay," August 5, 1909, p.3.

New Cents Will Stay

Not to be Called in Because of Designer's Initials

Precedent in Other Coins

All Except the Old Penny and the Nickel Give Credit to the Artist. Treasury Besieged by Mob Clamoring for Lincoln Penny, but It Is Said There Will Be Enough for All.

The demand for the new Lincoln cent almost has reached the stage of a frenzy throughout the country. In Washington it has assumed mob-like proportions, because of a false report that the issue was to be recalled. Persons of all races, sexes, and ages have become seized with a wild speculative mania. The United States Treasury sustained a three-hour "run" yesterday, unprecedented for tumult, and in all 80,000 of the ornate coins were given out - $800 worth.

From all the subtreasuries of the country requests poured in on the Philadelphia mint for new supplies of the coinage. The San Francisco mint is making a small quantity, about $5,000 so far, for the Pacific slope, but the rest of the country is being supplied from Philadelphia. Two hundred and sixty thousand dollars of the pennies have been coined there, and the minting will continue. There is no prospect that there will be a shortage of supply. According to the Treasury officials, the country gets excited over a new coin nowadays in a manner that must be described as nothing short of frenzy. In anticipation of the issue of the new pennies "orders" have been flooding the mint and Treasury offices. Banks have joined in the clamorous appeal, for to them it is becoming an important business advantage to be able to supply customers with shining new money.

About 2,000 persons, boys and old men predominating, were awarded allotments of 25 cents at the Treasury in this city yesterday. They began coming in large numbers shortly before 11 o'clock and kept surging and clamoring until the gates were peremptorily closed at 2 o'clock.

Doorkeeper Kept Busy

"In all my years on this post I never have seen the like," complained the veteran doorkeeper when 2 o'clock finally came and he could "shoo" the newsboys away. "I have had to stand here for hours fighting people off. I wonder what's the matter with the people, anyway? They're getting crazy. I haven't had a chance to get a bite to eat, and I am completely worn out."

The mob about the corridor and steps was at times 600 strong, desperately struggling to get to the window where the coins were issued. At first all was tumult, for it had never been dreamed that provide itself from the Philadelphia mint. The chief difficulty it has to contend with is the counting of the pennies from the large kegs in which they come, and the sealing up in the little envelopes, the working force not being adequate for a penny-mad population.[109]

There is a strong demand for coins fresh from the mint, but the erroneous report that the new pennies would be withdrawn from circulation because the initials of the designer, Victor D. Brenner, appear on them added greatly to the excitement in Washington. Such action would at once have sent them up to a high premium among coin collectors, and it was at once made apparent that a large part of Washington's population is keenly alert to pick up easy money. Unfortunately, the highly built hopes must be dashed to the ground, for the government is going to continue minting the pennies in abundant supply.

Designers Receive Credit

Almost all the coin in circulation bear the initials of the designers, the nickel and old penny being the only exceptions. Look at the handsome throat of the goddess where it begins to taper off on the dime, and you will see the letter B. That is the initial of Barber, the designer. The 25-cent and 50-cent pieces bear the same stamp, showing the same authorship. On the dollar the letter M is to be found – Morgan being its designer. The $5 and $2.50 pieces carry the initials of Bigelow Pratt [sic – BLP for Bela Lyon Pratt] down to posterity, and the $10 and $20 coins are initialed by Saint-Gaudens.

The practice of giving designers credit for their work, just as painters affix their names, was begun in 1849, when the letter L first appeared on the double eagle, a man named Longacre then being the chief designer for the mint. Brenner is a native of Russia.

The mint authorities do not undertake to account for the remarkable interest that is taken throughout the country for the new coins. In part, it is explained by the demand of fashionable women in the large cities to be supplied with clean, undefiled coin at the banks. Many bankers, therefore, are sending to the mints for new issues even though forced to pay the expense of expressage. The subtreasuries in the respective cities could furnish plenty of coin without this extra cost, but when milady imperiously throws back a money piece that has gathered a trifle of filth from circulation and makes the demand, "Oh, give me some new money," her desires must be gratified, just as it is always good

---

[109] It would be very interesting to locate a small hoard of these little envelopes and see exactly what the first Lincoln VDB cents handed to citizens looked like. Press reports say nothing about how the coins were packaged, if at all, in San Francisco or other major cities.

police regulation would be necessary. It was soon seen, however, that [a] system must be established, and a line of the penny applicants was formed from the window stretching, serpent-like, up and down the long corridor and out to the steps in front of the main entrance.

Boys at once set up a thriving business. The gatekeeper and Treasury officials had to accord them the same rights as any other citizen of the land, and as they could burrow through the crowd they got to the window first. Then they went out into the mob and began selling the coins to those who saw that it was impossible for them to reach the disbursing window in reasonable time. The rate fluctuated, from three pennies for 5 cents to 5 cents each, the latter being the prevailing price. About 400 persons who were turned away when the doors were closed at 2 o'clock afforded a harvest for the youthful speculators.

Eager for Speculation

Aged men also were numerous in the throng. One of them came rushing in perspiring and breathless, demanding to be shown where he might get the new coins. When the inquiry was made of him why he was so frantically eager for the pennies, he replied, "Don't you know they are going to sell for a big premium? I want to get $25 worth." He was very much crestfallen when informed that not more than 25 pennies could be had by one applicant.

From an office with a large working force came a young man with $4, "his fellow employees had entrusted to him to get a supply of the new pennies…" His role of purchasing agent did not work, however. He got 25 pennies for himself, but the rest of the office force must go to the Treasury in person.

It was explained yesterday that the Treasury has an abundant supply of the coins, or can easily policy to cater to the wishes of business customers.

Procured Clean Money

A New York bank ran out of clean, untainted money recently, and it found that it could obtain a supply of the shining, spick and span variety only at the New Orleans mint. Though the cost of this long-distance expressage was considerable, the bank unhesitatingly sent on for the money, in order to satisfy the requirements of petitioners.

Connecticut is said to be the only state from which no demand for freshly made coin has come, the explanation ventured being that up there the people are eager for any kind of coin, so long as it is coin of the realm.

The Treasury has a postal card prepared for answering inquiries in numismatics, and it is set forth that "no coins of the United States have been called in." The nearest thing to this was the suspension of the Saint-Gaudens double eagles, which was found necessary because they could not be stacked.[110]

New Yorkers Seek Coins

New York, Aug. 4 – Wall Street found diversion today in the sight of a line of applicants for the new Lincoln pennies which stretched out for the length of a block from the door of the United States subtreasury. A report that the coins might be withdrawn from circulation because of the questioned legality of the issue with the initials of the upon the face of the coin, drew the coin collectors to the financial district in swarms.

Not more than a dollar's worth was given each applicant, and a premium was demanded by the possessors of the bright, new 1-cent pieces, in the belief that official action might result in making the coins comparatively rare.

Assistant Treasurer Terry said today that his attention had been directed to the matter, but that he had received no instructions from Washington to discontinue the distribution of the pennies.

Not everyone had to wait in line for a few of the new coins. Congressman William Ashbrook, an active coin collector wrote in his diary:[111]

> The new Lincoln cents made their first appearance today and I got a bunch to take home.

Two days later he had secured an additional four hundred specimens to send back to his Ohio congressional district friends.[112]

> Sent 400 of the new Lincoln pennies to that many friends in the district, today.

With no mint director in office, the treasury department had to improvise its public statements. The confused and sometimes contradictory comments to newspapers encouraged reporters to improvise "facts" and only added to speculation about a recall of the new coins. Brenner's tiny initials, certainly less prominent than Saint-Gaudens' monogram or

---

[110] This was not the real reason. See Burdette, *Renaissance of American Coinage 1905–1908* for the compete story.
[111] William A. Ashbrook, *A Line A Day for Forty Odd Years; the Diaries of William A. Ashbrook*, vol. 2, entry for August 2, 1909.
[112] *Ashbrook*, op. cit., entry for August 4, 1909.

Pratt's on the gold coins, became the focus of newspaper attention. This fueled public speculation, get-rich-quick dreams and added to an already heightened interest in the coin.

Figure 17. Citizens wait to purchase new Lincoln cents at the New York subtreasury on August 4, 1909. The block-long line formed after rumors circulated that cents were going to be recalled due to the artist's "advertising" initials on the reverse. Many of those in line appear to be boys, probably newspaper sellers, waiting to purchase the coins for resale or holding places in line for adults. Note the New York City police officer present to maintain order. (Courtesy George Grantham Bain Collection, Library of Congress.)

By August 5 secretary MacVeagh had decided what was to be done about the artist's initials:[113]

> MEMORANDUM FOR ASSISTANT SECRETARY NORTON
> As to that cent, the policy will be to let those coins remain out which have been struck off; but I should like to have directions sent to the Mint to make no more of them and to rearrange the dies so as to omit those initials. At the same time, I do not see any reason for changing the rule – if it is a rule – that the designer should have in some hidden way, his initial on the coin; but I should want to be very sure that this was not objectionable in form.
> This plan of action can be made public. I spoke, indeed, to some newspaper men this morning, near the White House, about it.
> Franklin MacVeagh, Secretary

Assistant secretary Norton suspended coinage of the Lincoln cent and sent instructions to acting director Preston:[114]

> Please instruct the mints to coin no more of the Lincoln pennies until further notice. Request Engraver Charles E. Barber of Philadelphia to visit Washington in or-

---

[113] *US Mint*, NARA-CP, op. cit., entry 1A 328I. Memorandum dated August 5, 1909 to Norton from MacVeagh.
[114] *US Mint*, NARA-CP, op. cit., entry 1A 328I. Memorandum dated August 5, 1909 to Preston from Norton.

der to arrange with us a place to have the initial "B" placed upon the new one-cent pieces in an inconspicuous manner.

The production of Lincoln cents with initials V. D. B. on the reverse was terminated on August 5. Philadelphia had been making the coins for over a month and had produced nearly 28,000,000 pieces. San Francisco did not start production until late July and had struck somewhat less than 500,000 coins by the suspension date. Treasurer Charles Treat suggested that the treasury not accept cash or checks in payment for Lincoln cents after August 7. The purpose was to prevent speculators from buying most of the available coins and reselling them at a premium.[115] This limited acquisition to banks and sub-treasuries, effectively suspending distribution of the new coins.

On August 6, engraver Barber arrived in Washington on the 2 o'clock train and immediately entered a long meeting with assistant secretary Norton and acting director Preston. Norton's notes from the meeting, in the form of a memorandum, were sent to MacVeagh the same afternoon:[116]

> Mr. Barber the Coiner [sic] of the Philadelphia Mint is here and I should be glad to have you meet him before he returns to Philadelphia, if possible.
>
> The first issue of the Lincoln coin was exactly similar to the present issue except that the Lincoln head was placed near the top of the coin and more of the bust was showing and there was no motto "In God We Trust." In the second and final edition the only change was that the head was brought nearer to the center of the coin, part of the shoulders were cut off and the motto "In God We Trust" was set above. On the reverse side there has been no change. V. D. B's initials were in the samples which were showed to you and the President [Taft] – Mr. Barber states.
>
> The making of a coinage die is as follows: a "mother die" is cut, intaglio. From the mother die is made the "hub" which is a steel relief exactly the same as the coin. From this "hub" the coinage dies are produced by being driven into blocks of cold steel.
>
> The letter B could be engraved in the mother die easily but the letters V. D. B. cannot be erased from the mother die because it is intaglio. To make a new mother die with an inconspicuous B and without the V. D. B. would take at least fourteen days.
>
> This delay can be avoided by simply erasing the V. D. B. from the "hub" and having no B whatever on the coin. From this amended "hub" the coinage dies can be rapidly and promptly struck off within three days and the mint can continue the coinage of the pennies for which there is a great demand and in which there is a great profit to the government.
>
> Mr. Barber favors cutting off the initials and leaving them off the coin entirely. This is not unusual as there are no initials on the five-cent piece, and formerly there were no initials on the Eagle, Half-Eagle or Quarter-Eagle. On the other hand it is not unusual to have an initial show on a coin. St. Gaudens' initials appear on the gold pieces, Pratt's on the Half-Eagle and Quarter-Eagle, etc. I have before me a French five-franc piece coined in 1870 on which Barr's full name appears. On another piece coined in 1831, the name E. A. Oudine appears. An Italian 20 centime piece bears the full name of both the Engraver and Designer.
>
> There are two reasons why Mr. Barber favors erasing the initials from the new penny; First, because it involves a delay of only three days in coining operations instead of a delay of about fourteen days. Second, because if the B is placed in an inconspicuous place, he fears that it may be confused with the B which now appears on the half-dollar which was engraved by himself. He is not willing to be held

---

[115] *US Mint*, NARA-CP, op. cit., entry 1A 328I. Letter dated August 6, 1909 to MacVeagh from Treat.
[116] *US Mint*, NARA-CP, op. cit., entry 1A 328I. Memorandum dated August 6, 1909 to MacVeagh from Norton.

personally responsible for the Lincoln penny which he has always opposed and does not regard as a successful coin.

Shall we take fourteen days and insert a small B in an inconspicuous place, or three days and elide the initials entirely? If the former, what is the inconspicuous place? Mr. Barber states that it is very difficult to place it on the Lincoln shoulder inconspicuously because the bust comes to the edge of the coin. On the reverse side he thought that he had found the least conspicuous place for the initials which he regarded as very small, but the American newspaper reporters have made it very clear that the place was by no means inconspicuous and the initials were by no means small.

Assistant secretary Norton relied on Barber's expertise and Preston's experience as a former mint director, to provide him with accurate, dependable information on the problem and possible solutions. He was evidently not told that removing the initials from the reverse **and** adding an incuse "B" or "VDB" under Lincoln's shoulder on the obverse would take no longer than only removing the initials.[117] The memorandum makes it clear that Barber and Preston wanted Brenner's initials off the new cent's reverse, and found every excuse to prevent adding them to any other place on the coin.

Exclusion of Piatt Andrew, the new director-designate, would have worked in favor of Barber and Preston. Andrew was very knowledgeable in matters of art and was a close friend of several painters and sculptors.[118] Had he known of the problem with Brenner's initials, it is possible he would have asked to have Brenner contacted. It is also possible Andrew could have caught Barber in his distortions of the time required to add a "B" to the design. As events unfolded, and true to Mint Bureau past performance, the original artist was ignored when changes to a design were contemplated. Within hours, after discussing the problem again with MacVeagh present, Norton issued instructions to Preston:[119]

Confirming the conference between the Secretary, Mr. Barber, the Engraver at the Philadelphia Mint, Mr. Preston and myself, this evening, we all agreed:

1. That the initials V. D. B. on the new Lincoln head one-cent piece are too conspicuous.

2. That it would not be objectionable to display the single initial B in an inconspicuous place.

3. That serious difficulties present themselves in the effort to find any place less conspicuous than the present place by reason of the fact that Lincoln's bust comes to the edge of the coin and the usual inconspicuous place is therefore lacking.

4. Owing to the great public demand for the Lincoln head one-cent piece it is not in the public interest to suspend coinage for a great length of time. Considerable time must elapse if Mr. Brenner is to be requested to submit an artistic inconspicuous monogram similar to that placed by St. Gaudens on the Double Eagle. Mr. Barber is satisfied that no monogram can be submitted which will be sufficiently inconspicuous to satisfy the requirements of all of us. If he were to submit such a monogram and it were accepted, fourteen days more must elapse before coinage could be begun at the earliest.

5. This delay is highly objectionable on account of the public demand. The initials can be erased from the "hub" tomorrow and coinage resumed within three days.

---

[117] Adding a raised "B" would take a little longer but not fourteen days. Removing the raised initials from the master hub would actually take just an hour or two. Producing a large number of working dies would take only a few days.
[118] See Chapter 5, below, for more information about director Andrew.
[119] *US Mint*, NARA-CP, op. cit., entry 1A 328I. Memorandum dated August 6, 1909 to Preston from Norton.

6. Therefore, you are authorized to show the documents in this case to the Solicitor of the Treasury early tomorrow, and as soon as he has endorsed hereon that there are no legal objection to you so doing, return this memorandum and I will, with the Secretary's approval, issue an order to erase the initials V. D. B. from the "hub" and to coin the Lincoln "cent" hereafter with no initials of the artist whatever thereon.
C. D. Norton

Maurice D. O'Connell, Solicitor of the Treasury Department, examined the various letters and memoranda, then issued his opinion:[120]

> The initials are not part of the devices or legends required on coins. It cannot be claimed that such initials are a part of the design of the coin. I see no legal objection to omitting the initials.

Norton added his orders to the same memorandum, "Secretary MacVeagh authorizes me to direct you to erase the initials V.D.B. as above indicated."[121]

Had MacVeagh been more experienced in the job it is possible he would not have taken newspapers' comments as seriously as he did. Brenner's initials were small and significantly less obvious than those of Bela Pratt on the half eagle and quarter eagle coins issued in 1908. Saint-Gaudens' monogram was in a prominent place on the double eagle, like Pratt's, close to the date; Morgan's "M" was on both sides of the standard silver dollar. Former director Leach was not consulted, and new director Andrew was excluded, leaving only Barber and Preston to present the pros and cons to Norton and MacVeagh.

Victor Brenner wrote to secretary MacVeagh and director Andrew on August 7 after being contacted by newspaper reporters. The short letter to MacVeagh asked only if the initials were to be removed and indicated no objection:[122]

> Hon. [Franklin] MacVeagh,
> Secretary of the Treasury
> I am asked by the Newspapers whether I have received official notice that the initials are to be taken off the Lincoln Cent. Would you kindly advise me of your decision.
> Thanking you for an early reply. I am,
> Respectfully,

The longer letter to director Andrew indicates the real problem for Brenner was shortening the bust and changing proportion of the cent's design:[123]

> Hon. A. Piatt Andrew, Jr.
> Director, U.S. Mint
> Much has been said for and against my initials on the Lincoln Cent, and as the designer of same, it was natural for me to express indignation to their being taken off. In reality there is a feature in the new cent, which was brought in without my knowledge, and which concerns me most. Lincoln's bust in my design was to touch the edge of the coin – in the minted cents, the bust is separated from the border. This feature makes my coin loose much of its artistic beauty.
> I beg you Sir – before more cents are minted, and before new dies are made, to kindly consider and advise.

---

[120] *Ibid.* Typed addendum to the memorandum dated August 7, 1909.
[121] *Ibid.* Second typed addendum to the memorandum dated August 7, 1909.
[122] *US Mint*, NARA-CP, op. cit., entry 1A 328I. Letter dated August 7, 1909 to MacVeagh from Brenner.
[123] *US Mint*, NARA-CP, op. cit., entry 1A 328I. Letter dated August 7, 1909 to Andrew from Brenner.

Brenner failed to mention that he had previously been instructed by Leach to: "…drop the Lincoln portrait down so that the head would come nearer the center of the coin…"[124] on May 22.

The designer was not the only one suggesting changes in the new coins. Ordinary citizens such as William K. McAllister from Denver, Colorado thought the "…setting of the obverse of the new Lincoln pennies [is improper], because Lincoln faces…right or towards the east." He felt the rules of heraldry should have Lincoln "…facing westward just as the Eagle on our coat of arms and which represents the course of empire…"[125] Louis F. Wolfe from Clifton Forge, Virginia wrote to say he thought the coin "…would look much better by placing the word Liberty at the bottom of Lincoln's bust and the date 1909 put on the reverse side."[126]

Acting director Preston sent instructions to Philadelphia Mint superintendent John Landis to remove the artist's initial from the cent on August 7:[127]

> Referring to instructions given you this date by telephone relating to removing the initials "V.D.B." from the new Lincoln one-cent piece…you will…instruct the Engraver to prepare without delay dies for the coinage of the one-cent piece with the initials "V.D.B." omitted.
> We have received a complaint that the new one cent pieces will not fit in the slot machines. I will thank you to inform me if this is true…

During suspension of cent coinage, a more serious problem had become evident: the new coin was slightly thicker than the old cent. This had been noticed by the engraving department and by several vending machine businesses. Initial distribution had resulted in few coins entering circulation. Wide spread notice did not occur until production was resumed and the coin was available in large quantities for ordinary commerce. A cautious letter from the Stollwerck Company, maker of automatic vending machines in Stamford, Connecticut, requested information:[128]

> Can you advise the exact thickness of the rim around the new edition of pennies which I understand will be out very shortly? We find a variation of from .003 to .005 of an inch in the thickness in the pennies obtained from the sub-treasury last week.

A more detailed letter arrived on the 15th from Brandt Cashier Company in Chicago – one of the larger manufacturers of coin payment machines used by banks and business to help prepare weekly payrolls. Their patented equipment delivered a specified amount of coin based on the combination of keys pressed, or issued change from the amount tendered while rejecting slugs and some counterfeits.[129]

---

[124] *US Mint*, NARA-CP, op. cit., entry 1A 328I. Letter dated May 22, 1909 to Brenner from Leach.
[125] *US Mint*, NARA-CP, op. cit., entry 229, box 283. Letter dated August 7, 1909 to MacVeagh from William K. McAllister, General Agent, Southern Pacific Company.
[126] *US Mint*, NARA-CP, op. cit., entry 229, box 284. Letter dated August 9, 1909 to MacVeagh from Louis F. Wolfe.
[127] *US Mint*, NARA-CP, op. cit., entry 235, vol. 376, p.727. Letter dated August 7, 1909 to Landis from Preston.
[128] *US Mint*, NARA-CP, op. cit., entry 229, box 284. Letter (excerpt) dated August 11, 1909 to Treasury Dept. from William B. Haller.
[129] *US Mint*, NARA-CP, op. cit., entry 1A 328I. Letter dated August 15, 1909 to assistant secretary Norton from M. H. Mandelbaum, supervisor of the Chicago office of Brandt Cashier Co. The main office of the company was in Watertown, Wisconsin, with Chicago serving as a well-known location from which the company could do business. Most company records prior to 1917 were destroyed many years ago. See Burdette, *Renaissance of American Coinage 1916-1921* for more information about Brandt Cashier Co. and testing of the 1916 coins by "slot machine" manufacturers.

> You will be interested in knowing that the Lincoln pennies are causing annoyance to Bankers and others because they do not pay through the BRANDT AUTOMATIC CASHIER.
>
> The fault is that the pennies are not even in thickness. We make this remark because some of the pennies pay while others do not.
>
> We sincerely hope that the Government in placing cons on the market will consider machines that are used to expedite business, such as the BRANDT AUTOMATIC CASHIER, and in answering bankers in the past few days about the Lincoln pennies, we have told them that the coins varied in thickness.
>
> If there is any information that we can give you it will be our pleasure to do so by letter or in person, and we hope that in writing you we did what is proper on our part, and beg to remain,
> Yours sincerely,
>
> PS: Enclose [for] you [a] folder. There are today 5,000 BRANDT AUTOMATIC CASHIERS in use.

Landis already had the engraving department working on the problem but with little success:[130]

> As requested in your letter of the 9th instant we have experimented with the reduction of the thickness of the Lincoln cent. We cut down the border of the reverse side on some of the old dies after removal of the initials, and also reduced the height of the border on the reverse side on the hub and made working dies from this. In neither case were the coins after being struck of any less thickness than those struck from the dies with the initials. The thickness is entirely due to the design, and to reduce it the dies will have to be modified.

The next day Landis sent the director's office 100 of the new coins without initials on the reverse.[131] Acting superintendent Norris provided a more detailed explanation for the thickness problem in a letter to acting director Preston on August 13:[132]

> In accordance with your letter of the 11th instant, requesting that the Engraver go ahead and prepare as early as possible new dies or hubs by which the thickness of the Lincoln cent can be reduced, I beg to inform you that I communicated with Mr. Barber by telephone yesterday at his hotel at Cape May and requested him to come to the mint for consultation in the matter. He reported today and has written a letter to the Superintendent, copy of which I enclose.
>
> I also send you three specimens of the one cent piece, one of the old style, one of the new ones with greater thickness, and one which has been reduced by Mr. Barber since he reported today. There is also enclosed a gauge by which you can measure the thickness of these different coins. Mr. Barber states that the thicker specimen of the Lincoln cent is as far as he can reduce it without a radical change in the design.
>
> The Engraver will return to Cape May today and await further instructions. He stated, however, that even if new dies are made there is no certainty with the present design that the thickness will be materially changed. It would only be a matter of experimentation.
>
> If Mr. Barber made out a voucher for his traveling expenses from and to Cape May, would it be approved?

---

[130] *US Mint*, NARA-CP, op. cit., entry 1A 328I. Letter dated August 11, 1909 to Director from Landis. This letter seems to imply yet another variation of the reverse was tested. Nothing is known about the fate of these test pieces.
[131] *US Mint*, NARA-CP, op. cit., entry 1A 328I. Letter dated August 12, 1909 to Director from Landis.
[132] *US Mint*, NARA-CP, op. cit., entry 1A 328I. Letter dated August 13, 1909 to Director from Norris.

Only ten days earlier, Barber had counseled it would take two weeks to cut new hubs. Yet, in the above letter Norris indicates that Barber had cut a hub using the maximum reduction available on the Janvier lathe in less than a day. For the second time in three years Barber's summer vacation had been interrupted. Before returning to Cape May, he wrote to the superintendent giving more detail about the situation. His letter also indicated distrust of vending machine manufacturers, who seemed to complain about the slightest alteration in coins.[133] This attitude by Barber may explain, in part, his support for Fraser's Buffalo nickel in 1913.[134]

> In compliance with your request to make the new one cent the same thickness as the old I beg to state that I have made such changes as can be readily made without an entire reconstruction of the model.
>
> If it is desired that the new coin was to conform to all the conditions of the old coin it should have been so arranged and stipulated with the designer, as it is placing this department to great disadvantage to accept a model, from an artist who never has modeled for coinage and knows absolutely nothing of the process of coinage and then insist that this department shall make dies that shall answer all Mint conditions, even to the thickness of the pieces when struck.
>
> Independent of the fact that the model was made without any thought of this requirement, the change that takes place in hardening may be sufficient to create a difference in the convexity of the die which will show when the pieces are gauged in slot machines,[135] or piled fifteen or twenty high, and are we to sacrifice the appearance of the coin or limit our production to satisfy the manufacturers and vendors of slot machines, I think not, although if the change I have already made does not conform to these machines, the only possible thing to do is to remodel the design and alter it, that it will at least satisfy the slot machine manufacturers, although it may not be satisfactory to anyone, also.
>
> The change I have made may interfere with the average number of pieces per pair of dies that the Coiner expects and is almost necessary when the demand for one cent pieces is great, but it is the only change that can be made without, as I have already said, an entire reconstruction of the coin.
>
> The relief of the Lincoln head is so great that in order to protect it from abrasion the border must be higher than the highest point of the head and consequently to make both sides of the coin alike the reverse border must be high also and these two borders regulate the thickness of the coin. You will therefore see the difficulty is two fold, first if the borders are not the same height the two sides of the coin will differ, one from the other and the mechanical difficulty is, that the borders not being equal the strain on the lowest border is too great and the die cracks before a proper average of pieces is obtained. The change I have made does not reduce the thickness of the piece to the same thickness of the old coin which I do not hesitate to say cannot be done without new models and even then it will be only an experiment as the designs are so entirely different that it is impossible for any one to say how the metal will be swallowed up by the design, and [as] the law requires the diameter and weight of the piece, we have to remedy in this direction, and therefore I earnestly advise that the change I have made be accepted as final unless it proves to reduce our production in which case there is nothing to do but return to our present hub.

---

[133] Barber also had reason to believe that his Washington design would be used on the five-cent coin as a companion piece to the Lincoln cent.
[134] *US Mint*, NARA-CP, op. cit., entry 1A 328I. Letter dated August 13, 1909 to Landis from Barber.
[135] The "slot machines" Barber refers to are not the "one armed bandits" now seen in casinos. "Slot machine" was the commonly used term for any device that accepted coins through one or more slots or openings in the device. Pay telephones, streetcar ticket and candy vending machines were the most common slot machines in the 1909 era.

It took a week for assistant secretary Norton, acting for MacVeagh, to reply to Brenner's complaint about elimination of his initials. Permitted no access to discussions about his coin design, with the president completely uninterested, Victor Brenner was figuratively shown the back exit of the mint.:[136]

> In the absence of the Secretary I am replying to your letter of the 7th instant. It was the intention of the Department to display your initials in an inconspicuous manner on the new Lincoln one-cent piece. When the first issue of the coin appeared, the initials were found to be more conspicuous than was intended and the mint officials were unable to make them less so, without changing the design and die.
>
> In view of the urgent demand for the new coins it was deemed advisable to avoid delays and it was decided to erase the initials and proceed promptly with the coinage.

There was no suggestion of replacing his initials, or of consulting with the artist on how to make the initials less conspicuous. Brenner also expressed concern about reproduction rights to his Lincoln design and his last known letter on the subject went to director Andrew:[137]

> When your predecessor the Hon. Frank A. Leach gave me the commission for the models of the Lincoln cent, I promised to destroy the models for any other purpose. Previous to my obtaining the commission, I had sold the right to publish the model to the Gorham Co. in their tablet with the Gettysburg speech. At the time, I did not think of telling Mr. Leach of this fact, and since the adoption of the cent, I made another error in allowing the Gorham Co. to cast the medallion separately – three of them or so are cast, but I withdrew my permission to cast them and I shall have those that are already cast destroyed, unless I receive permission from you to publish this medallion.
>
> Thanking you for your kind advise, I am,
> Yours very respectfully,

There is no record of a reply from the treasury department. Brenner then wrote to Farran Zerbe, president of the American Numismatic Association explaining his feelings about the initials and design:[138]

> It is mighty hard for me to express my sentiments with regard to the initials on the cent. The name of an artist on the coin is essential for the student of history as it enables him to trace environments and conditions of the time said coin was produced.
>
> Much fume has been made about my initials as a means of advertisement; such is not the case. The very talk of the initials has done more good for numismatics than it could do me personally. The cent not alone represents in part my art, but represents a type of art of our period.
>
> The conventionalizing of the sheaves of wheat was done by me with much thought, and I feel that with the prescribed wording no better design could be obtained. The [new] cent will wear out two of the last ones in time, due entirely to the hollow surface. The original design had BRENNER on it, that was changed to the initials. Of course, the issue rests with the numismatic bodies, and Europe will watch the outcome with interest.

---

[136] *US Mint*, NARA-CP, op. cit., entry 1A 328I. Letter dated August 14, 1909 to Brenner from Norton.
[137] *US Mint*, NARA-CP, op. cit., entry 229, box 284. Letter dated August 15, 1909 to Andrew from Brenner.
[138] *The Numismatist*, September-October 1909.

On the difficult-to-take-seriously side of events was a lengthy letter from Joseph Farrar who described himself as the "Great Incohonee of the Great Council of the United States of the Improved Order of Red Men" in Philadelphia. His comments included this stern warning:[139]

> ...[we understand] the "Indian Head" on pennies is no longer to be in use and I, therefore, desire to call your attention to the fact that we represent the IMPROVED ORDER OF RED MEN, an order that has taken up the peculiarities, customs and traits of the North American Indian and can assure you I voice the sentiment that over 500,000,000 Red Men, earnestly protest the discontinuance of the "Indian Head..."

The engraved letterhead (above), printed in red ink, features distorted caricatures of Native Americans. The date is given as "19th Sun, Sturgeon Moon, G.S.D. 418 (August 9, 1909)." The early twentieth century was a time when membership in societies, orders and lodges was common. Men felt a shared bond by joining the rituals and practices of such groups. Many directed their energy toward philanthropic as well as social activities. The *Improved Order of Red Men* survive a hundred years later, although in nowhere near the 500 million Farrar once claimed.

The newspaper-fed public invective against Brenner's initials was good copy for the daily papers and was still a topic of misinformation in 1916. A small article in the October 31 issue of the *New York Times* used the Lincoln cent as precedent for its complaint about the new Winged Liberty dimes:[140]

May Remove Artist's Initials From New Dime
Washington, Oct 30. – Treasury officials are considering whether the initials of the designer of the new dime, put in circulation to-day, shall be eliminated and *coinage suspended temporarily as was done in the case of the Lincoln one-cent piece.* On the face of the dime the initials of the artist, A. Weinman, appear prominently in monogram. *The Treasury Department ordered the letters off the Lincoln cent under its ruling that no advertisement shall appear on any coin.*

---

[139] *US Mint*, NARA-CP, op. cit., entry 229, box 284. Letter (excerpt) dated August 19, 1909 to MacVeagh from Joseph Farrar. The *Improved Order of Red Men* is chartered by Congress and has its national headquarters in Waco, TX. In 1995 national membership was approximately 65,000.

[140] *Adolph Alexander Weinman papers,* Smithsonian Archives of American Art, reel 283, frame 891. October 31, 1916 newspaper clipping contained in Weinman's scrapbook. Emphasis added. Fortunately, secretary McAdoo ignored the newspapers' comments.

Assistant secretary Norton, evidently pleased with his performance for the new administration during the Lincoln cent "crisis," prepared a memorandum for his office files explaining the problems with the new design and how they were solved. He also was careful to blame the mess on the previous administration:[141]

> It was contemplated that the initials V. D. B. would be placed upon the new Lincoln cent in an inconspicuous place. They were placed in the least conspicuous place which the Engraver could find. The place where the initials of a designer usually appear is between the edge of the bust and the edge of the coin. In the case of the Lincoln one-cent piece the bust is brought to the edge of the coin so that it was not possible to place the initials in the usual place without stamping them on the shoulders of Lincoln. It was not deemed advisable to place the initials at that place; therefore they were placed on the reverse side of the coin.
>
> When the cent appeared it was apparent that the initials were conspicuously placed, contrary to the expectation of the engraver. The Department then decided to substitute the letter B for the initials V. D. B., but at this point a difficulty arose. It was not possible to place the B on the coin without modifying the mother die. A change in the mother die would have caused a delay of several weeks; the public demand for the coin was very great. It was decided therefore to erase the initials entirely which could be done in a short time and proceed with the coinage. This has been done.
>
> Further objections have been made to the coin that the rim is too thick to enter the slot machines, in some cases. The Mint has done everything possible to reduce the thickness of the rim. It must be borne in mind however, that according to law, the one-cent piece must weigh 48 grains, and that the rim must be sufficiently deep to protect the head of Lincoln.
>
> The design for the Lincoln cent was adopted during the last administration. There were some requirements which would have been obvious to the experienced engravers of the Mint and which perhaps did not receive sufficient consideration at the hands of designer Brenner who is without Mint experience.

The entire "V.D.B." affair had been nothing more than a non-event cooked up by newspaper reporters with little hard news to print during a lazy summer in Washington. MacVeagh, Norton and other neophytes in the treasury department were easily manipulated by hungry newshounds into thinking Brenner's initials were a major error requiring immediate, drastic action. A reasonable course would have been to fully understand the precedent involved, then, if necessary, make changes at the end of the calendar year. But sometimes a public press gives public figures little space in which to be thoughtful, and treasury officials set about burning down their chicken coop without realizing they were locked inside. The most favored person in all this confusion was former mint director Frank Leach, who was happily packing for a return to Oakland, California, while his former bosses flapped and clucked in the flames of publicity.

Distribution

The Treasury Department and Mint Bureau made every effort to distribute the new Lincoln cents as widely as possible. The following list shows the number of one-cent coins shipped to the states and territories during calendar year 1909. Although the Denver Mint did not strike cents in 1909, they acted as distributor of Philadelphia made coins to mid-

---

[141] *US Mint*, NARA-CP, op. cit., entry 1A 328I. Memorandum dated August 17, 1909 to personal file by assistant secretary Norton.

western states. Cents from the San Francisco Mint were disbursed to only five west coast states.[142]

State or Territory	Distributed From	One-cent Value	One-cent Quantity
Alabama	Philadelphia	$11,600.00	1,160,000
Arizona Territory	San Francisco	$10,750.00	1,075,000
Arkansas	Denver	$9,895.00	989,500
California	San Francisco	$12,860.00	1,286,000
Colorado	Denver	$10,680.00	1,068,000
Connecticut	Philadelphia	$45,565.15	4,556,515
Delaware	Philadelphia	$21,350.00	2,135,000
District of Columbia	Philadelphia	$43,980.18	4,398,018
Florida	Philadelphia	$11,310.00	1,131,000
Georgia	Philadelphia	$22,460.00	2,246,000
Idaho	Denver	$10,385.00	1,038,500
Illinois	Philadelphia	$56,850.00	5,685,000
Indiana	Philadelphia	$44,225.00	4,422,500
Iowa	Denver	$45,650.00	4,565,000
Kansas	Denver	$22,990.00	2,299,000
Kentucky	Philadelphia	$12,860.00	1,286,000
Louisiana	Philadelphia	$24,000.00	2,400,000
Maine	Philadelphia	$11,310.00	1,131,000
Maryland	Philadelphia	$35,840.00	3,584,000
Massachusetts	Philadelphia	$43,655.00	4,365,500
Michigan	Philadelphia	$11,855.00	1,185,500
Minnesota	Denver	$10,640.00	1,064,000
Mississippi	Philadelphia	$10,115.00	1,011,500
Missouri	Denver	$21,865.00	2,186,500
Montana	Denver	$9,840.00	984,000
Nebraska	Denver	$10,650.00	1,065,000
Nevada	San Francisco	$11,280.00	1,128,000
New Hampshire	Philadelphia	$9,115.00	911,500
New Jersey	Philadelphia	$45,105.25	4,510,525
New Mexico Territory	Denver	$11,995.00	1,199,500
New York	Philadelphia	$84,214.55	8,421,455
North Carolina	Philadelphia	$23,965.00	2,396,500
North Dakota	Denver	$9,845.00	984,500
Ohio	Philadelphia	$60,029.55	6,002,955
Oklahoma	Denver	$45,980.00	4,598,000
Oregon	San Francisco	$11,165.00	1,116,500
Pennsylvania	Philadelphia	$110,439.00	11,043,900
Rhode Island	Philadelphia	$22,880.00	2,288,000
South Carolina	Philadelphia	$11,610.00	1,161,000
South Dakota	Denver	$9,810.00	981,000
Tennessee	Philadelphia	$12,015.00	1,201,500

---

[142] *US Mint*, NARA-CP, op. cit., entry 229, box 287. Letter dated January 21, 1910 to Andrew from Landis. The report gives the total value of cents as $1,176,628.68 which is equal to the official mintage of cents for 1909. However, this is $233.95 more than the total of individual entries.

State or Territory	Distributed From	One-cent Value	One-cent Quantity
Texas	Denver	$10,800.00	1,080,000
Utah	Denver	$9,180.00	918,000
Vermont	Philadelphia	$10,665.00	1,066,500
Virginia	Philadelphia	$24,000.00	2,400,000
Washington	San Francisco	$9,605.00	960,500
West Virginia	Philadelphia	$23,000.00	2,300,000
Wisconsin	Philadelphia	$14,650.00	1,465,000
Wyoming	Denver	$11,800.00	1,180,000
Total	Philadelphia		85,866,368
Total	Denver*		26,200,500
Total	San Francisco		5,566,000
1909 Total	Distribution		117,632,868
1909 Total	Reported Mintage (all kinds)		117,686,263

* Cents struck at Philadelphia and shipped to Denver for regional distribution.

Strong demand for Lincoln cents continued through the end of 1909. Banks seemed to have an insatiable appetite for new cents although interest was in both the new design and bright new coins. A letter to the Murchison National Bank in Wilmington North Carolina is typical of many remaining in the archives:[143]

> In reply to your letter of the 24th inst, addressed to the Treasurer of the U.S., you are informed that, owing to the great demand for the Lincoln cent, our supply of that coin became exhausted. Your order will be filled in about a week, or sooner if possible.

Brenner Fades Away

Victor Brenner didn't give up the idea of designing additional coins for the government. On April 18, 1910 he wrote to director Andrew offering an "ideal head of Liberty" for use on any available coin.[144] In 1913 he wrote director George Roberts, "I have given considerable thought to designs suitable for the silver coinage and I am sure we could arrive at fine results."[145] Roberts might have expressed interest because on February 7, 1914 Brenner noted, "I take the liberty of sending to you three sets of sketches in the rough and upon your advice I will be glad to restudy and make models of them for you to approve."[146]

Brenner continued sending letters to the Mint Bureau offering his services until June 7, 1916 when he learned that MacNeil and Weinman had designed the new silver coins. "Had I known that they were considered for the silver series, I would not have inquired about it. At your convenience, kindly return sketches I sent [in 1914]."[147]

---

[143] *US Mint*, NARA-P, op. cit., entry 621. Letter dated December 28, 1909 to S. V. Grainer, Vice President, The Murchison National Bank, Wilmington, NC from Landis.
[144] *US Mint*, NARA-CP, op. cit., entry 229, box 290. Letter dated April 18, 1910 to Andrew from Brenner.
[145] *US Mint*, NARA-CP, op. cit., entry 229, box 299. Letter dated April 3, 1913 to Roberts from Brenner.
[146] *US Mint*, NARA-CP, op. cit., entry 229, box 300. Letter dated February 7, 1914 to Roberts from Brenner.
[147] *US Mint*, NARA-CP, op. cit., entry 229, box 300, file 313710. Letter dated June 7, 1916 to Robert W. Woolley from Brenner.

During the First World War, Brenner again offered his services "…for the duration of the War in some department where his knowledge and skill in designing and modeling for the fine arts as well as for the applied arts could be of use….Mr. Brenner is, as you know, a distinguished artist and sculptor, and as designer for the Lincoln penny, is well known in the country. Besides his ability as an artist, he is a charming man."[148] Mint director Baker reported that Brenner visited his office in early May, but it appears nothing further was done.[149]

He contracted lung cancer in early 1921 and his last medal was designed in 1923. Victor Brenner was probably the best of a small number of American artists who specialized in medals and other small *bas relief* works. In 1922 he was awarded the J. Sanford Saltus silver medal from the American Numismatic Society for achievement in medallic art. He left only one well-regarded large scale work, an ornamental fountain titled *Song to Nature (Zeus and Persephone)*, located in Schenley Park, Pittsburgh, PA. Although he is well known to collectors of U.S. coins as designer of the Lincoln cent, his artistic reputation faded quickly following his death. Brenner died from lung cancer in New York City on April 5, 1924.[150]

Figure 18. Obverse design for Lincoln cent by James Fraser. Originally prepared in 1911 (left) remodeled in 1952 (center); a normal rim was used on the patterns, not the wide one shown above. The proposed reverse of 1952 is on the right. (Left photos courtest American Numismatic Rarities; center photo by Bill Fivaz taken at the Philadelphia Mint,1996; right photo courtesy Fred Weinberg,)

Comments scattered among Mint Bureau correspondence over the 1909–1920 decade make it evident that many in the treasury department considered Brenner's Lincoln portrait weak and uninspiring. Only three years after its adoption, director Roberts commented to Jim Fraser: "…the present miniature Lincoln reproduction of a design originally made of a medal does not have a good effect. We would be willing to go to Congress if we had a suitable substitute."[151] This view surfaced again in the 1950s where we find director Nellie Tayloe Ross corresponding with Jim Fraser about a new Lincoln cent design. Fraser submitted an obverse similar to the one he prepared in 1911 accompanied by an oak tree reverse design. Ross had more than 100 pattern pieces struck from the new design dies.

---

[148] *US Mint*, NARA-CP, op. cit., entry 229, box 315, folder 'W'. Letter dated April 12, 1918 to Secretary William G. McAdoo from Thomas W. Woodward, Interstate Commerce Commission.

[149] *US Mint*, NARA-CP, op. cit., entry 229, box 315, folder 'W'. Letter dated May 3, 1918 to Woodward from Raymond T. Baker, Director of the Mint.

[150] David R. Lit, Brenner's nephew, donated what was left of the sculptor's numismatic collection to the American Numismatic Society in 1987.

[151] *US Mint*, NARA-CP, op. cit., entry 235, vol. 387. Letter dated June 9, 1911 to Fraser from Roberts. Paraphrase of a longer section.

She planned to replace the Brenner version with Fraser's in 1953, however increased demand for coins and Republican Dwight D. Eisenhower's victory in the 1952 presidential election ensured Ross would be replaced as director and the project was abandoned.

Chapter 4 – Patterns and Proofs

The Lincoln cent, like its immediate predecessor the half eagle, has left us with no known pattern coins. One or two lead impressions of the obverse without motto exist to tempt the collector, but little else. Contemporary documents attest to creation of pattern pieces, and also to director Leach's zeal in having them destroyed. Nothing was saved for posterity – not even for the mint's own cabinet of coins. The source of Leach's decision to destroy all experimental pieces was his distaste for coin collectors who might "pester" him with requests to buy the coins. Viewed in context of his extensive dealings with government officials and collectors in 1907 and 1908 when the Saint-Gaudens coins were new, one might understand Leach's avoidance of anything that might interest collectors other than normal circulation issues.[152] It is unfortunate that Leach saved nothing for posterity.

			Distributed			Returned	
Denomination	Judd No.	Quan.	To	Date	Quan.	To	Date
Cent #1	J-A1909-1	5	3 to Landis; 2 to Director	5/12/09	5	Mint	5/27/09
Cent #2		4 ?	Director	5/20/09	4 ?	Mint	5/27/09
Cent #3		2	Director	5/22/09	2	Mint	5/27/09

Figure 19. Pattern Lincoln cents documented as having been struck in 1909. All examples were destroyed on orders from mint director Frank Leach.

All that remains of the bronze Lincoln cent patterns is a short list of pieces struck, distributed and presumably returned for destruction. Over the century since the coin's introduction, there have been few rumors of extant specimens and nothing tangible. The three pattern Lincoln cent variations are more fully described as:

First Obverse:
Long, full bust extending nearly rim-to-rim; no motto. Reverse, as issued for circulation but probably with BRENNER in separated script characters. Documentation is not

---

[152] See Burdette, *Renaissance of American Coinage 1905-1908* for more information.

clear enough to be conclusive. Judd A1909-1, a uniface piece struck on a oversize lead disk, is the only known example.

Figure 20. Obverse of first pattern design of 1909 Lincoln cent, cataloged as J-A1909-1. No coins are known to have survived. (Courtesy private collection.)

First Reverse:

Available documents suggest it is likely the first pattern reverse included the sculptor's last name, BRENNER, not his initials. Director Leach objected to the artist placing his name on first the obverse model, and instructed him to discuss the matter with Barber. After meeting at the Philadelphia Mint on March 4, Brenner agreed to make changes in location of his name:[153]

> I saw Mr. Barber today and have taken the plaster models with me for some alterations.
> I fully agree with you that my name on the Obverse looks intrusive, and thank you for calling my attention to it. I shall take it out, and put it in small letters on the reverse near the rim.

The resulting reverse model, and a galvano made from it (per U. S. Mint photo), does not include VDB – it has the name BRENNER in tiny, separated script lettering. Apparently, Brenner thought this was satisfactory although it was clearly not what director Leach expected. On February 27, after the President and treasury secretary Cortelyou had examined the models, Leach wrote to superintendent John Landis:[154]

> ...I notice that Mr. Brenner insists upon putting his name in full on the obverse side. I am sorry to have to disappoint him in this matter, but after consultation with the Secretary of the Treasury upon the subject it was decided that only his initials could be permitted, and that in an unobtrusive way.

It appears that either no one made it clear to Brenner about limiting his recognition on the coin to initials only, or the artist decided to use his name anyway and hope it was accepted. There is no record of Brenner revising the reverse model to include only his initials. Additionally, the appearance of finished coins suggests that V.D.B. was not part of the original model or galvano. Further support for Barber removing the name from the reverse hub and substituting initials comes from a memorandum written by assistant secretary Norton on August 6. His comments suggest both the second and third pattern designs

---

[153] *US Mint*, NARA-CP, op. cit., entry 1A 328I. Letter dated March 4, 1909 to Leach from Brenner. Agreement to alter the models was confirmed by a note from Landis to Leach on March 5.
[154] *US Mint,* NARA-CP, op. cit., entry 1A 328I. Letter dated February 27, 1909 to Landis from Leach.

had VDB on the reverse, and that it was Barber who "found the least conspicuous place for the initials."[155]

> ...On the reverse side there has been no change. V. D. B's initials were in the samples which were showed to you [MacVeagh] and the President [Taft]....
> ...On the reverse side he [Barber] thought that he had found the least conspicuous place for the initials which he regarded as very small,

Figure 21. Sculptor's name on the reverse galvano of the Lincoln cent (left)) and his initials on reverse of Lincoln cent as issued (right). Note crooked, irregular letters and off-center position of the mint-created version. (Left, courtesy David W. Lange, original image from the Philadelphia Mint; right, courtesy Numismatic Guaranty Corporation.)

It appears Barber first made a galvano of Brenner's reverse model then cut a master hub (raised design) on the Janvier reducing lathe. He then carefully ground off the raised word BRENNER and struck a master die (incuse design). Using fine engraving tools, Barber manually cut the initials V.D.B. into the master die. Presumably, the engraver was under considerable pressure to complete the work: the tiny initials are off-center, irregularly formed and slightly crooked, with the periods unevenly spaced. The position midway between ends of the wheat ears aligns with the period after "D," considerably to the right of the letter's center. Had Barber started to cut a solitary "B" then decided to use the full set of initials? It is very doubtful that Brenner would have put his initials so crudely on any model. Nothing indicates why the change was not made on the galvano where better quality could have been obtained. When compared with the galvano other parts of the reverse design appear to be accurately reproduced, making it unlikely that only the initials were distorted. The altered master die was then used to strike a new master reverse hub from which all subsequent VDB reverse master dies and working dies would have been made.

This type of retouching and manipulation of master hubs and master dies was common procedure for Barber and Morgan. Both felt that direct reductions from the Janvier and other reducing lathes were incapable of producing the sharpness of detail they expected coins to possess. With this approach, adding or removing a few initials was not difficult; however, under close examination the irregularities of hand work were evident.[156]

The author's conjecture is that the first pattern coin reverse showed BRENNER just as on the U. S. Mint's galvano. The second and third pattern cents would have had the initials V.D.B. exactly as issued for circulation as confirmed by correspondence.

---

[155] *US Mint*, NARA-CP, op. cit., entry 1A 328I. Memorandum dated August 6, 1909 to MacVeagh from Norton.
[156] The retouching of master hubs occurred on every new circulating coin design during the 1907-1921 period except the Buffalo nickel. (One pattern Buffalo nickel was extensively re-engraved but the piece did not lead to a circulating coin design.) Skill and expertise culminated in Morgan's removal of a broken sword from the reverse of the Peace dollar in December 1921, blunting public criticism and allowing the coin to be released as planned.

Second Obverse:
Reduced height bust, head considerably distant from upper rim, and positioned more to the right than previously. There is a noticeable open space between head and rim, but no motto. LIBERTY and date are larger, and the date is higher in field. Lettering stronger and clearer than previous. The reverse apparently was the same as that issued for circulation with initials V.D.B.

Figure 22. Recreation of obverse of second Lincoln cent obverse pattern, based on descriptions in archive documents. No specimens are known to exist.

Correspondence suggests that a total of between eleven and thirteen pattern pieces of all three designs were struck, with all reported destroyed on May 27, 1909. An example of this version was shown to President Taft on May 26. Leach's disdain for coin collectors was probably why no examples were kept for the mint collection.

Third Obverse:
Reduced height bust as on second obverse, with head away from rim. The space at top is filled with the motto IN GOD WE TRUST in small letters. This arrangement was specified by director Leach, but not approved by the artist, so the mint changed the design anyway. Reverse, as issued for circulation with initials VDB.

Figure 23. Third design for Lincoln cent. This version was adopted for circulation use. Patterns appear to have been destroyed, although were likely similar in appearance to collectors' proofs struck a few weeks later. (Reverse image courtesy Numismatic Guaranty Corporation.)

President Taft approved this version on May 26, 1909, but there is no record of what happened to the specimen other than it was returned to Philadelphia. Presumably, it was destroyed along with other pattern pieces. If engraver Barber followed the same procedure in making the 1909 Lincoln patterns as he did for the 1908 gold half eagle, the coins would have been struck with dies aligned "medal turn" rather than normal "coin turn."[157] Any 1909-VDB cent with evidence of being struck on a medal press, but absent the normal matte finish, and with faces aligned medal-turn, should be examined carefully. No samples were provided to the artist and none left with President Taft. Additionally, there is no mention of the specimens being polished, so they were probably what was called "bright" specimens ("satin" is the modern descriptive term) – struck on a medal press from fresh dies but not brilliant, sandblast, or matte.

Proof Coins

Matte proof specimens of the new Lincoln cent were struck for collectors and were in high demand due to the novelty of the design. These collectors' specimens of the new Lincoln cent were struck at the same time as the Philadelphia Mint was striking circulation prices. Due to curvature of the dies, engraver Barber felt they could not be polished evenly.

Date/Variety	Quantity Cents	Quantity Nickels
1909 Indian	2,500	N/A
1909-VDB	1,194	N/A
1909	2,618	5,265

Figure 24. Collectors' proof coins produced by design type and variety. To obtain a complete set of 1909 proof cents, a collector had to place three separate orders at the correct times of the year. But success was not assured because the mint did not announce availability of proof specimens prior to release or accept advance orders. Quantities produced based on entries by assistant coiner Robert Clark in medal and proof coin journals. 1909 VDB is from entry 107-E.

He was also aware of specific objections by Saint-Gaudens, Pratt and other artists about "rubbing" or "polishing" the fields of their medal-like coin designs. These factors obviated making brilliant proofs as had formerly been done. Sandblasting, as was used for gold proofs of the new designs, was considered. However, the time required to individually sandblast thousands of cents (and nickels) was prohibitive. Therefore, Barber resorted to having the coining department make collector's proofs by striking the pieces on a medal press with dies that had been lightly sandblasted before being hardened. These are called "matte proof" by modern collectors. This was no more time consuming than making brilliant proofs, but the resulting specimens closely resembled ordinary circulation coins rather than a specially produced item for collectors. Rather than highlighting detail of the design, sandblasting the dies was just as likely to remove fine detail resulting in an unconvincingly special specimen. The edges of matte proof Lincoln cents have a brilliant mirror-like surface which is different than that on circulating coins. If the dies were used too long, the special surface degraded, leaving ordinary-looking coins.

This change in perceived quality was not popular with coin collectors, and orders diminished in future years. The mint also contributed to decreased proof coins sales by abandoning its old policy of notifying previous purchasers that proofs were available (see the letter from Giles R. Anderson, below). It is also interesting to note that the mint was selling the collectors' coins at, or slightly below, cost of production. (This did not include postage, handling, and cost of notifying previous buyers.) A table prepared by the coining department in early 1912 showed that each one-cent proof cost 1.5 cents to produce, and each nickel proof cost 2.03 cents to make. The two minor coins were sold for 8-cents to-

---

[157] See Burdette, *Renaissance of American Coinage 1905–1908* for further information on the 1908 gold patterns.

gether, or 2-cents for the cent and 6 cents for the nickel. Thus each set resulted in a production loss of slightly over ½-cent.

1909 proof cents were struck in ten batches during the calendar year. Five hundred Indian type coins were made in each batch on January 5, February 20, March 6, March 23 and May 19 for a total of 2,500 pieces. The only group of proof Lincoln cents with VDB on the reverse were struck on July 30 with 1,194 delivered and accepted by the coiner on August 2.[158] No further proofs with Brenner's initials were made in 1909. Matte proof Lincoln cents without the initials were struck on August 16 – one hundred; August 23 – eight hundred twenty; December 3 – five hundred; and December 23 – two hundred ninety-eight.[159] Presumably, a new batch of proofs were not struck until most of the pieces on hand had been sold. Anecdotal information from the Anderson, Lowe and Brand letters (see Chapter 5) indicate all 1909 Indian and Lincoln VDB proofs were sold well before the end of the year. An interesting, but unsubstantiated, comment occurs in The Numismatist of March 1959: "The [1909 V.D.B.] proofs were mostly purchased by mint employees who sent them to their friends, so that this variety in proof is very scarce."[160] Coins that were either rejected due to defects or unsold, were placed in circulation after the close of the calendar year, or when demand slackened.

Introduction of the Lincoln and Buffalo designs produced noticeable spikes in an overall decline in minor proof coin sales. From a high of over 6,000 one-cent proof pieces in 1909, production shrunk to ten percent that quantity by 1916 when only six hundred one-cent proofs were made.

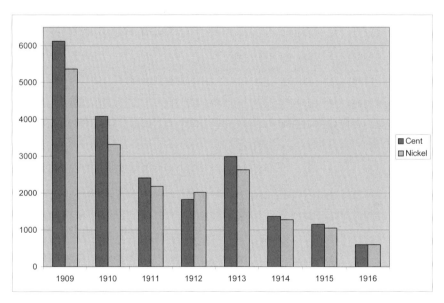

In 1911, the Mint Bureau decided production of proof specimens for collectors could not begin until the respective denomination had been issued for circulation. This had

---

[158] *US Mint*, NARA-P, op. cit., entry 107E, vol.1. Log book of delivered medals and proofs coins by Robert Clark, the assistant coiner. This is the only delivery of cents with VDB initials on the reverse.

[159] *US Mint*, NARA-P, op. cit., entry 107G "Medal and Proof Coins Book." This is an account book kept by Robert Clark, coiner of the Philadelphia Mint. These totals are different from those reported in most editions of *A Guidebook of United States Coins*.

[160] *US Mint*, NARA-CP, op. cit., entry 328I, folder "Lincoln Cent Inquiries." Article titled "The Old Lincoln Cent" attributed to Herman L. Boraker.

little effect on those who purchased only the minor coins – they were in almost constant production starting from the first days of January. Collectors of silver proofs saw only a short delay between placing an order and its delivery. However, collectors of gold sets had to wait until later in the year. Though small in number, they were very influential and particular customers. They typically bought their proof coins – cent through double eagle – all at one time. Although having to wait until November or December to order would be an inconvenience to ordinary collectors, these well-heeled persons expected to receive their sets early in the year – the better to show them off to friends and the curious. Reasonable on its own, the new policy was confusing to collectors who were accustomed to ordering proof coins soon after the beginning of the calendar year. It was especially unwelcome to wealthy gold collectors who provided the greatest revenue (and profit) to the mint.

Beginning in 1911 the policy change had a negative impact on both collectors and the Philadelphia Mint. Superintendent Adam Joyce explained in 1916:[161]

> Formerly the full set of proofs was made in January and February and orders could be filled when received, but since the manner of manufacture and issuing the proofs has been changed so that some of the denominations may not be issued until late in the year (we are only allowed to make each denomination after the regular coins for circulation have been issued), great dissatisfaction has been shown by persons desiring these proofs and a seemingly unnecessary amount of correspondence entailed on this office, returning orders and answering complaints.

The new policy led to customer dissatisfaction, complaints, delays, and wasted time and resources by collectors and the mint. Orders for proof coins, once a stable source of income and goodwill for the mint, declined precipitously, and their manufacture ceased in 1916.[162]

---

[161] *US Mint*, NARA-CP, op. cit., entry 229, box 305. Letter dated October 17, 1916 to director F.J.H. von Engelken from Adam Joyce, superintendent, Philadelphia Mint.

[162] The new policy appears to have resulted from changes in management procedures instituted by A. Piatt Andrew and continued by George Roberts. After his promotion to assistant secretary, Andrew maintained a close watch on the Mint Bureau. Andrew was also responsible for the orders to destroy all non-current dies, hubs, and partial hubs in May, 1910. See the next Chapter.

Chapter 5 – Novus Ordo Seclorum

With advent of the Taft administration on March 4, 1909, Franklin MacVeagh from Chicago replaced George Cortelyou as secretary of the treasury. MacVeagh owned one of Chicago's largest wholesale grocery and produce businesses, and was a long time director of the Commercial National Bank of Chicago.[163] He had little experience in economics or theoretical finance, and was ill prepared to lead the central bank concepts supported by President Taft and the Republican Party. When Frank Leach left the directorship at then end of July 1909 and began his journey back to San Francisco,[164] secretary MacVeagh saw his chance to bring one of the nation's foremost economic scholars into the treasury. There were no assistant secretary positions available at the time, so MacVeagh appointed A. Piatt Andrew, PhD, an Assistant Professor of Economics at Harvard, to the director's position at the Bureau of the Mint.[165] Although Andrew lived in Gloucester, Massachusetts, his family had a distinguished heritage in the mid-West. His father was active in Indiana banking circles, and his grandfather was founder of the city of LaPorte, Indiana. Andrew was also a widely published author on economics and banking and a principal editor of publications for the National Monetary Commission (a product of the Aldrich-Vreeland Act), in addition to his Harvard credentials. He was one of the few erudite, somewhat progressive souls in an otherwise conservative administration.

New Director, New Direction

Abram Piatt Andrew played no role in the removal of Victor David Brenner's initials from the Lincoln cent. He was appointed to the directorship on August 7, 1909 but did

---

[163] George E. Roberts became president of this bank after the left the Director's job in July 1907. He and MacVeagh were well acquainted and this partially explains Roberts' reappointment as Director of the Mint when Piatt Andrew left.
[164] Leach resigned because his family hated the Washington DC climate and missed the San Francisco area.
[165] Andrew was appointed on August 7, 1909 but did not assume the duties of Director until November 1. He was promoted to assistant secretary on June 7, 1910. Only F. J. H. von Engelken (September 1, 1916 to February 14, 1917) served for a shorter period during modern times.

not assume the duties of office until November 1. During the interlude, Robert Preston was again acting director. Andrew took this time to investigate the bureau, the treasury department, the sub-treasuries and the relationships between them. He also read letters and cards sent to the mint in complaint, inquiry and praise of its products.

An unexpected result of the 1907 Saint-Gaudens coinage was a huge increase in letters sent to the Mint Bureau in Washington and the Philadelphia Mint. Prior to 1907, the mint received a few letters per week asking about an old coin, requesting proof coins or inquiring about the amount of gold in a sample of ore. In most instances, the writers were sent individual typed replies including the requested information or pointing the writer to the correct government department to get an answer. Publicity attendant with the well-known sculptor Saint-Gaudens' work for President Roosevelt, the artist's death in August 1907, and later issue of his designs to mixed reviews, prompted many people to write the mint.

Through most of 1908 the mint attempted to respond to the increased flow of letters. Each letter had to be checked carefully because some contained orders for the new gold coins, and no one wanted Roosevelt to read a complain about having a coin request ignored. The small headquarters staff was overwhelmed with cards and letters, some in-

Figure 25. Abram Piatt Andrew former Director of the Mint in uniform as Major, United States Army 1918. (Courtesy American Field Service.)

cluding old coins, drawings of coin design ideas, and photos. By late 1908, director Leach and Margaret V. Kelly, who was in charge of administrative workers (including typists), decided to change how the mint answered mail. Individual replies were largely eliminated, except for known correspondents, business leaders and officials. As each new letter was opened, a secretary read it and wrote a response directly on the original, placed it in a fresh envelope, addressed it and sent it back to the writer. Some people received post cards with "stock" replies printed on them. No record was kept of who wrote, or when, or the subject, unless it seemed unusual to the mint employee reading it.

From this point until 1915, few letters to the mint were saved, aside from official correspondence and letters forwarded from the treasury secretary or White House. The result is an historical archive lacking in depth and connection with the common citizen. The return to something approaching previous practice occurred when Mary M. O'Reilley replaced Kelly in 1915. O'Reilley changed the way letters were handled, installing two "gatekeepers" to sort the material by topic, then parsing it out for pre-printed replies or individually typed responses as the subject and writer's status warranted.[166] Occasionally, a correspondent raised enough consternation among officials that we have a partial record of the event. That was the situation with Giles R. Anderson and his order for a minor proof set.

This Is Not A Square Deal – 1909

It must certainly have struck director Andrew as odd that the volume of public correspondence surged in autumn 1907, and that complaints of special deals, favoritism, irregularities and poor communication continued to increase with introduction of the Pratt designs and Lincoln cent. Rather than being appreciative of the new designs, citizens seemed to find more things about which to complain. Typical was the letter of Giles R. Anderson who wanted nothing more than a "square deal." The complaint discussed below differs from many others in that the writer was persistent in voicing his objections to a perceived injustice. Though, as a common type of objection it is entirely consistent with many the Mint Bureau evidently received. (Some of Anderson's correspondence appears to have survived because he wrote to President Taft, not the mint.)

On December 6, 1909 secretary MacVeagh forwarded a letter with enclosures to Piatt Andrew:[167]

> Dear Mr. Andrew:
> Here is a letter which came over from the White House, and I wish you would give it your personal attention. This is a matter that is Greek to me. The charge that there is something wrong in the handling of these numismatic matters in the Mint is something that needs investigation. Evidently this numismatist, Mr. Anderson, does not propose to let anybody or anything – not even the President nor any of his occupations – stand in the way of his coin fads. He is an American citizen, however, and his rights must be regarded.
> Very sincerely yours,

Giles R. Anderson, a coin collector from Waterbury, Connecticut, wrote President Taft in August 1909 to complain that he had ordered two sets of minor proof coins (including the VDB Lincoln cent) and not received his order or an acknowledgement from the Treasury. On December 1 he wrote a follow-up letter to Fred W. Carpenter, personal secre-

---

[166] When the Mint Bureau documents in the National Archives were "organized" in the early 1960s, most of the topical files maintained by the Mint Bureau were separated by origin and stored in a manner that has made it very difficult to find related documents. In some instances, topics were of sufficient notoriety to prompt archive searches and storage as new topical folders. This occurred with the Buffalo nickel, Lincoln cent, Peace dollar and in part with the Saint-Gaudens coinage. Yet, even within these well-known subjects, the GSA staff that performed the work often missed related letters and memoranda. To further confuse the mint archives, a decision was made in the mid-1980s to distribute the files among the Archive's facilities closest to each of the mints or assay offices. Thus the "San Francisco Mint" files went to NARA's Western Regional facility in San Bruno, California; Philadelphia Mint files went to Philadelphia, and so forth. As logical as this may seem, the dispersion of documents has made it extremely difficult to reassemble complete exchanges of correspondence. At least two regional facilities must be consulted to determine if relevant documents might exist. In many instances trips to three or more NARA facilities are required to be assured of reasonably complete coverage. Further, the size of the collection at each repository is too small to justify full attention of an archive specialist to assist researchers. After 1915, documents appear to have been organized alphabetically by correspondent, with only occasional topical or chronological episodes. Only 10 file boxes cover the period 1915 to 1925, with the entire decade's letters more or less alphabetized as a single "lump." Nearly all routine operational reports have not been located.

[167] *US Mint*, NARA-CP, op. cit., entry 229, box 284. Letter dated December 6, 1909 to Andrew from MacVeagh. Documents in this box are grouped approximately by subject, then by date; however, the first date in the subject group may not be the date under which the documents are filed.

tary to the president. The letter was passed to secretary of the treasury MacVeagh who sent it to mint director Andrew to handle.[168]

> Last August I wrote the President and received your reply of August 20th, stating that my remittance for the proof coins requested had been sent to the Secretary of the Treasury, for his consideration, but up to this date, I have heard nothing from the same at all.
>
> It is not the amount of twenty-five cents, but the principle involved in my not having any reply at all, when I make a remittance for a definite object, that I complain about.
>
> I desired to get one of the proofs of the first issue of the Lincoln cents. The cost of the minor proof set of one and five cent pieces is 8 cts. And I sent enough for two sets and the cost of registering the return package and one cent change.
>
> As stated in my previous letter, I wrote to the Superintendent of the U. S. Mint at Philadelphia, when I heard that the new Lincoln cents were in the engravers hands and asked when proofs could be obtained and received no reply, then finally saw that they were issued and sending for proofs, find that they are at once recalled and none can be obtained.
>
> These varieties are of interest to anyone who desires a complete collection of our country's coinage and I have the proofs from the date of my birth, to this present year and have regularly purchased the same from the Mint. Formerly the Mint would inform those who regularly purchased, if they did not get their order before the end of the year, so that the apparent oversight might be called to their attention, before it was too late to get them but during the past few years, in writing for information regarding any proposed new coinage and when proofs could be obtained, there was either no reply, or a very misleading one and then all of a sudden the news through the papers, come that the new coin is issued and for some reason, being imperfect, is recalled and a new one is out and a FAVORED FEW ONLY, get the first proofs issued.
>
> This is not a S Q U A R E   D E A L and as a citizen I have just as much right to the knowledge of when I can get proofs, so that I can have a complete set, as speculators have, who walk in and buy them up and charge me higher rates for them.
>
> I am well aware Sir, that this subject may seem a petty one when we compare the value of it to the country, to the investigation of the Sugar Trust etc., but it does seem to me, that when one has had his name on file, at the United States Mint in Philadelphia, as many years as I have, as a purchaser of the proof sets, that in the event of new coins being issued, I should have the chance to get them.
>
> An illustration of the above was in the issuing of the $20 gold piece.
>
> At the very first when the first specimen coins were submitted to Bankers and others, there was immediately raised an objection to them, which objection was stated publicly as a very decided one, viz., that the knee of the Liberty projected so much that the pieces could not be stacked, as money is in a Bank and that they would therefore be very objectionable. Notwithstanding this fact, well known in advance of their issue, a small lot of them were issued, delivered to the favored few and immediately a "great discovery is made:" Bankers do not like the new coins, call them in and change Liberty's knee. This is done and at once the first issue are selling at prices ranging from $25.00 to $35 for a twenty dollar gold piece.
>
> In this case, I had written the Mint B E F O R E they were first issued, asking when they could be had and received no reply for some time. I then had occasion to order some coins and asked the question again and with that package, written on an ordinary piece of scrap paper (not a Mint letter head) was the information,

---

[168] *US Mint*, NARA-CP, op. cit., entry 229, box 284. Letter dated December 1, 1909 to Fred W. Carpenter from Giles R. Anderson.

> that the new coins would not be issued "this year" and it was only a short time after, before they were issued and recalled.
>
> I know positively that in the time that was written to me, that the dies were in preparation, for their issue.
>
> I believe Sir, that you can take this matter up and see that I am forwarded for my remittance proofs of the first two issues of Lincoln cents which I desire and furthermore that such orders be given, that the Mint authorities would give notice by letter to all collectors who are getting proofs each year, of any new issues, so they could keep their sets complete without paying tribute to any speculators.
>
> Yours respectfully,
>
> P.S. Kindly take this matter up before the time when the annual destruction of dies occurs, so that I may not be informed that it is <u>too late.</u>

Anderson had a number of "facts" regarding the Saint-Gaudens coinage incorrect, but his overall opinion was consistent with other disappointed collectors who failed to locate one of the high relief MCMVII double eagles, or who did not receive a 1909 VDB proof cent with their order. Matters were further confused by inaccurate newspaper reports and wildly speculative estimates of the value of some varieties.[169]

Director Andrew checked with Preston and others at mint headquarters and with superintendent Landis in Philadelphia. He then prepared a memorandum for secretary MacVeagh:[170]

> I have made some inquiries with regard to the question of proof coins, referred to in the letter from Giles R. Anderson which you sent to me to-day. "Proof coins" are coins struck by hand by means of a hydraulic press upon discs which have been specially polished. The Mint is not obligated by law to sell such coins but makes a practice of doing so at a regular schedule of prices and the endeavor is to provide proof coins of the current year for all those who ask for them. The Mint, however, sells no such coins of other than the current date.
>
> Quite naturally, when a new coin is issued for only a few days and the design is suddenly changed, as was the case with the St. Gauden's [sic] coins and as was the case with the Lincoln cents bearing the initials "VDB", the proof coins of the early issue very soon command an extraordinary price. It does not seem to me, however, that we are in any way obligated to provide collectors or others with proof sets of designs whose coinage has been abandoned. Mr. Anderson and quite a number of other collectors have besieged the Department with demands for proof sets of the Indian Head type bearing the numeral "1909", of which a number were issued early in the year. As you know, the coinage of the Lincoln cent with VDB was stopped five days after the first issue and it appears that only one lot of proofs of that coin were made. Only a few of those who ordered proof coins of the Lincoln cents secured proofs from those early dies and the other would-be buyers are naturally disappointed.
>
> These proof coins are only struck at the Philadelphia Mint and Mr. Landis says that orders are always filled there as received. I shall look into the matter when in Philadelphia at the end of the week, but one can easily see how utterly impossible it would be to meet the demand for such hand-made coins in the case of new coin models which have been abandoned soon after they began to be issued.

---

[169] Speculative and ill-informed reporting in the present era, thus, has a long and sordid tradition resulting in similar public confusion, distrust and wasted effort. All eleven hundred proof VDB cents could have been purchased for less than $25.

[170] *US Mint*, NARA-CP, op. cit., entry 229, box 284. Memorandum dated December 7, 1909 to MacVeagh from Andrew.

Two days later Mr. Anderson received a courteous "brush-off" and refund from director Andrew:[171]

> Your letter of the 1st instant addressed to Mr. Fred W. Carpenter, Secretary to the President, has been referred to this Bureau by the Secretary of the Treasury. In reply you are respectfully informed that your former letter was referred to this Bureau by the Superintendent of the Mint at Philadelphia and it was supposed that officer would reply to you. Upon examination it appears that he returned your letter with the statement that there were no proof Lincoln cent with the initials "V.D.B." on hand. The Superintendent states that there was only one lot of proof Lincoln cents with the initials made, as the coinage of these pieces was stopped five days after the first issue. He also states that orders were filled as received and the stock was soon exhausted. Having been directed to discontinue the coinage of the Lincoln one-cent pieces bearing the initials "V. D. B." there was no alternative but to stop coining both the ordinary and the proof pieces.
>
> It is not considered a part of the duty of the Superintendent of the Mint to notify coin collectors when proof coins can be had. I regret that you did not file your application in time with the Superintendent of the Mint at Philadelphia to obtain proofs of the Lincoln one-cent piece with initials.
>
> In the examination of the letter of the Superintendent of the Mint at Philadelphia returning your former letter to the Bureau the 25 cents forwarded by you was found enclosed and is returned herewith.

Nothing more appears in the mint's archives regarding Anderson's search for 1909 proofs. It is likely he had to buy the coins from a dealer. Fortunately, the Mint Bureau's uncooperative attitude did not completely dissuade Anderson from his "coin fads." In 1921 we find him writing to the mint director in hopes of obtaining some of the new Peace dollars for his collection.[172]

Other collectors and coin dealers were also interested in the 1909 minor proofs, and it appears the mint had been dispensing incorrect or misleading information as a part of its normal business. New York coin dealer Lyman H. Low noted:[173]

> Under date of November 15th, you advised me that the matter of striking proof Cents of the Indian head type, and Lincoln with "V. D. B." of the present year, would be decided in the near future.
>
> As the last month of the year is fast passing on, I should like to know the prospect of the gladening [sic] of the hearts of hundreds of collectors of American coins – but for whose patronage proofs would not be struck.

A few days after Low's brief inquiry, Chicago beer magnate and coin accumulator Virgil M. Brand seemed equally concerned by the mint's silence:[174]

> I have been purchasing proof sets and minor proof sets from the Philadelphia Mint each year for about twenty years. On the seventh of the present month I sent P. O. money order to cover a stated number of sets and requested that I be in-

---

[171] *US Mint*, NARA-CP, op. cit., entry 235, vol. 380, pp.1577-1578. Letter dated December 9, 1909 to Giles R. Anderson, Waterbury, Connecticut from Andrew. A batch of five hundred proof 1909 Lincoln cents was struck on December 3, and another two hundred ninety-eight on the 23rd. It is strange that a coin or two could not have been located for Mr. Anderson.

[172] *US Mint*, NARA-CP, op. cit., entry 235, vol. 441. Letter dated December 27, 1921 to Anderson from Mary M. O'Reilly, acting director.

[173] *US Mint*, NARA-CP, op. cit., entry 229, box 286. Letter dated December 6, 1909 to Preston from Low.

[174] *US Mint*, NARA-CP, op. cit., entry 229, box 286. Letter dated December 16, 1909 to MacVeagh from Brand. The 1904 proof dollars were made in December – several months after circulation strikes were last produced.

formed if minor sets could be furnished containing the three varieties of bronze cents which have been made this year, namely the cent with the "Indian" head, the variety with bust of Lincoln and initials VDB, and the variety similar to the last without the initials. I received sets containing the last mentioned variety only. No answer was given to my question and I take it for granted that sets with the three varieties are not now on hand. I am informed by parties not in the mint, that early in the year sets had the first variety, that later the second variety was placed in the sets and that now the last variety only is furnished. I have always understood that it was the custom to furnish proofs of all the coins made during the year if requested any time during the year. In 1883 the three varieties [i.e.: shield, Liberty without 'cents', Liberty with 'cents'] on the nickel five cent piece were placed in the proof sets of that year, and again in 1904, purchasers of sets in the latter part of the year received at first no silver dollar, the coinage of that coin having been suspended, but were later notified that it had been decided to furnish the silver dollar in proof after all. This placed purchasers late in the year on the same basis as those who purchased early. I need one hundred minor sets containing the three varieties of the bronze cent and am prepared to remit the money for them as soon as the price is fixed. May I hope to receive an early reply to this communication, as time is getting short in which sets can be furnished. Thanking you for your courtesy in this matter, I am,

Low received a curt reply stating, "…there is no authority for striking additional proof pieces of the [Indian head and Lincoln VDB cents]."[175] The reply to Brand has not been located. Complaints, confusion and conflicting information all must have contributed to director Andrew's perception of the Mint Bureau as an agency in need to substantial reform.

In addition to collector and coin dealer complaints, there were multiple letters from Medallic Art Company of New York. Co-owner Henri Weil, who had helped engraver Charles Barber make hubs from the 1907 Saint-Gaudens extremely high relief double eagle models, and brother Felix insisted that Philadelphia Mint personnel were using government equipment to produce advertising medals for private sale. He also suggested that Barber and Morgan had a steady side-business cutting private commission dies during working hours. As if to reinforce Medallic Art's complaint, engraver Barber sent Andrew a sample of his commercial handiwork, to which the director took exception:[176]

> I return herewith the sample medal enclosed in your letter of the 28th ultimo. I do not think that the Mint should be engaged in the striking of medals which are for advertising purposes solely, as is evident in this case. You are authorized to notify the parties desiring the striking of these medals accordingly.
> The sample medal enclosed in your letter is returned herewith.

Andrew finally met with Medallic Art Company representatives in mid-March 1910 to listen to their accusations. The policy on private medal work for Charles Barber was no different from that for his predecessors at the Philadelphia Mint. All had been permitted – often encouraged – to design and produce non-government medals both within and outside the mint. The only restriction was that private commissions could not interfere with their required mint duties. This was also normal practice at European mints as Barber noted in the report of his 1905 overseas trip. "…the mint engraver is allowed the use of

---

[175] *US Mint*, NARA-CP, op. cit., entry 235, vol. 380, p.1582. Letter dated December 8, 1909 to Lyman H. Low from Andrew.
[176] *US Mint*, NARA-CP, op. cit., entry 235, vol. 386, p.375. Letter dated February 3, 1910 to Barber from Andrew.

mint machinery for the execution of such commissions. These commissions given the mint engraver, I was told, was a source of considerable revenue to the engraver and was done to encourage the medallic art."[177]

During the first 100 years of American independence, the only medal press in America capable of striking large diameter medals was at the Philadelphia Mint. Any American medal more than 1.5 to 2-inches in diameter had to be struck at the mint or the work contracted to European companies. The mint was the focus of some of the best die sinking/engraving talent in the country. Striking medals was also more profitable than producing coinage and mint engravers prepared private medals with the full approval and support of the Treasury department. Private medal work also allowed the mint to improve its medal production and finishing skills while materials and time were being paid for by the private commission.

The number of clients for which the mint produced medals is large and varied beginning with *Rickett's Circus*, produced circa 1794, until at least 1948. Subjects ranged from simple award medals for sporting and academic achievement, to university official and alumni honors and even wedding anniversaries (Julian, PE-5), and dog shows (UN-19, UN-20). By the early twentieth century, however, the medal production capacities of private companies (Tiffany's, Gorham, Deitsch Brothers and others) had increased to the point where businesses felt the mint was unfairly competing with private enterprise. This was the basis of Felix and Henri Weil's complaints to assistant secretary Andrew. The result was that mint engravers eventually built studios in their homes and sent models of their private commissions to Gorham, Keller, Medallic Art and other medal producers.[178]

The issue for proof coins and medals was not so much of isolated individuals complaining of favoritism, but of many in the coin collecting hobby accusing the mint of selling direct to dealers while collectors' orders were rejected, and of giving special treatment to well-connected politicians. All of this pointed to a lack of accountability, responsibility, consistency and integrity – factors which Andrew determined to correct.

Piatt Andrew was possibly the most intellectually gifted of all mint directors. He was also a tough-minded manager who "…did not suffer fools lightly." Later, during his service in France early in World War I, he would sometimes remove names from volunteer ambulance driver lists if the individual failed to agree with Andrew's opinions.[179] From the beginning of his term, Andrew questioned nearly everything about the Mint Bureau: how it operated, who was responsible for various actions, what its coin and medal products were

---

[177] *US Mint*, NARA-CP, op. cit., entry 229, box 232. Memorandum dated July 27, 1905 to Roberts from Barber.

[178] According to Dick Johnson, researcher and former employee of Medalic Art Co., commenting in the internet publication E-sylum on February 24, 2004: "John R. Sinnock was the first to do this in 1926, the year after his appointment as U.S. Mint Chief Engraver. This had the appearance at least of not conflicting with his mint duties. Every chief engraver since then did private medal jobs which were struck by American medal makers. Gilroy Roberts even modeled medallic portraits of Clyde C. Trees, his successor William Trees Louth, both as president, and all the directors of the board of Medallic Art Company over a 30-year period. (The relationship between Roberts and Medallic Art was quite close, until Joe Segel hired Gilroy away from the Philadelphia Mint to work for Franklin Mint.) American medal companies began forming in 1892 (thank you, Colombian Exposition!) and had full medal making capability by 1910, even for large-size medals. During depression years of the mid 1930s, however, Clyde Trees was attempting to keep his little company afloat by obtaining any medal job possible. It irked him to see private medals being struck by the U.S. Mint in direct competition. He mounted a campaign for the U.S. Mint to stop accepting such commissions. He insisted these should go to private American industry. Trees beat this drum constantly in the 1930s and 1940s, but it was not until 1948 that the mint stopped this practice for any new private medals. Even so, those private jobs, as award medals already in yearly production, did not run their course until 1962, when the last private medal was struck, two years after Trees had died."

[179] Per historian for the American Field Service, New York.

and what were the overriding economics of the mint. He followed these with the more difficult question, "Why?" and this was something many in the bureau had not asked themselves. The resulting changes had a profound impact on organization of the Mint Bureau and treatment of issues important to numismatists. So far as we can determine, the only numismatist to have any influence on Andrew was William H. Woodin, an acquaintance and occasional dinner companion in New York.[180]

Andrew began his term by reviewing mint operations and requesting a multitude of reports from the superintendents. This included detailed lists of dies used, coins struck from them and dies destroyed for 1909.[181] His curiosity included an interest in where the cents and nickels were distributed, for which he required yet another report.[182] He began an investigation of the Philadelphia Mint medal department based on complaints by Medallic Art Company of New York.[183] Engraver Barber was required to produce a complete list of all medals made and/or sold by the mint during the past decade.[184] During his pursuit of accountability, Andrew organized a conference of the superintendents in February 1910 asking each to provide topics for discussion.[185] He also established a committee of bureau employees to "…identify standard methods of filing and indexing…" documents.[186]

While exploring more efficient and productive operations at the mint, Andrew identified two areas of production that could be improved immediately: manual weighing of gold and silver coins, and manual feeding of presses. The director explained in a memorandum to secretary MacVeagh:[187]

> …Up to this time every gold coin has been weighed and adjusted in blank by hand and then weighed again in coin by hand, and every silver piece has been weighed after [sic – before] coining by hand as well. Last year [1909] the gold coinage of all the mints amounted to 8,144,457 pieces, all of which were weighed twice by hand, and the coinage of silver half dollars and quarter dollars amounted to 21,500,700 pieces, all of which were weighed once by hand. It is my belief that we should do away altogether with the hand weighing and hand filing, and as rapidly as automatic weighing machines can be constructed and sent to the other mints we should discharge the adjusters….

The weighing machines were made by the Napier Automatic Weighing Machine Company and purchased from England on Andrew's authority. A later report suggested the machines were not as accurate as had been thought. It wasn't until 1913 that mint officials realized that a simpler, four beam balance assembled by the machinists in the Philadelphia

---

[180] There are occasional letters from Farran Zerbe in the archives; however they are all of an official character, devoid of personal remarks or suggestions.
[181] *US Mint*, NARA-CP, op. cit., entry 229, box 291. Letter dated January 24, 1910 to Andrew from Landis. Other lists in Box 286.
[182] *US Mint*, NARA-CP, op. cit., entry 229, box 287. Letter dated January 21, 1910 to Andrew from Landis, with accompanying list of minor coins from each mint shipped to the various states and territories.
[183] *US Mint*, NARA-CP, op. cit., entry 229, box 285. Letter dated January 16, 1910 to Andrew from Medallic Art Co. Other letters in boxes 284, 286 and 288.
[184] *US Mint*, NARA-CP, op. cit., entry 229, box 288. Letter and list dated February 18, 1910 to Andrew from Landis.
[185] *US Mint*, NARA-CP, op. cit., entry 229, box 287. Letter dated January 20, 1910 to Landis, et al from Andrew.
[186] *US Mint*, NARA-CP, op. cit., entry 235, vol. 381. Letter dated January 19, 1910 to MacVeagh from Andrew.
[187] *US Mint*, NARA-CP, op. cit., entry 229, box 288. Memorandum dated February 28, 1910 to MacVeagh from Andrew. In 1905 Charles Barber reported that European mints used automatic weighing and adjusting equipment. He described several types of planchet shaving devices used in London and Vienna. Andrew does not mention automated adjustment, only suggesting that all planchets within tolerance be accepted and the others melted.

Mint was easier to use, faster and more accurate.[188] Later in the same memorandum Andrew discussed changes in the way planchets were fed into the presses:

> ...Up to a month ago one man was required for each of the 22 coining presses in the Philadelphia Mint to stack the blanks by hand in the feeding tubes. Through an ingenious...automatic coin feeding device...invented and constructed by A. Leslie Lambert, the assistant superintendent of machinery, large hoppers have now been constructed into which the blanks can be poured in sufficient quantity to last 40 minutes, from which they feed themselves automatically into the coining presses. This will make it possible for five or six men to do the work formerly accomplished by 21 or 22. It was thought at first that these coin feeds could not operate successfully without continual attendance for the reason that if the blanks ceased to be fed into them the dies would destroy themselves by the continued operation of the press. Mr. Lambert, however, constructed an ingenious electrical arrangement by which the press will be automatically stopped the moment that anything prevents the blanks from feeding into it. When it is remembered that the total coinage of the several mints last year amounted to 173,000,000 pieces and that these pieces have hitherto always been fed into the presses by hand, one can appreciate the vast improvement effected by the introduction of these automatic feeds....

Automatic weighing of gold and silver began in February. By the 14th Andrew had arranged for twenty-two women in the Philadelphia Mint adjusting department to be furloughed effective March 1. "In this case the 22 women...will be practically retired from the service. This step will probably cause some protest but the adjusters were warned six weeks ago that their tenure of office was uncertain."[189] He also ordered the dismissal of thirteen employees from the coining room as the "...automatic coin feed will be in operation by February 19th..."[190]

As the March first reduction in force date approached, Andrew, assisted by Margaret Kelly, settled on final numbers: thirty-four adjusters would be removed, fourteen coining room helpers, and "...31 additional laborers scattered through the several departments and offices of the Mint." The New Orleans Assay Office, which had been downgraded from a mint in May of 1909, lost nine employees.[191]

> The total reduction in force in Philadelphia amounts to 79 people with a resultant economy of $67,354.25; the total reduction in New Orleans amounts to 9 persons with a pay-roll of $7,859. This amounts to a reduction since the first of January in the two institutions of 88 persons and a reduction of the pay-roll amounting to more than $75,000...As soon as additional coin feeds and weighing machines have been constructed for use in Denver and San Francisco, and we have been able to make a personal visit to the Mint in San Francisco, we hope to make somewhat similar reductions in the service in the other mints.

---

[188] *US Mint*, NARA-CP, op. cit., entry 229, box 297, file 311716. Letter dated April 7, 1913 to J. S. Williams, assistant secretary of the Treasury from George Frist and C.N. McGroarty. [Signatures illegible; both names are probably incorrect.] The Mint device could "...weight either gold or silver with a degree of exactness that is almost uncanny." It was accurate to 1/5-grain.

[189] *US Mint*, NARA-CP, op. cit., entry 229, box 288. Memorandum dated February 14, 1910 to MacVeagh from Andrew.

[190] *Ibid.*

[191] *US Mint*, NARA-CP, op. cit., entry 229, box 288. Memorandum dated February 28, 1910 to MacVeagh from Andrew. Was this the first governmental use of the phrase "reduction in force"? Thankfully, Andrew did not add the acronym "RIF" to the official lexicon.

Andrew anticipated resistance to the firings – the seventy-nine positions were nearly one-fifth of the workforce – and advised MacVeagh, "I have warned Senator Penrose that the step is about to be taken because he will doubtless be pestered with complaints."[192] He likely did not anticipate the editorial cartoon that appeared in the Philadelphia *Record* on Sunday February 27.

Figure 26. Editorial cartoon showing Uncle Sam using the press of Economy to down-size mint staff. Other overstaffed (and overstuffed) government facilities – Army Arsenal, Navy Yard, Custom House, and Post Office – reluctantly await their turn. (NARA)

Receiving only slight mention in newspaper articles, memoranda and letters to secretary MacVeagh, were changes in the classification and salaries of many mint employees. Many workers who had been paid *per diem* (by the day) saw their compensation changed to an annual salary. Per diem workers received extra pay for overtime or Sunday work, but as salaried employees they received a fixed sum each week. Andrew felt this would simplify accounting, but also knew it would avoid extra expense during peak production periods. A few employees, such as Virginia Carpenter, a clerk who was also superintendent Landis' secretary, received small raises, but most lost $50 to $100 or more per year in regular pay plus additional money for overtime by being reclassified. In the engraving department, assistant engraver George T. Morgan saw his pay reduced from $10 per day ($3,130 per year based on the normal three hundred thirteen work days per year) to $3,000 per year; assistant engraver William Key lost $68 per year. Across all departments, remain-

---

[192] *US Mint*, NARA-CP, op. cit., entry 229, box 288. Memorandum dated February 14, 1910 to MacVeagh from Andrew.

ing per diem workers had their rates remain static, or reduced by 25¢ to 50¢ per day. A. Leslie Lambert, whose planchet feeding invention was to save the mint thousands of dollars each year, received an insulting raise of just $12 per year and nothing for his invention.[193]

Andrew's staff reductions came as Philadelphia was in the midst of labor strife which began in January. This had evolved into a call for a general strike by members of the Brotherhood of Railroad Trainmen against the Philadelphia Trolley Company. Railway workers throughout the northeastern states had been denied wage increases and the situation deteriorated daily. The mint dismissals and reductions in wages must have contributed to a tense situation in Philadelphia. On March 5, 1910 Andrew wrote to MacVeagh:[194]

> In view of the labor troubles and disorder in the streets now prevalent in Philadelphia, I am of the opinion that some additional protection should be given to the United States Mint....I would suggest applying to the War Department for the detail of a small guard to be maintained in the Mint night and day as long as unsettled conditions continue to exist.

On March 7 newspapers reported that Federal troops were prepared to enter the city "...in case Federal property should be endangered because of riots growing out of the general strike....the War Department feared that the United States Mint might be endangered, and no unnecessary risk was to be taken."[195] The situation was dangerous and one wonders why Andrew chose to fire employees at this time.

The long-term effectiveness of Andrew's reduction in force is questionable. As of April 1, 1909 there were four hundred ninety-seven employees on the Philadelphia Mint role. By April 1, 1911 the number was three hundred sixty – a reduction of nearly one hundred forty positions. However, in 1909 all positions were counted including potential part-time employees, whereas in 1911 only full-time staff were included. By 1912 women employees who were once titled "Adjusters" and fired by Andrew's order, were now called "Selectors" at the same per diem rate formerly paid to "Adjusters." Other departments had added staff or created new titles although most wages were still at the 1910 level.[196]

The Philadelphia "RIF" exposed another, more serious flaw in Andrew's approach to running the mint: he seemed completely unaware of the political ramifications of his decisions. Following the March 1 firings, mint files are filled with correspondence to and from the Civil Service Commission, lawyers, Congressmen and Senators. Responding to each letter must have placed an enormous burden on the small Mint Bureau staff in Washington.[197]

Andrew held strong opinions on governmental ethics and propriety, and his directness was applied to both superiors and inferiors in the Treasury. When a Congressman dared to introduce a commemorative coin bill (six versions of a half dollar with up to

---

[193] *US Mint*, NARA-CP, op. cit., entry 229, box 289. Letter dated April 5, 1910 to MacVeagh from Landis. The letter lists all changes in personnel during March including salary adjustments and reclassifications. The list includes nearly half the remaining employees of the Philadelphia Mint except for Department Supervisors.
[194] *US Mint*, NARA-CP, op. cit., entry 229, box 289. Letter dated March 5, 1910 to MacVeagh from Andrew.
[195] "May Call Federal Troops," *New York Times,* Mach 7, 1912, p1.
[196] *US Mint*, NARA-CP, op. cit., entry 235, vol. 388. Letter dated September 28, 1911, with attached supplement dated January 22, 1912 to MacVeagh from M. M. Kelly. This information is summarized from multiple employee registers and classification lists in NARA files.
[197] A sample count of pre- and post-March 1, 1910 correspondence indicates a more than ten-fold increase in this type of document.

300,000 pieces minted) to help fund the Washington Masonic Monument in Alexandria, Virginia, the director issued a four-page opinion to secretary MacVeagh summarizing the commemorative situation. It explained Andrew's opinion in rather direct language for the day:[198]

> ...The plan (to have six versions of the coin)...is objectionable because it is a fundamental perversion of the coinage. If a silver coin is issued at a fictitious value for the benefit of local organizations, why might it not be asked to go further and authorize the Bureau of Engraving and Printing to issue commemorative bills...[This is a...dangerously] easy and surreptitious use of the money providing function of Government.

The commemorative proposal failed in Congress.

General Washington's Nickel – 1909-1910

Suggestions for changing the nickel gained support during the administration of director Frank A. Leach. The grand plan of President Roosevelt had been for Augustus Saint-Gaudens to redesign all denominations from the cent through double eagle. Due to constraints of the Coinage Act of 1890, only the gold coins and bronze cent could be changed when the president and Saint-Gaudens began their collaboration in 1905.[199] When the gold dust had settled, this first effort resulted in eagle and double eagle coins by Saint-Gaudens and half eagles and quarter eagles by Boston sculptor Bela Pratt.[200] A completed cent design by Saint-Gaudens was submitted but not actively considered for adoption. Following the gold designs' introduction, President Roosevelt, now a lame duck and at odds with many in his political party, recommended to director Leach that Victor Brenner design a new bronze cent. Introduction of Brenner's Lincoln head design occurred after Roosevelt left office,[201] but the favorable public response to using Lincoln's portrait on a circulating coin encouraged director Leach to pursue changes in the nickel – the next denomination that could be changed without act of Congress.

For many years little was known about the pattern Washington five-cent pieces dated 1909 and 1910. The assumption had been they were designed by Charles Barber, but few ideas were offered about why they were made, or if they were intended for eventual replacement of the Liberty nickel first issued in 1883. Some believed them to be little more than a dead-end whim of engraver Barber.

The story of these pieces begins in September 1908. At that time, mint director Leach had Barber complete final modifications to Bela Pratt's half eagle design. A first pattern design was approved by President Roosevelt, but Barber and the director felt it needed more "sharpening" to make the Indian's feather headdress and other features clearer. Neither wanted a repeat of the headdress on Saint-Gaudens' 1907 $10 coin where the portrait had a soft, "washed out" look that mint officials felt encouraged counterfeiting. Barber made a new obverse hub based on Leach's suggestions during the last week of September. This time the feather and beading detail were sharpened and the entire design made slightly larger. The judgment of Bela Pratt when he saw the production coin was to

---

[198] *US Mint*, NARA-CP, op. cit., entry 235, vol. 381, pp.12-15. Letter dated January 6, 1910 to MacVeagh from Andrew.
[199] The sculptor died before any coins of his design were issued for circulation.
[200] See Burdette, *Renaissance of American Coinage 1905-1908* for details.
[201] By the time the Lincoln cent was released Roosevelt was busy shooting wild game in Africa. His personal papers include nothing to, or from Brenner, and say nothing about the one-cent coin.

complain about the ruin of his design. Director Leach, however, thought Barber's work was some of the best ever done.[202] About the same time, Leach learned from Barber that Victor Brenner had been preparing a medallic portrait of President Roosevelt,[203] and the president was also very impressed with the sculptor's portrait of Abraham Lincoln.

To a certain extent the 1909-1910 Washington five-cent coins may have been Leach's way of rewarding Barber for working on Pratt's sunken-relief half eagle dies. Under typical circumstances, Barber would have been expected to raise numerous objections to the novel sunken relief design. Apparently Pratt was better able to control the relief and scale than Saint-Gaudens and Hering, with the result that reductions were relatively easy to make. It is also possible that director Leach felt Barber should design the nickel because he would then be replacing his own design, with a presidential portrait. The director could do nothing about Roosevelt's instructions for the cent, but he could unobtrusively give the companion nickel design to Barber.

While the Lincoln cent was in it's formative stages director Leach commented in a letter to Victor Brenner:[204]

> ...We have only two coins on which we can make a change now, the penny and the nickel. For one of these coins I had already requested Mr. Barber to submit a design, and therefore I can only use your design, if it is accepted, on the penny or the nickel.

Soon thereafter it appears Leach gave Barber specific "...verbal instructions...to prepare certain designs and dies for a new five-cent nickel coin..."[205] featuring the portrait of George Washington. Many citizens, while appreciative of the Lincoln centennial, felt that if any person were to appear on a circulating United States coin, it should be the first president, Washington. Director Leach evidently intended the "Washington nickel" as a companion piece for the Lincoln cent, and anticipated its release in late 1909. Thus, the logic of design and of designer established, Barber proceeded to create seven different versions of a Washington five-cent piece, plus one preliminary design using shield and Liberty cap elements previously used on 1896 patterns.

Overall, the designs are stiff and old looking as if they were conceived in the 1880s instead of 1909. The portraits are no better, and possibly much worse, than ones on a plethora of Washington pieces popular during the civil war. Reverse designs are uniformly utilitarian and could have been copied from some grade school child's margin doodles in a reading book.

According to engraver Barber, a total of thirty-nine pieces of the new designs were struck and twenty-six melted. The remaining thirteen coins were apportioned among the designs as follows (in approximate order of production):[206]

---

[202] *US Mint*, NARA-P. op. cit., box 71. Letter dated October 16, 1908 to Philadelphia Mint superintendent John Landis from mint director Frank Leach.
[203] *US Mint*, NARA-CP, op. cit., entry 235, vol. 368, p.827. Letter dated October 1, 1908 to Landis from Leach. The portrait was used on the Panama Canal medal.
[204] *US Mint*, NARA-CP, op. cit., entry 1A 328I. Letter dated February 2, 1909 to Brenner from Leach.
[205] *US Mint*, NARA-CP, op. cit., entry 229, box 291. Letter dated May 26, 1910 to Landis from Barber.
[206] *US Mint*, NARA-CP, op. cit., entry 229, box 291. Statement dated May 26, 1910 signed by Barber. The information has been rearranged slightly to improve clarity, and photos of specimens in the Smithsonian, National Numismatic Collection have been added. Reference numbers from the 8th Edition of *United States Pattern Coins, Experimental and Trial Pieces* by J. Hewett Judd, Q. David Bowers, ed., Whitman Publishing Company LLC, 2003, have also been added.

Design No.	Quantity	Obverse	Reverse
8	1	Shield, word liberty on band crossing shield, flowing ends, liberty poles crossing shield, liberty cap on one and spread eagle on other, 1909 date between poles at bottom of coin, thirteen stars around. (J-1933)	Same as #4
7	1	Profile of Washington same as No. 4 only a trifle bolder, smaller date 1909. (J-1935)	Same as #4
6	1	Profile of Washington, date 1909 below bust, word liberty around head, stars between each letter. (J-1937)	Same as #5 [sic - 4]
5	1	Profile of Washington, date 1909 below bust, liberty in front of face, thirteen stars commencing in front of face and running around to point of shoulder, date 1909. (J-1936)	Same as #4

Design No.	Quantity	Obverse	Reverse
4	1	Profile of Washington looking left [sic - right], colonial coat, shirt ruff, date 1909 below bust. Liberty above head, seven stars at back of bust and six in front of face. (J-1934)	Olive branch, arabic numeral 5, word cent below, encircled by the olive branch. United States of America running around outside of branch. E Pluribus Unum below wreath.
3	1	Profile head of Washington looking left slightly smaller head [than #2], same arrangement of date 1909 and word Liberty. (J-1938)	Arabic numeral 5, cents underneath, encircled by an olive branch. E Pluribus Unum below, United States of America in large letters.
2	2	Profile head of Washington looking left, bust running down to border, queue tied low, 1909 in front of face and Liberty at back of head. (J-1939)	Same as No. 1 only In God We Trust is omitted, olive branch a trifle larger.
1	5	Profile head of Washington looking left, large head with coat stock and shirt ruff, queue tied with bow. Liberty in front of face and 1910 at back of head. (J-1942)	Arabic numeral five, outlines, cents running across olive branch on either side of coin. In God We Trust at bottom of coin. United States of America and E Pluribus Unum at top of coin.

(All photos courtesy Smithsonian National Numismatic Collection, Douglas Mudd.)

Numbering of the patterns (left column) is from Barber's original 1910 list, and the quantities are those reported remaining after twenty-six were melted. An interesting transition occurs between coins #4 and #3 (J-1934 and J-1938) where the portrait becomes much larger in size. It is possible this was due to Mint Bureau dislike of the small scale of Lincoln on the new cent, something that was still considered objectionable when the Buffalo nickel was proposed in 1911. Note that the motto IN GOD WE TRUST was omitted from all but the last version.

If director Leach had long-term plans for the Washington nickel, they vanished with his resignation in July 1909. He and his family returned to Oakland, California to escape Washington's climate – meteorological and political. His successor, A. Piatt Andrew, didn't assume office until November 1, and then immediately became embroiled in reorganizing the Mint Bureau.

During mid-November 1909 a newspaper ran a story announcing the mint would soon issue new nickels featuring a portrait of George Washington. With the Lincoln cent a popular success, a Washington nickel was a logical coin to produce. Several banks wrote to the director asking about the new coins:[207]

> We understand through the newspapers there will soon be some "new nickels" or new 5 cent pieces made with a new design - (Washington head). If this information is correct we would like to get our order in now for $100 to $200 of these to be sent to us by Express, of the very first of these that are made. Please advise how soon you think these will likely be ready to ship?
> Respectfully,
> J. L. McCulloch, President
> The Marion National Bank

On the bottom of the letter is a handwritten note, "We have received no orders to make such a coin. Probably a newspaper yarn. A. A. Norris." A similar inquiry came from The National Recording Safe Company in Chicago asking if the new coins would differ from the old Liberty nickels in size or shape. By December 7 the Farmers and Mechanics' National Bank in Philadelphia wrote to U. S. Treasurer Lee McClung, "We are having very many inquiries concerning Washington Nickels…when [will] an order be accepted for these coins."[208]

Early in 1910 Barber made final obverse and reverse hubs and struck a few examples of what he felt was the most mature design. Director Andrew, distracted with other matters of Mint Bureau administration, showed little interest in either the Washington nickel or the trouble of bringing out a new design. Barber's pattern coins and hubs escaped destruction in May, 1910 because they had been authorized by director Leach and were still a pending matter for the director's decision. Evidently, the patterns remained in Barber's office until after June 13, 1911 when coin collector William Woodin wrote to director Roberts:[209]

---

[207] *US Mint*, NARA-CP, op. cit., entry 229, box 286. Letter dated November 17, 1909 to Andrew from McCulloch. The bank was in Marion, Indiana.
[208] *US Mint*, NARA-CP, op. cit., entry 229, box 286. Letter dated December 7, 1909 to McClung from Oscar K. Weiss, Asst. Cashier.
[209] *US Mint*, NARA-CP, op. cit., entry 229, box 296. Letter dated June 13, 1911 to Roberts from Woodin. This information had probably come to Woodin through either his friend Louis Comparette, or assistant secretary Andrew. Woodin had also promoted publication of Comparette's catalog of the U.S. Mint collection in February 1911.

> May I be permitted to offer a suggestion in regard to some designs of nickels that have been executed by Mr. Charles Barber, in the Mint at Philadelphia? In company with Dr. Andrew, a year ago, last Summer, I had the pleasure of seeing these and I understand that none of them have been placed in the Mint cabinet in Philadelphia. Whether these designs are accepted or not, it seems to me very important that one specimen of each design should be placed in the coin cabinet, as these pieces were designed by the Chief Engraver and Coiner of the United States Mint, and a metallic record of this ought to be put in the Government's pattern collection.
>
> I am emboldened to write this to you for fear that these pieces might be destroyed.

Examples of the remaining coins were placed in the mint's collection and reside in the Smithsonian National Numismatic Collection to this day. A few specimens of J-1939 and J-1942 are known to be privately held. There is no information about how these pieces escaped the Philadelphia Mint, although it is likely they were inadvertently distributed by the director's office in Washington. Accounting for pattern coins remained haphazard despite the 1910 controversy between mint and coin collectors about ownership of pattern and experimental pieces.

Victor Brenner's Lincoln portrait was not popular with director Andrew or his successor George Roberts. It was felt there was "too much bust and not enough Lincoln" on the small coin. In 1911 Roberts seriously considered requesting Congressional approval to replace Brenner's version with one by James Fraser similar in scale to Barber's 1910 Washington design. Nothing came of the idea for the cent, but Fraser's enthusiasm eventually led to adoption of the Buffalo nickel in December 1912.

Some Practices at the Mint

Pattern and experimental coins had been a recurring problem for the Mint Bureau. Samples of proposed designs were needed by officials and members of Congress to visualize coinage concepts. Yet, once the coins left the Philadelphia Mint building, they were subject to loss, "forgetfulness," Congressional "borrowing" and a host of other misadventures. Naturally, coin collectors were extremely interested in new designs and took every opportunity to place patterns in their collections. As a partial stop-gap, and a convenient fund-raiser for the mint, patterns, experimental and off-metal coins had been openly sold by the Mint Bureau. Sometimes the sales were by the piece, sometimes by the set. Favored collectors and dealers usually got first pick of available examples, and Congress occasionally dipped into the trough by authorizing large numbers of patterns of unusual denominations, such as four hundred twenty-five of the $4 "Stella" and Goloid and metric dollar coins of 1879 and 1880.[210]

Charles Barber's Washington five-cent patterns had been made on verbal orders from director Frank Leach, the last of them produced in early 1910 before director Andrew halted further work. At nearly the same time, controversy raised its head in the form of "pattern, experimental and trial pieces." These were another of the "irregularities" Andrew

---

[210] *US Mint*, NARA-CP, op. cit., entry 235, vol. 386, p.503. Letter dated April 2, 1910 to T. Douglas, Shawnee National Bank, Shawnee, Oklahoma from Andrew. This is one of several inquiries about the Stella received by the mint director's office over a period of years.

perceived in need of fixing. Engraver Barber explained these coin-like pieces in a letter intended for Andrew on May 14, 1910:[211]

> A <u>pattern</u> piece or die is one made for the purpose of displaying a certain design for a coin, whether for a contemplated change in design or some existing coin or merely to exhibit the design.
>
> An <u>experimental</u> piece or die is made for the purpose of testing some proposed change in metal or alloy, such as that made for the goloid dollar, the pure nickel and aluminum coins, coins with holes in the center and with points projecting from the periphery, etc.
>
> A <u>trial</u> piece is made from dies for coin to be issued, in order to prove the correctness of the die, that is, to test whether the dies fully answer the mechanical requirements of coinage, for example: the trials made in the last designs for the double-eagle, eagle and cent.

Although these special pieces were generally thought of by Andrew as property of the U.S. Mint Bureau, there had been many occasions when specimens were given or sold to members of congress. At various times the same pieces had been considered non-monetary since they were not officially adopted designs or alloys, and thus had no value except as scrap.[212] (This parallels the earlier attitude regarding used dies which were once felt to be nothing more than old iron, until it was realized that they had to be defaced before being sold.) Over a period of several decades these special coins were sold or given to a great many people – coin collectors as well as non-collectors – and the question for Andrew in 1910 was: "Could coin collectors legally own these pieces?"

Examples of patterns being given to congressmen abounded within the memory of current representatives, the 1896 metallurgical patterns being a prime example. Acting superintendent Albert Norris recalled:[213]

> …There were many more of these pieces struck, as some of the employees in the Coining Department, who were present at the time, remember that the members of the [Congressional] Committee carried off specimens…

In 1907 President Roosevelt encouraged the sale of pattern and experimental pieces to anyone who wanted one (or more), and specifically authorized their sale.[214] Mint director Frank Leach and assistant treasury secretary Edwards accepted payment and delivered the coins to applicants ranging from ordinary collectors to senior administration officials and the Chief Justice of the United States.[215] Members of the 1908 Assay Commission each were sold one of the fifty remaining $10 eagles from the second hub that was quickly abandoned for production. One of these was sold the next day for $150.00.[216]

---

[211] *US Mint*, NARA-CP, op. cit., entry 229, box 290. Letter dated May 14, 1910 to Landis from Barber. The letter was intended to be forwarded to Andrew.
[212] Mint director James R. Snowden called them "unauthorized coins…which do not belong to the national authorized series, being of an experimental character…" in his 1860 book *A Description of Ancient and Modern Coins in the Cabinet at the Mint of the United States*.
[213] *US Mint*, NARA-CP, op. cit., entry 229, box 296. Letter dated August 28, 1911 to Roberts from Norris.
[214] It could be argued that Roosevelt's order "grandfathered" any patterns then held by collectors and by its open-ended character, also applied to future pattern and experimental pieces.
[215] See Burdette, *Renaissance of American Coinage 1905–1908*, for the President's orders and a list of coins sold.
[216] William Albert Ashbrook, *A Line A Day for Forty Odd Years; the Diaries of William A. Ashbrook*. Johnstown, Ohio, 1939. Ashland University Archives, Ashland, OH 44805. Entries for February 13, 14 1908. Ashbrook was a member of the commission and purchased all of the $10 eagles from the other members.

Today, in the early twenty-first century, numismatists admire and covet the many striking and unusual pattern and experimental coins made by the Philadelphia Mint, although few can afford to own them. But in 1910 the field of pattern and experimental coins was largely unexplored ground to both collectors and the Mint Bureau. William Woodin was the then-current expert on the subject, it would be another three years before his 1913 book would lift some of the mystery.

The Director's Sting

Farran Zerbe of Tyrone, Pennsylvania was one of the nation's leading coin dealers and promoters. He, along with Ben Green, the brothers Samuel H. and Henry Chapman, John Haseltine, Lyman Low, Thomas Elder and the young B. Max Mehl, constituted the "elite" of numismatic purveyors of the era. On December 23, 1909 Zerbe wrote the director complaining about unethical and illegal practices at the Philadelphia Mint. These likely paralleled some of Andrew's concerns about how the mint was being operated. Andrew replied to Zerbe on January 5, 1910:[217]

Referring to your letter of December 23rd which has just come to my notice upon my return from the West, I should be glad if you would let me know frankly and confidentially the "facts regarding some practices at the Mint" which you say "if brought to official attention and investigation would lead to that which is now, apparently, a source of individual profit to those in public position being diverted." I should be glad to receive a detailed statement of what you have in mind.

Figure 27. Collector William H. Woodin paid $10,000 each for two $50 gold pattern pieces that had been sold by the Philadelphia Mint to A. Loudon Snowden for approximately $100. The sale evidently precipitated director Andrew's attempt to confiscate pattern coins as "stolen government property." (Courtesy Library of Congress, George Grantham Bain Collection.)

Obviously Andrew wanted as much information as possible on Zerbe's accusations and was prepared to listen to the dealer's comments in confidence if that would help him learn more about the situation. It appears that about this time someone, possibly Zerbe, brought to Andrew's attention an article in the October 1909 issue of the *American Journal of Numismatics* in which it was stated that two $50 gold pattern pieces had been sold by collector/dealer John Haseltine to New York collector William H. Woodin for $10,000 each. This was an astounding sum of money for any coin and must have attracted special attention because of the unusual circumstances under which the coins might have left the mint collection. According to an article in *The Numismatist* of June 1909:[218]

---

[217] *US Mint*, NARA-CP, op. cit., entry 235, vol. 386, p.21. Letter dated January 5, 1910 to Farran Zerbe from Andrew.
[218] *The Numismatist*, June, 1909, p.170. Unsigned article, possibly by Farran Zerbe who was publisher at the time. The collection curator was R. A. McClure until 1905 when T. Louis Comparette was appointed to the position.

> ...The piece in the Mint [collection] was originally represented by a gold specimen, but some ten or more years ago, the one in charge of the cabinet at the time, considered $50 too much to be confined in one specimen when he could have the type duplicated in copper. The mint specimen is said to have been sold to the bullion department and melted up and the proceeds of it used in the purchase of a lot of very ordinary Spanish and Mexican dollars.

The two gold half-union ($50) patterns had not been melted, but more about these coins, later.

Mint correspondence during Andrew's tenure is silent on the subject of pattern coins until February 17, 1910 when a series of telegrams traveled between the director, J. Whitaker Thompson, the United States District Attorney in Philadelphia, and James H. Manning an officer of the National Savings Bank in Albany New York. The exchange took place over a week's time:

February 17, 1910[219]
From: Andrew
To: James H. Manning, Albany, NY

   Please wire whether you have received any news from Philadelphia.

February 22, 1910[220]
From: Andrew
To: J. Whitaker Thompson

   Manning telegraphs impossible to leave Albany before Sunday, that letter will follow.

February 24, 1910[221]
From: Andrew
To: James H. Manning, National Savings Bank, Albany, NY

   Can you meet me District Attorney's office, Post Office building Philadelphia Saturday morning at eleven bringing coins.

February 25, 1910[222]
From: Andrew
To: J. Whitiker Thompson, District Attorney

   Will meet you and Manning at your office Saturday at eleven.

James Manning had been Mayor of Albany and served on the Assay Commission several times. He was also was a coin collector who had made prior purchases from Philadelphia collector/dealer John Haseltine. Haseltine was the son-in-law of collector/dealer William Idler who had amassed a huge collection of pattern and experimental pieces during the nineteenth century. Idler had particularly close dealings with employees of the Philadelphia Mint and his name is associated with several unusual transactions involving the exchange of duplicate specimens from the mint's collection.

---

[219] *US Mint*, NARA-CP, op. cit., entry 235 vol. 386, p.267. Telegram dated February 17, 1910 to Manning from Andrew.
[220] *US Mint*, NARA-CP, op. cit., entry 235 vol. 386, p.287. Telegram dated February 22, 1910 to Thompson from Andrew.
[221] *US Mint*, NARA-CP, op. cit., entry 235 vol. 386, p.294. Telegram dated February 24, 1910 to Manning from Andrew.
[222] *US Mint*, NARA-CP, op. cit., entry 235 vol. 386, p.298. Telegram dated February 25, 1910 to Thompson from Andrew.

Manning ordered a selection of 24 pattern coins on approval from Haseltine in early February 1910. The package included the following pattern and experimental pieces:[223]

1859 cent, bronze	1859 cent, bronze	1863 cent, copper
1863 two cents, copper	1868 five cents, nickel	1864 two cents, copper-nickel
1866 half-dollar, copper	1863 ten dollar, copper	1874 twenty cents, silver
1875 dollar, copper	1881 three cents, copper	1885 dollar silver
1870 dollar, silver	1881 cent, copper	1881 five cents, copper
1882 five cents, nickel	1882 five cents, nickel	1882 five cents, copper
1882 five cents, nickel	1882 five cents, nickel	1882 five cents, copper
1882 five cents, nickel	1882 five cents, copper	1883 five cents, nickel

Figure 28. Coins shipped to James Manning of Albany, New York and later returned to John Haseltine. At the instigation of director Andrew and Philadelphia District Attorney J. Whtiker Thompson, the package was siezed by Secret Service agents when it was deliverd to Haseltine.

Haseltine's affidavit (later given to the United States Circuit Court of Philadelphia) gives examples of recent sales of these varieties, but does not provide further description of the coins. This makes it impossible to determine which varieties were included in the package. The exceptions are the 1885 silver dollar, which must have been the Morgan-design lettered edge experimental since there were no other dollar patterns made in that year,[224] and the 1863 $10 in copper which was probably from the GOD OUR TRUST dies.

Based on the telegrams, above, it appears that Manning did this as part of a plan by director Andrew to entrap Haseltine in the sale of pattern and experimental coins. The first telegram, February 17, suggests that Manning had not received the coins, but that Andrew knew about the transaction and was anxious to have the pattern pieces in his possession. By February 24, Manning had received the coins from Haseltine and agreed to bring them to a meeting with Andrew and Thompson the following Saturday morning (the 26th), as instructed.

Evidently the meeting took place, and Manning was instructed to prepare a letter to director Andrew asking for information about the coins and specifically requesting a legal opinion from the director regarding ownership. The letter was prepared and sent to Andrew on February 28, who replied on March 11:[225]

> I beg to acknowledge the receipt of your letter of February 28th, asking for data with regard to certain pattern pieces struck at the Mint of the United States at Philadelphia, with an enclosed list of the models concerning which you desire to know the number issued and the various metals in which they were struck.
>
> An examination of the records of this Bureau reveals no authority for the issue of these pieces and I would call your attention to Section 3516 of the Revised Statutes, which states that "no coins either of gold, silver or minor coinage shall hereafter be issued from the Mint other that those of the denominations, standards and weights set forth in this title." Since the passage of this act in 1875 there has

---

[223] American Numismatic Association Library. [no entry or file number]. *Affidavit of Defense* dated June 23, 1910 to United States Circuit Court, Eastern District of Pennsylvania from John W. Haseltine. The coins sent to Manning are listed in Exhibit 4 of the statement.

[224] See Burdette, *Renaissance of American Coinage 1905–1908* for additional information on the lettered edge experimental dollars of 1885.

[225] *US Mint*, NARA-CP, op. cit., entry 235, vol. 386, p.386. Quoted in letter dated March 24, 1910 to Thompson from Andrew. The Director's March 11 letter is not in the volume of press copies in NARA files. The quotation also matches that in *the Numismatist* for July, 1910, p.162.

> been no authority of law for the distribution of experimental or pattern pieces and any such pieces as have been taken from the mints have been taken unlawfully and without authority. No title has passed to any individual and the pieces are still the property of the United States.

Andrew's reply is tightly focused on the alleged illegality of the patterns, and may be interpreted as suggesting a prearranged situation. The director was not a legal authority and had no valid standing in giving an opinion – it was nothing more than his personal view – but others did not know that. On March 23 Andrew received a letter from Manning "…stating to my great surprise that he had not sent the coins but was awaiting a legal opinion in regard to them."[226] Andrew telephoned Manning asking him to forward the coins without further delay. The director's original letter to Manning says nothing about sending the coins to the Mint Bureau, which makes it evident that delivery of Haseltine's consignment and the "legal opinion" had been prearranged between Manning, Thompson and Andrew.[227]

To further complicate matters, District Attorney Thompson had visited the Securities Trust Company in Philadelphia in an attempt to confiscate the Idler/Haseltine collection from a lock box in the bank. The box was missing which prompted Andrew to comment, "…and [I] hope that Mr. Griffin (Special Agent for the District Attorney's office) will be able to follow the matter up with Mr. Idler [sic – Haseltine] that you will be able to locate the collection if it still exists."[228]

By April 21 Andrew made no excuses about his intentions. In a letter to New York coin dealer Tom Elder the mint director went straight to the point:[229]

> I have your letter of April 20th and will say that you are correct in that it is my intention to test in the courts the title to various sorts of experimental, pattern, false metal coins, etc. which have been struck in the United States Mint. I am aware that in 1888 at Mr. Linderman's sale some of the exhibits were seized by the Secret Service and that afterward certain exhibits were allowed to be sold. Among these, however, were not included any false metal pieces and the ruling at that time was that such pieces could never be disposed of by Mint officials. I should be glad to talk the subject over with you some time when I am in New York.

However, Andrew failed to tell Elder the complete Linderman pattern collection story, possibly because he wanted to create some level of apprehension in Elder's thoughts. There was no legal "ruling at that time" because the case never came to trial. The Linderman coins were returned to his widow and son after Stephen A. Walker, United States Attorney for New York, found that the mint had misinterpreted both law and department regulations. There was, "…no statute provision, governing pattern pieces, and the like; that there is no statute provision governing the sale of pattern pieces, struck in any metal, whether adopted designs or not…"[230] (It may have helped that Henry Linderman, Jr. was

---

[226] *US Mint*, NARA-CP, op. cit., entry 235, vol. 386, pp.461-462. Letter dated March 24, 1910 to Thompson from Andrew.
[227] Further speculation is that Manning was supposed to deliver the coins to Andrew and Thompson in response to the "legal" opinion of March 11. However, it appears Manning got "cold feet" at the prospect of double crossing John Haseltine and Idler, and sent the coins back to Haseltine.
[228] *US Mint*, NARA-CP, op. cit., entry 235, vol. 386, pp.461-462. Letter dated March 24, 1910 to Thompson from Andrew.
[229] *US Mint*, NARA-CP, op. cit., entry 235, vol. 386, p.586. Letter dated April 21, 1910 to Elder from Andrew.
[230] *US Mint*, NARA-CP, op. cit., entry 229, box 3. Case file relating to the Linderman auction scheduled for June 28, 1887. The U.S. Attorney's opinion was presented in October 1887.

an attorney.) The pattern coins were not only legal to own but substantial evidence pointed to the mint as primary agent in selling the pieces to collectors with proceeds credited to the government. Circulars had been issued offering Trade Dollars and other selected pattern coins for sale. Other coins – including ones in non-standard metals – were sold or given to people outside the Mint Bureau. In 1876 director Linderman stated: "Under present regulations a few sets of pieces from [experimental] dies are struck and sold at fixed rates to numismatologists."[231] Recipients included Thomas Acton, superintendent of the New York Assay Office (1877 pattern dollars in copper), President Hayes (pattern dollars in silver) and other government officials. Goloid pattern coins were popular,[232] and included authorization to strike extra specimens for personal use,[233] and for members of congress[234] or the President.[235] Congress also passed specific resolutions requiring that certain pattern coins be struck and sold to members, such as a request for one hundred of the Goloid dollar, metric dollar, stella sets.[236] Private citizens could also purchase these patterns as did Edwin Einstein of New York in June, 1880.[237] Some of the items in Linderman's sale were similar to those later seized from Haseltine. In 1907 President Roosevelt and directors Roberts and Leach (confirmed in 1908) waived all regulations relating to pattern and experimental coins so that collectors could purchase examples at face value. Andrew may have known this, but would not be dissuaded.

On April 24 the director reported a "…collection…was taken from Mr. Haseltine"[238] and Andrew was searching mint files for anything he could find to support his case, including going back to the 1792 coinage laws. He also wrote to the London and Paris mints asking for information on how they handled pattern and experimental coins and dies.[239] On April 29 the director ordered a set of the last thirty-six volumes of the ANS journal for delivery to bureau headquarters in Washington.[240]

The director was determined to stop all potential for future embarrassment. He requested a complete inventory of all pattern and experimental coin, dies and hubs in the Philadelphia Mint. Engraver Charles Barber replied on April 30:[241]

> In making out the list of dies and hubs in this department that have been made for display of designs for coins of the United States, and struck as pattern pieces under direction of the Directors Linderman and Pollock I beg to say; that those dies and hubs I have marked as being engraved between the dates 1836 and 1844,

---

[231] *US Mint,* NARA-CP, op. cit., entry 235, vol. 11, p.146. Letter dated December 28, 1876 to Rep. Roscoe Conkling from Linderman.

[232] *US Mint,* NARA-CP, op. cit., entry 229, box 16 of 18. Letter dated December 29, 1877 to Linderman from John B. Haverty, acting treasury secretary.

[233] *US Mint,* NARA-CP, op. cit., entry 235, vol. 14, p.200. Letter dated January 12, 1878 to Pollock from Linderman.

[234] *US Mint,* NARA-CP, op. cit., entry 229, box 13 of 18. Letter dated January 21, 1878 to Linderman from Secretary, House Committee on Coinage.

[235] *US Mint,* NARA-CP, op. cit., entry 235, vol. 21, p.180. Letter dated January 26, 1880 to Hayes from Burchard.

[236] *US Mint,* NARA-CP, op. cit., entry 235, vol. 21, p.344. Letter dated March 3, 1880 to Snowden from Burchard.

[237] *US Mint,* NARA-CP, op. cit., entry 235, vol. 22, p.220. Letter dated June 9, 1880 to Einstein from Preston. Similar letters to other individuals.

[238] *US Mint,* NARA-CP, op. cit., entry 235, vol. 386, p.603. Letter dated April 25, 1910 to Jasper Yates Brinton, assistant United States Attorney for Philadelphia from Andrew.

[239] *US Mint,* NARA-CP, op. cit., entry 235, vol. 386, p.606. Letter dated April 25, 1910 to Mr. Ellison-Macartney, Deputy Master, Royal Mint, London from Andrew. The *Monnais de Paris* letter is on page 607.

[240] *US Mint,* NARA-CP, op. cit., entry 235, vol. 386, p.632. Letter dated April 29, 1910 to Bauman L. Belden, ANS from Andrew. Had these been intended for use of the mint collection curator, they would have been shipped to Philadelphia, not Washington.

[241] *US Mint,* NARA-CP, op. cit., entry 229, box 290. Letter dated April 30, 1910 to Andrew from Barber.

> also those between 1844 and 1869 we have no record of, and therefore, that which I have said regarding Linderman and Pollock does not apply to these hubs and dies, as said before, I know nothing more.
>
> Since 1869 to the present date no design for any coins or die whether for pattern, experimental or regular issue, has been engraved without instructions from the Directors or Superintendents of this Mint.
>
> We have no written instruction ordering these several dies and hubs, they are the result of consultations and verbal requests and suggestions from those having authority on these matters at the time, and when the dies had served their purpose they were destroyed.
>
> The dies I have called finished are of no use other than as samples of design for the engraver's aid, they are without date and there are no obverse dies to make a pair, from which anything could be struck. The unfinished dies are those having a part of a design leaving space for inscription, etc.
>
> The finished hubs are only for the purpose of displaying the design and are without date.
>
> The largest number of hubs are those designated unfinished, these are heads of Liberty and eagles in different treatment, displayed with and without shield, and are of no use of themselves, but could be utilized if some experiment was desired in haste, and are only preserved with that in view.
>
> As before reported I have the finished hubs without date for the experimental fifty dollar coin, but no dies.
>
> If I have omitted any part of your inquiry be so kind as to so indicate.

Barber's list covered nine pages describing each different die or hub, including the mint engraver responsible for the work. His descriptions indicate the hubs and dies are of "…no use other than as samples of design for the engraver's aid…" making it obvious he was trying to persuade director Andrew to retain the materials.

Andrew was evidently not convinced the list was complete and wrote on May 10 "…requesting that the engraver furnish a specific and itemized account of the experimental dies and hubs now in his possession."[242] Barber responded with a second list which included hubs and "mother dies" for most of the previous circulating coin types, plus all of the Saint-Gaudens patterns of 1907 and the 1906 Barber-Morgan double eagle.[243] (It is interesting to note that the Saint-Gaudens list included hubs for all versions of the 1907 patterns, including the extremely high relief double eagle and the small diameter double eagle, but no edge dies were included.)

Andrew and William Woodin visited the Philadelphia Mint on May 23, examined the dies and hubs, and issued verbal orders which were followed-up by written instructions to destroy all hubs and dies on Barber's lists:[244]

> As a safeguard against possible irregularities in the issue of coins in future years, the following instructions should be carried out at the earliest possible date:
>
> There should be defaced and destroyed in the presence of the Superintendent, and Assayer, first, the dated hubs of past years. Second, the hubs and dies of superseded design. Third all dies including "mother" dies, obverse and reverse, dated and undated, except the working dies of the current year and one "mother" die of each obverse and reverse of each current design upon which is based the manufacture of the hub for the working dies. Fourth, all hubs, dies and "mother"

---

[242] *US Mint*, NARA-CP, op. cit., entry 229, box 290. Letter dated May 13, 1910 to Andrew from Landis.

[243] This latter pattern, J-773, was long thought to be the sole work of Charles Barber. The inventory reveals it was the work of both engravers. This information also changes the 1891 pattern half dollar (J-1776) to a joint effort since the obverse is clearly the same design as the 1906 reverse – both by Morgan.

[244] *US Mint*, NARA-CP, op. cit., entry 235, vol. 385, p.738. Letter dated May 23, 1910 to Landis from Andrew.

dies for experimental and pattern pieces. Hereafter, all dies and hubs of whatever character, except those used for the production of dies for the current coins of the United States should be destroyed at the end of each calendar year.

Until the end of this calendar year, the pattern hubs and dies for the new 5-cent nickel piece need not be destroyed, but the Engraver should furnish a written statement as to the number of each such pieces which have been struck, and the number which have been destroyed, and the number which are still in his possession.

The only pattern dies permitted to remain untouched were those for the 1909-1910 Washington nickel, which Andrew felt might be of use in the near future. With this action a significant portion of the mint's historical heritage – and some of the finest work of its engravers – was lost forever.

We don't know if Woodin's involvement occurred before or after the deal was struck for return of the two $50 gold patterns. Persistent numismatic rumor has been that Woodin received large quantities of excess pattern coins from the mint in compensation. If the visit occurred after Wooden and Andrew had agreed on some form of remuneration for the $50s, then Woodin's presence could be as interpreted as his personal verification that the pattern dies would be destroyed and his "compensation" in excess pattern coins protected. A letter from Woodin's attorney to District Attorney Henry Wise (below) is dated only two weeks after the dies were destroyed. It mentions the agreement in the past tense implying that it took place at a time proximate to the pattern dies destruction.

Certificates of destruction dated May 24 and May 25 were attached to copies of each list:[245]

> We, the undersigned, have witnessed this twenty-fourth day of May, 1910, the destruction of the ninety-four (94) above described hubs and dies.
> (signed)
> John Landis, Superintendent
> Charles E. Barber, Engraver
> Jacob B. Eckfeldt, Assayer
> Rhine H. Freed, Coiner

The certificate for May 25 included a statement signed by Barber of what was not destroyed (or at least part of it):[246]

> I hereby certify that the above described one hundred and thirty-six (136) dies and hubs for experimental and pattern pieces are all the dies and hubs for experimental and pattern pieces in the possession of the engraving department at the Mint of the United States at Philadelphia, excepting the pattern hubs and dies of the new 5-cent nickel piece, which have been retained in accordance with the instructions of the Director of the Mint in his letter of may 23, 1910. It is understood, however, that this statement refers solely to the United States coins and in no manner applies to dies and hubs held by the Engraver for foreign governments.

In a separate letter to director Andrew, Charles Barber sadly reports:[247]

---

[245] *US Mint*, NARA-CP, op. cit., entry 229, box 290. Affidavit dated May 24, 1910 signed by Landis, Barber, Eckfeldt and Freed.
[246] *US Mint*, NARA-CP, op. cit., entry 229, box 290. Affidavit dated May 25, 1910 signed by Barber; also by Landis, Eckfeldt and Freed.
[247] *US Mint*, NARA-CP, op. cit., entry 229, box 290. Letter dated May 25, 1910 to Andrew from Barber.

> All that now remains in the custody of the engraver is such hubs and dies as are required for the production of dies and hubs for the current coins of the United States….

The mint director also instituted a new policy of monthly reports from Barber, which must have seemed like a vote of "no confidence" in the engraver's integrity:[248]

> Beginning June 1st the Engraver should prepare each month a statement with regard to the work of his department during the preceding month, the number of hubs and dies prepared, the number of pattern or experimental pieces made and the number of such pieces returned to the Superintendent for destruction. On the first working day of each new year the Engraver should turn over to the Superintendent the hubs of all coins along with the dies for destruction.
> On the first working day of each year, and at other times if he so desires, the Superintendent of the Mint should inspect the Engraver's department and personally examine all dies, hubs, and pattern and experimental pieces that have been struck, in order to insure compliance with the regulations.

With the pattern dies and hubs destroyed, Andrew wrote to secretary MacVeagh explaining what had been done. It is of special interest that he not only consulted with pattern specialist William H. Woodin just before having the hubs destroyed, but that Woodin accompanied him to the mint, lending expert numismatic authority to his actions:[249]

> In pursuance of the effort to guard against irregularities in the future in the issue of coins of unadopted and abandoned patterns, I visited the Mint in Philadelphia on May 23rd with William H. Woodin, a coin collector in New York who has an expert knowledge of American coins. I found that the Engraver retained in his possession 136 dies and hubs for experimental and pattern pieces and 94 dies and hubs formerly used for United States coinage. The regulations of the Mint for the last 22 years have provided that all dated dies shall be defaced at the end of each year and that all dated or obverse dies cannot lawfully remain in existence after the year of their date. The Engraver had interpreted this law literally and had not considered it applicable to the hubs or mother dies of adopted coins, or to any dies of earlier date than 1888, when the present regulations went into operation, not to undated dies. This interpretation was, I believe, within the letter of the regulations but contrary to their intentions and I therefore gave instructions that all dies and hubs of whatever character, except those used for the production of dies for the current coins of the United States, should be destroyed and in consequence I have received a signed statement of the Superintendent, Engraver, Assayer and Coiner that they had jointly witnessed the destruction of 230 such dies and hubs on the 24th and 25th days of May, 1910. Mr. Barber, the engraver, writes that there now remain in his custody only "such hubs and dies as are required for the production of dies and hubs for the current coins of the United States."
> When we issue the new set of regulations I shall endeavor to reword them with regard to dies and hubs so as to provide safeguards against all of these irregularities in the future.

Andrew's decision to bring in an expert on patterns suggests he was fully informed about the nature and collector interest in these pieces. It is likely he was also aware that hubs and dies could have been placed in the mint collection under the protection of Louis

---

[248] *US Mint*, NARA-CP, op. cit., entry 235, vol. 385. (Note: page numbering ends with #738.) Letter dated May 23, 1910 to Landis from Andrew.
[249] *US Mint*, NARA-CP, op. cit., entry 235, vol. 381. Letter dated May 27, 1910 to MacVeagh from Andrew.

Comparette, and there retained for the benefit of future artists and collectors. If he had other motives for destroying the pattern hubs, they may remain forever unknown.

Andrew left the director's job on June 6, 1910 – two weeks after having all remaining pattern hubs destroyed. Considering the publicity and Congressional inquiries generated by firing of mint staff, and the legal action brought against collector/dealer John Haseltine, it is possible that secretary MacVeagh promoted Andrew, in part, to keep him out of more trouble.[250] Correspondence in mint files concerning pattern and experimental pieces ends abruptly with Andrew's promotion. Unfortunately, his assistant secretary's files, which might contain further insights, have not been located.[251] His new position brought the Mint Bureau under his supervision, and Andrew continued to show considerable interest in details of its operation. For the balance of 1910 through mid-1912, Andrew occasionally acted as a "super" mint director examining the work of director George Roberts (back for a second term at MacVeagh's request), encouraging redesign of the five-cent coin, supporting a catalog of the mint collection, and giving orders.

Events surrounding the $50 half-union gold patterns were clarified in a letter written to the U. S. Attorney in Philadelphia, Henry W. Wise. The coins were originally saved from destruction by Col. Archibald Loudon Snowden, former coiner and superintendent of the Philadelphia Mint:[252]

> ....Col. [A. Loudon] Snowden, who had originally purchased these coins from the Director of the Mint in Philadelphia by depositing the bullion value and the charge for pattern pieces to save them from being melted down, in the course of negotiations between himself and Dr. Andrew, Director of the Mints, came to an agreement with the latter over all matters in dispute between them, and proposed to Mr. Woodin to repay him the $20,000 he had paid for these pieces, in order that he might carry out his arrangement with Dr. Andrew. Mr. Woodin after numerous visits to Philadelphia and Washington and conference with Dr. Andrew, both there and in this city, decided to accept this offer, returned the 50's to Col. Snowden, and I thereupon notified Mr. Pratt, as did Mr. Woodin, that the incident was closed, and we requested a letter from your office confirming the same. In view of the trouble and expense to which Mr. Woodin was put to facilitate Dr. Andrew in the adjustment of a very difficult situation, your letter seems a little unfair, in that it would tend to create the appearance of a record some time in the future that Mr. Woodin had been compelled to give up something of which he was improperly in possession.

The two coins, which Woodin had so proudly purchased from John Haseltine, were given back to Col. Snowden, who then presented them to the Philadelphia Mint collection.

By autumn 1910 collector's journals were reporting that the two $50 gold patterns had been returned to the mint collection, but no details were given. A few tantalizing hints exist. In a letter to assistant secretary Andrew, William Woodin writes:[253]

---

[250] One could speculate that had Andrew been promoted a month earlier, a substantial portion of the nation's numismatic art heritage would still exist within the safety of the Smithsonian.
[251] If these files still exist, they should be in Record Group 56, in the NARA-College Park, Maryland facility. The author has not been able to locate them.
[252] Stacks' John J. Ford numismatic library catalog. Letter dated June 7, 1910 letter to Henry W. Wise from Woodin's attorney. Ford's library was sold at auction in June 2004. No one except Ford and possibly Walter Breen had ever seen the letter.
[253] *US Mint*, NARA-CP, op. cit., entry 229, box 295. Letter dated August 25, 1910 to Andrew from Woodin.

> ...I have not heard anything from you in regard to the pattern proposition. I trust this will come in due course.

Andrew replied on August 31:[254]

> ...I have not yet found time to formulate a plan with regard to the pattern pieces, but I presume it would be wiser anyway to wait until the court has settled the case in Philadelphia.

When combined with accounts published in *American Journal of Numismatics* and *The Numismatist*, this letter helps focus on what might have occurred. First, Col. Snowden bought the two $50 gold patterns from Robert McClure, the Curator of the Mint Collection before 1905 with the approval of either Mint Directors Robert Preston or George Roberts. He "rescued" the coins when McClure wanted to melt them for their gold value. Snowden paid for them in gold plus the charge for striking the pieces. Woodin purchased them from Snowden for $20,000. Thus, ownership went from the Mint Bureau to Snowden to Woodin. (Some speculate that John Haseltine and Stephen Nagy brokered the deal between Snowden and Woodin and received a commission on the $20,000 purchase.)

The June letter notes that as part of the settlement between Andrew, Woodin and Snowden, both coins were returned to Col. Snowden. He returned them to the Philadelphia Mint Collection. The gold patterns have remained in the mint collection and the Smithsonian ever since.

As of June 7, it appears the coins were back at the mint. Although the deal seems to have been completed, Woodin's letter of August 25 and Andrew's reply indicate that Woodin had, as yet, received nothing in compensation. Andrew's comment suggests that the former director had not actually come up with a plan of compensation. From here forward things become very murky. Apparently, the Mint Bureau was to compensate Snowden, who was obligated to repay Woodin his $20,000. The mint did not have $20,000 sitting around and could certainly not have paid such an amount to anyone without Congress raising an investigation. But, did the mint have to give Snowden anything more than a refund of his original money – $100 plus the minting charge? Thus, Snowden could have been compensated with something that had little or no value on the mint's books. The curator's purchase fund was appropriated $500 per year from the Philadelphia Mint's contingency fund. Use of this money in 1910 or 1911 would require only approval from the mint director or acting director Preston – or Andrew.

Wise's letter is also revealing in that it mentions "... numerous visits to Philadelphia and Washington..." by Woodin to negotiate the deal. This must have included Woodin's visit in May 1910 to the Philadelphia Mint during which Andrew ordered all old pattern hubs destroyed.

A Speculative Scenario

Absent further documents the author offers the following.

Farran Zerbe's December 1909 letter dealt with sale of the Half Union patterns. In it, he claimed the coins were illicitly obtained from the mint collection and sold for a huge private profit. Andrew was concerned by Zerbe's letter and after limited internal discussions, decided the sale was illegal and that government property had been stolen. Once an

---
[254] *US Mint*, NARA-CP, op. cit., entry 229, box 295. Letter dated August 31, 1910 to Woodin from Andrew.

opinion was formed, Andrew was not one to change his mind readily or to admit he was wrong. The director determined to recover the Half Unions – the world's most valuable coins – for the mint collection.

In January and February 1910, Andrew and U.S. Attorney J. Whitaker Thompson hatched a plan to put pressure on Woodin to return the Half Unions by taking legal action to confiscate pattern coins from John Haseltine. Haseltine was well known to collectors and had an established trade in pattern and experimental pieces. For entrapment purposes, Andrew selected James Manning (possibly on Zerbe's recommendation as a pattern collector) who had been on the 1909 Assay Commission.[255] Once a solid case was established against Haseltine, prosecuting Woodin, or persuading him to avoid a legal battle, would be much easier.

By late April, after Manning's reticence and deeper research by the U.S. Attorney's office, Andrew realized his entrapment plan threatened to draw the treasury into a long, and ultimately futile legal battle. The fight would not only be with some very wealthy and politically-connected collectors, but with current and former members of Congress and Executive Department officials. These politically prominent persons held $4 Stellas, off-metal proof sets, Goloid dollars, copper examples of pattern silver coins, Saint-Gaudens Extremely High Relief double eagles and other items obtained during their official terms of office. (Whether they were obtained legally or paid for would be immaterial to newspapers.) They included former President Roosevelt, the estate of former President Hayes, and a host of former cabinet officers and lesser political figures of both parties. Woodin's wealth, Haseltine's connections, and cooperation from Tom Elder and other coin dealers, ensured that defense attorneys would dig out politically connected owners of pattern pieces and have them testify to buying coins direct from the Mint Bureau. Newspapers would love the story and none of the publicity could possibly benefit the treasury department. Secretary MacVeagh would quickly be made to look like he didn't know what was happening in his department. Publication of the U.S. Attorney's 1888 opinion in the attempted suppression of the Linderman pattern auction – that the Mint Bureau had no claim of title to the pieces – would certainly make the Taft Administration look foolish.

Being tight fisted but stubborn by nature, Andrew proposed to drop all legal actions against Haseltine and anyone else regarding pattern and experimental pieces, if the two $50 Half Unions were returned. The mint would refund Snowden's money, approximately $106.00, from the contingency fund for the mint collection. To take care of the $20,000 market value of the coins, Snowden would take his refund in gold and silver pattern and experimental pieces up to $106 in metal value. He would also be allowed to purchase all other gold and silver pattern pieces (except examples in the mint collection) held by the director's office or the Philadelphia Mint at bullion value. Lastly, Col. Snowden would receive all other base metal pattern pieces as if they were scrap. For his part, director Andrew agreed to guarantee that no more could be struck by having all pattern hubs destroyed. Snowden's purchase would then be given to Woodin and the $20,000, or a large part of it, forgiven. If Haseltine and/or Nagy received a commission on the original sale, they likely returned the value to Woodin in pattern coins.

---

[255] Cortelyou, George B., papers, *Library of Congress*, box 16. "Annual Assay Commission" [1909]. Zerbe was also a member of the 1909 commission. It is natural that Zerbe, Manning and Ambrose Swasey (another coin collector on the commission) would have discussed their collections and numismatic interests during the event.

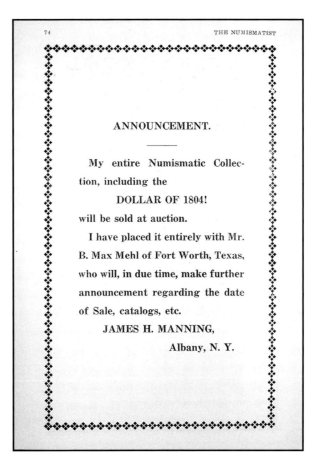

Figure 29. James Manning's advertisement in the February 1921 issue of The Numismatist indicating his collection, including an 1804 dollar, would be sold at auction by B. Max Mehl. (Image from *The Numismatist* February 1921, courtesy Mark Coffey.)

Woodin evidently also received from Snowden a large group of pattern coins which Snowden had previously purchased from the Philadelphia Mint. Illustrations of many of these pieces later turned up with descriptions in the Adams-Woodin book on pattern coins.

At its conclusion, this speculative scenario would have given Woodin the world's largest pattern and experimental coin collection; assured him that no coins would ever be restruck; returned the Half Unions to Philadelphia Mint Collection custody; given Snowden most of his $20,000 selling price; and halted possibly embarrassing litigation. Engravers Barber and Morgan (and future numismatists) came out losers with much of their most creative work destroyed. The mint also lost because not only was its artistic heritage gutted, but nothing remained from which to prepare future pattern and experimental pieces. Lastly, Farran Zerbe, if he encouraged Andrew's confiscation attempts, would have become a pariah to Haseltine, Chapman, Snowden, Elder and other numismatists.

James Manning continued collecting coins, although it is doubtful if he did further business with John Haseltine. Over a decade after the pattern coin debacle, Manning announced that his collection, including an 1804 dollar, were to be auctioned by Texas entrepreneur B. Max Mehl.[256] The collection, consisting of 1,860 lots, was sold on May 17, 1921. The 1804 dollar (aka Cohen-duPont specimen) ended up in the collection of Willis duPont

---

[256] *The Numismatist*, February 1921, p.74. Issue information and image courtesy of Mark Coffey.

Pattern Hub Destruction – An Inventory

The following table reproduces most of Barber's inventory. The only exceptions are the dies and hubs of obsolete circulating coinage. Information in the table is presented in the order and as organized by Barber. Cross references to the Judd pattern books were provided by Saul Teichman with additional material supplied by Mark Hagen.

As working dies of patterns accumulated at the mint, the temptation to make a "few extras" for well-connected collectors became too great, and during the late 1860s many earlier-dated designs were restruck for sale to collectors. Special versions and "mules" of unrelated designs were also prepared and sold. Mint director Linderman insisted in 1871 that all pattern dies had been destroyed, yet examples continued to "leak" from the mint. The ensuing scandal helped define the Coinage Act of 1873 which placed the mint firmly under treasury department control and moved the director's office from Philadelphia to Washington.

Extensive pattern and experimental coin designs were made in the 1870s and 1880s. Although most pattern coins were intended for internal Mint Bureau or treasury department examination – by the director, secretary of the treasury, etc. – others were occasionally given wider distribution such as 1873 Trade dollars or the 1896 metallurgical patterns that ended up in many congressmen's pockets as souvenirs.[257]

This section presents a list of all hubs, dies, master dies and incomplete dies inventoried by engraver Charles Barber between April 30 and May 24, 1910, except current and obsolete circulating coins. The inventory was prepared by Barber at Andrew's request. According to affidavits signed by superintendent Landis, engraver Barber, assayer Jacob Eckfeldt, and coiner Rhine H. Freed all listed items were destroyed on May 24 and 25, 1910.

There are three original lists dating from 1910. One, typed on normal mint correspondence paper, appears to be the master list. A partial copy of this list, number two, exists as a typed carbon copy that appears to be contemporary with the original, but is not a carbon of the original. This may have been a copy made by mint clerks so the list could be filed by other treasury offices. A third list consists of two typed pages, one on correspondence paper, the other a typed carbon copy. This third list shows hubs and master dies for obsolete circulating designs from the mid-nineteenth century on the first page. (Not illustrated in the table, below, since the designs are well known.) The second page briefly describes hubs made for the Saint-Gaudens pattern and circulating designs of 1907, and the 1906 pattern double eagle by Barber and Morgan. The cover letters state the total number of dies and hubs destroyed, and these figures match the totals on the accompanying lists, so we can be reasonably certain that we have at least the main body of correspondence.

All of this was prepared several years before the Adams-Woodin book on U. S. Pattern coins was published. The descriptions are short and sometimes ambiguous, although pattern experts Saul Teichman and Mark Hagen were able to associate many of Barber's descriptions with known pattern coins represented by the hubs. Some descriptions do not appear to match any known pattern or experimental pieces. These may never have been used to strike samples, or possibly all examples have been lost. In many instances, the same design was used on obverse hubs of several sizes, and in these cases, the images have not been duplicated.

---

[257] *US Mint*, NARA-CP, op. cit., entry 229, box 296. Letter dated August 28, 1911 to Roberts from Norris.

Barber's lists do not appear to be in any order. The only organization is by "heads," "eagles" and "wreaths," and by engraver, although it is not entirely consistent in any of these. The table consists of several columns:

Quan. is the quantity of dies/hubs of this description indicated on Charles Barber's lists.

Description is Barber's written description of each design. These have been edited slightly to improve clarity.

Engraver is the person or persons credited with engraving the hubs or dies as stated by Barber. Several of these brief entries indicate that current pattern catalogs may attribute designs to the wrong artist(s).

Photo is the Judd reference number and a photograph of a sample pattern piece that most closely matches the description. It is not possible to identify minor differences between hubs based on Barber's descriptions. Some descriptions cannot be matched with any known pattern coin. Other descriptions indicate the dies were not hardened, implying that no examples had been struck. Many different patterns may have used the same design; however, only one example is illustrated. The hubs would have been dateless or had only a partial date. *These images are not to scale.*

Quan.	Description	Engraver	Photo
\multicolumn{4}{c}{**Six hubs made between 1836 and 1844 probably for half dollar, supposed to be the work of Kneass and Gobrecht.**}			
1	#1. Eagle with upraised wings, head looking to right, standing upon shield, shield pointing to right.	Kneass or Gobrecht?	Unidentified
1	#2. Eagle looking to left standing upon shield, shield pointing right.	Kneass or Gobrecht?	Unidentified
1	#3. Eagle looking down, shield pointing right.	Kneass or Gobrecht?	Unidentified
1	#4. Eagle looking left, shield pointed left, wings upraised.	Kneass or Gobrecht?	Unidentified
1	#5. Eagle looking right, shield left, upraised wings.	Kneass or Gobrecht?	Unidentified
1	#6. Eagle standing on top of shield, looking right with raised wings.	Kneass or Gobrecht?	Unidentified
\multicolumn{4}{c}{**Three Unfinished Dies Supposed to be by Longacre, Purpose Unknown.**}			
1	#1. Wreath similar to wreath on dime, diameter 1 1/8-inch.	Longacre?	Unidentified
1	#2. Spread eagle, shield upon breast, arrows and olive branch in claws.	Longacre?	Unidentified
1	#3. Spread eagle, shield upon breast, flowing ribbon from beak surrounded by thirteen stars, inscription half dollar	Longacre?	Unidentified

Quan.	Description	Engraver	Photo
	Ten unfinished reverse dies without date.		
1	Eagle, head erect, drooping wings; United States of America two stars and one dollar around the eagle, E Pluribus Unum in old English.	William Barber	J-1554  Image courtesy Mark Hagen.
1	#1. Half dollar size. Profile eagle, looking left, standing upon tablet surrounded by United States of America, half dollar and beads.	Morgan	J-1512  Image courtesy Mark Hagen.
1	#2. Half dollar size. Eagle on shield with wreath, In God We Trust over shield surrounded by United States of America, half dollar.	Morgan	J-1503  Courtesy Bowers & Merena Galleries.
1	#3. Half dollar size. Eagle on shield with wreath, inscription United States of America, half dollar.	Morgan	J-1504?  Image courtesy Mark Hagen.

Quan.	Description	Engraver	Photo
1	#4. Half dollar size. Eagle on shield surrounded by wreath and United States of America, half dollar.	Morgan	J-1506? *Courtesy Bowers & Merena Galleries.*
1	#5. Half dollar size. Spread eagle standing on tablet, inscription United States of America, half dollar.	Morgan	J-1516 *Image courtesy Mark Hagen.*
1	#6. Half dollar size. Spread eagle standing on tablet same as No. 5 with feathers more developed, inscription United States of America, half dollar.	Morgan	J-1514 *Image courtesy Mark Hagen.*
1	Size five cent, cotton, corn, tobacco wreath, roman V in centre. E Pluribus Unum above wreath.	Charles Barber	J-1680 *Courtesy American Numismatic Rarities.*

Quan.	Description	Engraver	Photo
1	Dime. Olive wreath, one dime, thirteen stars, and E Pluribus Unum.	Morgan	J-1588 Image courtesy Mark Hagen.
1	Gold dollar. Standing eagle with shield to right, United States of America, one dollar.	William Barber	J-1224 Courtesy Heritage Auctions.

Seventeen Unfinished Dies Without Date.

Quan.	Description	Engraver	Photo
1	Head of Liberty, thirteen stars, In God We Trust, size 1½-in design for standard dollar.	Charles Barber	J-1554 Image courtesy Mark Hagen.
1	Wreath for five cent nickel. Cotton, corn, tobacco.	Charles Barber	Unidentified
1	Head of Liberty looking left, flowing hair, liberty cap, size of dime.	Charles Barber	Unidentified. Possibly a quarter eagle in the style of J-1575.
1	Eagle, size of dollar, spread wings looking left, standing erect.	Charles Barber	J-1565 Courtesy Bowers & Merena Galleries.

Quan.	Description	Engraver	Photo
1	Eagle, size of half dollar, spread wings, looking left, standing erect.	Charles Barber	J-1597 ? *Courtesy Heritage Auctions.*
1	Eagle, size of quarter dollar, spread wings, looking left, standing erect.	Charles Barber	J-1590 *Image courtesy Mark Hagen.*
1	Eagle, profile looking left, standing upon arrow and large olive branch.	Morgan	J-1616 *Image courtesy Mark Hagen.*
1	Spread eagle looking right, standing upon tablet with motto In God We Trust.	Morgan	Unidentified
1	Wreath design for dime. E Pluribus Unum, and thirteen stars.	Morgan	J-1587 *Image courtesy Mark Hagen.*
1	Eagle looking right, wings pointed down, olive branch and arrow in claw, suitable for quarter dollar.	Morgan	Unidentified

Quan.	Description	Engraver	Photo
1	Liberty head same as three cent nickel, looking left, Liberty upon tiara, thirteen stars, size suitable for eagle.	Longacre	J-663 *Image courtesy Mark Hagen.*
1	Liberty head, same design as above, size three cent nickel.	Longacre	[Standard 3 cent obverse for reference] *Courtesy Heritage Auctions.*
2	Liberty head, same design, suitable for gold dollar.	Longacre	J-224? *Courtesy Heritage Auctions.*
1	Head of Liberty looking left, word Liberty on band around head, size for five dollar.	Morgan	J-1568 *Courtesy Heritage Auctions.*

Quan.	Description	Engraver	Photo
1	Five pointed star with inscription: one stella four hundred cents.	Charles Barber	J-1635 Image courtesy Mark Hagen.
1	Laurel wreath, size of five cent.	Charles Barber	Unidentified

Eight Finished Hubs Without Date.

Quan.	Description	Engraver	Photo
1	Fifty dollars, obverse, head of Liberty, the word Liberty on tiara with row of beads, surrounded by thirteen stars.	William Barber	J-1546 Courtesy Smithsonian National Numismatic Collection.
1	Fifty dollars, reverse, spread eagle upon shield husk and scrolls with E Pluribus Unum, rays above In God We Trust, thirteen stars among rays, inscription: United States of America, fifty dollars.	William Barber	J-1546 Courtesy Smithsonian National Numismatic Collection.
5	Five unfinished hubs for reverse of half dollar, no date, designs fully described in list of finished dies, No. 1, 2, 3, 5, and 6.	Morgan	[See above]
1	Dime: Corn and cotton wreath surrounding one dime and E Pluribus Unum, encircled by row of beads.	Morgan	J-1586 Image courtesy Mark Hagen.

Quan.	Description	Engraver	Photo
	W. Barber's Designs for Liberty Heads.		
4	Head of Liberty looking right, hair tied in knot, band with Liberty, tobacco and olive leaves in hair, four sizes: dollar, half, quarter and dime.	William Barber	 J-733 Courtesy Heritage Auctions.
5	Head of Liberty looking left, with cap, and hair flowing from under cap. Dollar, half, quarter and two sizes for dime.	William Barber	 J-1603 Courtesy American Numismatic Rarities.
2	Sitting figure of Liberty. Left arm resting upon shield, sword in left hand, eagle standing in front of figure, size dollar and half dollar.	William Barber	 J-1200 Courtesy Heritage Auctions.
2	Head of Liberty with cap which extends down side of head, facing left, word Liberty upon cap, two sizes [for] half and quarter dollar.	William Barber	 J-1575 Courtesy Goldberg's Coins and Collectibles.

Quan.	Description	Engraver	Photo
3	Head of Liberty looking right with Liberty cap and two large stars upon cap, size half dollar, quarter dollar and dime.	William Barber	J-721 and "Standard Silver" Courtesy Heritage Auctions.
1	Head of Liberty with band around head with word Liberty and wheat and cotton coming from under band, hair tied with ribbon. Size half dollar.	William Barber	J-1535 Courtesy Heritage Auctions.
1	Head of Liberty with helmet with eagle rampant upon helmet, size half dollar.	William Barber	J-1526 Courtesy Bowers & Merena Galleries.
2	Head of Liberty looking left, tiara and flowing hair, sizes dollar and half dollar.	William Barber	J-1502 ? Courtesy Bowers & Merena Galleries.
3	Head of Liberty looking right and up, tiara, hair in knot and flowing down neck, sizes half dollar, quarter dollar and dime.	William Barber	Unidentified. Possibly J-861

121

Quan.	Description	Engraver	Photo
3	Head of Liberty looking right and up, band around head with one star in front of forehead, flowing hair and light drapery on neck. Three heads probably for half dollar, quarter dollar and dime.	William Barber	J-733 ? Courtesy Heritage Auctions.
1	Head of Liberty with tiara, row of beads upon tiara, flowing hair, knot of hair held with ribbon.	William Barber	J-1459 ? Courtesy Heritage Auctions.
1	Sitting figure of Liberty with shield in right hand, flag, staff, and Liberty cap at back of figure.	William Barber	J-996 or ? Courtesy Stack's Rare Coins New York.
1	Sitting Liberty with globe and sheaf of wheat, and flags at rear of figure. Steamer in the offing.	William Barber	J-1399 Courtesy Heritage Auctions.

Quan.	Description	Engraver	Photo
1	Head of Liberty looking left, hair smooth not flowing, band across head with word Liberty, size dollar.	Charles Barber	J-1655? *Courtesy American Numismatic Rarities.*
1	Head of Liberty looking left, hair braided and coiled on top of head, band across head with Liberty, size of stella four dollar coin.	Charles Barber	J-1638 *Courtesy Goldberg's Coins and Collectibles.*
1	Head of Liberty looking left, flowing hair, band with word Liberty and pearl in front of band.	Charles Barber	J-1659 *Image courtesy Mark Hagen.*

W. Barber's Designs for Standing Eagles.

Quan.	Description	Engraver	Photo
4	Four standing eagles with wings lowered, sprig of olive in right claw with three leaves projecting beyond wing and arrows in left claw with three arrow points beyond wing. Probably dollar, half dollar and quarter dollar.	William Barber	J-1304 ? *Courtesy Stack's Rare Coins New York.*

Quan.	Description	Engraver	Photo
			J-1206 and 1872 "Amazonians"
3	Three standing eagles with wings lowered, shield supported by left claw of eagle, band crossing shield from right to left.	William Barber	Courtesy Heritage Auctions.
3	Three standing eagles with lowered wings, olive branch with six leaves in right claw and three arrows with heads showing. In dollar size but not in half and quarter size.	William Barber	Unidentified
2	Two standing eagles looking left, lowered wings, arrow in left claw and olive branch in right, arrow heads and leaves resting upon the wings of eagle.	William Barber	Unidentified
1	Standing eagle, lowered wings, supporting shield in left claw beneath eagle, tablet with E Pluribus Unum.	William Barber	See J-1539
1	Shield decorated with standing eagle, lowered wings, arrows and olive branch in claws of eagle. Half dollar size.	William Barber	J-1526 Image courtesy Mark Hagen.
1	Eagle standing partially lifted wings, head looking left, size twenty cent.	William Barber	J-1399 Courtesy Heritage Auctions.

Quan.	Description	Engraver	Photo
	Morgan's Designs – Eagles.		
2	Eagle standing upon tablet with In God We Trust, eagle looking left, wings in position of bird rising, olive branch thirteen leaves and three arrow heads. Two of the above, dollar and half dollar.	Morgan	J-1608 Courtesy Bowers & Merena Galleries.
1	Eagle standing [upon tablet] with In God We Trust, eagle looking left, wings in position of bird rising, olive branch thirteen leaves and three arrow heads. As above but with feathers on arrows more developed.	Morgan	Unidentified
4	Eagles same design as standard dollar reverse, exception only in olive leaves and arrow heads: three leaves and three arrows.	Morgan	J-1550 Courtesy Michael S. Fey, PhD
3	Three standing eagles for dollar, half dollar and quarter dollar, wings in position of alighting, head thrown up looking right, three arrows and six olive leaves in talons.	Morgan	Unidentified. Similar to J-1702 reverse, but leaf count is different.
3	Three standing eagles, lowered wings, head turned left, seven olive leaves and three arrows in talons. Dollar, half dollar and quarter dollar.	Morgan	J-1611? Image courtesy Mark Hagen.
1	Spread eagle looking left, In God We Trust and part of inscription below, unfinished, soft steel, size of dollar.	Morgan	Unidentified
1	Heraldic eagle, tablet In God We Trust, head turned right.	Morgan	Unidentified

126

Quan.	Description	Engraver	Photo
	Morgan's Designs for Liberty Heads.		

Quan.	Description	Engraver	Photo
9	Nine heads of Liberty looking left, flowing hair, band across head with word Liberty, wheat, cotton and tobacco in hair, and liberty cap, same design as standard dollar. Nine of these heads for dollar and subsidiary coins.	Morgan	J-1504  Image courtesy Mark Hagen.
3	Three Liberty heads looking right, with flowing hair held at back by ribbon with word Liberty; dollar, half dollar, and quarter dollar size.	Morgan	J-1698  Courtesy American Numismatic Rarities.
1	One head of Liberty looking left, flowing hair, liberty cap with band and word Liberty, four olive leaves held by band of cap.	Morgan	[See below]
1	One head of Liberty same as above without olive leaves and slight change in detail of hair about the neck.	Morgan	J-1577  Courtesy Goldberg's Coins and Collectibles.
1	One head of Liberty looking left, very youthful face and flowing hair held at back by ribbon, band across top of head with word Liberty.	Morgan	J-1608  Courtesy Bowers & Merena Galleries.

Quan.	Description	Engraver	Photo
	[No title to this section]		
4	Four spread eagles with shield upon breast, shield ornamented with scrolls, flowing ribbon in beak of eagle, crossing shield from right to left. All soft, never been used, size ten dollar, five dollar, two and a half dollar, and dollar gold coin.	Longacre	Probably an unknown design.
2	Head of Liberty looking left, flowing hair held at back by ribbon, bow tiara with pearls, three cent size and gold dollar.	Longacre	Unidentified
1	Eagle profile, wings raised, head turned right, standing upon shield prone, arrows and olive branch in talons. Size quarter dollar.	Bailly	J-1315 ? Courtesy Superior Galleries.
	Wreaths		
2	Corn, cotton & wheat held together by ribbon bow at bottom of wreath, size dollar and half dollar.	William Barber	J-1120-1125 Courtesy Heritage Auctions.
1	Wreath, corn and cotton ornamented at top with scrolls and in lower part by husk, size dollar.	William Barber	Unidentified J-565?
1	Wreath, corn, cotton and wheat held together by bow of ribbon; size five cent.	Charles Barber	Unidentified
1	Wreath, corn, cotton, and wheat, soft, reduction from model unfinished, size about quarter dollar.	Longacre	Unidentified
1	Wreath, corn, cotton & wheat, bow knot to hold wreath, suitable for five cent nickel.	Charles Barber	Standard five-cent piece ? Courtesy Heritage Auctions.

Quan.	Description	Engraver	Photo
2	Olive wreaths, suitable for five cent nickel.	Charles Barber	J-1770? Image courtesy Mark Hagen.
2	Shields with ribbon crossing from left to right, and crossed liberty poles with liberty cap, suitable for five cent.	Charles Barber	J-1770? Image courtesy Mark Hagen.

Saint Gaudens

Quan.	Description	Engraver	Photo
2	Double eagle, obverse and reverse, first reduction from model high relief, too high to coin.	Saint-Gaudens	J-1907 Courtesy Smithsonian National Numismatic Collection

Quan.	Description	Engraver	Photo
2	Same design, second reduction, obverse and reverse reduced relief, but still too high. Model changed by Saint Gaudens.	Saint-Gaudens	#2 models *Courtesy Smithsonian National Numismatic Collection.*
2	Same design, third reduction, greater reduction in relief, detail lost in reducing the relief to such an extent, in trying to come to coin relief. Model changed by Saint Gaudens. These double eagle hubs were made acceptable by the engravers restoring the detail in the hubs.	Saint-Gaudens	#3 model; #4 model version
1	Liberty head design for obverse double eagle, high relief; afterward reduced in relief and used for eagle. The model was changed by Saint Gaudens.	Saint-Gaudens	J-1905 *Courtesy Saint-Gaudens National Historic Site.*

Quan.	Description	Engraver	Photo
3	Saint Gaudens' design, high relief reverse for twenty dollar, standing eagle. One hub, two dies.	Saint-Gaudens	Judd p.270, illus. Courtesy Saint-Gaudens National Historic Site.
2	Double eagle, obverse and reverse. Barber and Morgan design, hubs.	Barber & Morgan	J-1773 Courtesy Smithsonian National Numismatic Collection.
2	Double eagle high relief, diameter of eagle. Obverse one, reverse one.	Saint-Gaudens	J-1917 Courtesy Smithsonian National Numismatic Collection.

Quan.	Description	Engraver	Photo
2	Ten dollar gold. Saint Gaudens design obverse and reverse hub from which present design is a modification. Obverse one, reverse one.	Saint-Gaudens	

Charles Barber's descriptions indicate several designs long assumed to be by one engraver, are really by a different person. The 1891 half dollar and 1906 double eagle are notable instances. In both cases the assumption has been that they were the sole work of engraver Barber. However, the inventory suggests the 1891 pattern half (J-1766) obverse was prepared by George Morgan and the reverse by Barber. Likewise, the 1906 $20 gold pattern (J-1773) has an obverse portrait by Barber and the reverse is an adaptation of Morgan's 1891 half dollar obverse. The biggest surprise is that according to the inventory, Barber designed both of the 1879/1880 $4 Stella patterns (J-1635, J-1638).

That there are errors in our previous knowledge of pattern coin designers is not unexpected. The series is poorly documented and many patterns were produced on verbal orders, much as the 1909-10 five-cent Washington designs. With the incomplete state of much mint documentation, opportunities to incorporate information from reliable sources – such as Charles Barber's inventory – are always welcome.

Chapter 6 – A Better Metal

During 1911 the mint continued its experiments with various alloys and planchet sizes. Much of this work appears to have duplicated efforts from 1885 and 1896, although the mint director said he considered the older work unsuitable. Some may also have been related to former director Andrew's interest in a "uniform coinage" system. Andrew was now an assistant secretary of the treasury and kept a close watch on director Roberts, who may have felt it desirable to continue work along lines suggested by Andrew.

Alloy Experiments

Complaints about tarnishing of bronze cents had been around nearly as long as the cent had been coined. As the small coin began to be used in vending machines and other coin operated devices, it became apparent that minor corrosion – normal for a coin composed of 95% copper – was sufficient to cause the coins to stick in the mechanisms or to be rejected. Letters to the Mint Bureau mentioned this and the perceived hygiene problems of a "dirty" coin.

Extensive tests had been performed in 1896 using more than twenty different alloys to strike experimental cents and nickels from pattern dies. Samples were sent to the Pittsburgh Reduction Company to be tested for abrasion and discoloration, with a printed report of the results delivered to Congress.[258] The final recommendation was to make no change in alloy for either the cent or five-cent coin. But all this was before A. Piatt Andrew became director in late 1909. As part of his examination of coinage operations, Andrew ordered new somewhat less complicated tests to be made. Although he left the director's position in 1910, he seems to have been deeply involved in most decisions relating to the Mint Bureau until his resignation from the treasury in July 1912.

---

[258] *US Mint*, NARA-CP, op. cit., entry 229, box 296. Letter dated July 27, 1897 to Director Robert Preston from Alfred E. Hunt, President *The Pittsburgh Reduction Company*.

Interest in changing coinage alloys included experiments with aluminum. On February 10, 1911 engraver Charles Barber wrote to director Roberts enclosing sample one and five-cent coins struck in aluminum. Presumably, these were made using normal dies for the current year:[259]

> I send you the coins mentioned yesterday, namely one and five cent struck in aluminum.
> If you will look at the report of the Royal Mint, London 1908, page thirteen you will see that the aluminum coinage made for East Africa has been found unsuitable. I do not know how it stands in France as I have no direct information, all that I know of aluminum coinage for France I have learned through the press.
> Personally I know of no advantage in using this metal for coinage and Mr. Eckfeldt tells me that he mentioned some of the disadvantages when the subject was discussed with you yesterday.
> I would beg to suggest that if the enormous amount of one cent coin already in circulation does not offer any obstacle to making a change, why not use the same alloy as we are now using for the five cent, it would avoid all complications in handling the clipping and scrap, in fact the same ingots could be used as the demand might be either for one or five cent coin.
> The alloy of the five cent does not corrode to any great extent.

By June 1911 director Roberts, at assistant secretary Andrew's urging, authorized the mint to strike additional Lincoln cents in non-standard alloys to test the coinage characteristics of alternative metals:[260]

> In accordance with the instructions contained in your letter of the 26th ultimo, approved by the Assistant Secretary of the Treasury, I have today had struck by the Engraver six (6) one cent pieces upon blanks composed of twelve per cent nickel and eighty-eight per cent bronze coin, which I have forwarded herewith by registered mail. But six impressions were made.

If the experimental coins were made of the alloy described by Landis - 12% nickel and 88% bronze – the actual composition would have been approximately 84% copper, 12% nickel, 2% tin, and 2% zinc. If, however, Landis meant "copper" when he wrote "bronze" the experimental pieces would have been of the same alloy as the so-called "white cents" of 1857.

Roberts instructed superintendent Landis to give Philadelphia Mint assayer Jacob Eckfeldt some of the blank planchets "...to experiment with by exposing them to corrosion and ascertain what advantage in this respect they possess over the present bronze coins."[261] Eckfeldt offered his comments about the "nickel – bronze" alloy on June 21:[262]

> I have examined a lot of the nickel-bronze alloy (blanks), nickel 12%, copper, etc. 88%.
> I have subjected these blanks to a number of different re-agents, to observe what oxidation or discoloration might be expected to take place under certain con-

---

[259] *US Mint*, NARA-CP, op. cit., entry 229, box 296. Letter dated February 10, 1911 to Roberts from Barber. These experimental pieces may still exist in the collection of an error specialist, misidentified as struck on foreign coin planchets.
[260] *US Mint*, NARA-CP, op. cit., entry 1A 328I. Letter dated June 8, 1911 to Director from Landis. (File #304815 written at top of letter.)
[261] *US Mint*, NARA-CP, op. cit., entry 229, box 296. Letter dated June 22, 1911 to Roberts from Landis. Quoting instructions of June 9.
[262] *US Mint*, NARA-CP, op. cit., entry 229, box 296. Letter dated June 21, 1911 to Landis from Eckfeldt.

> ditions in circulation. These experiments or tests were also made with a number of one cent blanks, for comparison.
>
> The nickel alloy would discolor pretty much the same as the bronze, but I might say, possibly a little slower and a <u>trifle</u> less, though there was not much difference. I am of the opinion, however, that no laboratory test would compare with what the pieces would be subjected to in circulation.

An undated memorandum found adjacent to the Eckfeldt's letter in mint archives analyses the potential seigniorage on one-cent pieces made from the ordinary bronze alloy and the copper-nickel alloy used in the five-cent pieces. Calculations showed the cost of copper, tin and zinc to make $100 in bronze cents was $8.7615, but the same $100 if coined with 75% copper-25% nickel would cost $13.4133. It further states that in 1911 the mint earned $1,804,668.88 in seigniorage on one-cent production, but that if the copper-nickel alloy had been used the seigniorage would have been $1,712,657.74 or a reduction of over $92,000.[263] Although the analysis does not consider other cost savings derived from simplifying mint operations or the longer circulating life of a copper-nickel cent, the reduction of seigniorage must have been a strong argument against changing the one-cent alloy.

Experiments with alloys continued during the summer months. On July 15, Roberts asked the mint to produce one-cent-size blanks "…composed of 75% bronze coin and 25% nickel,"[264] an alloy nearly the same as that used for the current five-cent coin.[265]

A letter from Edmund S. Hoch to secretary MacVeagh conveyed a commonly held opinion about the lowly one-cent bronze coin. After a lengthy introduction Mr. Hoch writes:[266]

> …[these] suggest to me the possibility of your giving the everyday citizen a service, in the improvement of our coinage, in one important detail, by replacing our copper cents with a coin of exactly the same size, style and denomination, made of a cleaner, whiter metal – german silver or otherwise.
>
> The copper coin is a dirty coin. This is very noticeable in France and England, also in Canada where the large copper pieces are still used, and the crudity of these copper coins is emphasized by contrast with the white metal coins of Germany, which serve the people so much better, in similar capacity.
>
> I realize that objections which will be offered against such a change as is here suggested, such as the possibility of mistaking the one cent piece for the dime, etc.; but these objections are trivial, when compared with the great service of cleanliness and stimulus to refinement, which the whiter metals will give. The special objection named is unsound, because the coins may be so made as to be unmistakable for any other coins, except by the most careless or ignorant; and evolution out of such state, effected by a few mistakes of this character, would be obtained at very low cost, indeed.

---

[263] *US Mint*, NARA-CP, op. cit., entry 229, box 296. Memorandum titled "Memorandum on the One-Cent Proposition" undated (but must have been after December 1911 since it quotes 1911 production figures) to "unknown" from "unknown".

[264] *US Mint*, NARA-CP op. cit., entry 229, box 296. Letter dated August 22, 1911 to Roberts from Norris.

[265] Use of the term "bronze" in the alloy instead of "copper" or specifying the proportions of metals in the mix, may have come from a misinterpretation of the term "nickel-bronze" used by Royal Mint Master William G. Ellison-McCartney. The Royal Mint called a mixture of 25% nickel and 75% copper "nickel bronze" meaning a "bronze alloy containing a significant percentage of nickel." The bronze alloy used by the U. S. Mint was called "French bronze" in Great Britain and other parts of Europe.

[266] *US Mint*, NARA-CP, op. cit., entry 1A 328I. Letter dated November 13, 1911 to MacVeagh from Edmund S. Hoch. (File #308449 written at top of letter.)

You have already inaugurated one great service, the benefits of which are felt, generally, by the people, viz., the facilitation of the return of old bills to be exchanged for new bills, if you could supplement this by eliminating the dirty copper coin by gradual substitution for it of a coin in white metal, there is no man, woman or child in the country who will not be thankful for the change; verdigris is poisonous, and coins travel far....

Trusting that my suggestion will not be considered impertinent or unwise and assuring you that it is sincerely made, I am
Very respectfully,

P.S.: It is not presumed that the change here suggested has not come to the [attention of] Treasury Department, frequently, heretofore; but the writer feels that the great benefits and desirability of the reform in question have been improperly and unwisely subordinated to the difficulties in the way; and recent improvements in metallurgy offer greater opportunities and possibilities than have been available in the past.

In a subsequent letter to MacVeagh, Hoch suggests potential confusion with the dime could be avoided if the "white cent" were:[267]

...of the same size, thickness and face as our present piece, but slightly changing the form – varying from the circular to a polygon shape, employing as many sides as may be desired...This suggestion was made by Mr. Frederick J. V. Skiff, Director of the Field Museum, a mutual friend, who is familiar with the coinage of the various nations of the world.

I note the information [in your reply to my previous letter] that other coins of small denomination are proposed. These, of course, would not supplant the cent piece – the fitness of which should have first consideration.

A July 29, 1912 letter from George E. Kinney offers another idea for a new alloy for the cent:[268]

Dear Sir:
By enclosed clipping I am led to believe that you desire a new formula for the ever popular penny, therefore I submit a formula which I think will fill the bill in regards to its retaining its natural brilliancy and as it is nearly as hard as iron, it will out wear the present penny.
Rx: Copper   95%
     Aluminum   4-1/2%
     Tin   ½%
If amiable I await your reply
Yours truly,
George E. Kinney
Box 57, Arctic, R.I.

The Boston *Sun American* newspaper clipping from the of the previous day provided by Kinney, condemned both the alloy and design of the Lincoln cent:[269]

The Director of the Mint is dissatisfied with the makeup of the one-cent piece. He recommends that it be altered.

The reason why the copper cent is unsatisfactory is that it is almost wholly copper – in exact figures, 95 percent copper, and 5 percent tin and zinc. Copper rapidly oxidizes and the penny soon becomes dull and dirty.

---
[267] *US Mint*, NARA-CP, op. cit., entry 1A 328I. Letter dated December 13, 1911 to MacVeagh from Edmund S. Hoch.
[268] *US Mint*, NARA-CP, op. cit., entry 1A 328I. Letter dated July 29, 1912 to Director from Kinney.
[269] *US Mint*, NARA-CP, op. cit., entry 1A 328I. Annotated newspaper clipping accompanying Mr. Kinney's letter.

> The old copper cent was, in point of design, the handsomest coin we had. The penny with the Lincoln head is said to be the ugliest and least artistic. The director of the Mint offers no criticism on this point but complains that the coin quickly becomes unfit for circulation.
> This is especially true when the penny comes in contact with the salt air....

The article goes on to misinform readers that prior to 1857, "...our cents contained 22 per cent of nickel." Despite the errors, it is clear the Mint Bureau was looking for some type of substitute for the bronze alloy then in use.

Coinage Bill of 1912

As early as August 1909, secretary MacVeagh had suggested the idea of reforming and beautifying the paper and metallic currency. These ideas included a reduction in the size of bills by about one-fourth, a uniform system of design and of portraits, uniformity of color on the same denomination. Coins would be designed by America's best artists, with their size directly related to value. All unnecessary weight and diameter would be eliminated and large, non-circulating pieces such as the silver dollar, would be abandoned.[270] Only small portions of MacVeagh's grand currency reform were adopted during his administration. The near-term changes were redesign of the $100 bill reverse and the Buffalo nickel.

In late 1911 Representative Robert J. Bulkley (D-Indiana) proposed adding ½-cent and 3-cent coins to the monetary system.[271] Originally entered as HR 14042, then as HR 23291, the final bill was HR 23570 which went to Representative Ashbrook's (D-Ohio) Committee on Coinage Weights and Measures on April 20. The bill was reported out of committee on May 1 with two amendments, debated and passed May 6 as part of the Unanimous Consent Calendar. The full text of the final bill was:[272]

> That as soon as practicable after passage of this act there shall be coined at the mints of the United States a 3-cent piece of the standard weight of 60 troy grains and a ½-cent piece of the standard weight of 30 troy grains, with no greater deviation from the standard weight than 2 grains each piece, and said coins shall be composed of 75 percent copper and 25 percent nickel. The diameters and devices of said coins shall be fixed by the Director of the Mint with the approval of the Secretary of the Treasury: Provided, however, That upon one side there shall be an inscription of the word "Liberty" and the year of the coinage, and upon the reverse there shall be an inscription of the words "United States of America" and a designation of the value of the coin. Said 3-cent pieced shall have one perforation in the center, and shall be a legal tender in any payment to the amount of 30 cents. The ½-cent piece shall be a legal tender in any payment to the amount of 25 cents.
> SEC. 2. That all laws now in force relating to the minor coins of the United States and the striking or coining of the same, regulating and guarding the process of coinage, providing for the purchase of material and for the transportation, distribution, and redemption of the coins, for the prevention of debasement or counter-

---

[270] *The New York Times,* "MacVeagh to Urge Uniform Currency," August 16, 1909, p.7. Based on an article by an unnamed Boston correspondent. Eames MacVeagh was very interested in coins and currency; see below.
[271] The whole idea of reinstating the ½-cent and three-cent denominations seems peculiar. There appears to have been little economic or practical reason for the new coins, and almost no public interest aside from places were streetcar fare was three cents. Both had been discontinued due to lack of demand and public dislike for the coins. When the 2-1/2 cent coin was proposed in 1920, it was promoted as a commemorative for Theodore Roosevelt, and acknowledged as having little real economic value.
[272] *Congressional Record.* 62nd Congress, 2nd Session; p.5978. This is the language as reported out of Committee.

feiting, for the security of the coin, or for any other purpose, whether said laws are penal or otherwise, shall, so far as applicable, apply to the coinage herein authorized.

    SEC. 3. That from and after the passage of this act all 1-cent pieces coined at the mints of the United States shall be of the standard weight of 48 troy grains, with no greater deviation from the standard weight than 2 grains each piece, and shall be composed of 75 percent copper and 25 percent nickel.

    SEC. 4. That all acts or parts of acts in conflict herewith are hereby repealed.

During floor debate a committee amendment to eliminate the center perforation in the three-cent coin was approved. Another amendment was approved to prevent the new coins from having the same diameter as any existing U.S. coins.

Representative Austin (R-Tennessee) asked what was the necessity for a ½-cent coin. Ashbrook replied:[273]

> …it was the opinion of the Secretary of the Treasury that there would be a very great demand for it. This bill was originally introduced for the 3-cent piece only, but after conference with the Secretary of the Treasury he recommended, as will be seen by the printed report, that it should include the half-cent piece…
>
> …It is believed that with a half-cent piece the people would get the benefit. The half-cent now goes to the grocer and merchant in making change, and if there is a half-cent piece the people will get the benefit in making change.

Rep. Austin also asked if the motto IN GOD WE TRUST had been considered, and Ashbrook replied, "I am in favor of it, but we have not included it, because these coins never had this motto on them." Representative Mann, Republican Minority Leader, scolded Ashbrook about the form of the committee report, but raised no formal objection.[274]

Perforated Planchets – The Mint Experiments

Director Roberts followed the legislation closely as it moved through the House of Representatives. Letters traveled between the Philadelphia Mint and those in London and Brussels dealing with potential coin alloys, diameter and shape. The earliest noted in mint correspondence was a letter of December 6, 1911 to superintendent Landis from Charles Barber:[275]

>   Mr. Rigg of the Royal Mint, London sent a communication to this office asking for information on this subject, namely the alloy of nickel coins, and states that he is preparing a statement of the nickel coinages of the World and that he wishes to classify them under the two heads, pure nickel and nickel-bronze.
>   He states that he can get much of the desired information for the currency laws dealing with the question, but as some of the reports are silent on the subject he has addressed letters to the following Mints, Paris, Berlin, Belgium, Copenhagen, Vienna, Japan and Buenos Ayres [sic], no doubt Mr. Rigg would gladly state the result of his inquiry.
>   I enclose a statement furnished Mr. Rigg at his request made up from the coins in our cabinet and those coins that were made at this Mint, those marked with an

---

[273] *Congressional Record.* 62nd Congress, 2nd Session; pp.5978-5979.
[274] In August 1921 Mann was the only House member to object to the Peace dollar legislation. See Burdette, *Renaissance of American Coinage 1916-1921* for more information.
[275] *US Mint*, NARA-CP, op. cit., file 308449. Letter dated December 6, 1911 to Landis from Barber.

asterisk we gave the composition the others we could not. The coins marked are seventy-five copper and twenty-five nickel.

The only coins of Europe that I can give the composition are those of Belgium and Switgerland [sic]. At the time I visited those countries [1905] Belgium was using the same alloy as our own seventy-five copper and twenty-five nickel, these coins had a round hole in the center. Switzerland was making a five and ten centimes coin the same as ours, 75 and 25, and a 20 centimes piece pure nickel. You will see by the enclosed list that my statement that many countries are using nickel alloy or as Mr. Rigg calls it nickel-bronze is correct. I regret that I am not able to furnish the proportion of the composition used by the various countries contained in the enclosed list.

Barber's list included 24 coins from twenty countries. Of these, six were struck in pure nickel, the remaining 18 were made with a copper-nickel alloy.

On February 29, 1912 superintendent Landis wrote to director Roberts regarding the alloy proposed in the draft coinage bill. An early draft of the bill called for use of an aluminum alloy – something the mint had tested in the past but found unsatisfactory.[276]

In reply to your letter of the 24th instant, in reference to House bill 14042,[277] which provides for a coin of the value of three-cents, to be made of 95% aluminum and 5% copper and to weigh 24 grains, I beg to inform you that in accordance with your request I have conferred with the operative officers on the matter and there seems to be very little I can learn of such a coin. 24 grains of the alloy mentioned would make a coin of the size of the present five-cent nickel piece. By increasing the thickness the coin could be made smaller in diameter or vice versa. In 1896 experiments were made in this mint with pure aluminum and alloys containing 97 and 98% aluminum. All of these were found to be too soft and clogged the dies. It is not thought that the further addition of 2% copper will very much change the qualities of the alloy. About 1860 the French Government struck a number of aluminum coins containing 4% copper. This coinage was not continued.

After diligent search and inquiry I can find nothing relative to the condemnation of aluminum coins from a medical standpoint.

The market quotations for aluminum are .1825¢ per pound in ton lots.

Roberts asked for more information about use of aluminum in coinage on March 7, but was told by Landis that he didn't know anything more:[278]

In reply to your letter of the 7th instant, in further reference to the proposed new 3¢ piece, I beg to say that owing to our very limited experience with aluminum, I have nothing further to add to my letter of February 29th. I do not, however, consider aluminum a suitable metal for coins and I would recommend that the new coin be composed of 75 per cent copper and 25% nickel.

The director kept pushing Landis to supply more information. After all, Congress was actively considering the bill and this was the mint's best chance to affect the legislation. Evidently no one remembered the aluminum proof sets made by the mint in the 1860 to 1880 period. One might have expected Dr. Comparette, curator of the mint coin collection to have heard about the new coinage bill, and offer information, but that apparently did not occur. During this time, Rep. Bulkley was also in regular communication with Rep. Charles A. Korbley, also from Indiana, and A. Piatt Andrew, assistant secretary of the

---

[276] *US Mint*, NARA-CP, op. cit., file 308449. Letter dated February 29, 1912 to Roberts from Landis.
[277] This was an earlier version of the bill which was later withdrawn.
[278] *US Mint*, NARA-CP, op. cit., file 308449. Letter dated March 13, 1912 to Roberts from Landis.

treasury (and former mint director).[279] All three were from Indiana, suggesting the possibility of Andrew's support of the coinage bill.

Writing on March 27 Roberts asked to have some experimental pieces struck in aluminum-nickel alloy. These could be shown to influential Congressmen and might help the mint get changes to the bill. Landis replied the next day:[280]

> In reply to your letter of the 27th instant, asking that we try the aluminum-nickel composition under a die, I beg to say that as all experimental dies and hubs have been destroyed we have nothing on hand from which we could strike these experimental pieces. If it is your desire that we shall make an experimental coinage die for this work I would respectfully request the necessary authority, and also, in conformity with Article 15, Section 11, that you state the number of pieces you desire us to strike and such instructions as you may see fit to give us with reference to design and size.

On receiving this officious sounding letter, Roberts phoned the mint and instructed Landis to make several planchets according to the draft bill's specifications but using alloys the mint had available (he also sent written instructions). The samples were intended for Congressman Bulkley[281] who was the bill's sponsor.[282]

> In accordance with the request contained in you letter of the 28th instant I beg to enclose herewith specimens of blanks of different diameter and thickness conforming to the conditions of Congressman Bulkley's Bill.

A year earlier, samples had been struck using ordinary coinage dies. It is not clear why Landis now suggested making experimental dies, although the inconvenience of having no old hubs or dies available was evident. The director appears to have succeeded in getting the use of aluminum eliminated from the bill. Events now focused on the copper-nickel alloy used in the current five-cent piece. The congressman wanted to see more samples and Roberts arranged to visit the mint on April 1 to examine copper-nickel planchets made in different sizes, with and without central perforations.[283]

> In accordance with your request when at the mint on the first instant I beg to forward herewith samples of 3-cent blanks made from our standard nickel alloy.
> The plain blanks are of the diameter selected by you, .793". Some of the plain blanks have been milled and others reeded. I send blanks with two sizes of hole;

---

[279] *Charles A Korbley; papers.* Indiana University, Lilly Library, Manuscripts Department. Letter dated March 11, 1912 to Korbley from Andrew. Asst. Sec. Andrew's grandfather was a founder of LaPorte, Indiana and the family was prominent in state political and social circles.

[280] *US Mint*, NARA-CP, op. cit., file 308449. Letter dated March 28, 1912 to Roberts from Landis. All pattern coin dies and hubs were destroyed in May 1910 on Andrew's orders.

[281] Robert Johns Bulkley was a Congressman and later Senator from Ohio. Born in Cleveland, Cuyahoga County, Ohio, October 8, 1880, he attended the University School, Cleveland, Ohio, and graduated from Harvard University in 1902. He studied at Harvard Law School, was admitted to the bar in 1906 and commenced practice in Cleveland, Ohio. He was elected as a Democrat to the Sixty-second and Sixty-third Congresses (March 4, 1911–March 3, 1915). During the First World War Bulkley served as chief of the legal section of the War Industries Board 1917–1918. After the war he resumed the practice of law, and was elected as a Democrat to the United States Senate on November 4, 1930, to fill the vacancy caused by the death of Theodore E. Burton. He was reelected in 1932 and served from December 1, 1930, to January 3, 1939 when he was defeated for reelection in 1938. Engaged in banking and resumed the practice of law; during the Second World War served as a member of the board of appeals in visa cases; died in Cleveland, Ohio, July 21, 1965. Source: http://bioguide.congress.gov. It is not clear why, as a freshman member of Congress from the Democratic party, Bulkley's coinage bill got support from the Taft Administration or why the House passed it.

[282] *US Mint*, NARA-CP, op. cit., file 308449. Letter dated March 29, 1912 to Roberts from Landis.

[283] *US Mint*, NARA-CP, op. cit., file 308449. Letter dated April 4, 1912 to Roberts from Landis.

the smaller, 3/16", is the one selected by you, but the larger, 7/32", is one we think would work more satisfactorily as the weak part of the punch will be the portion that cuts out the center hole and the greater the diameter here, the less risk of breakage.

The primary issue was what sizes and weights of new coins would not conflict with the present one-cent, five-cent, ten-cent and twenty-five cent coins. Within a week Roberts asked for additional samples of perforated blanks:[284]

As requested in your letter of the 10th instant I enclose herewith samples of perforated blanks with diameters of .870 and .750 of an inch, composed of standard nickel alloy.

By cutting a hole in the center of a planchet, the coin could be made larger in diameter while retaining a relatively low weight. This could have been effective in preventing new three-cent or ½-cent coins from being used in five-cent or twenty-five cent coin slots.

It was apparent that much additional testing had to be performed before the best size for a new coin could be determined. To help with this, the director and Landis obtained examples of pay telephones from several phone companies. Roberts also had a slot-type pay telephone made by the Gray Telephone Company[285] sent to the mint for additional tests.[286] This was the mechanism used by most of the telephone companies in the country.

I beg to acknowledge receipt by express today of a package containing a Gray slot machine of the type used by the Bell Telephone Company, as mentioned in your letter of the 12th instant. I communicated by telephone with the Keystone Telephone Company in this city and they informed me that they used the Gray slot machine and also one known as the Baird machine, a sample of which they sent to the mint.

The Bell Telephone Company, in this city, stated that the principal machine used by them is the Gray machine, but they also had two other types, specimens of which they sent to the mint for trial.

I also telephoned the Horn and Hardardt Baking Company, proprietors of the Automat lunch houses in this city.

We find that the diameter of the coin seems to be the only essential part of the working of these machines, although some of the companies claim that the thickness also plays some part on the working. Our experiments, however, seem to negative this. After a trial of blanks of a large variety of diameters between the one cent and the quarter dollar in the different types of Bell and Keystone telephones, we find that the only pieces which do not conflict with existing coins and which will not work in these machines are the following:

First, the piece .875" in diameter, weight 50.35 grains, which is nearly as large as the quarter dollar. This piece is too large for the five cent slot and passes through the twenty-five cent slot without ringing the bell.

Second, the piece .870" in diameter and 1/32" larger than the nickel five cent piece. This is too large to enter the five cent slot.

---

[284] *US Mint*, NARA-CP, op. cit., file 308449. Letter dated April 12, 1912 to Roberts from Landis. The Gray pay phones were the most widely used at the time.

[285] Officially named the *Gray Telephone Pay Station Company* in Hartford, Connecticut. The devices were often called "slot machines" from the slot into which the coin was inserted. It was several years later that the term began to be applied exclusively to gambling devices.

[286] *US Mint*, NARA-CP, op. cit., file 308449. Letter dated April 13, 1912 to Roberts from Norris, acting superintendent.

142

> Third, the piece .750" in diameter, the same size as the one cent bronze piece. This piece falls through the five cent slot and does not ring the bell.
>
> The last two mentioned pieces weigh 60 grains each and specimens were forwarded to you yesterday by registered mail. Samples of the first mentioned piece were sent you some time ago.
>
> We find that the piece a trifle smaller than the five cent nickel piece will ring the bell.
>
> Of these three pieces mentioned above, not one will work the machine. The two larger are too large to enter the nickel slot and too small to ring the quarter dollar slot.
>
> The conclusion we have arrived at is that the coin must be of the one cent size, or too large or too thick to enter the five cent slot.
>
> Respectfully,

Roberts requested additional samples for congressman Bulkley, and coiner Robert Clark sent them on Saturday, April 20:[287]

> Replying to your inquiry by telephone today I enclose Philippine Half-cent and sample of nickel pieces same size. The dimensions etc. you will find marked on enclosed envelope. Will ascertain Monday if this piece will ring the One Cent slot machines. Places are closed this afternoon.

Robert Clark had continued his correspondence with Edward Rigg of the Royal Mint. On February 27 he received a letter from London enclosing several coins and planchets of varying diameters and weights. Rigg discussed the different shapes used in the Royal mints in Bombay and London including holed, square with rounded corners, and scalloped edge.[288] These were forwarded to Roberts and were mentioned by him in a letter of April 20 in which the director asked Clark about testing different shapes of coins in the telephone slot machines.[289]

> Your letter of the 20th instant referring to Mr. Rigg's letter in which he says he sent a number of blanks and finished coins of different shapes, was received. Replying to the same I would say that I sent you these coins and blanks with Mr. Rigg's letter. I however retained one piece of each, and enclose [for] you a coin and blank of the square and round cornered shapes as requested. In addition to the above I am sending you a few blanks .700 diameter, size of Philippine half cent. The alloy is 75% copper and 25% nickel, and the weight is 42.50 [grains]. These pieces can be either scalloped, or made square and round cornered. Can also be made a little thinner and of course weigh less. I think a scalloped piece about this size would make a very pretty coin. The square piece with round corners would be easy to work.
>
> As soon as the manufacturer sends in the one cent slot machine I will give you the result. In case the enclosed size rings the one cent slot machine I have made two pieces slightly smaller, one .600 and the other .650.

A one-cent telephone slot machine loaned by Bell Telephone Company arrived at the mint on April 22.[290] Clark immediately began testing Philadelphia Mint and Royal Mint planchets and coins in the mechanism. He reported to Roberts on April 23:[291]

---

[287] *US Mint*, NARA-CP, op. cit., file 308449. Letter dated April 20, 1912 to Roberts from Clark.
[288] *US Mint*, NARA-CP, op. cit., file 308815. Letter dated January 4, 1912 to Clark from Edward Rigg, Royal Mint, London.
[289] *US Mint*, NARA-CP, op. cit., file 308449. Letter dated April 22, 1912 to Roberts from Clark.
[290] *US Mint*, NARA-CP, op. cit., file 308449. Letter dated April 22, 1912 to Roberts from Norris, acting superintendent.
[291] *US Mint*, NARA-CP, op. cit., file 308449. Letter dated April 23, 1912 to Roberts from Clark.

> I enclose [for] you a few blanks that we tried in the one cent slot machine, none of which will work the machine. The piece in envelope marked No. 1, is too thick and the piece in No. 2, (Mexican cent) is too large in diameter to enter the slot. The other pieces in envelopes 3 and 4 will enter but will not operate the machine. The piece in No. 3 envelope is the same size as the Philippine half-cent .700, and the piece in No. 4 envelope is slightly smaller being .650 in diameter. Either would be a nice size for a coin. I also enclose [for] you a few square pieces with round corners. They will not ring the one cent slot machine.

No one had tried well-worn bronze cents in telephone slots and the director asked the mint to also test them. Albert Norris wrote back on April 23 stating that the mint did not "…have…uncurrent one-cent bronze pieces on hand and therefore cannot forward any in bad condition."[292] Roberts asked for additional sample planchets in different sizes and weights and the mint provided them accompanying a letter prepared the morning of April 26:[293]

> In accordance with your suggestion in letter of the 24th instant I am enclosing herewith additional experimental blanks – five samples of the small piece, .650 in diameter, weight 53 grains and five samples the size of the Philippine half-cent, .700 in diameter, weight 60 grains, standard nickel alloy. Neither of these blanks will operate the one or ten cent slot machines, both being too thick to enter. The square piece with round corners, sent you a few days ago, if made this thickness, will not operate the one or ten cent slot machines. This same size and thickness, scalloped, will not operate the one or ten cent slot machines.
> In reference to your inquiry of April 24, as to whether the proposed 3-cent piece would have to go through the punching machine an extra time in order to make the hole in the center, I beg to say the whole thing is done with one stroke when the piece is cut out.
> As stated in my letter of April 23rd we have no one-cent pieces returned for redemption on hand. They have all been melted.

By afternoon, superintendent Landis provided a further update when he noted that changes in legislation had altered the weight of the proposed coins:[294]

> Since preparing the .650 and .700 diameter blanks, mentioned in my letter of this morning, neither of which will operate the one and ten cent slot machines, we find the Bill provides for a piece to weigh 30 grains and have prepared the enclosed blanks – one .625 in diameter, weighing 33 grains and .600 diameter, weighing 30 grains as provided for in the Bill. These pieces will enter the slot machines but will not operate them. We find a piece above .625 to the size of a dime will operate a dime slot machine.

Director Roberts and secretary MacVeagh continued to struggle with the proposed legislation, and on April 27 still more sample planchets were requested from the mint.[295]

> As requested in your letter of the 27th instant I have forwarded by registered mail today three varieties of blanks (milled), one .625 diameter, .048 thick, weight 33 grains, another, same diameter, .053 thick, weight 37 grains, and still another,

---

[292] *US Mint*, NARA-CP, op. cit., file 308449. Letter dated April 23, 1912 to Roberts from Norris.
[293] *US Mint*, NARA-CP, op. cit., file 308449. Letter (AM) dated April 26, 1912 to Roberts from Norris.
[294] *US Mint*, NARA-CP, op. cit., file 308449. Letter (PM) dated April 26, 1912 to Roberts from Landis.
[295] *US Mint*, NARA-CP, op. cit., file 308449. Letter dated April 30, 1912 to Roberts from Landis.

sample of the same diameter, .055 thick, weight 38 grains. We think the most suitable piece would be the .625 diameter, weight 33 grains. This could be reduced to 30 grains and would still be thick enough to protect the dies in operation. By making the legal weight of the half-cent 30 grains, the one-cent 48 grains (the present weight) and the proposed three-cent piece 60 grains, the weight of a dollar in half-cent and one-cent pieces, and of three dollars in three-cent pieces would be easy of calculation, coming our even and doing away with fractions, which is very desirable.

We know of no provision in the law which regulates the diameters of any of our coins, the weight and fineness only being fixed by the statutes. Mr. Barber and Mr. Eckfeldt concur in this opinion, a letter from the former being enclosed.

It is interesting that Landis should make the comment about coin diameter, although he was referring only to the current bill. This subject had been examined in excruciating detail in January and February, 1908 by the Philadelphia Mint staff (including engraver Barber) and director Leach; the opposite conclusion was reached.[296] The following figures may help visualize the proposed coins and their configuration.

Date	Diameter (inches)	Weight (grains)	Thickness	Shape	Alloy	Denomination
4/4	.793	U/K	U/K	Round, 3/16" hole	U/K	3-cent
4/4	.793	U/K	U/K	Round, 7/32" hole	U/K	3-cent
4/12	.870	U/K	U/K	Round, perforated	75% Cu, 25% Ni	3-cent
4/12	.750	U/K	U/K	Round, perforated	75% Cu, 25% Ni	3-cent
4/13	.875	50.35	U/K	Round	75% Cu, 25% Ni	
4/13	.870	60	U/K	Round	75% Cu, 25% Ni	
4/13	.750	60	U/K	Round	75% Cu, 25% Ni	
4/20	Philippine half-cent	U/K	U/K	Round	95% Cu, 5% Sn	Half centavo
	Size of Phil ½-cent .700	U/K	U/K	Round	75% Cu, 25% Ni	Half centavo
4/22	.700	42.5	U/K	Round	75% Cu, 25% Ni	U/K
4/22	.600	U/K	U/K	Round	75% Cu, 25% Ni	U/K
4/22	.700	U/K	U/K	Round	75% Cu, 25% Ni	U/K
4/22	.650	U/K	U/K	Round	75% Cu, 25% Ni	U/K
4/26	.650	53	U/K	Round	75% Cu, 25% Ni	U/K
4/26	.700	60	U/K	Round	75% Cu, 25% Ni	U/K
4/26	.625	33	U/K	Round	75% Cu, 25% Ni	U/K
4/26	.600	30	U/K	Round	75% Cu, 25% Ni	U/K
4/30	.625	33	.048	Round, milled	75% Cu, 25% Ni	U/K
4/30	.625	37	.053	Round, milled	75% Cu, 25% Ni	U/K
4/30	.625	38	.055	Round, milled	75% Cu, 25% Ni	U/K

Figure 30. Summary of experimental planchets tested in 1912.

---

[296] See Burdette *Renaissance of American Coinage 1905–1908*.

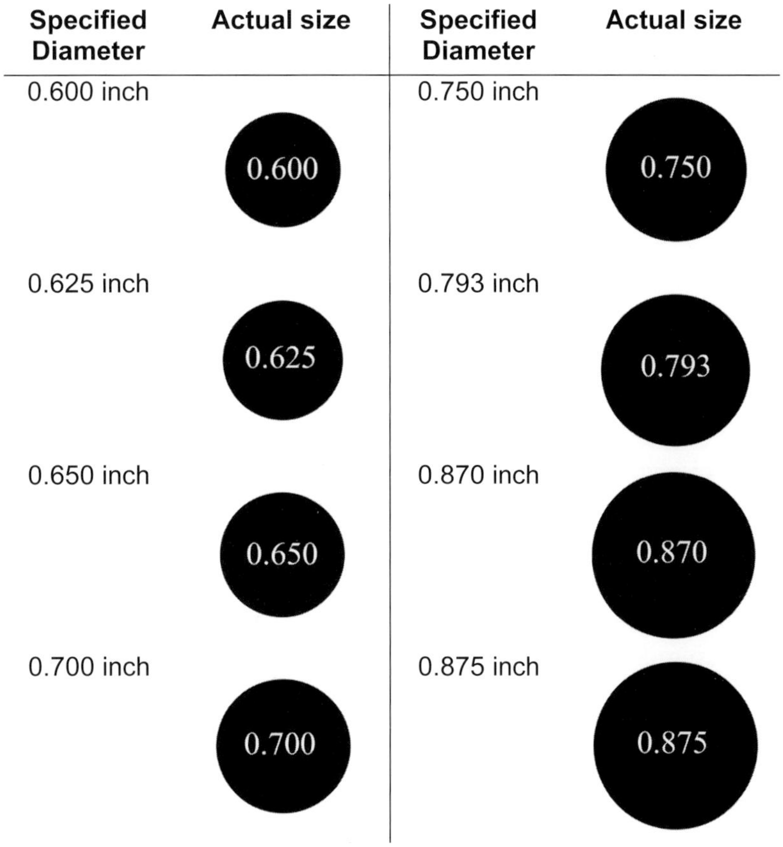

Specified Diameter	Actual size	Specified Diameter	Actual size
0.600 inch	0.600	0.750 inch	0.750
0.625 inch	0.625	0.793 inch	0.793
0.650 inch	0.650	0.870 inch	0.870
0.700 inch	0.700	0.875 inch	0.875

Figure 31. Diameters of proposed new coins (actual size). The five-cent piece is 0.835-inch (21.21 mm) in diameter.

Date	Diameter (inches)	Weight (grains)	Thickness	Coin Slot Mechanism Yes = operates; No = does not operate			
				1-cent	5-cent	10-cent	25-cent
4/4	.793	U/K	U/K	U/K	U/K	U/K	U/K
4/4	.793	U/K	U/K	U/K	U/K	U/K	U/K
4/12	.870	U/K	U/K	U/K	U/K	U/K	U/K
4/12	.750	U/K	U/K	U/K	U/K	U/K	U/K
4/13	.875	50.35	U/K	N/A	No (large)	N/A	No (small)
4/13	.870	60	U/K	N/A	No (large)	N/A	No (small)
4/13	.750	60	U/K	U/K	No (small)		No (small)
4/20	Philippine half-cent	U/K	U/K	U/K	U/K	U/K	U/K
	Size of Phil ½-cent .700	U/K	U/K	U/K	U/K	U/K	U/K
4/22	.700	42.5	U/K	U/K	U/K	U/K	U/K
4/22	.600		U/K	U/K	U/K	U/K	U/K
4/22	.700	U/K	U/K	U/K	U/K	U/K	U/K
4/22	.650	U/K	U/K	U/K	U/K	U/K	U/K
4/23	#1	U/K	U/K	No (thick)	U/K	U/K	U/K
4/23	#2 Mexican cent	U/K	U/K	No (large)	U/K	U/K	U/K
4/23	.700	U/K	U/K	No (small)	U/K	U/K	U/K
4/23	.650	U/K	U/K	No (small)	U/K	U/K	U/K
4/26	.650	53	U/K	U/K	U/K	U/K	U/K
4/26	.700	60	U/K	U/K	U/K	U/K	U/K

4/26	.625	33	U/K	No (small)	U/K	Larger than .625 up to dime size will operate	U/K
4/26	.600	30		No (small)	U/K	U/K	U/K
4/30	.625	33	.048	U/K	U/K	U/K	U/K
4/30	.625	37	.053	U/K	U/K	U/K	U/K
4/30	.625	38	.055	U/K	U/K	U/K	U/K

Figure 32. Test results for various planchet dimensions using Gray Telephone Co. coin box mechanisms.

The coinage bill passed the House of Representatives on May 6, 1912, but did not reach the Senate floor. Assistant secretary Andrew had been the bill's primary administration supporter. His strained relations with MacVeagh and resignation on July 2 may have marked the end of congressional interest. Timing of the proposed coinage bill, and extensive changes in the minor coin system that it contemplated, worked against adoption of a new nickel design. The difficulty was not the change of design, as much as sensitivity of the vending machine manufacturers to *any change* in the physical characteristics of the minor coins. It is evident from tests made by the mint on telephone pay boxes that a combination of diameter, thickness and alloy had to be discovered for the 3-cent piece which would not operate the mechanisms for a higher-denomination coin. The mint also considered round, perforated pieces, and non-round pieces in order to help distinguish the new coins from existing ones of almost the same diameter.

All of the mint's tests were done with blank planchets. Some were milled to raise the edge as would normally be done prior to striking a coin, others had plain or reeded edges to simulate struck coins. However, with the exception of the Philippine and Mexican coins, and ones sent by the Royal Mint or acquired from other sources, no struck U. S. coins were tested. It appears that the mint felt only the legal specifications were important, and the details of a design were of no consequence. This latter item is important because Hobbs Manufacturing Company (from which more will be heard) apparently based their counterfeit detection mechanism on portions of the design, not just diameter and weight.

The Treasurer's Treasure

Rumors about existence of a "secret" stock of gold dollars had floated about Washington for some time. It is not known how long the treasurer's private supply of obsolete gold coins had existed but it must have been well established before 1907. Representative William Ashbrook reported in his diary for December 20, 1907: "Got several $3 and $1 gold coins from the U.S. Treasury and some more of the double eagles. All command a premium."[297]

On August 8, 1911 Senator John D. Works (R-California)[298] wrote to Secretary of the Treasury Franklin MacVeagh about the coins:[299]

> I understand that there are certain souvenir gold dollars that may be distributed at the request of Senators. If so I should be glad to have a couple of them, in exchange for the bills enclosed.

---

[297] *Ashbrook*, op. cit., vol. 2, entry for December 20, 1907.
[298] John Downey Works, March 29, 1847 – June 6, 1928. Senator from March 4, 1911 to March 3, 1917. He did not seek reelection.
[299] *US Mint*, NARA-CP, op. cit., entry 229, box 297. Letter dated August 8, 1911 to MacVeagh from Works.

The Senator was sent one gold dollar and his other paper dollar was returned with a note apologizing for MacVeagh's inability to provide more than one coin.

On December 16, 1911 Representatives William Ashbrook (D- Ohio)[300] and Arthur W. Kopp (R-Wisconsin)[301] approached assistant secretary of the treasury A. Piatt Andrew (former director of the mint) with an unusual request.[302] The Congressmen were the only active coin collectors in congress and were eager to find specimens for their collections.[303] Both were members of the American Numismatic Association and Ashbrook had also been on the Assay Commission. In 1908 Ashbrook bought one of the high relief double eagles from director Leach as well as multiple examples of the 1907 Saint-Gaudens gold eagle with normal rim and periods. He was a member of the House Coinage Committee and fully aware of the collector value of the one dollar and three dollar gold coins. Their joint request was, "… to examine the one and three dollar gold pieces now in the hands of the Treasurer with the idea of securing therefrom any such as may be of peculiarly rare date or mintage."[304]

Andrew immediately discussed the request with Treasurer Lee McClung, under whose jurisdiction the $1 and $3 gold pieces were held in the Treasurer's Cash Room at face value. During the conversation, Andrew learned that Treasurer McClung also had additional coins that might be of special value to coin collectors. These "forgotten" coins were the balance of special 1907 eagles and double eagles of the Saint-Gaudens designs transferred to the Treasurer in December 1907 on orders of then assistant secretary John Edwards. Andrew prepared a memorandum for secretary MacVeagh explaining the situation and describing what had been done with the coins between 1907 and 1912:[305]

> I have talked with Mr. McClung about the question of the rare coins in the Treasurer's Office. It appears that there are 320 one dollar gold pieces, 337 three dollar gold pieces, 129 ten dollar St. Gauden's [sic] pieces of rare and early strike, and 58 twenty dollar St. Gauden's pieces of an early strike, all of which have a market value considerably above their face value. The one dollar and three dollar pieces ceased to be coined in 1889, and the rare strikes of the St. Gauden's ten dollar and twenty dollar gold pieces were issued only in 1907. It is possible that some of the individual pieces bearing special dates or the marks of particular mints have a value considerable above the rest. All of these coins are held in the Treasurer's cash room and constitute part of his cash at their face value. They have been given to applicants from time to time at the discretion of yourself or of the Treasurer. For about a year the distribution of the twenty dollar gold pieces has been confined entirely to your option. The unsatisfactory feature of this present method is the necessary discrimination between the applicants. If a school teacher from New Hampshire were to ask for one of these dollar pieces as a souvenir of her visit, she would undoubtedly be refused. On the other hand, an application by a Congressman or a Senator would probably never be denied. An application en-

---

[300] William Ashbrook (July 1, 1867 – January 1, 1940), Democrat from Ohio, was a coin collector and member of the American Numismatic Association. He was primarily responsible for the ANA receiving a national charter from Congress. He served on the Assay Commission six times, and attended many ANA conventions. He ceased active collecting in 1919 after his coins were stolen in a bank robbery.

[301] Arthur William Kopp (February 28, 1874 – June 2, 1967). Progressive Republican Member of Congress March 4, 1909 to March 3, 1913, from Wisconsin. Lawyer and later Circuit Court Judge. ANA member #1502 from June 1911 to June 1967.

[302] *US Mint*, NARA-CP, op. cit., entry 229, box 297. Memorandum dated December 18, 1911 to Andrew from MacVeagh.

[303] *Ashbrook*, op. cit., vol.2, entry dated December 14, 1911.

[304] *US Mint*, NARA-CP, op. cit., entry 229, box 297. Letter dated February 12, 1912 to Ashbrook from MacVeagh.

[305] *US Mint*, NARA-CP, op. cit., entry 229, box 297. Memorandum dated January 29, 1912 to MacVeagh from Andrew.

dorsed by a Senator or Congressman might or might not be granted according to circumstances.

The issue of these pieces involves the conferring of a favor which has a certain financial value and ought, therefore, to be carefully considered. A request from such as that recently presented, to be allowed to select from among those more or less valuable pieces those of peculiarly rare dates or mintage involves the conferring of a favor of possibly very large financial value and is open to serious objection on the grounds of propriety and of precedent. Such permission might yield the beneficiary a very considerable profit which, if known, might subject the Treasury to disagreeable criticism, and the precedent established, of allowing outsiders to examine coins in the cash room for the purpose of obtaining rare pieces, might lead to undesirable results.

As regards the stock of rare coins now in the cash room, there are several possible alternatives:

1. To continue the present policy of leaving the distribution to the discretion of the Secretary and the Treasurer.
2. To limit the distribution to Senators and Congressmen at their personal request for their personal ownership and enjoyment, and
3. To transfer the present supply to the Mint with orders for their melting and recoinage.

Mr. McClung favors the first alternative, believing that no harm comes from the present practice and that if embarrassment should arise in the future then reconsideration may be given the question in the light of developments. I am inclined to the third alternative – the recoinage of these pieces – on the general ground that it is peculiar and not quite proper for the Treasury to be distributing, through its cash room, to selected recipients, coins of exaggerated market value.

Former director Andrew's memorandum explains what happened to the Saint-Gaudens coins Edwards sent to the treasury department. They were used as personal favors distributed at face value by the treasurer and secretary of the treasury to members of Congress and others of influence. Except for the list of purchasers identified in other mint documents,[306] there appears to have been no record kept of who received the special coins or when they were sold to individuals. This method of distribution must have been known only to a few in the treasury department since there is no other known description of the practice.

Secretary MacVeagh read the memorandum with considerable interest. His awareness of coinage and numismatics had been enhanced by his contacts with Kenyon Cox (paper currency design) and James Fraser (Buffalo nickel samples) and Andrew's earlier explanations of numismatic inquiries. The next day he sent a short letter to mint director Roberts:[307]

Assistant Secretary Andrew has brought this matter, which has been suggested by the request of Representatives Ashbrook and Kopp, to my attention for consideration. What do you think about the matter? It is something I had not thought of before. I didn't know even how many pieces there were.

Roberts immediately saw the situation in a different light than the assistant secretary and wrote his own memorandum to Andrew the same day:[308]

---

[306] See Burdette, *Renaissance of American Coinage 1905–1908* for a list of purchasers of $10 and $20 Saint-Gaudens pieces.
[307] *US Mint*, NARA-CP, op. cit., entry 229, box 297. Letter dated January 30, 1912 to Roberts from MacVeagh.
[308] *US Mint*, NARA-CP, op. cit., entry 229, box 297. Memorandum dated January 30, 1912 to Andrew from Roberts.

> Referring to the $1 and $3 gold pieces and other coins worth a premium now held by the Treasurer, and the desirability of disposing of them in some way in order to avoid the private applications for them, I beg to suggest that they be sold at their face value to the Superintendent of the Philadelphia Mint for the coin collection at the Mint. The Superintendent is authorized to expend each year $500 out of the Contingent Fund of the Mint for coins for this collection; if he buys these pieces worth a premium he can use them to advantage in purchasing other rare pieces for the collection. In fact, they will have greater purchasing power than the same amount of ordinary cash and perhaps in effect amount to doubling his appropriation for one year. A special regulation should be adopted providing that all purchases or exchanges made with these coins shall have the approval of the Director of the Mint or that an annual report be made to the Secretary of the Treasury in which all transactions in which these coins are involved are specifically described.
>
> The amount now available in the appropriation is probably not sufficient to purchase all of these coins outright but if it is definitely settled that they are to be disposed of in this manner they can be considered sold, payment to be made as soon as funds are available.

Coincidentally Roberts had been director during much of the Saint-Gaudens design work in 1907, and owned one of the extremely high relief patterns made in February of that year. His knowledge of the mint's coin cabinet, the curator's expertise and details of the bureau's operations, gave his suggestion unique status and brought the immediate support of Andrew:[309]

> Dear Mr. Secretary:
> Attached herewith is a memorandum prepared by Mr. Roberts in regard to the disposition of the rare coins at present held as cash by the Treasurer. This idea has occurred to Mr. Roberts since I submitted the memorandum to you upon this subject yesterday, and I am inclined to regard his suggestion as better than any of those made in yesterday's memorandum. Congress is very loath to make any increase in the appropriations for the Mint collection at Philadelphia. We have, however, quite an important collection which has accumulated at the Mint during the century or more of its existence. We have a competent curator of scholarly training, who, with small salary and little encouragement, works hard to develop the collection with the meager funds at his disposal. We are just about to publish an important catalogue of our collection which he began to prepare when I was Director of the Mint and which will, I think, rank high in numismatic literature. I should be glad if we could encourage him in this way by turning these coins over to him to use as a part of the appropriation for the purchased of coins and medals for the Mint, with special instructions, which Mr. Roberts could prepare, requiring the purchases or exchanges made with these coins should have the approval of the Director, so insuring a careful accounting of all transactions in which these coins are involved.
> If this plan meets with your approval and you will so indicate either upon this letter or upon the memorandum of the Director of the Mint, I will see that the proper steps are taken for the transfer of these coins to the Mint for the purpose indicated and that proper arrangements are devised for the supervision of their use.

The plan would have turned over all the Treasurer's coins to the mint collection. Curator Comparette could then add pieces to the collection, exchange any of the pieces for others he felt were needed, or sell the coins and use the proceeds to buy additional coins. Implicit in this arrangement was the authority of the curator and director to approve the

---

[309] *US Mint*, NARA-CP, op. cit., entry 229, box 297. Letter dated January 30, 1912 to MacVeagh from Andrew.

sale or exchange of coins from the mint collection. This had been done on previous occasions, but apparently without the requirement to report transactions.

Director Roberts prepared another memorandum for secretary MacVeagh regarding the Congressmen's request on February 9. At the bottom of the page, assistant secretary Andrew wrote a short note, "This is quite in accord with my memorandum of January 29, dictated in Mr. McClung's presence and with his approval. APA."[310]

> In regard to the request of Congressmen Ashbrook and Kopp for permission to examine the one and three dollar gold pieces now in the hands of the treasurer, and to be allowed to buy them at their face value, I beg to refer you to my previous recommendation that these pieces be sold to the Superintendent of the Philadelphia Mint for the benefit of the coin collection in that institution. All of these pieces are now understood to be worth a premium, and some of them may be worth considerably more than others. If the Curator of the collection does not desire to retain these coins he will be able to use them advantageously in making exchanges for other rare pieces. If Messrs. Ashbrook and Kopp desire any particular pieces to fill out their collections they will perhaps be able to effect such exchanges with the Curator to the mutual advantage of themselves and the Mint collection. If, however, these gentlemen are allowed to take their pick of the lot at face value other collectors or applicants cannot fairly be refused the privilege of doing the same and the entire plan to benefit the Mint collection will have to be abandoned.

Clearly Roberts and Andrew were in agreement on how to handle the coins and that did not include permitting a couple of Congressmen to "cherry pick" the hoard. They recognized the greatest benefit to the mint collection (and to the nation) was to turn the coins over to the curator and use the profits to improve the scope and quality of holdings.

But the director and former director did not have the support of a key treasury employee – Treasurer of the United States Lee McClung, how controlled access to the gold pieces. McClung's memorandum of February 10 supported the *status quo*:[311]

> I have you memorandum with regard to the desire of Congressman Ashbrook to go over the stock of coin in the Cash Room of the Treasurer's Office with the idea of securing therefrom any coins that may be found of rare dates, and in reply would say that my opinion is that to grant this request may establish a precedent that might be embarrassing to us in the future. From personal observation I am inclined to think that as practically all of the coins in our Cash Room are current – and by that I mean in actual circulation, with the exception of the premium gold coins – I am inclined to think that there are among these no pieces of rare dates, as the St. Gaudens double-eagles are all of the 1907 coinage, and all of the $1 gold pieces are of the 1889 mintage (the last year in which these coins were minted). As far as I know, there are no rare dates with respect to the $3 gold pieces; all of these $3 gold pieces that are in our Cash Room have been in circulation. This is not true of the other three kinds of gold coins referred to, namely, the St. Gaudens 20s, the St. Gaudens 10s and the one-dollar gold pieces.
> If the Secretary wishes to be relieved of any annoyance in the matter of these applications I would suggest that he simply refer the applicants directly to me.

McClung's comments make it evident he wanted to retain control of the gold coins and continue his policy of handing them out as special favors. He may have viewed the coins as one of the small "perks" of the otherwise low-profile job of treasurer, and was

---

[310] *US Mint*, NARA-CP, op. cit., entry 229, box 297. Memorandum dated February 9, 1912 to MacVeagh from Roberts.
[311] *US Mint*, NARA-CP, op. cit., entry 229, box 297. Memorandum dated February 10, 1912 to Andrew from McClung.

hesitant to give up anything under his control. Assistant secretary Andrew sent McClung his response – which sounded a little like an order – the same day:[312]

> The Director of the Mint, on behalf of the Superintendent of the Mint at Philadelphia, has submitted a request that all of the one-dollar and three-dollar gold coins and other rare pieces now in the Treasury be sold at their face value to the Superintendent of the Mint for the numismatic collection at that institution. I agree with this proposal and should be glad if you would carry it into effect and would arrange with the Director of the Mint for so doing.

Although there was no agreement about disposition of the coins, everyone in the top ranks felt that allowing members of Congress to examine the coins was a bad idea. A polite rejection letter went out to congressman Ashbrook on February 12:[313]

> I have had the Director of the Mint, the Treasurer, and the Assistant Secretary in charge of fiscal bureaus give careful consideration to the request made by you and Representative Kopp for permission to examine the one and three dollar gold pieces now in the hands of the Treasurer, with the idea of securing therefrom any such as may be of peculiarly rare date of mintage. The unanimous opinion of those who have considered the matter is that the granting of this request might establish a precedent which would be embarrassing in the future, and that the conferring of this favor or allowing an examination of coins in the cash room for the purpose of obtaining rare pieces might possibly be subjected to criticism on grounds of propriety. On these accounts I am very sorry not to be able to extend you this courtesy.

Apparently, Ashbrook spoke with Roberts about the coin transfer plan and decided it was a good idea. Congress was considering the treasury appropriation bill during March, and Ashbrook took the opportunity to offer to add a clause benefiting the mint's collection:[314]

> I have been endeavoring to have…authority for the Secretary…to have coined and for sale at the Mint at Philadelphia a small medalet, the profit of which is to go to the Mint Cabinet…Now I believe if you will write me a letter endorsing the same, that I can get the present Committee to include it in the bill…I would also be glad to have you draft the clause to be added to the bill. I understand that employees in the Mint are no longer allowed to sell a medal and I believe by the passage of this legislation it would result in a profit of two or three thousand annually for the Mint Cabinet…

The congressman was not easily dissuaded from his "coin fad," however. On January 17, 1913 an entry in his diary states: "I spent three hours in the Treasury looking over a bag of 5,000 quarter eagles, but did not find one that I wanted. I expect it is foolish, but I enjoy my coin fad." He returned to the treasury on January 18, 20 and 21 and spent the bet-

---

[312] *US Mint*, NARA-CP, op. cit., entry 229, box 297. Letter dated February 10, 1912 to McClung from Andrew.
[313] *US Mint*, NARA-CP, op. cit., entry 229, box 297. Letter dated February 12, 1912 to Ashbrook from MacVeagh. A copy of the letter was sent to Representative Kopp.
[314] *US Mint*, NARA-CP, op. cit., entry 229, box 297. Letter dated March 16, 1912 to Roberts from Ashbrook. In previous years, mint employees gave educational tours to visitors of the mint and mint collection. Visitors were offered the opportunity to purchase a descriptive pamphlet and small medallion as a memento of their visit. The medal and pamphlet were privately produced and mint staff kept the profits as supplement to their income. Director Andrew halted this procedure, to the dismay of both employees and visitors. Ashbrook's clause in the appropriation bill was intended to restore part of the former process but distribute profits to the mint collection.

ter part of each day looking through a total of 30,000 quarter eagles without finding anything needed for his collection.[315]

Treasurer McClung still objected to sending the coins to the mint, so director Roberts sent a more formal request on March 19.[316]

> The Treasurer of the United States:
> It is requested that the Bullion Fund of the Mint of the United States at Philadelphia be increased in the sum of $3,781, by a transfer of that amount in gold coin of the following denominations from the Treasury of the United States:
>
> | | | |
> |---|---|---|
> | $1 | 320 | $320 |
> | $3 | 337 | $1,011 |
> | $10 | 129 | $1,290 |
> | $20 | 58 | $1,160 |
> | Total | | $3,781 |
>
> Respectfully
> George E. Roberts
> Approved: R. C. Bailey, Assistant Secretary

The treasurer now decided there had to be a legal reason not to turn the coins over to the mint, and he found a possible excuse:[317]

> I have yours of March 19th requesting that the bullion fund of the Mint of the United States at Philadelphia be increased in the sum of $3,781, by the transfer of that amount in gold coin of $1, $3, $10 and $20 denominations from the Treasury of the United States.
>
> Leaving out the question for the moment the merits or propriety of the suggestion, I express the opinion that in submitting your request the following existing Statute which has a bearing on this subject may have been overlooked:
>
> *Section 3545 R. S. – "<u>For the purpose of enabling the Mints and the Assay Office in New York to make returns to depositors with as little delay as possible, it shall be the duty</u> of the Secretary of the Treasury to keep in such mints and assay-office, when the state of the Treasury will admit thereof, such an amount of public money, or bullion procured for the purpose, as he shall judge convenient and necessary, out of which those who bring bullion to the said mints and assay-offices may be paid the value thereof, in coin or bars as soon as practicable after the value has been ascertained. On payment thereof being made, the bullion so deposited shall become the property of the United States. The Secretary of the Treasury may, however, at any time withdraw the fund, or any portion thereof."*
>
> The following statute also has particular bearing with regard to the $1 and $3 gold pieces.
>
> *Act of September 26, 1890. "Chap. 945 – An Act to discontinue the coinage of the three-dollar and one-dollar gold pieces and three-cent nickel piece."*
>
> *Be it enacted by the Senate and House of Representatives of the United States of America in Congress assembled, That from and after the passage of this act the coinage of the three-dollar gold piece, the one-dollar gold piece, and the three-cent nickel piece be, and the same is hereby, prohibited, and the pieces named shall not be struck <u>or issued by the Mint of the United States</u>"*

---

[315] *Ashbrook*, op. cit., vol.2 , p.772, entries for January 17, 18, 20 and 21, 1913.
[316] *US Mint*, NARA-CP, op. cit., entry 229, box 297. Letter dated March 19, 1912 to McClung from Roberts.
[317] *US Mint*, NARA-CP, op. cit., entry 229, box 297. Letter dated March 21, 1912 to Roberts from McClung.

> SEC. 2 That as fast as the said coins shall be paid into the TREASURY OF THE United States they shall be withdrawn from circulation and be recoined into other denominations of coins."
> Respectfully,

McClung seemed to be grasping for any possible argument which would permit him to retain control over the coins and continue his privilege of dispensing them as he determined best. It is interesting that his letter to Roberts completely ignores possible ethical implications of the treasurer selectively selling coins with known numismatic value. Two weeks later assistant secretary Andrew wrote to McClung with a copy for secretary MacVeagh:[318]

> Dear Mr. McClung:
> The Secretary has been over the correspondence in regard to the transfer of the one and three-dollar gold pieces to the Mint in Philadelphia and is still of the opinion that these and the St. Gaudens pieces should be sent as asked by the Director of the Mint in his letter to you of March 19th, approved by Assistant Secretary Bailey. The Act of September 26, 1890, which you cite in your letter to the Director of the Mint, dated March 21, 1912, stating that the one and three-dollar gold pieces shall not be struck or issued by the Mint of the United States, also states "That as fast as the said coins shall be paid into the Treasury of the United States they shall be withdrawn from circulation and be recoined into other denominations of coins." This would seem to place the issue of these coins in the Treasurer's office on the same basis as their issue from the mint. I trust therefore that the request of March 19th made by the Director of the Mint for the transfer of the one and three-dollar gold pieces and the ten and twenty-dollar St. Gaudens pieces will be complied with as it has been passed upon by the Secretary as well as by Assistant Secretary Bailey.
> Sincerely yours,
> A. Piatt Andrew

Andrew's argument was simple: if the Mint Bureau had issued the coins originally, then they should be returned to the mint's control. Therefore the only thing to do was send them to the Philadelphia Mint for disposition as "uncurrent" coin. But McClung was not about to give up his prerogative and sent Andrew a letter indicating his intention to appeal to MacVeagh in person.[319]

> I have yours of April 4th in regard to the suggested transfer of the one and three-dollar gold pieces and the St. Gaudens pieces to the Philadelphia Mint. I quite appreciate your views in this matter, but at the same time I am inclined to think the matter is of sufficient importance to warrant a conference with the Secretary on the subject; so if you will be good enough to hold the matter in abeyance for the time being I shall seek an interview with the Secretary.
> As to your comment on the Act of September 26, 1890, I assume you do not know that the one and three-dollar gold pieces which are now in the Treasury were not paid therein after the act in question.

---

[318] *US Mint*, NARA-CP, op. cit., entry 229, box 297. Letter dated April 4, 1912 to McClung from Andrew; copy to MacVeagh.
[319] *US Mint*, NARA-CP, op. cit., entry 229, box 297. Letter dated April 5, 1912 to Andrew from McClung. The last sentence indicates the $1 and $3 pieces had been under the Treasurer's control prior to the 1890 law.

McClung also wrote to secretary MacVeagh requesting an interview:[320]

> As you have not had my views with respect to the suggested transfer to the Philadelphia Mint of the one and three-dollar gold pieces and the St. Gaudens ten and twenty-dollar gold pieces, all of which now constitute a part of the Treasurer's cash, I beg to seek from you a conference, at which time I may be afforded an opportunity to present such views to you.

Secretary MacVeagh attempted to put and end to the disagreement with a terse letter to Treasurer McClung on April 8:

> Dear Mr. McClung
> I have your letter of April 5th. Your views on the subject of the $1.00 gold pieces, etc., were expressed to the Assistant Secretary of the Treasury and were submitted by him, with the other papers, to me at the time I approved his suggestion.
> Very truly yours,

However, the treasurer sent Andrew yet another version of his April 5 letter. Andrew complained to MacVeagh on April 11 that there was nothing more he could do to get the treasurer to comply with his requests:[321]

> In regard to the transfer of the one and three dollar gold pieces and the St. Gaudens coins to the Mint in Philadelphia, which was agreed upon last week, I enclose a further letter from Mr. McClung in which he says he thinks "that the matter is of sufficient importance to warrant a conference with the Secretary on the subject" and asks that the matter be held in abeyance until he can have that interview with you. Apparently there is nothing more that I can do in the matter. I have several times asked that the transfer be made, and Mr. Roberts has made the request according to the usual form.

MacVeagh evidently talked with McClung, insisting that the coins be transferred to the Philadelphia Mint. By April 17, the treasurer advised he was arranging for the transfer:[322]

> Referring further to your letter of April 4th, I am to-day arranging for the transfer to the Philadelphia Mint of the following gold pieces:
>
> | | | |
> |---|---|---|
> | $1 | 313 | $313 |
> | $3 | 335 | $1,005 |
> | $10 | 129 | $1,290 |
> | $20 | 58 | $1,160 |
> | Total | | $3,768 |
>
> As for the number of $1 and $3 gold pieces stated in Director Roberts' letter of March 19th, I do not know where that information was secured; it was not gotten through me.
> The number stated above constitutes all the $1 and $3 gold pieces that we have and all that we have had for sometime past.

Andrew sent the letter on to director Roberts with a note stating, "...I think it would be advisable if you would prepare some sort of instructions to the Superintendent of

---

[320] *US Mint*, NARA-CP, op. cit., entry 229, box 297. Letter dated April 5, 1912 to MacVeagh from McClung.
[321] *US Mint*, NARA-CP, op. cit., entry 229, box 297. Letter dated April 11, 1912 to MacVeagh from Andrew.
[322] *US Mint*, NARA-CP, op. cit., entry 229, box 297. Letter dated April 17, 1912 to Andrew from McClung.

the Mint in Philadelphia which will provide for a careful report to you as to the disposition made of all of these coins."[323]

As requested, Roberts prepared an advisory letter to mint superintendent Landis listing what coins he could expect to receive, and how to handle their disposition by the curator:[324]

> The Treasurer is transferring to you and charging in the Bullion Fund the following gold pieces which are believed to be worth a premium:
>
> | Denomination | Number | Value |
> |---|---|---|
> | $1 | 313 | $313 |
> | $3 | 335 | $1,005 |
> | $10 | 129 | $1,290 |
> | $20 | 58 | $1,160 |
>
> You are instructed to have a strict account kept of these coins all of which are to be held by you and turned over to the Curator of the numismatic Collection from time to time as the appropriation for the collection will allow and as he, with your approval, may desire to use them, either by adding them permanently to the collection or by using them for the purchase of other rare pieces.
>
> All such purchases are to be specifically approved by you and reported to this Bureau with a statement setting forth the coins purchased, a description of the rare coins or medals purchased. Hereafter it is desired that a regular monthly statement of all coins and medals purchased shall be made to the Bureau.
>
> The rare coins now being transferred are to be held and used for no other purpose than the one set forth in this letter, to wit: For the use of the Numismatic Collection, and your records be made to show the disposition of every coin.

Detailed reports would be a nuisance but the additional funds derived from sale of the coins was a windfall to the mint collection. For a collection whose curator had aspirations of international recognition, the present $500 purchase fund was far too small to do more than buy a few duplicates from relatively minor collections. Treasurer McClung, in a last bit of pique at having to hand over his "personal treasure" to some academic at the mint, had the transfer order made on the standard form used for "Uncurrent and Light Weight Coin." The numismatic pieces were dumped in a small bag and shipped as so much damaged goods on April 20, 1912[325] and received by the mint on the 22nd. Albert Norris reported, "No advice of the forwarding of this coin was received from the Treasurer, the tag on the bag being simply marked 'Uncurrent Gold Coin.'"[326]

On receipt, curator Comparette went through the hoard looking for anything that might be added to the present collection. He noted the gold dollars "…were all of one date [1889] with a single exception, and that specimen was considerably worn…. The three-dollar pieces had all been in circulation and were not a little worn and nicked."[327]

With substantial purchasing power available for the first time Comparette's first transaction was with Philadelphia coin dealer Henry Chapman. On June 28 and 29, 1912 Chapman acquired all three hundred thirteen gold dollars at $2.00 each and thirty-six of the

---

[323] *US Mint*, NARA-CP, op. cit., entry 229, box 297. Memorandum dated April 18, 1912 to Roberts from Andrew.
[324] *US Mint*, NARA-CP, op. cit., entry 229, box 297. Letter dated April 19, 1912 to Landis from Roberts.
[325] *US Mint*, NARA-CP, op. cit., entry 229, box 297. U. S. Mint transfer form #777 dated April 20, 1912.
[326] *US Mint*, NARA-CP, op. cit., entry 229, box 297. Letter dated April 22, 1912 to Roberts from Norris.
[327] *US Mint*, NARA-CP, op. cit., entry 229, box 297. Letter dated August 16, 1912 to Landis from Comparette.

three dollar pieces at $4.00 each.[328] In his report of the transaction dated August 16, Comparette felt the need to explain the prices obtained, "…Perhaps I may anticipate a natural inquiry by stating that the prices obtained…are certainly favorable to the Government and all that could be expected."[329]

This initial expedition into the commercial coin market netted the mint collection one hundred five new specimens on June 28 and an additional nineteen pieces on June 29. The first group consisted primarily of ancient Greek and Roman coins featuring such items as a tetradrachm of Demetrius Poliorestes bought for $42.50, a gold distater of Alexander the Great for $80 and an aureus of Lucilla (C-69) for $31.00, along with a dozen French seventeenth century gold and silver pieces. The June 28 group included a 1912 gold proof set, several colonial pieces and a scattering of European gold. The grand total of the first Chapman purchases was $773.20 in dollars or, as Comparette preferred to figure the prices in the gold coins from the treasurer's office, $423.81.[330]

By September 3, Norris reported the original $3,768 in rare coins transferred from the Treasury had been reduced to $3,327. All expenditures were accounted for in the transaction with Chapman except for one double eagle which was sold to representative William M. Calder on May 7 by order of the secretary of the treasury. This left a balance of fifty-seven double eagles, one hundred twenty-nine eagles, and two hundred ninety-nine three dollar coins in the mint collection account. The Saint-Gaudens design coins consisted entirely of high relief double eagles and high relief eagles from the #1 dies as struck in late August-early September 1907. The $10 and $20 coins were all that remained of five hundred of each transferred to the treasurer in December 1907, plus fifty-one additional double eagles sent to Washington in May, 1908.

The curator was anxious to make additional purchases and wrote to Landis on December 13, 1912:[331]

> The present season is probably favorable for the dispersion at good prices of the rare Eagles and Double-eagles held by the Cashier to be sold and the premiums utilized for the purchase of coins for the Cabinet. I beg leave, therefore, to request that authority be sought from the Director to dispose of a portion of each lot at the most advantageous prices procurable.
> It might be well to add for his information, that the Three Dollar gold pieces, which we were authorized to dispose of, are nearly all gone out, and the balance on hand will soon be sent out on terms already agreed upon. We secured for the pieces the highest retail-market value.

Comparette's next report on February 12, 1913 showed considerable change in the coins held for resale:[332]

> …I beg to make the following report on the special gold coins transferred to this Mint, from the Treasurer's office, to be sold and the profits used for the benefit of the Numismatic Collection:

---

[328] *US Mint*, NARA-CP, op. cit., entry 229, box 297. Letter dated September 3, 1912 to Roberts from Norris. The receipt from Chapman was dated July 18 suggesting that either there was a delay in transferring the coins to him, or Comparette had neglected to obtain a receipt as required by Roberts.
[329] *US Mint*, NARA-CP, op. cit., entry 229, box 297. Letter dated August 16, 1912 to Landis from Comparette.
[330] *US Mint*, NARA-CP, op. cit., entry 229, box 297. Letter with inventory included dated August 29, 1912 to Landis from Comparette. The inventory is approximately four pages. Valuing purchases in the treasury coins at a discount allowed Comparette to stay under the $500 appropriation ceiling.
[331] *US Mint*, NARA-CP, op. cit., entry 229, box 297. Letter dated December 13, 1912 to Landis from Comparette.
[332] *US Mint*, NARA-CP, op. cit., entry 229, box 297. Letter dated February 12, 1913 to Roberts from Landis.

	On hand at last report	Sold	On hand Feb 1
$20's	57	0	57
$10's	129	0	129
$3's	299	259	40

The 259 $3.00 gold pieces were sold to Mr. Thos. L. Elder of New York City at a profit ranging from $1.00 to $1.50 apiece, the total profit received on their sale being $271.65. Out of this profit, the following medal and coins were purchased by the Curator:

Art Institute of Chicago, Bronze Replica of the Potter Palmer medal	$7.00
Henry Chapman, Philadelphia. Roman coin	$2.50
Indian, Roman, Mexican, Peruvian, and other coins	$64.85
Rudolph Rauer, Philadelphia. British colonial and Chilean coins	$5.25
Cashier Mint US Philadelphia. Set of 1913 US Gold Proof coins	$37.50
Royal Mint, Ottawa. Canadian gold, silver and bronze coins	$16.01
F. Redder, Leipzig, Germany. Coins of German States	$32.66
C. G. Thieme, Dresden, Germany. German and other Foreign coins	$52.59
Total	$218.36

His report of March 13 indicated that most of the remaining coins had been sold, although this time he did not specify the purchaser(s):[333]

...I beg to make the following report, for February, on the special gold coins transferred to this Mint, from the Treasurer's office, to be sold and the profits used for the benefit of the Numismatic Collection:

	On hand 2/1/13	Sold	On hand 3/1/13	Profit
$20's	57	57	none	$171.00
$10's	129	24	105	$120.00
$3's	40	39	1	$43.95

Out of the profits, the Curator purchased and paid for during the month the following coins for the Numismatic Collection in this Mint:

From Cashier, US Mint, Philadelphia. Specimen (pyx) coins from the other mints	$16.45
From Royal Mint, Copenhagen. New coins of Denmark	$9.53
Henry Chapman, Philadelphia. African, Italian, Roman, Syrian and other coins	$128.80
Total	$154.78

The one $3.00 piece still on hand is mutilated and therefore unsalable – it has several initials stamped on it.

Using the reported profit to calculate the selling price, the mint sold high relief double eagles for $23 each, the #1 model eagles for $15 each and the $3 pieces for an average of $3.30 a piece. These prices suggest there was little market for either of the Saint-Gaudens coins although collectors were willing to pay a higher premium for the $10 #1 design pieces than for its larger cousin.

By July 18 Comparette reported that all coins had been sold with the exception of "…about eighty (80) eagles, for which we are asking $15.00 each."

---

[333] *US Mint*, NARA-CP, op. cit., entry 229, box 297. Letter dated March 15, 1913 to Landis from Comparette. The eagles were likely sold to Chapman, if later reports of his inventory are correct.

Although the project seemed to be going well and had been particularly effective at allowing the curator to purchase a wide range of coins for the collection, the change of executive administration in 1913 brought new questions for the mint to answer. A new assistant secretary of the treasury, John Skelton Williams, knew nothing about numismatics and had several questions about the gold coin transactions. He first wanted assurance that the mint was obtaining an affidavit of authenticity for all of the coins purchased.[334] Once this was settled, he wanted to know if there were any gold dollars at the mint and if not who had bought them.[335]

When acting director Frederick Dewey replied on July 26, Williams annotated the letter with further questions:[336]

> The one dollar gold pieces which were transferred from the Office of the Treasurer of the United States to the Mint in Philadelphia in April 1912, for the benefit of the Numismatic collection of the Mint at Philadelphia have been sold. The last sale of these pieces was made to Mr. Henry Chapman of Philadelphia who paid two dollars each for them...
>
> [*At the bottom in bold writing:*]
> On what date?
> Who is Chapman?
> JSW

Dewey responded by providing the date the last sale was made and noting that "...Mr. Henry Chapman, a well known coin dealer of Philadelphia...paid two dollars each for three hundred and thirteen pieces..."[337]

It appears that assistant secretary Williams was not entirely trusting of the Mint Bureau's explanation and the next day he had W. U. Thompson, possibly a treasury employee, write to Henry Chapman in Philadelphia asking if he had any gold dollars for sale. Chapman replied the next day:[338]

> Mr. W. U. Thompson,
> Dear Sir:
> Replying to your letter of 29th inst. I can supply you small gold dollars extremely fine condition, at $2.40 each. Large size very good to fine at $2.10 each, uncirculated, $2.25 each.
> Shall be glad to have your order,

At a profit of just 25¢ per coin for Chapman, this exercise must have satisfied Williams for nothing more appears in mint records.

The curator was well acquainted with most of the prominent numismatists and museum collections in the eastern United States and had ample opportunity to let them know of any coins the mint had for sale. With only a small number of coins remaining – a mutilated $3 piece, seventy-six 1907 eagles from the #1 dies, and one eagle from the #3 normal circulation dies – Comparette had little that was of interest to collectors or his dealer con-

---

[334] The mint did not obtain such a certificate. Comparette argued that an honest dealer would take a fake coin back, and a dishonest one would sign anything to make the sale, then vanish.
[335] *US Mint*, NARA-CP, op. cit., entry 229, box 297. Memorandum dated July 23, 1913 to Williams from Frederick P. Dewey, acting director.
[336] *US Mint*, NARA-CP, op. cit., entry 229, box 297. Memorandum dated July 26, 1913 to Williams from Dewey.
[337] *US Mint*, NARA-CP, op. cit., entry 229, box 297. Memorandum dated July 28, 1913 to Williams from Dewey.
[338] *US Mint*, NARA-CP, op. cit., entry 229, box 297. Letter dated July 30, 1913 to W. U. Thompson from Chapman (signed by Ella B. Wright). There is no address for Mr. Thompson.

tacts. He had sold twenty-eight #1 eagles in December to bring the stock to its present level,[339] and by August 1914 he recommended "…[sale of] the balance of the first pattern Saint Gaudens eagles, at $15.00 each for those in perfect condition, and the unsalable pieces at face value."[340]

On October 19, the sale of another four eagles was reported bringing the total remaining to seventy-two coins. Two more were sold on November 17, 1914. With no interest in the remaining coins Comparette filed his last report on June 9, 1915 listing seventy eagles of the Saint-Gaudens design, #1 models. In response to an inquiry on June 14, 1918 from director Raymond T. Baker, Philadelphia Mint superintendent Adam Joyce commented:[341]

> …I beg to inform you that the 70 eagles which were reported as on hand at my last report, June 9, 1915, have all been melted. None has been sold since that time, and of the profits reported on hand…24 cents, 21 cents was paid out the next day for expressage on medals which were donated to us, leaving 3 cents still on hand.

Thus, the unusual tale of the treasurer's treasure came to a quiet end.

The last 1907 gold eagles, once eagerly sought by a few collectors, promoted as being worth hundreds of dollars each, could not be sold at $15 apiece, and met oblivion in the melt of obsolete and defective coin. It was nearly a century before anyone figured out what happened to the Saint-Gaudens pieces. By that time the golden orphans were prized by numismatists and routinely sold at auction for thousands of times their face value.

---

[339] *US Mint*, NARA-CP, op. cit., entry 229, box 297. Letter dated January 8, 1914 to Director of the Mint from Landis.
[340] *US Mint*, NARA-CP, op. cit., entry 229, box 297. Letter dated August 25, 1914 to superintendent of the mint from Comparette.
[341] *US Mint*, NARA-CP, op. cit., entry 229, box 297. Letter dated June 14, 1918 to Baker from Joyce.

Chapter 7 – Something of Real Merit

While Andrew adapted to life in Washington, DC of 1909, he became acquainted with Eames MacVeagh, the only surviving son of secretary Franklin MacVeagh. The two were nearly the same age and shared an interest in art and culture not well represented in the new political administration. By fortunate coincidence Andrew took a personal interest in earlier redesign work done under Leach's direction, and shared Eames' interest in improving the appearance of our coinage. For his part, Eames was interested in national currency and coinage, and had given several illustrated lectures on the subject in Chicago.[342] It is possible that Eames was the source of secretary MacVeagh's ideas for uniform currency and improvements in the artistic style of circulating media. These would later come to fruition as the Buffalo nickel and Kenyon Cox' reverse for the Series 1914 one hundred dollar Federal Reserve Note. Eames and director Andrew evidently corresponded from 1910 through the first part of 1912, after which the strained relationship between Andrew and secretary MacVeagh probably discouraged communication.

The Fraser Approach

Sculptor James Earle Fraser knew how to manipulate bureaucracies to achieve his goals. Fraser was familiar with previous coin design efforts and how easily mechanical requirements could override creativity. Accompanying his superior artistic talent and prodigious technical skill, his ability to comprehend the mechanics of coinage (possibly acquired from his father who was a railroad civil engineer) was possessed by only a handful of his contemporaries. Fraser, like Adolph Weinman, Paul Manship, Robert Aitken and a few other sculptors, negotiated with and through government agencies, memorial commissions and corporate boards with remarkable success. Others, notably Bela Pratt and An-

---

[342] *US Mint*, NARA-CP, op. cit., entry 229, box 288. Letter dated February 15, 1910 to Andrew from Eames MacVeagh. His lecture was titled "The Symbolism of our National Currency" and illustrated both coins and paper currency.

thony de Francisci, became burdened by demands, often concluding a commission in frustration or disillusionment.

The Buffalo nickel is "classic" Fraser in subject, style, method of creation and popular appeal.[343] By preparing several strong designs and paying for initial work from his own pocket, Fraser was able to focus treasury interest on his work and his designs alone. There is no record of anyone outside the mint bureaucracy being asked to submit a drawing or model for the nickel. Concurrently, he arranged for letters of praise from individual members of the Commission of Fine Arts, thus ensuring expert support for treasury officials' decisions, and approval from the Commission as a whole. Fraser's skill even subdued the "mint's blacksmith," engraver Charles Barber, who supported Fraser in the fight over Clarence Hobbs' counterfeit detection device.[344]

By the time mint director Roberts offered Fraser a commission to design the nickel, the artist had produced rough sketches, life studies and finished drawings, plaster models, and electrotypes of several designs for the cent and nickel in multiple sizes. Before there was an official commission, treasury secretary MacVeagh and director Roberts had already approved the Indian-Bison design. Fraser was also the first coin designer to benefit from support of the Commission of Fine Arts, an organization that would have considerable influence on circulating and commemorative coins in the future. Except for the self-serving interference of Clarence W. Hobbs,[345] President of Hobbs Manufacturing Company and principal in American Stamp and Ticket Vending Machine Company (known as Astumco),[346] the first Buffalo nickels might have been released in the fall of 1912.[347]

When compared to all coin designs in the 1907-1921 period for the U. S. Mint, Fraser's nickel is closer to the artist's original concept that any other. This can be attributed in part to the sculptor's careful preparation of preliminary models, yet much of this success was due to Fraser's assertiveness in insisting on the fundamental validity of his designs. Saint-Gaudens' concepts suffered due to his illness and President Roosevelt's "suggestions." His death before acceptance of final models left the work in the competent but un-

---

[343] The author will, to the consternation of purists, refer to the animal in Fraser's five-cent coin design as "buffalo" or "bison" as may seem appropriate to the context and ordinary usage. The artist and everyone else connected with the project seems to have known that the animal was an American bison.

[344] This term first appears in a letter written in late October 1908 by Bela Pratt after he had seen samples of the circulation strikes of his Indian head design half eagle. "…[The Mint] let their die cutter spoil it…the $5 is a sight! I could not sleep for a night or two after I saw it. The first impression, which Dr. Bigelow showed me at the Symphony two weeks ago, looked quite well. [This was a unique pattern piece struck from the original design.]…. With a few deft touches the butcher or blacksmith, who is at the head of things there, changed it from a thing that I was proud of to one [of which] I am ashamed!" The reference is to engraver Charles Barber. See Burdette, *Renaissance of American Coinage 1905-1908* for additional information.

[345] This was Clarence W. Hobbs, Sr. His son, Clarence, Jr., became an actuary and was active in actuarial business organizations.

[346] Did Hobbs substitute a "U" for a "V" on the corporate initials in reverse imitation of artists using the Roman "V" for the modern "U" in inscriptions? By 1916 "ASTUMCO," or its progeny, had turned into "American Sales Machine Company" of the same address.

[347] As will become evident, Mr. Hobbs apparently had a talent for exaggeration and misrepresentation in 1912 that carried through to the 1916 subsidiary silver redesign. In 1901 Clarence W. Hobbs was involved in a patent infringement case that ended in the U.S. Supreme Court. Clarence W. Hobbs et al., Petitioners, v. Fred H. Beach, 180 U.S. 383 (1901) was argued January 16-17, 1901 and decided against Hobbs on March 5, 1901. This was a bill in equity by Fred H. Beach against Clarence W. Hobbs and Richard Sugden, deceased (whose estate was represented by his executors), doing business under the name of the Hobbs Manufacturing Company, for an injunction and recovery of damages for the infringement of patent No. 11,167 dated May 26, 1891, for a *Machine for Attaching Stays to the Corners of Boxes*. The Court found that Hobbs had copied Beach's machine for reinforcing paper and cardboard box corners.

inspired hands of his assistant and at the mercy of the mint's engravers.[348] Bela Pratt's half eagle began as a private commission for a technical model, not an artistic one, for the paltry sum of $300. The artist's gentle nature left him without influence at the mint or direct support from President Roosevelt. The artist complained of being taken advantage of, and unilateral degradation of his work by the Mint Bureau's engravers. Victor Brenner, Fraser's closest contemporary and designer of the Lincoln cent, compromised his artistic credibility when he initially submitted designs copied from current French coins. It fell to James Fraser to become the first sculptor to work with the mint free of compromises artistic and personal.

Lastly, success of the Buffalo nickel could also be attributed to use of a private firm – Medallic Art Company – to produce all except the last reductions and hubs from the artist's models. By avoiding use of the mint's Janvier reducing lathe and the inadequately trained mint staff, Fraser retained maximum supervisory control over this critical production step.[349] Although Barber cut the last pair of hubs used to make production dies, Fraser and Medallic Art had set the standard for quality and Barber had no latitude to tinker with the design.

MacVeagh and Company

The treasury department and its Bureau of the Mint were no less formidable in Fraser's time, than when Saint-Gaudens and President Roosevelt pried open a reluctant bureaucracy. It was also a much changed place. Director Leach had dealt with significant morale problems in connection with the Saint-Gaudens design project, and all concerned had learned from the experience. In a lengthy missive to superintendent Landis in January, 1908, the director commented in part:[350]

> ...What I want is results, and questions of detail like these must be settled in your institution.
> Again, I fully appreciate the very many difficulties attending such a radical change in the coinage operations as we have had to meet, and the only way to reach satisfactory results is for all hands to enter into the work with a harmonious spirit – each to do his best to the best of his ability.
> You have accomplished a great deal, and I think the worst is passed, but there are many more difficulties ahead of us to be overcome, and I trust the officers of the Philadelphia mint will meet the issues in the proper spirit, dropping any petty differences as trifling and as sources of interference to obtaining results....

The letter was prompted by his earlier discovery that experimental small diameter double eagles had left the Philadelphia Mint, a 1908 suggestion by Barber to increase the size of edge lettering on the double eagle, excessive fin on the high relief $20 coin, inconsistency in the diameter of the 1907-dated circulation coins, and several other problems related to the new designs. The primary difficulty was the tendency of superintendent Landis

---

[348] The much praised extremely high relief double eagle was actually Hering's test model intended to experiment with the mint's capabilities. Only the best of the 12,667 high relief coins struck in August-September and November 1907-January 1908 embody the detail approved by Saint-Gaudens.

[349] In 1922 Fraser and Anthony de Francisci supervised the mint's production of new hubs from de Francisci's low relief models for the Peace dollar. Unfortunately none of those present knew how to properly control the Janvier machine, and sending the models to a private contractor who understood the complicated equipment was not considered.

[350] *US Mint*, NARA-P, record group 104, box 71, folder "Gold Coin Designs." Letter dated January 29, 1908 to Landis from Roberts.

and engraver Barber to ask the director for solutions to every problem that occurred. This created long-winded discussions over minor issues and caused delay in producing the new coins. It was Leach whom President Roosevelt leaned on for results and the director put the Philadelphia Mint staff on notice of his expectations.

Superintendent Landis, in particular, had been subject to persistent complaints including one from MacVeagh: "What is Landis doing at the Philadelphia Mint? Is he attending closely to business and is he efficient?"[351] To which director Roberts replied:[352]

> Mr. Landis has been far from satisfactory as a Superintendent. He has no initiative and it has been necessary to go around him to subordinates in order to get any real touch with operations....No other person in the Service has tried my patience so sorely. Six or seven years ago I made a recommendation to Secretary Shaw (1906) that a change be made....Mr. Landis is an honest man, well intentioned, tractable and ready to obey explicit instructions....he conforms to the Civil Service regulations.

After being pushed into action, Barber and Landis assumed a greater role in deciding on alterations to new designs. This led to more efficient production, but created increased friction with non-mint artists designing the coins. Bela Pratt was ignored after he submitted his models in June, 1908. Victor Brenner found his design unilaterally changed by order of director Leach although he had been authorized to make the steel hub. The increased initiative shown by mint engravers could also be used to advantage: when instruction came from the director, the staff were more likely to perform the work without questioning the artist.

The treasury department had also changed. At the beginning of the Taft administration in March 1909, the urbane, politically experienced George Cortelyou had been replaced with Franklin MacVeagh, a wholesale grocer from Chicago who had limited banking experience. Whereas Cortelyou's career had encompassed the role of private secretary to Presidents McKinley and Roosevelt, Teddy's campaign manager in 1904 and Republican Party Chairman, the new secretary's contacts were almost exclusively wholesale trades and limited service on various museum boards. His appointment as secretary shifted influence toward many of the large financial houses that President Roosevelt had viewed with suspicion. MacVeagh was deeply committed to reforming the management of the treasury department, but did not comprehend the sophistication of the nation's finances. The most important creative light in the new treasury and mint was Abram Piatt Andrew, a young economics professor from Harvard University who replaced Frank Leach as mint director on November 1, 1909.[353] Andrew had impeccable credentials to support the Taft administration's fiscal policies. He was one of the most learned promoters of a central bank and was a framer of the Aldrich-Vreeland Act. He was also a close friend and confidant of artist Cecilia Beaux, frequently attending parties and art events in Boston and New York. It is possibly through Beaux that Andrew was introduced to sculptor Jim Fraser.

---

[351] *MacVeagh papers*, LoC. op. cit., box 7, press copy book, p.110. Letter dated February 18, 1913 to Roberts from MacVeagh.
[352] *MacVeagh papers*, LoC. op. cit., box 16. Letter dated February 19, 1913 to MacVeagh from Roberts.
[353] The appointment was made on August 6.

Figure 33. Treasury Secretary Franklin MacVeagh (right) with son Eames in 1912. Eames was instrumental in encouraging his father to change the nickel design and secure new designs for paper currency. Secretary MacVeagh approved James Fraser's nickel design in 1913 – only three weeks before leaving office. (Courtesy Library of Congress.)

Andrew's term as director was short, only seven months, because the mint was a "holding pen" for him before he moved into an assistant secretary's position in June 1910. He was also one of the few creative, innovative minds in the Taft administration, which was dominated by solid but uninspiring business managers. Andrew retained oversight of the mint in his new job and appears to have taken the responsibility to heart. There are nearly as many extant letters to him on numismatic/mint matters as assistant secretary than when he was director. It was as assistant secretary that Andrew took the suggestions of Eames MacVeagh and approached sculptor James Earle Fraser about coin designs in general and specifically the nickel. His position gave him ample opportunity to influence the nickel in both design and artist. According to a memorandum written by George Roberts,[354]

> The first step in the negotiations for the new nickel piece was taken by Assistant Secretary Andrew in 1911. As a result of his interest in the subject Mr. J. E. Fraser of New York, upon his own initiative, prepared several small wax models showing the Indian head and buffalo as they now appear on the coin, although in somewhat higher relief.

With Eames MacVeagh pressing his father to redesign the coin, and assistant secretary Andrew orchestrating Fraser's introductions to secretary MacVeagh and the new mint director, George E. Roberts, the design and commission were fixed with little artistic inter-

---

[354] *US Mint*, NARA-CP, op. cit., file 305310. Memorandum dated March 18, 1913 to Secretary of the Treasury William G. McAdoo from Roberts.

ference. President Taft, a former protégé of President Roosevelt but now at odds with "Teddy" on almost everything, showed little interest in the project.[355] With Taft uninvolved nearly all responsibility for the new design fell to director Roberts and Fraser, with Andrew and Eames MacVeagh giving an occasional push when bureaucratic wheels got stuck.

Roberts was as cautious as any civil service bureaucrat, although in his second term as director. He approached the new design with circumspect intent. He had dealt with "outside" artists before – specifically Augustus Saint-Gaudens – and was wary of balancing artistic ideals against practical coinage. In 1906 he had stated his objections to Saint-Gaudens' plans, and been ordered by President Roosevelt to proceed in spite of his bureau's objections. His previous experience had included little contact with the artist; only an assistant, Henry Hering, visited the mint or Washington. Saint-Gaudens, in rapidly declining health, corresponded with the mint and President Roosevelt, but he and director Roberts never met. Absent his formidable presence, Saint-Gaudens' designs received less than Robert's full attention until the director resigned in July 1907 to take a banking job in Chicago.

However, from 1909 to 1912 there was no micromanaging Chief Executive pounding fists and brandishing rhetoric: Roberts had to make his own decisions. This time around, Roberts faced the talented, vigorous and somewhat manipulative James Earle Fraser, and Fraser had a plan to get his designs on a coin. But first, Roberts had to deal with a nickel design left over from Frank Leach's directorship.

This was the treasury department and mint into which Fraser immersed himself in early 1911.

Fraser Meets the Mint

As discussed in Chapter 5, design work for a cent and nickel by Charles Barber were authorized by director Leach in 1908. Barber completed several versions of a Washington design dated 1909 and 1910. The first serious mention of redesigning the nickel using something other than Barber's Washington head composition is in a letter from assistant secretary of the treasury A. Piatt Andrew to Eames MacVeagh on May 2, 1911.[356]

> My dear Eames:
> You are quite right – the nickel is the only coin which can be changed during this administration except by vote of Congress. The present nickel was designed in 1883 and therefore has been subject to change since 1908. The present designs for our silver coins were adopted in 1892, the gold coins in 1907 and 1908, and the bronze coins in 1909. When I was in the Mint I was much interested in the plan of arranging for competition among medalists for an ideal set of coins and had it in mind that if anything satisfactory resulted from it we could appeal to Congress to have them adopted, and I succeeded in getting Mr. Archer Huntington of the

---

[355] Theodore Roosevelt was affectionately known as "Teddy" or "Teddykins" by his first wife, Alice. When Washington Post newspaper cartoonist Clifford Berryman showed President "Teddy" refusing to shoot a chained bear, the public latched onto both bear and President as "Teddy." The "Teddy bear" became one of the first popular toys inspired by a politician. This popularity encouraged the Taft presidential campaign of 1908 to offer its own pet: "Billy Possum." Merchants produced sets of children's china and utensils, buttons, and stuffed opossums, but to little gain. Political and satirical cartoons soon turned Billy Possum into something less than a pleasant icon and poor Billy vanished. (The author has a silver plated spoon and fork with little Billy's name and image stamped on them. They were a gift to the author's father at age 2 from a family friend and Taft Republican.)
[356] *US Mint*, NARA-CP, op. cit., file 305927. Letter dated May 2, 1911 to Eames MacVeagh from Andrew.

> American Numismatic Society interested in the plan, but since I left the Mint the matter has been dropped and so far as I know nothing has been done about it. I am glad you have recalled the matter of the nickel to my attention and I will take it up again with the Director of the Mint.

The letter suggests Eames had contacted Andrew and mentioned redesigning the nickel sometime before that date, and may have suggested a specific artist. According to mint director Roberts, "The first step in the negotiations for the new nickel piece was taken by assistant secretary Andrew in 1911. As a result of his interest in the subject, Mr. J. E. Fraser of New York, on his own initiative, prepared several small wax models showing the Indian head and the buffalo about as they now appear upon the coin..."[357] It also indicates that Andrew had attempted to develop support for an "ideal set of coins," probably ones that had a logical relationship between dimensions, metal content and face value. These would certainly have been consistent with MacVeagh's ideas expressed in August 1909.

Andrew wrote to Roberts the same day asking for information on having a non-mint artist prepare designs:[358]

> Will you please send me the following information:
> (1) The legal restrictions as to size, weight, material, design and inscriptions which would have to be observed by a medalist in preparing a pattern for a new five-cent piece.
> (2) Is there any fund which could be made available to employ a designer or medalist outside of the present service to design such a piece?

The idea of changing the nickel design may not have belonged exclusively to Eames MacVeagh, but he seems to be the person who got the idea "off the ground" and stirred his father to action. In a short letter written on May 4, 1911 to his father he said:[359]

> A little matter that seems to have been overlooked by all of you is the opportunity to beautify the design of the nickel or five cent piece during your administration, and it seems to me it would be a permanent souvenir of the most attractive sort. As perhaps you are aware, it is the only coin the design of which you can change during your administration, as I believe there is a law to the effect that the designs must not be changed oftener than every twenty years. I should think also it might be the coin of which the greatest numbers are in circulation.
> The attached letter from Mr. Andrew explains the matter further and shows his interest in it, and I feel quite sure that the present director of the Mint would also be interested if he were stirred up about it. He is himself the possessor of a very rare and beautiful Greek coin.
> Affectionately yours,

Although the younger MacVeagh had a few details incorrect, the general idea of this being his father's only chance to associate his name with a new coin design is clearly stated. His comment about director Roberts owning a rare Greek coin is interesting in that Roberts had at least one of the extremely high relief Saint-Gaudens double eagles in his possession. By 1911 the first experimental Saint-Gaudens double eagles, produced in February 1907, were trading hands among collectors for $800 to $1,000 each,[360] however the other special gold pieces were available at little premium.

---

[357] *US Mint*, NARA-CP, op. cit., file 305310. Memorandum dated March 18, 1913 to William G. McAdoo from Roberts.
[358] *US Mint*, NARA-CP, op. cit., entry 229, box 296. Letter dated May 2, 1911 to Roberts from Andrew.
[359] *US Mint*, NARA-CP, op. cit., file 305927. Letter dated May 4, 1911 to Franklin MacVeagh from Eames MacVeagh.
[360] See Burdette; *Renaissance of American Coinage 1905-1908* for more information.

Secretary MacVeagh forwarded the two letters to director Roberts the following week along with a note:[361]

> Dear Mr. Roberts:
> Here is some correspondence about the nickel. It brings up the general subject of the designs of coins. This will be an interesting matter to discuss with you at your convenience. Please consult with Mr. Andrew first. He has given a good deal of thought to the matter and is greatly interested in it.

In the formal language of the time, MacVeagh was instructing Roberts to immediately discuss the matter with Andrew, then visit the secretary's office as soon as he could schedule a meeting. The redesign was important to the secretary and his son, and Roberts was expected to begin working on it.

Roberts and Fraser met in Washington in early June with the result that Roberts was impressed with the artist's ideas and probably with the artist himself:[362]

> The Belgian coin bearing the portrait of King Leopold which you showed me when here made a great impression upon me. Dr. Andrew and I have been wondering whether some such effect might not be obtained with the Lincoln head instead of the present miniature reproduction of a design originally made for a medal. We would have to get an act of Congress to allow us to change the present design, it having been adopted only a few years ago, but we would be willing to try if we had such a substitute at hand. What do you think of it?
> I want to get one of those Leopold coins; will you please let me know the denomination in order that I may order one.

The coin Fraser showed to Roberts was probably similar to the 5 franc piece showing a strong, large scale portrait of the Belgian King. The style on this piece was completely different than that used by Victor Brenner on the current Lincoln cent and it is clear

Figure 34. Belgian coin featuring a large portrait of King Leopold II. This was the style preferred by Roberts and Andrew for the Lincoln cent and lead to adoption of Fraser's large portraits on the new nickel.

that Roberts was very favorably disposed toward Fraser's stylistic suggestion. The artist replied on June 13 offering to make several sketches and send them to the mint director for discussion. The designs could have been used for a cent or nickel, although it would seem

---
[361] *US Mint*, NARA-CP, op. cit., file 305927. Letter dated May 13, 1911 to George E. Roberts from Franklin MacVeagh.
[362] *US Mint*, NARA-CP, op. cit., entry 235, vol. 387. Letter dated June 9, 1911 to Fraser from Roberts.

unreasonable to attempt to change the cent after only three years. However, Roberts encouraged Fraser to work on both the Indian design and a portrait of Lincoln as a possible substitute. The sculptor reported his progress:[363]

> The Belgian coin which you admired so much is, I believe, in circulation at the present time; I will get one for you and send it on.
> I think your idea of the Lincoln head is a splendid one and I shall be very glad to make you some sketches as soon as possible and let you see them. I think they should be reduced to the actual size of the coin; otherwise we will not be really able to judge them, even in the sketch period. I will have that done here, where I can watch the process.
> I have numerous sketches underway, some of which I hope may be of value.
> Yours truly,

Sketches, as referred to in Fraser's letters, usually were not drawings but small sketch models in plaster or wax. It was these which Fraser had reduced by Medallic Art company, and ¾-inch diameter bronze casts created. The casts were rough because they were made quickly and because the sketch models were not finished compositions. This is the point in design creation where the sculptor separated himself from his predecessors (and successors). Instead of expecting non-artists, such as the director and secretary, to look at drawings or models and imagine coins, Fraser took the extra time and expense to make coin-like medals. These could be handled and examined as if they were real coins, and helped "sell" Fraser's designs to officials.[364]

Figure 35. Electrotypes of design experiments by Fraser for a new Lincoln portrait. Both pieces are dated 1911 and may have been made from the same model. Compare to the 1952 version, in Chapter 3, above. (Left, Lepczyk catalog, right photo courtesy American Numismatic Rareties)

While working directly with Roberts, Fraser was also writing to assistant secretary Andrew. His letter of July 20 is typical of the artist lining up support for his work:[365]

> Dear Mr. Andrew:
> You will find enclosed a photograph of Saint-Gaudens' letter, concerning which I spoke to you. It may be of no value but I will leave it to your discretion to use as you like.
> I am having some electro-plates made of the small sketches and I will send them to you when they are completed.

---

[363] *US Mint*, NARA-CP, op. cit., file 305310. Letter dated June 13, 1911 to Roberts from Fraser.
[364] This is analogous to sculptors and architects making scale models of proposed statues and buildings.
[365] *US Mint*, NARA-CP, op. cit., file 305310. Letter dated July 20, 1911 to Andrew from Fraser.

> In reference to competition, I think that a great trouble is that you may have numbers of sketches in the competition one of which you choose and, if I'm not mistaken, you will be forced to stick very closely to that design, even though it might not be quite up to what you would want. Whereas, working with a competent man, there would be no doubt that a great many designs would be made; in fact, you would go on working till something of real merit was produced. You may say, if you like, that I would be perfectly willing to satisfy the Art Commission Mr. MacVeagh spoke of.
>
> I will send you a few photographs of my work provided you wish to use them for reference.

Fraser was willing to do whatever Andrew and MacVeagh wanted to get the commission. If that meant contacting the newly formed Commission of Fine Arts and getting their approval, that was fine.[366] Andrew was probably not aware that Fraser knew all the artist members of the Commission and had shown drawings to Daniel Chester French and possibly others. The Buffalo nickel would become the first coin design officially reviewed by the members, although the Commission as a whole never acted on the design. Andrew passed the letter on to Roberts along with the copy of Saint-Gaudens' note praising Fraser's artistry.

The coin-sized electrotypes were evidently a significant factor in encouraging the mint and treasury department to actively consider commissioning Fraser to design a coin. These small, bronze or nickel plated facsimiles were the equivalent of pattern coins of the proposed designs. In an unusual letter to Fraser, director Roberts offered to pay for the sample designs and appeared to view them as prototypes of the coinage:[367]

> After considering further the subject of designs for the five-cent nickel piece it has been decided to have you present your ideas in the form of models of the same size as the legal coin, provided you will accept the sum of one hundred fifty dollars ($150) as full compensation for your labor and any expenses incident to preparing and submitting them, with the understanding that if these designs are accepted and used for the regular coinage a new agreement is to be made as to the amount of your compensation, and the one hundred and fifty dollars payment now contemplated will apply thereupon. If, however, the designs are not accepted for use the payment of one hundred and fifty dollars will be final and in full for all services. Payment will be made from the Contingent fund of the Philadelphia Mint, fiscal year 1912.

Secretary MacVeagh's reaction to the electrotypes must have been extraordinary for the tight-fisted treasury department to offer payment, without any commission or agreement to design a coin. These little experimental design pieces were made with the full knowledge, authorization, encouragement and involvement of the mint director and secretary of the treasury just as would have occurred with an experimental design produced at the Philadelphia Mint. The differences being that Fraser's electrotypes were cast not struck, and the work was done outside the mint. The secretary's offer to pay for the pieces is further evidence of their being considered design prototypes. The pieces also conform to

---

[366] The Commission of Fine Arts was established by Congress on May 17, 1910. It replaced the Council of Fine Arts that had been established by President Roosevelt on January 18, 1909 by Executive Order. The first Chairman of the Commission was Daniel H. Burnham, an architect and one of four members of the Senate Park Commission which had begun to fulfill and expand L'Enfant's 1791 plan for Washington, DC. Augustus Saint-Gaudens was one of the other members. See Kohler: *The Commission of Fine Arts – A Brief History* listed in the bibliography.

[367] *US Mint*, NARA-CP, op. cit., entry 235, vol. 387. Letter dated July 29, 1911 to Fraser from Roberts.

Barber's May 14, 1910 definition of a pattern: "A <u>pattern</u> piece or die is one made for the purpose of displaying a certain design for a coin, whether for a contemplated change in design or some existing coin or merely to exhibit the design."[368]

On August 1 Fraser advised director Roberts that payment was not necessary, a gesture of cooperation which likely ensured there would be neither competition nor consideration of anyone else's designs:[369]

> I am very sorry that I happened to be away from New York the day you called; I would like to have shown you some of the various things I am doing.
>
> When you say "the new models" do you mean the designs for the nickel? I have the sketches which I took to Washington in a better condition that they were then; they are now electro-plates. I will send you some copies.
>
> It's very kind of you to suggest paying my expenses in regard to the work I have done; but I don't feel that you ought to trouble too much in that direction. I am certain you wanted me to do this work and it will be no fault of yourself or Dr. Andrew if I do not receive it.
>
> I myself feel most confident over the result which I attained through doing the sketches; I know of no coins which were studied in just this manner, and I feel sure that is the only way of arriving at satisfactory results.

Most of Fraser's early letters concerning the Buffalo nickel project included a medallic sample, photo or other item designed to engage the reader and keep them involved in the project. As letters hurried back and forth, Treasury officials became more deeply entangled in the sculptor's ideas until Fraser's artistic concept became normal and any alternatives were quickly dismissed. To secretary MacVeagh, he wrote:[370]

> Although I realize that no definite commission has been given me in regard to the designs for the new coins, I have become so much interested in the sketches that I have pushed them a little farther and now they are in the shape of electrotypes which I should like to submit for your consideration. Of course, this means that they are still merely sketches and not finished products, but I have had them reduced and made into their present form for the purpose of showing exactly what I would wish done, provided I finish them.
>
> At present, they are the size of the penny but they could easily be enlarged to any size desired. The idea of the Indian and the buffalo on the same coin is, without doubt, purely American and seems to be singularly appropriate to have on one of our national coins. You will see that the Indian is entirely different than any that has ever been used on a coin. Most of the heads have been Caucasians with an Indian head-dress; in this case I have avoided using the war-bonnet and have made a purely Indian type. Therefore, I should like to ask whether or not you would consider placing these designs on the new nickel.
>
> I have also carried the Lincoln head farther, not only because I was personally interested in it, but because Mr. Roberts has rather encouraged the idea of doing so.
>
> Possibly you will be interested in knowing that the Italian Government has purchased a collection of my medals for its National Museum in Rome. The Belgian Government obtained a somewhat similar collection of my work last year.

---

[368] It is suggested that the Lincoln, Buffalo and Indian electrotypes be placed adjacent to the previously accepted pattern buffalo nickels of 1913 in listings of pattern and experimental pieces.
[369] *US Mint*, NARA-CP, op. cit., file 305310. Letter dated August 1, 1911 to Roberts from Fraser.
[370] *US Mint*, NARA-CP, op. cit., file 305310. Letter dated September 19, 1911 to MacVeagh from Fraser.

The cent-size electrotypes mimic the smallest diameter coin on which any of the designs might have been used. With the project soon to be limited to the five-cent piece, all future electrotypes were approximately the size of a nickel.

Figure 36. Electrotype patterns for the Buffalo nickel. Left, obverse sample dated 1911, note position of date, shape of chin and other differences from later versions. This is the only known version with an elongated, protruding jaw. Right, reverse probably 1911, note different treatment of background, very small lettering and distance between rim, design and motto. (Courtesy Fred Weinberg.)

Little work was done on the new nickel design during the balance of 1911, however by January 1912 the topic again had secretary MacVeagh's attention:[371]

> I am now writing to Mr. J. W. [sic] Fraser in acknowledgement of the attached letter[372] and apologizing for the fact that we have not heretofore been able to give the matter our careful attention. I am also telling him that he may expect, within a day of two, to hear directly from you.
>
> The sketches submitted by Mr. Fraser are in every way so satisfactory and he is a man who stands so high in his profession, that I am glad we all have agreed to let him continue with the matter without looking further or incurring additional delay. Will you, therefore, please write to him and tell him that the nickel five-cent piece is the coin for which we have been considering his designs and the only one that is available at this time. Tell him that of the three sketches which he submitted we would like to use the sketch of the head of the Indian and the sketch of the buffalo, subject to adaptation; the head of the Indian to appear on the obverse and the figure of the buffalo on the reverse. Only such inscriptions as the law requires should, of course, go on the coin, in order not to mar its beauty and to avoid crowding.
>
> Please state to Mr. Fraser exactly what the requirement and restrictions of the law are in this respect, and ask him to submit a completed model and to state his price.

Thus, by January 1912 secretary of the treasury MacVeagh had selected both designer and designs for the new nickel.[373] There would be no competition as assistant secre-

---

[371] *US Mint*, NARA-CP, op. cit., file 305310. Letter dated January 13, 1912 to Roberts from MacVeagh.
[372] Based on context, this is likely Fraser's letter of September 19, 1911.
[373] It is likely Eames MacVeagh had considerable influence with his father's decisions. Eames had prepared a lantern slide presentation on United States currency and which he presented several times in the Chicago area. He also occasionally wrote to Director Andrew about pattern coins, medals struck by the Philadelphia Mint and other issues relating to coinage and the Mint Bureau. The Franklin MacVeagh papers in the Library of Congress include only a few relevant letters from Eames, and the full extent of his involvement awaits further research.

tary Andrew preferred, and the inscriptions were limited only to those specifically required by law. Director Roberts took a few days to permit the secretary's short letter to reach Fraser then followed-up with a long set of instructions. He also took the opportunity to explain potential use of the new Lincoln portrait and offer his view on problems with the Saint-Gaudens designs of 1907:[374]

> I presume you have received within a few days a letter from the Secretary of the Treasury indicating that your designs have received such favorable consideration that the way is now open to deal more definitively upon the subject.
>
> We cannot, as you understand, change the design on the one cent piece unless we can get Congress sufficiently interested to grant special authority as the law forbids changes by executive action oftener than once in 25 years. We all like your Lincoln head very much better than the Lincoln Bust which now appears upon this coin and it is possible that we may be able to bring the matter to the attention of the Coinage committees of Congress. At present, however, we propose to deal only with the nickel piece. We would like to have you perfect the Indian Head and Buffalo for the obverse and reverse of this coin and to proceed with the matter as rapidly as practicable. We wish you to submit the designs complete in every respect, including the inscriptions required by law. I invite your attention to the statute as given below:
>
> *SEC.3571. Upon the coins there shall be the following devices and legends: Upon one side there shall be an impression emblematic of liberty, with the inscription of the word "Liberty" and the year of the coinage, and upon the reverse shall be the figure or representation of the eagle, with the inscriptions "United States of America" and "E Pluribus Unum," and also the designation of the value of the coin; but on the gold dollar and three-dollar piece, the dime, five, three, and one cent piece, the figure of the eagle shall be omitted; and on the reverse of the silver trade-dollar the weight and the fineness of the coin shall be inscribed.*
>
> The Indian head has always been accepted as "an impression emblematic of liberty." You will note that the word "Liberty" and the year of coinage are to go upon this side, which is the obverse, and that upon the other side there must be the inscriptions "United States of America" and "E Pluribus Unum," and also the designation of value. The motto "In God We Trust" is not required upon this coin and I presume we are agreed that nothing should be upon it that is not required.
>
> I am anxious that in the preparation of the design you shall take into account the technical requirements which must be observed in order that the work of striking the coins in great quantities may be facilitated. These have to do particularly with the degree of relief of the coin but there are certain other details concerning which I think it would be advisable for you to confer with the engraver of the Mint. I should like to avoid a repetition of the misunderstanding and friction which developed between Mr. St. Gaudens and the people of the Mint, most of which I am sure was due to Mr. St. Gaudens' attitude. He started out with the determination to make the coins in an impossible relief and attributed all opposition from the Mint to jealousy and a determination to make his plans a failure. There will be no trouble with the Mint of we go about the matter in the right way.
>
> It will be necessary, of course, for us to reach an early understanding as to the terms upon which this commission is to be executed but perhaps a personal interview will be the best means of reaching this end. You can do as you like about coming to Washington at once for this purpose or leaving it to be adjusted at a later meeting when a further conference is desirable.

---

[374] *US Mint,* NARA-CP, op. cit., entry 235, vol. 395. Letter dated January 18, 1912 to Fraser from Roberts. Complaints about Saint-Gaudens appear in Mint Bureau documents with unexpected frequency during the first decades of the twentieth century. In commissioning America's best sculptor to design the gold coins of 1907, it is possible President Roosevelt also selected the artist with the least potential for working successfully with the Mint Bureau.

Roberts gave first priority for the Indian-Buffalo nickel design. Changes in the Lincoln cent, however much they might be desired, would have to wait until completion of the nickel. Charles Barber's portrait of Washington, completed two years before, was ignored.

Eames MacVeagh was anxious to learn the status of the nickel project and wrote a short, somewhat tongue-in-cheek note to Roberts on January 20. In it he alluded to considerable delay in communicating with the sculptor for the previous six months:[375]

> Did you see Mr. Fraser, the medalist, when you were in New York, and if so, did he throw you out bodily into McDougal's Alley, as a result of the neglectful treatment he had received, or did he invite you in to talk that matter over?
> If you can find the time, would you drop me a line and let me know how the matter now stands, or would you ask Miss Kelly to do so?
> Was any conclusion reached between you and Mr. Fraser as to what he would do with the inscriptions?

The relaxed tone of Eames' letter suggests things were going very well on both a business and personal level between treasury officials and the sculptor. On January 27 Fraser sent a short note to the mint director:[376]

> Your letter of January 18 asking me to complete the designs for the five-cent piece contains my idea of what should be done in relation to the coins. I believe in placing as little lettering as possible on the coin, since the design will be just so much better for the fewer things it contains. I am very anxious to go on with the designs and make them as perfect as possible, then have them reduced to the nickel size, after which I believe it would be wise to confer with the Mint in Philadelphia. Possibly it would be better for me, before going to Washington, to complete the coins and have the reductions to bring with me.
> I will let you know how the work goes on.

With the Mint Bureau deeply involved in responding to Representative Bulkley's coinage bill, emphasis shifted away from the Buffalo nickel. During this critical period of early-1912, Eames MacVeagh kept up a steady stream of inquiries to his father, Fraser and director Roberts, all of which must have helped push the project forward. By June 26, Fraser advised Roberts he had completed the models and more coin-size electrotypes. These were now the size of the standard five-cent coin:[377]

> The models for the five cent piece have been finished and reduced in several heights of relief, and therefore I am ready to come and explain, and have explained to me what is necessary and to talk over some changes that I now think, since seeing the reductions, would prove advantageous.
> Will Secretary MacVeagh be in Washington? He asked me to let him know when I came on.

Fraser and Roberts agreed to meet on July 10 when the secretary would be in Washington.[378] The models and coin-size electrotypes were shown to the director and secretary, and met with enthusiastic approval. Deftly using the nickel-sized electrotypes to

---

[375] *US Mint*, NARA-CP, op. cit., file 305310. Letter dated January 20, 1912 to Roberts from Eames MacVeagh. Fraser's studio was located at 3 MacDougal Alley, New York City.
[376] *US Mint*, NARA-CP, op. cit., entry A1 328I, box 1, folder "Coins. Buffalo Nickel 1911-1938, Volume #1." Letter dated January 27, 1912 to Roberts from Fraser.
[377] *US Mint*, NARA-CP, op. cit., file 305310. Letter dated June 26, 1912 to Roberts from Fraser.
[378] *US Mint*, NARA-CP, op. cit., entry 235, vol. 395, p.284. Letter dated July 6, 1912 to Fraser from Roberts.

build interest in officials, Fraser had eliminated all thought of a competition and ensured that his design would be the only one considered by the treasury department.

Andrew Leaves the Treasury Department

Assistant Secretary of the Treasury A. Piatt Andrew resigned on July 2, 1912, writing to President Taft that the treasury department had been hampered by the idiosyncrasies and incapacity for decision of secretary MacVeagh. In 1910 he had replaced assistant secretary Charles D. Norton (who had been appointed personal secretary to President Taft) and became the senior advisor to secretary MacVeagh on matters relating to the proposed central bank. He spent much of this time traveling to conferences and meetings to explain reserve bank concepts to financial leaders throughout the country. He also wrote several articles for banking publications and the general public.

After holding office for about eighteen months, Andrew became uncomfortable with the style of treasury secretary MacVeagh. He stated that he had been "...hampered and discouraged at every turn by secretary MacVeagh's idiosyncrasies, his astounding capacity for procrastination, his incapacity for decision, and the peculiar moods of suspicion and aversion to which he is constantly subject."[379] He also felt the secretary was not paying enough attention to the Aldrich Commission, and was more interested in delegating work to others rather than taking a leadership position. During the time when Andrew was actively championing transfer of the treasurer's gold to the mint collection, he was also discussing problems in MacVeagh's administration with other treasury officials including Treasurer Lee McClung; Commissioner of Internal Revenue, Royal E. Cabell; Director of the Bureau of Engraving and Printing, J. E. Ralph; Comptroller of the Currency, Lawrence O. Murray and others. The secretary and assistant secretary became increasingly estranged, and after Andrew disobeyed a direct order not to attend the Republican Party convention in Chicago, MacVeagh requested Andrew's resignation.[380] The public excuse was that Andrew was "inefficient" in tending to his duties.

Andrew spoke with President Taft on July 2 for about an hour. That afternoon, Taft wrote to Andrew, "It is perfectly clear to me that your relation with the Secretary of the Treasury can not continue and that either you must resign or I must have a new Secretary of the Treasury."[381]

According to MacVeagh, the resignation was requested three times. Only on the fourth attempt, after several senators had lobbied President Taft to keep Andrew, did the assistant secretary provide the required letter.[382] It was not, however a simple document. Andrew sent it directly to the President, attacking MacVeagh for poor management of the treasury department and naming several senior officials, including McClung, as agreeing with him. The "attempted mutiny" was front-page news in major eastern papers. Some members of Congress immediately became upset and there was talk of a Congressional investigation, but President Taft insisted on a truce until after the November election, and the matter quickly faded.[383]

---

[379] *The Washington Post,* "Chaos In Treasury Department" July 4, 1912, p.1.
[380] The 1912 convention was a battle between Taft's conservative supporters and Theodore Roosevelt's progressive Republicans. Andrew was clearly in the progressive camp and MacVeagh didn't want him near the delegates.
[381] Hayden, et al., *Beauport Chronicle,* p.70. Excerpt from Taft's letter to Andrew date July 2, 1912.
[382] *The Washington Post,* "Andrew Ousted, Says MacVeagh" July 5, 1912, p.1.
[383] *New York Times,* "Treasury Row Finds Victim in McClung" November 15, 1912, p.6.

Andrew also resigned as treasurer of the American Red Cross, of which Taft had been elected honorary president and whose Central Committee included several conservative Republicans. Within weeks, Andrew decided to run for the Republican nomination for congress from his Gloucester, Massachusetts district and was planning his campaign. His position at treasury was taken by Robert C. Bailey, formerly personal secretary to MacVeagh.[384]

But A. Piatt Andrew did not simply fade into the shadows as many former officials had done. His congressional nomination campaign failed in 1912, and he was unsuccessful again, two years later in the primary election. Inspired by Theodore Roosevelt's rhetoric and the Wilson administration's hands-off response to the outbreak of war in Europe, Andrew sailed for France in December 1914 hoping to find a position at the American Hospital in Paris. He went to France in search of a larger purpose for himself and his talents. At the hospital he found a muddled volunteer ambulance driver service – perfect for Andrew's organizational drive. Before he could attempt to reorganize and improve the ambulance corps, he had to prove his value as a driver. He wrote in his journal:[385]

> I spend most of my days kneeling in the mud in the freezing rain, practicing the business of painter, carpenter, chauffeur and washer in turn. My section is made up of a fine lot of fellows; two or three were artists in peace time, one an architect in New York; some are students just out of college; some, like Regis Post, are millionaires, some paupers. There is even one ex-Assistant Secretary of the Treasury. We are like *les cadets de Gascogne*.

He was soon at work driving wounded soldiers from the train station to the hospital. Although rewarding, this did not save many lives. The key to saving the lives of soldiers was quickly transporting them from the frontline trenches to aid stations located in nearby towns. Andrew saw this as not a medical problem but a logistical one. By April 1915 he had devised a plan to improve the ambulance service and cajoled the French into allowing a meaningful test of the volunteers. A section of Americans would be permitted to prove their worth. If they were successful, restrictions on volunteer ambulance drivers at the front would be relaxed. "This was all Andrew needed. Returning to Paris, he immediately formed an elite section of ten cars and thirteen men under the aegis of three fellow Harvardians: Lovering Hill, Richard Lawrence, and Dallas McGrew. Telling them that the future of the service now lay in their hands…" they dispatched to the front lines.[386]

"Conveying freshly wounded men from the front throughout frosty nights and along slippery mountain roads without lights was only part of their accomplishment. For sheer military bravura…they had their little Ford ambulances punctiliously lined up and polished every morning at six o'clock, radiators and tanks filled, for inspection by a French officer. When this officer appeared, he invariably found the drivers standing at attention next to their cars, one foot placed on the crank protruding from the radiator. At a signal from the section chief the drivers would stamp heavily on the cranks and ten motors would spring to life simultaneously. The French had never seen anything like it. Ecstatic reports

---

[384] *New York Times*, "Takes Andrew's Duties" July 12, 1912, p.7.
[385] *American Heritage Magazine*, Andrew Gray, "The American Field Service." December 1974. Andrew Gray was the nephew of A. Piatt Andrew.
[386] Ibid.

went back to French army headquarters, and the American Field Ambulance Service was in business."[387]

Figure 37. Profile of an American Indian as used on some of the ambulances under A. Piatt Andrew's command in France, 1915. The image was painted on wooden side panels of the Ford ambulances. It was later replaced with the standard red cross. Right, one of James Fraser's initial Indian portraits for the nickel, 1911, that had probably been examined by Andrew. (Left, courtesy American Field Service archives; right, courtesy Wayne Wilcox.)

Andrew not only led the organization of the American ambulance corps, along with former driver Stephen Galatti, but used his connections in the United States to secure money and equipment. When the American army arrived in France, the American Field Ambulance Service was merged into the army's ambulance fleet. Andrew was made a Major, then later Lieutenant Colonel, but lost command of his ambulance corps.

"After the armistice in 1918, Andrew stayed in Paris long enough to attend the founding convention of the American Legion at the Cirque d'Hiver in March, 1919, and to ponder how his service could be revivified. For it was inconceivable to him that such fierce dedication to the French cause – *Tous and tout pour la France* had been the motto he had given the service – would not find embodiment in a lasting institution. At length he hit upon the idea of transforming the American Field Service into a program of fellowships for American students at French universities. This idea was well received, and with more than three hundred thousand dollars still in the till from unexpended donations the program could be put into effect immediately."[388] Today, the organization known by its initials – AFS for American Field Service – sponsors international exchange programs for students throughout the world.

Andrew's term as mint director had been one of the most tumultuous in the nation's history, punctuated with exceptional innovation and impetuous destruction. As assistant secretary Andrew aggressively supported the mint collection and publication of its catalog, continued the search for greater efficiency in coinage production, and promoted use of Fraser's designs on the nickel.

---

[387] Ibid.
[388] Ibid.

During the spring of 1912 the Mint Bureau was under pressure to supply samples and information to Congress in response to Representative Robert J. Bulkley's coinage bill. Internal disagreement over use of the treasurer's hoard of gold coins and the Andrew resignation controversy further distracted officials. The new design nickel, seemingly close to formal acceptance and production, would be further delayed by persistent objections from one very small but very self-important business. The Buffalo nickel would not be seen by the working public until the last days of the Taft administration, nearly a year later.

Chapter 8 – Hobbs Goblins

Although distracted treasury officials played a role in delay of the buffalo nickel, the primary impediments to approval were the objections of one man and one company: Clarence W. Hobbs, Sr., president of Hobbs Manufacturing Company of Worcester, Massachusetts. Word of the new designs had been leaked in June 1912 and by July 5 a description of the new design had been provided to newspapers by director Roberts. In response, several manufacturers of coin-operated vending machines wrote the treasury and mint.[389] Business owners had two concerns: first, that the Coinage Act of 1912, which would add half-cent, and three cent coins to the monetary system, be defeated; and, second, that any new-design nickels be of the same size and weight as the old ones. The first concern deserves additional discussion, because the possibility of one or more *new* coin denominations was a direct threat to most vending machine manufacturers.

A letter dated July 10, 1912 from The Recording and Register Fare Box Company is indicative of the attitude of many vending machine business owners:[390]

> We understand from the Washington newspapers and other sources that you are considering changing the five cent coin and we earnestly protest against this continued agitation regarding United States coins. The senseless coinage bill recently passed by the House and now before the Senate has nearly ruined our business, and this continued agitation will finally drive us and many others into bankruptcy unless the same is discontinued immediately.
> We therefore respectfully and earnestly protest.
> Sincerely yours,
> G. B. Kennedy, Secretary

---

[389] *The Washington Post*, "Buffalo Nickel is Assured" July 11, 1912, p.6.
[390] *US Mint*, NARA-CP, op. cit., file 308449. Letter dated July 20, 1912 to MacVeagh from G. B. Kennedy, Secretary, *The Recording and Register Fare Box Company*. The business, located in New Haven, Connecticut, made fare boxes, ticket dispensers and other supplies used by transit and interurban railways.

With congress actively considering additional coin denominations, vending equipment businesses were in a very difficult situation. Railroads, street car companies and others would not buy new fair boxes and ticket vending machines until the coin legislation was settled. Manufacturers of this equipment saw a significant reduction in sales, and they also had to plan for new coins that might be similar in size and weight to existing small change. Unknown to business owners, the mint had been conducting tests of various alloys, and sizes and shapes of coins for several months.

Kennedy's other concern, the possibility of physical changes to the new nickel, was also of importance to vending machine companies. Questions from vending machine and telephone manufacturers were not new to the mint. Occasional letters appear in the correspondence files throughout the early part of the century, and were common in late 1909 when newspapers announced a "Washington nickel" would soon be issued. Typical of earlier letters was one from the New England Telephone and Telegraph Company written on December 23, 1907:[391]

> Will you kindly advise if during the past two or three years the dimensions of the United States nickel five-cent coins have been changed?
> My object in asking this information is that we are experiencing some trouble with automatic coin collectors used in telephone pay stations, newly minted coins of this denomination clogging the chutes in the same.

Similar letters complaining about nickels, cents or other coins sticking in the chutes of coin-operated devices, occur from the mid-1890s forward. They seem to have been nearly as common before introduction of the Buffalo nickel as after.

The Johnson Coin Counting Machine Company of New York, Brandt Cashier Company of Chicago, American Telephone and Telegraph of New York, Chicago Telephone Company, and several others wrote to MacVeagh or Roberts asking: "…Will you kindly advise us whether this provides for any change in the diameter, thickness or form (shape) of the present five-cent coin…"[392] These were the only potential problems mentioned by any of the vending machine companies. MacVeagh wrote to each stating there would be no change in diameter, thickness or weight of the nickel. This seemed to satisfy virtually everyone, except for Clarence W. Hobbs. His first letter to the treasury was dated July 11. Without knowing anything more than general information in newspaper stories, Hobbs objected to any change in design:[393]

> We see by the Public Press that your Department is considering the issue of a new nickel coin to replace the Goddess of Liberty piece now in use.
> We wish to enter our protest in the change in this coin and for the following reasons:
> There have been very large sums of money expended during the past few years in perfecting Coin Detecting Machines, same as to be used in connection with machines for automatic sale of postage stamps, railroad tickets and other arti-

---

[391] *US Mint*, NARA-CP, op. cit., entry 229, box 260. Letter dated December 23, 1907 to Comptroller of the Currency from G. R. Manson, Asst. Chief Engineer, New England Telephone and Telegraph Company, Boston, Massachusetts.
[392] *US Mint*, NARA-CP, op. cit., file 308449. Letter dated July 10, 1912 to Roberts from C. H. Birdsall, president of Johnson Coin Counting Machine Company.
[393] *US Mint*, NARA-CP, op. cit., file 308449. Letter dated July 11, 1912 to MacVeagh from C. W. Hobbs, president of Hobbs Manufacturing Co. Clarence W. Hobbs. Sr. had written to the Mint Bureau on several occasions in addition to introduction of the Lincoln and Buffalo coins. In letters of May 24, 1911 and June 8, 1911, Hobbs asks the cost of acquiring proof coins including the 1904 silver dollar. The mint replied that a proof set cost $1.50 and the silver dollar (evidently not a proof) was $1.00 plus postage. (See NARA-CP RG-104, entry 235, vol. 387.)

cles of like nature. These machines are now ready to go on the market and orders for them are already placed.

There has been a very great popular demand for a successful apparatus of this kind, particularly on the part of railroad companies who desire automatic sales machines for selling local tickets on surface lines, elevated roads, etc., and these machines all call for 5 cent detectors.

This development has been based upon the standard form of nickel 5¢ token, and to change the design at this time will not only render valueless the expenditure that has already been made, largely by this company, but will also postpone to an indefinite date the time when the public transportation companies can avail themselves of a safe apparatus to use upon their platforms for selling their tickets.

We therefore beg your careful consideration of this highly important matter.

Mr. Ralph of the Bureau of Engraving and Printing, is well informed upon the work that has been done, and we suggest that his opinion will be of value.

Yours truly,
C. W. Hobbs

Hobbs carefully tried to suggest that his concern with a new design was widespread among equipment manufacturers; however, he admits writing only for himself by stating, "…the expenditure that has already been made, largely by this company…." MacVeagh passed the letter to director Roberts who wrote to Hobbs asking for more information on how his company's apparatus worked. Hobbs, who does not appear to have actually sold any of the devices, and probably pleased with the attention, wrote back on July 15:[394]

In order to successfully detect coins and separate same from counterfeit coins and from checks and slugs, and other articles of like nature which are used in automatic machines in place of genuine coins, it has been found necessary to take certain points upon the face of the coin as standard marks. This is arrived at after extremely careful investigation, and upon these standard points the Coin Detector is built up.

Machines as these have been greatly desired for very many years, as for instance, by the telephone companies. In Chicago it is stated that the telephone companies loose over $1000.00 per week in slugs taken at various telephone booths. The same thing has been true in New York City. The adoption of five cent ticket selling machines on railroad platforms has been abandoned because of the fact that there has been no efficient means of separating false coins and slugs from genuine coins.

The invention which has just been perfected and which is going into use very shortly on certain lines in New York is based upon the selection of certain proof points on the head of the <u>five cent</u> coin. It has been brought to such a state of perfection now that out of 1000 coins and about as many slugs, every genuine coin was accepted and every slug was rejected.

The machine has been brought to such a state of perfection that it will operate just so long as the figure of the head is visible.

It may be possible that the new coin would offer similar points which could be used identically with the other coins, but that of course is not known as we have not had the opportunity of seeing the new design, but unless there was such an agreement of test points upon the two coins, you can readily see that the scheme of having a machine which will accurately separate genuine coins from false coins would have to be abandoned, because the public could not be expected to discriminate between the old and the new, but would use the one or the other as they happened to have them in hand.

---

[394] *US Mint*, NARA-CP, op. cit., file 308449. Letter dated July 15, 1912 to Roberts from Hobbs.

With the two designs of one cent coins we have been able to make a Detector which would accept both, but that involved a very long study and was a very difficult proposition.

Our object in bringing up the matter of this five cent coin at this time, is that it would seem a very great misfortune if the public are to be deprived of this opportunity to use automatic sales machines, as is done in foreign countries. The conditions in this country are very different from those abroad on account of the large use of gambling machines in this country, which employ slugs and checks exactly the size of the five cent coin. These have gone into the possession of the people to a very great degree. There are also innumerable slugs and checks issued by restaurants and other places for coat checks, meal checks, beer checks, etc., all of which are based upon the size of the five cent coin.

There have been many attempts made to get a machine for selling a five cent cigar, also for selling newspapers, but these have all had to be abandoned because of the lack of an efficient coin detector.

Now after having just succeeded in perfecting such an instrument and after expenditure of over $50,000.00 in doing so, it comes as a great surprise to find that the pattern of the five cent coin is to be changed, and from the description that has been published that the Liberty head is to be replaced by the figure of a buffalo, it seemed to me that undoubtedly the coin would be so far changed that any Detector would be unable to accept both these coins and at the same time reject all others.

It was not our object in writing to you to attempt to say that there should never be any improvement in coin, but the interests of the people are so closely connected with the coinage, and the economy which is to be affected [sic] by the use of automatic machines is so very great, that it would seem wise to have the matter fully considered before any radical change in the face of the coin which is most generally used of any, should be made.

This has been called by very many a five cent country, and it is probable that more transactions are made with the 5 cent coin than with all other coins put together, not excepting the one cent.

It might be added that we are now designing for the use of the Post Office Department, in the postal savings work, a machine for selling the ten cent savings stamp which is based upon the standard ten cent coin, and although there are two figures on these coins, one on the old pattern and the other on the new, we have succeed in making a Detector which will accept them both. The same might be true of the five cent coin taking the old and the proposed new ones, but the object in bringing this matter forward is that the matter be considered before it is too late.

With much respect and thanking you for your response, and trusting that the matter will be looked into very carefully, we remain,
Sincerely yours,
Hobbs Manufacturing Co.
C. W. Hobbs, Pres.

PS: If it would shed any light upon the subject and enable you to come to a more definitive conclusion, a five cent coin detector might be sent to you for trial, and then you would readily see how important such a machine might become in the business of the country.

This long letter sets out Hobbs' claims and objections to changing the nickel:[395]
1. Many items valued at five-cents are sold from vending machines;
2. Some owners of these machines loose substantial amounts of money to counterfeits, slugs, gambling tokens, service checks, and non-U.S. coins;

---

[395] When one considers this must have been a strictly mechanical device with no electrical input, it must have been unusually delicate, slow to operate, and in need of frequent adjustment.

3. Detection of counterfeit nickels is desired to prevent loss to businesses;
4. Hobbs' device is capable of separating good coin from bad with 100% accuracy;
5. It uses carefully selected points on the obverse of the nickel to determine a coin's validity;
6. Hobbs does not know if the new design will work correctly in their mechanism, and does not mention tests of the old shield nickel.[396]

While stating his objections to the buffalo design (or any new design) Hobbs also weakens his argument by describing their success in adapting machines to use both the Indian and Lincoln cent in 1909.[397] He further boasts of being able to operate satisfactorily with both Seated Liberty and Barber design dimes.

Hobbs forwarded Roberts' reply, including the suggestion to contact Fraser, to Edward F. Henson, his business partner on the coin detector mechanism. Henson owned a lumber and millwork company in Philadelphia and Hobbs apparently believed that his connections in Philadelphia could be used to influence the mint's decision. Henson wrote to director Roberts on August 3, 1912:[398]

> Mr. Clarence W. Hobbs, of Worcester, informs me that he has written to you regarding the coin testing machines in the development of which we have both taken part, and particularly in regard to new designs for coins which will not interfere with a proper testing.
>
> The Post Office Department is interested in the development of this Patent and we expect soon to submit to that Department postage stamp vending machines which will prove satisfactory. You will appreciate that if coins be so changed as to make it necessary for a buyer of postage stamps to go to one vending machine with one design of coin and to another with another design of coin, such an arrangement would not be satisfactory to the Post Office Department. I do not mean you to understand that the coin testers require no change in designs. We have built a coin tester which accepts both the old Indian head and the new Lincoln head in the one cent. We have built a nickel machine which accepts all good, unmutilated coins, even though much worn, but will refuse the Philippino nickel, which is on practically the same size. We cannot, however, build a one cent machine which will accept the Lincoln and the Indian head and the old white nickel cent without building it so that it will take slugs.
>
> If you would like to see the device, the writer will endeavor at no distant date to submit same to you for your information. It is a very interesting little machine.
>
> You wrote to Mr. Hobbs suggesting that he communicate with Mr. J. E. Frazier [sic], the artist, in New York. Will you oblige me with his address?
>
> Very truly yours,
> Edward F. Henson

---

[396] It should be noted that according to the *Report of the Director of the Mint – 1883*, the new Barber nickels were the same weight but larger diameter than the old shield type. See page 4, paragraphs eight and nine of the report.

[397] The 1909 Lincoln cents were slightly thicker than previous "Indian Head" design and caused minor problems for many vending and telephone coin slot mechanisms. Equipment was quickly adapted as the mint simultaneously reduced the new cent's thickness.

[398] *US Mint*, NARA-CP, op. cit., file 308449. Letter dated August 3, 1912 to Roberts from Edward F. Henson, president of *Edward F. Henson & Co., Lumber & Millwork*. Henson was one of the founders of the *Pennsylvania Lumbermen's Mutual Insurance Company* in 1898, and was influential in Philadelphia business. In February 1913 he encouraged several Philadelphia owners of coin-operated devices to write to the mint about the new nickel, and gave distorted stories about the coin to local newspapers.

Roberts sent copies of the Hobbs and Henson letters to Fraser in New York, and the sculptor replied on August 12:[399]

> Dear Mr. Roberts,
> If you wish me to do so I will leave Monday night for Worcester to see about the coin detecting machine and show them the new design.
> I can't go before on account of press of work. It seems to me, that as the coins are changed only once every twenty years new detectors could be made in accordance.
> In Europe, I believe, when a new coin comes out the old ones are called in within the space of two years. Is that right?

Before Fraser could leave for Worcester, Henson contacted him and arranged to visit Fraser in his New York studio. Henson examined the models for the new nickel, then wrote a non-committal letter to director Roberts:[400]

> I am in receipt of you letter of August 23rd. I have already seen the proposed design at Mr. Fraser's office, but I am obliged to bring the inventors to view the coin, as I do not feel competent to determine whether the present design can, without some changes, be adapted. The coin detector measures into the ten thousandths of an inch, and if the new coin possesses some dimensions in common with the old one, it will be possible to adapt the detector to both, and that without robbing the new coin of its artistic merit.

Figure 38. Fraser's final 1912 model for the buffalo nickel. This might be the version discussed in the sculptor's letter of August 26, 1912. (Courtesy Bill Fivaz; photo taken at the Philadelphia Mint.)

On August 26, as Henson was writing his letter, Fraser telegraphed the director in response to a request to bring the final models to Washington:[401]

> I am ready to come to Washington with the models at once. Let me know when you want me.
> J. E. Fraser

---

[399] *US Mint*, NARA-CP, op. cit., file 305310. Letter dated August 12, 1912 to Roberts from Fraser.
[400] *US Mint*, NARA-CP, op. cit., file 308449. Letter dated August 26, 1912 to Roberts from Henson
[401] *US Mint*, NARA-CP, op. cit., file 305310. Telegram dated 11:02 am August 26, 1912 to Roberts from Fraser.

Clarence Hobbs and Edward Henson visited Fraser again in September, but in August the artist paid little attention to the mechanical needs of a single manufacturer – he had more important things on his mind.

A Ferocious Looking Animal

Surviving letters to the mint and treasury were not all from hard-nosed businessmen and bankers. On July 1, 1912 Mrs. Orville B. Lake of Philadelphia wrote one of the more interesting letters to secretary MacVeagh:[402]

> My dear Sir:
> I notice in today's papers the anticipated change in the five cent piece and forthwith send my emphatic protest. It is quite enough to have the Indian on the one cent piece. As for the five dollar gold piece that is too, too bad! The Indian will never be forgotten. All children of every class sometime or other wear an Indian suit, mimic war dances and pow wows.
> If it is necessary to make a change could it not be as artistic as we have now!
> I can fancy in A. D. 2012, a Continental traveler doing the United States and upon seeing the five cent piece with the Indian—soliloquizing, "So ziz was ze great Franklin MacVeagh. But, why did he wear so many 'plumes' in his chapeau;" and upon looking on the reverse side – "I wonder if zee people of that time rode that ferocious looking animal – ."
> Please Mr. Secretary use your influence to have the Indian and the Buffalo placed somewhere else, than upon our nice little five cent piece.
> Very truly yours,
> Elizabeth Willard Lake
> (Mrs. Orville B. Lake)

MacVeagh replied several days later in his best diplomatic style:[403]

> ...I quite agree with you that if we are to make a change, the new piece should be at least as artistic as the old one but is this so very difficult? A coin to be artistic should be suggestive and in some sense characteristic of the country to which it belongs. This cannot be said of the present 5¢ piece. The Buffalo and the Indian are both peculiar to the United States, identified together with its past and worthy of such a memorial as an artistic coin would be. The merit of the idea seems to depend upon the ability of the artist to give us something distinctive, pleasing and of really national significance. Nothing has been determined upon but if such a result could be achieved we should count confidently upon your approval.

The secretary's reply is of more than passing interest because it uses phrases that echo Fraser's language in describing the new designs of Saint-Gaudens: "suggestive," "characteristic of the country," and "distinctive, pleasing and of really national significance."[404] Since Fraser had spoken with the secretary several times, it is likely that MacVeagh was fully convinced of the new designs' merits, and subconsciously accepted them as "normal" for the nickel.

---

[402] *US Mint*, NARA-CP, op. cit., file 308449. Letter dated July 1, 1912 to MacVeagh from Mrs. Orville B. Lake. She appears to mimic the spoken accent of a European visitor – possibly French.
[403] *US Mint*, NARA-CP, op. cit., file 308449. Letter dated July 12, 1912 to Lake from MacVeagh.
[404] See also Fraser's newspaper quote on the Peace dollar in Burdette, *Renaissance of American Coinage 1916-1921*.

Figure 39. Left, package illustration for J. Brown & Co. Echo Chewing Tobacco. Right, children observing an American bison at the National Zoo, Washington, DC circa 1899. (Left, courtesy Library of Congress Prints and Records Division; right, photo by Francis B. Johnston, courtesy Smithsonian Institution Archives.)

However ferocious a beast the buffalo may have seemed to Mrs. Lake, by 1912 the American Bison was only one of many exotic curiosities to be seen in city zoos. It had been more than a generation since the last great herds roamed American prairies and few citizens had first-hand knowledge of the creatures. To most, probably including Mrs. Lake, American bison populated a world of nostalgic advertising images, calendars, nostrums and the occasional Sunday supplement rotogravure feature. The romantic, ennobled view so thoroughly cast by popular magazines, novels, cinema and Wild West shows left little space for reality of the animal's near-extinction in the wild.

The Commission of Fine Arts

Fraser spent July and early August lining up support among members of the Commission of Fine Arts. The Commission was newly established – May of 1910 – and still testing its jurisdiction. Secretary MacVeagh wanted Commission approval for any new coinage designs and director Roberts was prepared to do whatever the Commission wanted.[405] Unfortunately, the members were scattered during the summer of 1912: some in Chicago, some in Europe, others at summer vacation homes. The Commission could not meet as a whole, but this did not stop Fraser. He knew that the most important members were Chairman Daniel Chester French, a sculptor like Fraser, the artist members Edwin Howland Blashfield and Cass Gilbert, and architect Thomas Hastings.

Fraser started with French to whom he showed the nickel models on July 15:[406]

> Mr. James E. Fraser tells me that you wish my opinion on the artistic qualities of the designs which he has made of the obverse and reverse of the five cent piece. I have examined them carefully and with keen interest and I have no hesitation in giving them my hearty approval. They are very fine both in design and in execution and I think you have reason to take great satisfaction in the thought that this beautiful coin has been made by your direction and is to be struck during your administration. Mr. Fraser has my sincere congratulations on the result of his labors.
>
> Mr. Fraser has also shown me the design containing the head of Lincoln and I cannot help expressing the hope that this may be utilized for one of the other

---

[405] The Commission had also reviewed currency designs by Kenyon Cox.
[406] *US Mint*, NARA-CP, op. cit., file 305310. Letter dated July 17, 1912 to MacVeagh from French.

coins. It would seem a pity to loose so charming an example of the medallic art and so striking a portrait of the man.
Very respectfully,

With America's most respected living sculptor on his side, Fraser corralled the others one by one. He kept in touch with director Roberts to make sure the commendations arrived:[407]

> Dear Mr. Roberts,
> Mr. French wrote a letter to Mr. MacVeagh several days ago. Did it arrive? Mr. Hastings is away in Europe so I could not get him to write. Mr. French didn't think it necessary to have any other letters. What do you think about it? I am having other reductions made so as to be well fitted the next time I come to Washington.
> Very sincerely yours,

Chairman French's approval was very important, but MacVeagh wanted as much support from the Commission as possible, so French contacted Edwin Blashfield and Cass Gilbert and asked them to write letters of support to the secretary.[408] By August 28 Gilbert had seen the models and wrote an enthusiastic letter praising the nickel designs. Gilbert wrote:[409]

> My Dear Mr. MacVeagh:
> I have just received a letter from Edwin H. Blashfield of the Commission of Fine Arts asking me to look over some models of the new five cent piece made by Mr. Fraser and to express to you my opinion of them. It gives me great pleasure to say that they impress me most favorably. The use of the buffalo and the Indian as the insignia on the coin is admirable in itself and the modeling is done with rare skill and beauty. I wish it were possible that the <u>coin could be struck with the deeper relief which Mr. Fraser has shown in some of the models he has brought with him</u>, but he tells me that some practical objections are raised by your department.
> It gives me very great pleasure to express to you my admiration for the work Mr. Fraser has done and congratulate you on the step you are taking in securing really artistic coins.
> I remain,
> Sincerely

Secretary MacVeagh had an extended conversation with Edwin Blashfield on the morning of August 27 while he was in New York. The secretary discussed the nickel design and asked Blashfield to examine Fraser's models. The result was a letter from Edwin Blashfield to secretary MacVeagh on the 28th:[410]

> Dear Sir:
> I saw Mr. Fraser's designs yesterday and quickly approved of them.
> I like the Indian and am <u>delighted</u> with the Bison, which would give us, it seems to me, a distinctively national American coin. Our national Eagle is a supremely decorative bird and should always remain on some of our coins, but we share him with Germany, Russia, Austria and other States, the Bison is all ours.

---

[407] *US Mint*, NARA-CP, op. cit., file 305310. Letter dated July 22, 1912 to Roberts from Fraser.
[408] *US Mint*, NARA-CP, op. cit., file 305310. Letter dated February 8, 1913 to MacVeagh from Fraser; p.2. This ten page letter summarizes events beginning in July 1912. It mentions documents and conversations not otherwise recorded.
[409] *US Mint*, NARA-CP, op. cit., file 305310. Letter dated August 28, 1912 to MacVeagh from Cass Gilbert.
[410] *US Mint*, NARA-CP, op. cit., file 305310. Letter dated August 28, 1912 to MacVeagh from Edwin Howland Blashfield.

> I wish that Mr. Fraser's profile Lincoln could be used in some way. It seems to me fine in the rather high relief treatment which he has accorded to it and the silver is handsome in its color-effect of surface.
>
> I remain, yours faithfully,

The secretary replied from his summer residence in Dublin, New Hampshire:

> Very many thanks for your letter of the 28th of August, which has followed me here, and which I am forwarding to George E. Roberts, Director of the Mint. I will ask Mr. Roberts to go ahead with the matter.
>
> I am not surprised, but I am very greatly pleased that you so warmly commend Mr. Fraser's designs.
>
> I will take the liberty of advising you of my communication with Mr. Kenyon Cox. I shall not attempt this for a little while yet as I am going to try to take a little rest.

As a result of MacVeagh's discussions with the Commission artists and examination of the models and electrotypes Fraser had prepared, the secretary told Roberts in a letter written later the same day:[411]

> ...If I were you I would not wait any longer. It is evident that we can have the complete approval of the Fine Arts Commission. Mr. Hastings I see from the newspapers is still abroad, though he will now of course come home very quickly because his house in the country burned down the day I was in New York.

With commission approval assured and a "nudge" from secretary MacVeagh, Roberts wrote to Fraser offering him the commission.[412] Fraser's first part of the nickel plan had succeeded – now he had to engineer the more difficult part: getting the coin his way. Because of the interference of Hobbs, which produced nearly as much animosity among the mint staff as it did Fraser, the sculptor and mint ended up on the same side of the argument against Hobbs. Evidently, this avoided most disagreement and production turned out to be relatively painless.

When secretary MacVeagh visited President Taft at his family home in Beverly, Massachusetts,[413] he told him about the nickel project and showed the Chief Executive letters from Commission of Fine Arts members. MacVeagh described the meeting:[414]

> ...He told me he did not know anything about it before; and I think felt as though I had not wished to appeal to his artistic sense. He asked me if I had the "things" along; but of course I did not have them. He was extremely nice about it; and the interview of course left me free to go ahead; and he expects nothing further.

President Taft was not previously aware of the nickel redesign project. Without ever seeing a model or drawing of the new coin, he left the matter completely in MacVeagh's hands. Attempts were made to schedule a visit for Fraser with the president,

---

[411] *US Mint*, NARA-CP, op. cit., file 305310. Letter dated August 30, 1912 to Roberts from MacVeagh.

[412] MacVeagh must have been feeling particularly pleased with his work toward improving the artistic value of circulating currency. He had just completed agreement with noted artist Kenyon Cox to redesign the reverse of the National Currency paper notes. Cox' design was approved in February 1913, and used on the reverse of the Series 1914 $100 Federal Reserve Note.

[413] President Taft maintained his "Summer White House" (also known as "Parramatta") at 70 Corning Street in the town of Beverly, Massachusetts. The town was convenient to Senator Henry Cabot Lodge's summer retreat at Nahaut, and popular with many other Republicans including Theodore Roosevelt's daughter, Alice Longworth. President Taft arrived on August 31 and departed abruptly on October 26, 1912. It was during this time secretary MacVeagh attempted to have Fraser show his design to the President.

[414] *US Mint*, NARA-CP, op. cit., file 305310. Letter dated September 14, 1912 to Roberts from MacVeagh.

but Taft was in the thick of a nasty three-way presidential campaign against Theodore Roosevelt (Progressive – Bull Moose) and Woodrow Wilson (Democratic), and political obligations superseded other matters. By October 24, MacVeagh had given up on the artist's visit and asked director Roberts to notify Fraser. The internal Treasury memorandum included a terse postscript which Fraser probably did not see: "Mr. Forster wired department that the president had been consulted and had no interest in seeing Mr. Fraser."[415]

Rostron Medal

Sinking of the steamship *RMS Titanic* on April 14, 1912 had been a great blow to Americans. Although the ship was British, many of the passengers were Americans from some of the nation's finest families. President Taft felt the tragedy personally with the loss of his trusted military aide and friend Colonel Archibald Butts. Also lost was artist Frank Millet who had designed many of the government's military medals, and recommended Saint-Gaudens to President Roosevelt for design of the 1905 Inaugural medal.[416]

On August 17, 1912 President Taft wrote to seven artists inviting them to compete for the design of a Congressional Gold Medal to be awarded to Capt. Arthur H. Rostron. As skipper of the *USS Carpathia*, Rostron had rescued survivors of the *Titanic*. Based on recommendation of the Commission of Fine Arts the artists were: James Fraser, John Flanagan, Hermon MacNeil, Evelyn Longman, Adolph Weinman, Kenyon Cox and J. E. Roine. All except Longman and Roine would eventually design circulating coins or paper currency for the United States. The government was prepared to pay $1,000 for the best design. Cox was presently involved in redesigning the reverse of U. S. paper currency: a project of personal interest to secretary MacVeagh. Fraser was designing the new nickel.

The Commission reviewed the medal submissions and accepted Flanagan's design on November 11, 1912 rejecting several others, and not considering Fraser's at all. Apparently Chairman Daniel French felt this result sent a mixed message to the administration about Fraser's capabilities, and made a point of writing to President Taft's secretary:[417]

> It has occurred to me that it might be well in acquainting the President with our verdict in the case of the Rostron medal to tell him that Mr. Fraser's designs were not considered because he did not comply with the conditions of the competition, not having sent a design of the obverse of the medal. I should be sorry to have the President think that the man who is making the designs for the coins was not equal to any medalist in the land. You remember how very much we all admired Mr. Fraser's designs.

Flanagan completed the medals in time for a March 1, 1913 ceremony during which President Taft personally presented the gold medal to Captain Rostron.

---

[415] *US Mint*, NARA-CP, op. cit., file 305310. Memorandum dated October 24, 1912 to F. W. Taylor for Roberts from MacVeagh. Compare with Roosevelt's persistent enthusiasm when working with Saint-Gaudens.

[416] Millet had suggested to Edith Roosevelt, the President's wife, that Saint-Gaudens redesign the coinage in 1904. Millet and Butts were sharing a cabin on the voyage from England to New York. Three years later Alfred Gwynne Vanderbilt went down with the Lusitania; his widow, Margaret Emerson McKim Vanderbilt, married Raymond T. Baker in 1917 – Baker was Director of the Mint. To continue the nautical tragedy connection, the Gloucester fishing schooner *A. Piatt Andrew* was sunk by a German U-boat on August 28, 1918 with no loss of life. The schooner's namesake, the former mint director, was in France having reorganized the American Field Ambulance Service.

[417] *Taft papers*, LoC. op. cit. Microfilm reel 442, file 3346. Letter dated November 21, 1912 to Charles D. Hilles, Secretary to the President from Col. Spencer Cosby, secretary, Commission of Fine Arts. Includes the quotation from chairman Daniel C. French.

A Great Waste of Time

During autumn weeks consumed by attempts to schedule a meeting with the President, the mint had done little about the new design. However, Clarence Hobbs and his associates had been busy meeting with Fraser, examining the models and consulting among themselves about their counterfeit detector. After cooling his typewriter since late August Clarence Hobbs, possibly feeling ignored by the director, wrote to Roberts on November 2:[418]

> Some two weeks ago I addressed you requesting an appointment for the purpose of discussing the matter of the Five-Cent Coin which it is proposed to issue; also for the purpose of showing you the Coin Detector which has been perfected for the handling of the coin now in use; and to see what can be done toward combining the proof points upon the two coins so that one coin detector will permit the use of both coins by the public, and still the public gain the advantage of automatic sales mechanism, which are now ready to go upon the market.
> At that time, it was stated that you were out of the city and would return in two weeks. Will you kindly advise by return post when you will be in Washington and on what day it will be agreeable to you to have the undersigned call upon you on the errand as specified above. We believe this to be a matter of very great importance, else we would not trouble you with the matter, but believing it to be so, would urgently request the favor of the interview.
> Yours truly,
> HOBBS MANUFACTURING CO.

Hobbs and Reith showed up uninvited at Fraser's New York studio on November 7. After considerable conversation, Fraser provided them with "...electro-plate reductions of the two sides...made...since the latter part of August."[419]

Roberts wrote to Hobbs on November 12 suggesting they meet at Fraser's studio in New York to examine the models and electrotypes together. He also recommended Hobbs contact Fraser and obtain his concurrence. Hobbs replied that he would be able to meet in New York anytime during the next two weeks, and would await the director's notice of a day and time.[420] A further exchange of letters and phone calls fixed the meeting at 9am on November 19, at Fraser's studio.[421] Roberts held an internal conference about the nickel at the mint on November 18.[422]

The larger meeting took place as planned with Hobbs, the counterfeit detector's inventor Reith, Roberts and Fraser in attendance. Nothing was resolved and by November 22, Hobbs' examination was complete. He returned the two coin-size electrotypes to Fraser "...sweated together with all the changes made on both sides that he [Hobbs] stated were necessary in order to make the new nickel work satisfactorily with his detecting machine."[423] Hobbs also wrote to Roberts:[424]

---

[418] *US Mint*, NARA-CP, op. cit., file 308449. Letter dated November 2, 1912 to Roberts from Hobbs.
[419] *US Mint*, NARA-CP, op. cit., file 305310. Letter dated February 8, 1913 to MacVeagh from Fraser, p.3. These incorporated all the changes Fraser had previously made to the designs.
[420] *US Mint*, NARA-CP, op. cit., file 308449. Letter dated November 13, 1912 to Roberts from Hobbs.
[421] *US Mint*, NARA-CP, op. cit., file 308449. Letter dated November 15, 1912 to Roberts from Hobbs.
[422] *MacVeagh papers*, LoC. op. cit., box 7, lettercopy book, p.61. Memorandum dated November 18, 1912 to Roberts from MacVeagh.
[423] *US Mint*, NARA-CP, op. cit., file 305310. Letter dated February 8, 1913 to MacVeagh from Fraser, p.3.
[424] *US Mint*, NARA-CP, op. cit., file 308449. Letter dated November 22, 1912 to Roberts from Hobbs; enclosure, copy of letter same date to Fraser from Hobbs.

>...As you will see by the letter [I am sending to Mr. Fraser], upon examination of the coin we find that the change necessary will be extremely slight, consisting principally of reducing the height of the buffalo figure a little more than 1/16" and providing a ring around inside the rim, both on the Indian side and the Buffalo side.
>
>We feel sure that Mr. Fraser will be able to make those changes without in any way detracting from the appearance of the coin, in fact most of the critics who have looked at it while the coin has been in my possession have felt that the Buffalo figure was rather large for the coin and that the coin would be improved by reducing this figure even so slightly as suggested.

His letter to Fraser was more detailed:[425]

>Dear Mr. Fraser:
>I am returning to you today by Registered Post the two proof coins[426] which you entrusted to me for measurement. In our study of these in connection with the current five-cent coin, and the coin testing machines, we find that there will be needed no change in design of the Buffalo side but only a slight change in proportion – or size.
>
>The absolute requirements are:-
>(1) A root circle inside the rim of the reverse
>(2) A root circle inside the rim on the face which in this connection is the Buffalo
>(3) A broken circle inside the inscription
>(4) A bearing on the face (body) of the figure
>(5) A center bearing
>
>With the proof coins I am sending to you a standard five-cent coin marked with the circles indicated, 1, 2, and 3; also the center point, 5. Herewith I hand you a drawing which gives the diameters and heights upon which we must rely to successfully test the old and the proposed new coins, and to separate them from foreign, false, and imitation coins and tokens.[427]
>
>The design of the Buffalo and the Indian are so excellent that it would be asking too much to have them changed, but the results desired can all be achieved by reducing the Buffalo figure 8/100 of an inch in length and otherwise in proportion. This will give ample space for the outside circle, and the broken circle will then fall just outside the hump. The height between the root circle 2, and the circular bearing 4 and the center point 5 are easily accomplished without in any way altering the general design. The foundation for the feet could be lowered a trifle and the root circle 2 pass over it without altering the design. It is nearly low enough now.
>
>There should also be a root circular bearing around the Indian head inside the rim, as shown upon the reverse of the marked coin. This is for the purpose of getting the standard thickness upon which the test measurements are based.
>
>The bottom of the broken circle 3 need not be flat, but may be more or less so, provided we have approximately the root depth at all points.
>
>With the slight changes indicated I cannot see that the appearance of the coin will be marred and the public will then be given the full advantage of the automatic sales devices which I described to you.
>
>I am requesting Mr. C. U. Carpenter, our New York associate, who will have to meet the public in introducing these machines as sales agent of the American Stamp and Ticket Vending Machine Co., No. 30 Church street, for whom this com-

---

[425] *US Mint*, NARA-CP, op. cit., file 308449. Letter dated November 22, 1912 to Fraser from Hobbs.

[426] Hobbs refers to the two electrotypes, not actual coins. "Proof" is used in the sense of "sample," or "test."

[427] Hobbs did much the same thing in 1916 when he objected to the Winged-Liberty dime. He marked one of the high relief coins from the first trial production run with concentric circles. These showed where space was needed so his company's latest counterfeit detector would work with Adolph Weinman's new design. He also included a drawing on the back of one of his 1916 letters. See Burdette, *Renaissance of American Coinage 1916-1921* for details.

pany is acting to call upon you and he will make any needful explanations of these matters.

Thanking you for the courtesy of your reception and greatly appreciating the interest shown by you and Mr. Roberts on the whole matter, I remain.

Fraser took a few days to digest Clarence Hobbs' technical letter. Roberts had sent him a copy of Hobbs cover letter, so the artist was aware of the opinions expressed in it. The manufacturer had explained about bearing points and root circles during previous visits, but that did not make the artist comfortable with what was being requested.

As Fraser tinkered with the requested changes, he became increasingly uneasy about making them. The proportion of his designs had been worked out over months of sketches, models and electrotypes, now Hobbs not only suggested changes in scale, but had presumed to tell Roberts the coin would be improved by the modifications.

On December 1 Fraser wrote to Roberts:[428]

> I am in receipt of a letter from Mr. Hobbs – which I am enclosing – in reference to the five-cent piece.
>
> I notice that there is no concession whatever on his part; he asks me to reduce the size of the buffalo, inscriptions, etc, eight-one-hundredths of an inch which, practically is one-tenth of an inch. I have carefully considered every space surrounding the buffalo and have changed them all back and forth many times, arriving at this design only after the utmost care. So you see how radical any change approximating one-tenth of an inch would be in the relation of the spacing in a coin of this size.
>
> Not only that but it is no sure thing that the coin-detector will be a practical success. I suggested that the first rim of the nickel be used instead of the circle inside the fretwork and also to bring the second circle nearer the stars.[429] This I am sure can be done.
>
> It is plain to be seen that they are trying to get everything they can at my expense; and I hardly think that the government should be forced to accept a design which is inferior to the present one when the machine could be changed without altering to any great degree its effectiveness, thus leaving the [new] coin nearly in its present state. There would have to be a slight reduction even in the event of using the first rim of the nickel. In the future, this would eliminate the wide rim which, on the present coin, is wholly out of proportion to its size thereby adding to the difficulty in making the design. We should think of the future, also, so that it will not be possible to have this trouble again. I called on Mr. French and he thinks it would be nearly out of the question to make so great a change in my design
>
> I only received the coin from Mr. Hobbs last Saturday so have had little time to work on them. I am perfectly willing to [do] anything to help them without making the design bad.
>
> As I understand it now, I am to make the reductions, send them to the Mint and see what the result will be. I will have Mr. Weil send you the price on the reductions; it may be cheaper than usual as this is a trial.
>
> Faithfully yours,

With backing from the chairman of the Commission of Fine Arts, Fraser rejected Hobbs' request for a reduction in the size of the buffalo and Indian. He also proposed an

---

[428] *US Mint*, NARA-CP, op. cit., file 305310. Letter dated December 1, 1912 to Roberts from Fraser.

[429] This phrase has caused considerable speculation about there being stars on one of Fraser's nickel designs. Fraser is referring to the beading, or fretwork, inside the rim of the old Liberty-design (by Barber) and the obverse stars. His suggestion is that by using those points for measurements on the current coins, the new nickel design would not have to be changed.

alternative, similar to that mentioned during the November 19 meeting at his studio. Lastly, he encouraged the director to move ahead with plans for trial strikes by stating he will have Henri or Felix Weil, from Medallic Art Company, send the mint a quote for making steel hubs for the nickel.

Figure 40. Buffalo nickel model dating from November (?) 1912 or February 1913 (?). Note differences between this version and the one later used to create the first hubs in December, particularly the extra space between obverse rim and design, and reverse where the bison's forelegs are on higher ground than the back legs. (Courtesy James Earle Fraser and Laura Gardin Fraser Studio Collection, series 1, box 2, folder 7. National Cowboy & Western Heritage Museum, Oklahoma City, OK.)

The director wrote to Fraser on December 3 encouraging the artist to contact Hobbs about the nickel design. Roberts stated he did not want to do anything to damage the design; however, he also did "…not want to block the development of an improved automatic machine." Fraser was instructed to "…perfect the design going as far in the matter as I think I can without impairing the artistic effectiveness."[430]

On December 11 Fraser advised he would be in Washington on the following Monday (December 16) and wanted to show the director and secretary the "…electro-plate reductions changed by the Hobbs Manufacturing Company." During the meeting the three again examined the coin-sized replicas altered by Hobbs. According to Fraser, secretary MacVeagh "…and Mr. Roberts both objected to the reductions as they then appeared most emphatically."[431] After the meeting director Roberts asked Fraser to make what changes he could to the design without altering the artistry of the work. He also was "…urged …to make great haste in the matter, particularly in the making of the dies." Fraser phoned Medallic Art Company and had them send the mint a quote of $200 to make both reductions and hubs from Fraser's models, and Roberts approved the expenditure on the 14th.[432]

---

[430] *US Mint*, NARA-CP, op. cit., file 305310. Letter dated February 8, 1913 to MacVeagh from Fraser, p.4. The sculptor paraphrases from a now-lost letter written by Roberts.
[431] *US Mint*, NARA-CP, op. cit., file 305310. Letter dated February 8, 1913 to MacVeagh from Fraser, p.5. Fraser's letter states the date was December 15, but that was a Sunday and not a likely day for a meeting. Treasury letters confirm Monday the 16th. In his later summary of events Fraser says Roberts and MacVeagh "…would not have the designs such as they then were [with Hobbs' alterations] whether or not I would pass them myself."
[432] *US Mint*, NARA-CP, op. cit., file 305310. Letter dated December 12, 1912 to Roberts from H. Weil.

Unlike Brenner's experience in 1909, Fraser seems to have had the support of mint officials in having steel hubs cut outside the mint.

Official Acceptance

On December 18 Roberts set a letter officially adopting Fraser's design and authorizing him to "…complete and perfect the design's obverse and reverse heretofore submitted and now approved by the Department for a new five cent nickel piece." Final acceptance would depend "…upon completion of the same and the final acceptance of the models and after successful working test of the dies…," after which Fraser was to be paid $2,500 for his work.[433]

Fraser's relations with the mint director in Washington and the Philadelphia Mint staff were among the best enjoyed by any outside artist of the era. When the sculptor asked to be present for the striking of experimental pieces of the new nickel, superintendent Landis wrote:[434]

> As Mr. Fraser has expressed a desire to be present at the experimental striking of the new five-cent piece, I beg to inform you that we will be ready for this trial on Tuesday morning, January 7th. Will you kindly arrange for Mr. Fraser to be here at that time, or if that date should not suit, have him name as early a date as possible advising me of the same.

This first hubs had been prepared from Fraser's models by Medallic Art Company and delivered to the mint sometime before December 31, so there was little for the mint to do except make dies.[435] Medallic Art had left the hubs unhardened so they could be touched up by Fraser if necessary. Barber hardened the hubs and made experimental dies. Neither hubs nor dies could be used for production since they likely were dated 1912, but, for test purposes they were acceptable.[436] On the morning of January 7 Fraser, director Roberts, Eames MacVeagh, engraver Barber, superintendent Landis, coiner Robert Clark and medal room superintendent Samuel E. Hart were present as Barber struck the first experimental Buffalo nickels on a medal press. Everything went as planned and the coins appeared to be completely satisfactory to all present. Fraser later wrote "…I heard some of the men that were actually engaged in striking the coins say that the coins struck easier than the old nickel with less pressure."[437] These experimental coins were nearly identical to the version used in February to strike circulation pieces. The most obvious differences were the rim was wider than on the 1913 version and the hair tie ended before the rim on the 1912 version. It is the author's speculation that the dies tested on January 7, 1913 were made by Medallic Art Co. from the 1912 model, and that the pieces were dated 1912. There was nothing prohibiting this – the design had been accepted but not finalized for

---

[433] *US Mint*, NARA-CP, op. cit., file 305310. Letter dated February 8, 1913 to MacVeagh from Fraser, p.6 The quote is from the now-lost letter of December 18 by Roberts.
[434] *US Mint*, NARA-CP, op. cit., file 305310. Letter dated December 31, 1912 to Roberts from Landis.
[435] Landis' letter of December 31, 1912 states that the trial striking would take place on January 7. This indicates the hubs had been received on or before the 31st, since it is unlikely Landis could have named a specific date without the engraving department having examined the hubs and approved them.
[436] This was normal procedure at the mint and at commercial medal firms. Soft dies could be used for only a few strikes, but that was sufficient for test purposes. In 1916 the unhardened experimental dies were of such poor quality that they may have contributed to reworking of all three silver coin designs. See Burdette, *Renaissance of American Coinage 1916-1921* for more information.
[437] *US Mint*, NARA-CP, op. cit., file 305310. Letter dated February 8, 1913 to MacVeagh from Fraser, p.6.

production so the pieces struck were not real money. Once the test was completed, there was nothing to prevent changing the date to 1913 and making all the working dies for the next several months.

After the experimental striking Roberts asked Fraser if the Hobbs people were satisfied with the design. When Fraser said that additional changes were wanted, he was asked by Roberts to work with Hobbs and the inventor, Reith, to make any adjustments that could be done without harming the design; this Fraser agreed to do. No other objections to the new design were noted in existing mint correspondence. Engraver Barber wrote to the director on January 7 recommending the mint take possession of all models, reductions and other design materials for the new nickel. "I wish to call your attention to this matter because from the character of the design and execution of the same I am convinced that it would be an easy matter to counterfeit the new coin…"[438]

Barber made plans to prepare working dies as Landis reported on the morning of January 11:[439]

> In reply to your letter on the 10th instant, in reference to the new 5-cent piece, I beg to inform you that the Engraver states that he intends to harden the hubs today and will be ready to begin the manufacturer of the working dies on Monday. If he stops all other work he can have a supply of dies sufficient to start all the presses in this mint and also ship to the Denver and San Francisco mints in ten days after receipt of your order. The Superintendent of the Coining Department states he can turn out $15,000 [i.e.: 300,000 pieces] per day if all the presses are put on this coin.
> In accordance with your conversation over the telephone this morning, we will start the making of the dies on Monday and push the matter.

The mint was ready to make working dies for 1913 and everything seemed ready to produce the new nickels. At 3:08 pm that afternoon Fraser sent a telegram to the treasury department updating Roberts on his progress in working with Reith:[440]

> Geo E. Roberts, Director of the Mint,
> Department of the Treasury, Washington, D.C.
> Am working on models with the inventor of machine [;] expect finished dies next week, very difficult problem.
> J. E. Fraser

Fraser, taking to heart the earlier suggestion from director Roberts about working with the Hobbs Company, was now preparing new models in an attempt to meet demands of the "coin detector." During the week Fraser worked with George Reith, the Hobbs Company mechanic who invented the counterfeit detector, to change the design to suit Reith. Medallic Art cut a new pair of hubs from Fraser's models and shipped them to the mint.

Meanwhile, Barber moved ahead with the new design and struck seventeen experimental pieces (J-1950) on January 13. Two of these were placed in the Philadelphia Mint collection and the others made available for examination top treasury officials. These are the only pattern Buffalo nickels that were produced from dies intended for possible circulation use.

On January 20 telegrams shot between Roberts, Fraser and Hobbs' sales agent:[441]

---

[438] *US Mint*, NARA-CP, op. cit., file 305310. Letter dated January 7, 1913 to Roberts from Barber.
[439] *US Mint*, NARA-CP, op. cit., file 305310. Letter dated January 11, 1913 to Roberts from Landis.
[440] *US Mint*, NARA-CP, op. cit., file 305310. Telegram dated January 11, 1913 to Roberts from Fraser.
[441] *US Mint*, NARA-CP, op. cit., file 305310. Telegram dated January 20, 1913 to Roberts from Fraser.

> The dies [hubs] are finished and will be in Philadelphia tomorrow, delay caused by working with inventor until he was satisfied. The coin is practically the same.
> J E Fraser, 11:30 am

Next came a message from Hobbs' agent in New York:[442]

> Am wiring you at suggestion of Mr. Fraser, advising you our inventor Reith, will visit Philadelphia Mint tomorrow to go over suggested modifications in new five cent coins. Will you kindly wire proper authority there to take this up with Reith.
> American Stamp and Ticket Vending Machine Co
> C U Carpenter, VP and GM
> 1:11 pm

Lastly, another telegram from Fraser:[443]

> I think it wise to meet me in Philadelphia tomorrow as the Hobbs people want to try the coin detector on the dies and there may be rubbing down necessary.
> Fraser, 1:52pm

The Hobbs Company, now using the name American Stamp and Ticket Vending Machine Co. (ASTUMCO) to market its "coin detector," also wrote to director Roberts summarizing events:[444]

> As Mr. Fraser has probably informed you, we, by acting on your suggestion of working together, have come to the conclusion that certain modifications can be made in the new five cent coin which will make it possible it [sic] to be used on our machines and at the same time not detract from its artistic value.
> Mr. Fraser has sent the modified dies to Philadelphia today and our inventor, Mr. George Reith, will be in Philadelphia tomorrow morning to go over the matter very carefully with the die makers. I therefore sent you a telegram asking you to be kind enough to wire authority to the Philadelphia Mint to take this matter up with Mr. Reith.
> We greatly appreciate the attitude of yourself and Mr. Fraser in this matter for it was a question of the most serious import to us. Our machines are now in daily use in the Hudson Tunnels and will soon be in many other important places in this City and Boston.
> Thanking you most sincerely for your past consideration. I remain,
> C. U. Carpenter, VP & GM

The new hubs arrived at the mint on schedule, and Barber quickly made a pair of experimental dies. With production delayed until the changes were evaluated, everyone except the Hobbs people were anxious to resolve the difficulty and start striking coins. On January 21 superintendent Landis sent director Roberts a sample of the coins struck earlier that day:[445]

> I beg to enclose one of the new 5-cent nickel pieces struck today from the dies as modified by the Engraver. The only change is in the border, which has been made round and true. The model was all freehand work and therefore not mechanically correct, which it had to be in order to conform to the requirements of modern coinage. The change was approved by Mr. Fraser this morning and he expressed himself as highly pleased, considering we had improved the piece.
> Respectfully,
> PS: The dies that Mr. Barber is working on are the improved design.

---

[442] *US Mint*, NARA-CP, op. cit., file 305310. Telegram dated January 20, 1913 to Roberts from Carpenter.
[443] *US Mint*, NARA-CP, op. cit., file 305310. Telegram dated January 20, 1913 to Roberts from Fraser.
[444] *US Mint*, NARA-CP, op. cit., file 305310. Letter dated January 20, 1913 to Roberts from Carpenter.
[445] *US Mint*, NARA-CP, op. cit., file 305310. Letter dated January 21, 1913 to Roberts from Landis.

The work Barber performed was simply to make the rim (or border) circular on dies made from the new hubs. This was relatively minor touch up, and Landis reported that Fraser not only approved but thought it was an improvement. Coins from the modified design are nearly indistinguishable from the first experimental pieces. The most noticeable differences are the narrower rims on both sides, and the contour of the cliff under the buffalo. As Fraser stated earlier "The coin is practically the same." Barber reported the experimental striking to superintendent Landis:[446]

> In compliance with instructions of the Director of the Mint received in letter of the 20th inst., namely, that we should confer with Mr. Fraser, also with parties interested in a certain coin detecting device and report the result, I beg to state that I held such a conference and found that I had already anticipated all that the patentee of the said device required. Therefore to satisfy both Mr. Fraser and the manufacturer of the coin detecting device it was necessary to strike some pieces for the inspection of both parties concerned. Forty blanks were procured from the Superintendent of the Coining Department and nine pieces were struck in the presence of the Superintendent and Chief Clerk. One of the pieces was sent to the Director on the 21st inst. And eight pieces I am holding until we hear from the Director after his examination of the coin submitted, when we can destroy them according to the regulation. The remaining 31 blanks I have returned to the Superintendent.

Figure 41. Recreation of the Buffalo nickel pattern coin struck from the #2 model dies of January 21, 1913. Note improvements to the date, overall reduction in texture and the narrower rim. The inscription Liberty still remains somewhat indistinct and would not be strengthened until 1916. This version was apparently used for circulation coins.

In his report Landis listed those present as "…Messrs. Barber, Norris, Hart, Mr. Fraser, the designer, and two representatives of the automatic vending machine."[447] Fraser reported that Reith (who was in attendance) "…found so little difference in the two sets of dies that he told Mr. Barbour [sic], Mr. Hobbs, and myself that the difference was so slight that he could overcome all difficulties by the use of a flexible die in his own machine such as the company used on the one-cent piece. Mr. Reith also distinctly stated that coining

---

[446] *US Mint*, NARA-CP, op. cit., file 305310. Letter dated January 24, 1913 to Landis from Barber.
[447] *US Mint*, NARA-CP, op. cit., file 305310. Letter dated January 24, 1913 to Roberts from Landis. The two unnamed people were Reith and Henson.

should, as far as his machine was concerned, begin immediately under the *first set of dies* that had been prepared under my supervision."[448]

The next day, tests were conducted to determine what type of milling (i.e.: edge upsetting) would produce the best looking coins.[449]

> Today, in the presence of Messers. Clark, Buckley, Bird, Hewitt, Proud and myself 60 milled nickel blanks, in three lots of 20 each of different cutting and milling, were used in experimental strikes with a view of ascertaining the most suitable blank for the new design five cent nickel piece. After these experimental pieces had been completed the 60 pieces were destroyed in the presence of Mr. Clark and myself.

An additional 13 experimental pieces were struck on January 24 with Landis reporting that all had been destroyed in his presence.[450] The mint and Fraser seemed pleased with the results as the sculptor mentioned in a letter on January 26:[451]

> Dear Mr. Roberts:
> As you know, we found the dies which were both worked over with Mr. Reith the inventor and myself to be very little more aid than those which were done the first time.
> I don't know whether you understood that the first models were carefully worked over to fit the coin-detecting machine and in making the second dies, I tried to have them absolutely correct. But, as we have seen, the difference after the reduction was made was so slight that my two-weeks work went for nothing.
> The Hobbs people have offered to pay me for my time but I am not sure if that would be proper or the right ethics. You understand that the designs were finished six months ago, to our satisfaction and to the satisfaction of the Art Commission; so that all the work done since then has been at the instigation of the Hobbs Manufacturing Company. I could have done several medals in the time I have spent in changing the design to the one-thousandth-part of an inch, back and forth, innumerable times.
> I find the engraving which was necessary to make the two sides of the coin fit exactly, the reduction of the edge and the simplifying of the background under the Buffalo's head is beautifully done, showing no difference between the surface which I put on the models and the one they have made. I am delighted with their work at the Mint.
> I shall see that all the models are destroyed, except those which will most likely be wanted at the Mint in Philadelphia.
> Many thanks for your interest and perseverance in trying to preserve the artistic effect of my design and, at the same time, meet the requirements of the public at large.

With the coin project apparently at an end, Fraser sounded genuinely pleased with the results and offered praise for Barber's work and appreciation of Roberts' efforts. He was probably anxious to get back to other, much more profitable commissions awaiting his attention. Unfortunately, the project was not over. It would be nearly a month before production could begin and the culprit was again Clarence Hobbs. While the mint had been

---

[448] *US Mint*, NARA-CP, op. cit., file 305310. Letter dated February 8, 1913 to MacVeagh from Fraser, pp.7-8; emphasis added.
[449] *US Mint*, NARA-CP, op. cit., file 305310. Letter dated January 22, 1913 to Roberts from Landis.
[450] *US Mint*, NARA-CP, op. cit., file 305310. Letter dated January 24, 1913 to Roberts from Landis.
[451] *US Mint*, NARA-CP, op. cit., file 305310. Letter dated January 26, 1913 to Roberts from Fraser.

testing planchets with the new design, Hobbs was becoming increasingly agitated about the new nickel and his counterfeit detector.[452]

> Mr. Reith has just returned from Philadelphia where he went with Mr. Fraser, the artist, to examine the new dies for the five-cent coin which is being prepared. I am quite disturbed this morning at the report which he brings back that the changes which were promised by Mr. Fraser have not been made in the dies, and that one hundred sets of dies of a pattern which practically precludes us from using the coins in our machines, have been prepared ready for use.
>
> We were not aware that the matter had gone so far and can we now arrange with you to allow us to have one or two of these coins to make a careful survey of them, so as to determine just whether or not our business is ruined, or whether we can adopt [sic] our machines to the new coin as it is being made?
>
> I feel sure that you would not knowingly have forwarded the matter at the so great disadvantage of this enterprise, had you been fully aware of all the circumstances.
>
> I trust that I may have word from you by return post that permission will be given the Director of the Mint to supply us with some of these coins for testing.
> Yours truly,
> American Stamp & Ticket Vending Mach. Co.
>   by: C. W. Hobbs, Treasurer

George Reith and Edward Henson were the two Hobbs Co. representatives at the mint on January 21, and it appears that neither raised any objection at the time. It was only after considering matters on the train ride back to Worcester and in his workshop, that Reith decided the coin had to be changed again. Director Roberts, the consummate gentleman, wrote back to Hobbs offering to do what he could to resolve the problem. He contacted Henson in Philadelphia and Fraser in New York to discuss what had occurred during experimental striking. He also authorized Landis to loan the Hobbs employees one of the experimental nickels for testing in their equipment.[453]

> Your esteemed favor of the 26th is received…. I find on further inquiry of Mr. Reith that he expressed to Mr. Fraser and to the Engraver the opinion that he possibly could use the new coin in the form in which it has been put through the efforts of the Engraver to make it mechanically symmetrical.
>
> But we shall have to change our entire mechanism over in order to handle the new coin, whereas, had the changes been made as suggested to Mr. Fraser, this would not have been necessary….
>
> I am advised by our Philadelphia associate, Mr. Edward F. Henson, that he has received authorization from you to have one of the new nickels sent to us. We are expecting to receive this, perhaps tomorrow, and we shall then be in a better position to determine just where we stand in relation to this matter. I sincerely trust that the easy optimism of our Mr. Reith was in this instance well placed, and that my anxiety as to the event will prove to have been unfounded.

Roberts also sent a copy of the letter to Fraser and the artist returned a somewhat irritated reply the next day:[454]

> My dear Mr. Roberts,
> I really can't understand Mr. Hobbs letter. In the first place I worked on the models until Mr. Reith the inventor said they were perfect.

---

[452] *US Mint*, NARA-CP, op. cit., file 305310. Letter dated January 23, 1913 to Roberts from Hobbs (received January 25).
[453] *US Mint*, NARA-CP, op. cit., file 305310. Letter dated January 28, 1913 to Roberts from Hobbs.
[454] *US Mint*, NARA-CP, op. cit., file 305310. Letter dated January 29, 1913 to Roberts from Fraser.

Then we had the die cut and afterwards in Philadelphia we found one little point outside what it should be, and as he found that was the only trouble in the first die, it made no difference, which one was used.

Mr. Reith distinctly said to Mr. Barber, Mr. Henson (his own partner), and myself that it would make no difference, that it was alright to go ahead with the coining, and that he could arrange his dies to suit the coins and could do so without any doubt. Mr. Henson said "Are you sure" and he said "I am sure." He said he would make a flexible die like the one he made to fit the one cent piece. I asked him how that worked and he said it worked perfectly.

What I was expected to do was to make a large model so perfect that when it was reduced five times it would open a combination lock on being run through it. That is rather a difficult task and I only let it go when Mr. Reith was satisfied after measuring it day after day. I really could do no more.

As I have told you in a previous letter I feel that the work done at the Mint – the engraving, truing up the edge, smoothing the background where I suggested, is perfect. It couldn't have been done better. I have showed the trial nickel you gave me to Mr. French, Adams, and a number of other artists. They all tell me that this is our best coin.

Will you please tell Secretary MacVeagh that I am satisfied with the coin as it was struck from the present die.

Sincerely yours,
J. E. Fraser

As requested by the director, Barber provided his recollection of events on January 21. His detailed account supported Fraser's statements and helped lead to rejection of further assistance to the Hobbs Company.[455]

My recollection of the conference held on the 21st instant with Mr. Fraser and Mr. Reith, also Mr. Henson, in regard to the new Five Cent coin is perfectly clear.

Mr. Reith came to my office first and explained what was required to make the coin acceptable to the Vending Company. Mr. Henson, also a representative of the Company, came next and Mr. Fraser last. The subject was fully discussed in all its bearings. Mr. Fraser was more than satisfied with the hubs as made by me, and disapproved of the new reductions from his altered model. As Mr. Reith could not judge from the hubs whether a coin made from the dies would be satisfactory to him and suitable to his device, I proposed that a coin should be struck in the presence of these three gentlemen. This suggestion was gladly accepted. The regular blanks were procured and the first pair of finished dies that my hand rested upon in the die drawer was taken. We then proceeded to the medal room, and, in the presence of the three gentlemen mentioned, Mr. Hart, foreman of the medal room, struck the coins as I suggested – that is, one piece would be struck and then measurements would be made by Mr. Reith; then another piece would be struck and the same process would be gone through; this was done until nine pieces had been struck and measured by Mr. Reith. I proceeded in this manner, to give Mr. Reith full opportunity to see what difference there was likely to occur in different pieces arising from different degrees of malleability. I found Mr. Reith had provided himself with a micrometer gauge with adjustable points, making a most delicate instrument, as it allowed him to measure the smallest points of a coin. He was given every opportunity to satisfy himself that the coins were all that he needed or desired for the device he was making. He was given his own time, not hurried, or in-

---

[455] *US Mint*, NARA-CP, op. cit., file 305310. Memorandum dated January 29, 1913 to Landis from Barber. The number of working dies that had been made is unclear. Barber implies there were several pair in the die drawer, yet the new hubs by Medallic Art had arrived only that morning. Barber had also taken time to "true up" the hubs so they were exactly circular. Later comments suggest that Barber had made the hubs, but that is not possible since he didn't have the models.

fluenced in the least. After deliberating and measuring in every way he desired, he expressed himself as entirely satisfied.

Mr. Henson, who I understand is the capitalist, asked Mr. Reith in the presence of several of us who were standing around, if he, Reith, was fully assured that the piece was all that he required, and he answered Mr. Henson by telling him he was.

Having all parties so fully satisfied the conference broke up in the full belief that there was nothing more to be desired.

The parties present when the pieces were struck consisted of the Superintendent, Chief Clerk, Mr. Hart, the foreman of the medal room, and the three gentlemen who came to have the conference. [Barber was, of course, also present – RWB]

There was no suggestion that any change was advantageous or desirable. I must think there is some confusion of dates and that the letter to the Director was written before the conference, as every test made by Mr. Reith while here only appeared to confirm and strengthen his opinion that the coin was suitable for his device. He assured Mr. Henson that it was only a matter of a few days when he would be ready, as he would make some slight change. As Mr. Reith has not had in his possession one of the new coins, he could not have made any other tests, therefore it appears impossible that he should reverse his opinion of the 21st instant on the 23rd. Unless there is some mistake, Mr. Hobbs' letter is incomprehensible.

I have just finished a conversation over the phone with Mr. Henson, before mentioned, and he confirms my statement that Mr. Reith expressed himself as satisfied that the coin was all that he found necessary for his device, but qualifies this by saying that Mr. Reith is sometimes "over sanguine." Mr. Henson also says that he has had a conversation over long distance 'phone with Mr. Hobbs and that he, Hobbs, was very much disappointed at not receiving the coin to make further tests and that he, Henson, is of the opinion that that caused Hobbs to write his letter of the 22nd instant, but that now the coin has been furnished, Henson would suggest that no further notice be taken until a report is furnished after further tests have been made where the devices are constructed.

Respectfully,
Chas. E. Barber, Engraver

Barber's letter confirms everything Fraser had said and adds corroboration from Hobbs' business partner, Edward Henson, based on a telephone conversation with him the same day. Barber's report also suggests that Henson was already beginning to hedge Reith's acceptance of the new coin by typifying the inventor as overly confident. On the 31st we find C. U. Carpenter further justifying Reith's change of opinion:[456]

…As a matter of fact we find that Mr. Reith was quite naturally influenced by the fact that such a large number of dies had already been made and, instead of pointing out clearly just what the situation demanded, agreed to adapt our device to the coin more readily that he was warranted in doing….

After receiving the sample coin, Hobbs wrote that they would have to make "…a very great change in the detector…" and asked for an extension of the February 10 deadline to return the coin.[457] By January 31 Hobbs had decided that contrary to the inventor's statements while in Philadelphia, the new design was not suitable for their equipment. Like

---

[456] *US Mint*, NARA-CP, op. cit., file 305310. Letter dated January 31, 1913 to Roberts from Carpenter.
[457] *US Mint*, NARA-CP, op. cit., file 305310. Letter dated January 29, 1913 to Roberts from Hobbs.

Henson and Carpenter, he began to disparage Reith and suggested the inventor was subject to undue influence.[458]

> ...There has been a most unfortunate misunderstanding about this coin matter. I understood from what you said to Mr. Fraser when in New York that he was to have charge of making the dies for the new coin, and Mr. Fraser told me that same thing later on. Consequently I spent the two months of intervening time very largely with him, very much to his annoyance, and in the face of several complaints on his part that he was wasting his time in the matter as his duties had been paid for, and what he was then doing was being done without charge. This, however, only came out in the last few days previous to going to Philadelphia. But at the end of our conferences he had agreed to produce the results in the new coin which we were asking for, viz., a depression of .007 of an inch immediately around the rim so as to give us a root depth.
>
> When we were summoned to go to Philadelphia, I supposed, and so instructed Mr. Reith, that he was to go down to check the changes which had been made, as was supposed, by Mr. Fraser. Therefore I did not think it would be necessary for me to go.
>
> When Mr. Reith with Mr. Henson arrived at the Mint, he was confronted with a new state of facts, viz., that the dies had been made, and that all of our work with Mr. Fraser had gone for naught, because the dies had been made without reference to the changes which he had agreed to make. *In the mechanical work at the Mint it was found that certain changes from Mr. Fraser's design had been made.*
>
> Mr. Reith is not an expert engineer but a common workman of rather more than average capacity and ingenuity. He thinks slowly and has not the gift of expression, and he appears to have been rather surprised into making some statements which he now considers to have been premature, to the effect that he thought that the coin as designed and made by the dies could be successfully used. What he intended to say was that he thought he could devise a machine which would combine the points on the old die with some of the points on the new coin. He has been engaged upon this night and day since we received the new coin on Thursday morning. It will not be possible for him to reach a certain conclusion before Monday next, which will necessitate his working over Sunday.
>
> It is greatly to be regretted that the writer had not been informed that the matter of making the dies was not in the hands of Mr. Fraser but in the hands of the Engraver at the Mint. Arrangements could have been made that I work directly with the Engraver, and the necessary depth attained without in the least marring the design of the coin, or producing any difference in it that the eye would detect unless that attention was specially directed to it. The .007 of an inch depression around the rim could not have been seen by any person who was not looking for that particular thing, and then not with the naked eye, and only with very accurate instruments; but as this was not done, we are up against an exceedingly difficult proposition.
>
> We are using all due speed to get accurate data upon it. We recognize the fact that we are not the United States Government, and if it were only a question of our own interests in the matter we should not have troubled you at all. But this question of automatic sales is one which interests the general public to such a degree, as evidenced by our late trials in the station of the Hudson Terminal in New York, that it seems to me, and to others with whom I have conferred, to be quite worthy of you attention as it will reach on into the future as long as these 5¢ coins are used, and the security of the public is the great desideratum.
>
> I am therefore asking that you defer your order to proceed with the coinage until Monday afternoon or Tuesday morning [February 3 or 4 – RWB]. I will wire you just the earliest moment that we can come to a definite understanding of the situation.

---

[458] *US Mint*, NARA-CP, op. cit., file 305310. Letter dated January 31, 1913 to Roberts from Hobbs. Emphasis added.

> You will recall that we have been working on a blind lead for two months, and have only had accurate data to go from the past two days.
>
> Had we been informed by Mr. Fraser in New York when he showed us the sample coin [electrotypes shown Hobbs in November - RWB] that it was a matter that was up to the Engraver in Philadelphia, we would then have arrived at the end desired with trouble to no one, but he gave us distinctly to understand that the needed change in the coin would be made at his direction.
>
> This misunderstanding was most unfortunate all around, but because several persons were concerned in it I am venturing to make the request stated above, and will follow this letter by a telegram at the earliest possible moment as suggested.

The letter must have struck Roberts as accusatory and unappreciative of the efforts the mint and Fraser had been making to satisfy Hobbs' business interests. He accused the mint of making changes in Fraser's design then blamed the artist as well. According to Hobbs he had been mislead for two months by Fraser. He would have gone directly to the mint engraver is he had known that Barber would be making the dies. Further, Hobbs explains that his inventor is really "...not an expert engineer but a common workman...He thinks slowly and has not the gift of expression..." For Roberts, an additional question seemed to be Hobbs' claims of great public interest in the counterfeit detector. The revelation that the inventor of the "perfected" coin detector was not a skilled machinist, as Hobbs had intimated, must have reduced the confidence the director had in Hobbs Manufacturing Company.

By February 3 ASTUMCO had completed some of their tests with the sample buffalo nickel:[459]

> We have carried out tests upon the new coin today to the point where we can speak definitely in regard to the present situation.
>
> The thickest part, just inside the rim on the new coin, is at the head of the Buffalo. At this point the new coin is .006 thicker than the old coin in the same relative place. This extra thickness will prevent us from working close enough to be safe, by which is meant that the chance of slugs passing through and being accepted is increased by about 20%. The present percentage of uncertainty is only about ½ of 1%.
>
> There are two ways of meeting the difficulty.
>
> First, to sink the head of the Buffalo .006 of an inch. This could be done without in any way altering the design or making any change in it which would be visible to the observer, but the writer is not prepared to say just what affect [sic] this alteration might have upon your die, i.e., whether it would require to have the die re-engraved or whether the change could be made at that particular point.
>
> Second. The alternative way of meeting the difficulty would be to grind off from the face of the dies at the rim, .003 upon each side, which would give us the total adjustment of .006 which marks the difference between the old and the new coins. This would be the least trouble and would require no alteration in the engraved section of the die, and would result only in the slightly deeper embossing of the whole engraved portions upon each side. In other words, the rim on the coin would be .003 higher, as compared with the engraved portion than on the sample coin.
>
> The labor of making this change would be but a few minutes and when done the coinage could proceed at once, so far as this problem which we are considering is concerned.

---

[459] *US Mint*, NARA-CP, op. cit., file 305310. Letter (excerpt) dated February 3, 1913 to Roberts from Hobbs. The letter also reveals that Henson went to the mint with the same request on February 1, but Barber had refused. The difference amounts to the device missing five out of one thousand bad coins versus six out of one thousand using the Buffalo nickel.

> ...I urgently request that you authorize Mr. Barber to make this change as specified in Section 2, above.

Hobbs, Reith, Fraser and Roberts met at the Philadelphia Mint at 10:30 am on February 5 to see a new coin detector Reith had made. Fraser reported the new machine did not work to Hobbs' satisfaction with the new coin "...and thereupon asked me again to change the design according to their suggestions, always re-approaching the general mechanical effect of the old nickel."[460] The discussions on the 5th failed to resolve anything and Fraser, frustrated and feeling that his time was being wasted, wrote a long letter to secretary MacVeagh summarizing the Hobbs Manufacturing Co. situation since July, 1912.[461]

> ...I feel very confident that unless some immediate action be taken your iniation [sic – initiative] to improve the standard of our coinage...will be entirely lost.
>
> ...May I also submit for your consideration whether such as concession in this case by the Government would not set, by precedent, the preponderance in importance of the new coin detecting machines, <u>operated largely for private gain</u>, over the artistic value of the U.S. coinage, in which the whole public has an interest. In speaking to me the Hobbs Manufacturing Company have said that the "whole public" had an interest in their machine, and yet they speak almost entirely of the time <u>when</u> their machine is used <u>everywhere</u>, and I cannot but feel that this may be much further away than their hopes place it, and also that it is quite in order that other machines should come into the market "better," "as good," or "nearly as good," and then it would seem that the Government would either have to give a <u>practical monopoly</u> to, say, the Hobbs Manufacturing Company, or go change the coin [so] that it would be satisfactory to all the other *bone fide* and well constructed machines.
>
> Also if it becomes an established fact that practically only one kind of machine is in use for detecting coins, the color, feel, weight, etc. of which is in no way connected, would it not be worth considering whether such a machine, practically universal in use, would encourage the manufacture of counterfeit coinage with the sole purpose of passing it successfully in such a machine.

Fraser closed his ten-page opus by reminding MacVeagh that all the meetings, tests and time sitting on the train between New York and Washington, had taken away from productive time and that he had obligations to those who depended on him. Secretary MacVeagh forwarded the letter to director Roberts with a short note:[462]

> After you have considered this letter please let me know what you want. I hesitate to cause Fraser more trouble and loss of time.

Roberts determined that he needed to get everyone together and, with the secretary making the final decision, resolve matters.

> I think you should give an interview to Mr. Hobbs, who represents the Automatic Vending Machine Company, before you give you final order for coinage to proceed. I would have suggested such an interview before but I have always been confident that he and Fraser would reach an agreement there has always seemed to be so little between them. I am greatly disappointed by their failure to do so. I met them at the Mint last week and failing to achieve an agreement, sent them away with the understanding that Mr. Fraser would report to me today. I have now

---

[460] *US Mint*, NARA-CP, op. cit., file 305310. Letter dated February 8, 1913 to MacVeagh from Fraser, p.8.
[461] *US Mint*, NARA-CP, op. cit., file 305310. Letter dated February 8, 1913 to MacVeagh from Fraser, p.2, p.10.
[462] *US Mint*, NARA-CP, op. cit., file 305310. Manuscript note [ND] to Roberts from MacVeagh. Originally attached to the Fraser letter of February 8.

> requested both him and Mr. Hobbs to come here on Friday, next, for a final conference. I feel that you should meet and hear Mr. Hobbs and be fully informed before final action is taken. The importance of the automatic vending machine has grown upon me during the negotiations and I think the question of whether it shall be ignored or not should be decided now upon broad grounds of public policy without regard to the history of the negotiations with Mr. Fraser up to this time. That the latter has done his work cannot be questioned but we can better pay him and throw his work away than adopt it if to do so is contrary to sound public policy. I am not saying that this should be done but I am sure that the matter is important enough for you to hear both sides and make the decision yourself. Of course, the question is much larger than that of consideration for a private industry. It is that of dealing with a private utility.
>
> I am sorry not to have the conference before Friday but Mr. Fraser could not come tomorrow and I must be in attendance upon the Annual Assay Commission at Philadelphia on Wednesday and Thursday.
> Respectfully,

Roberts' natural caution and dependence on the accuracy of Hobbs' claims led him to shift the final decision to secretary MacVeagh, despite the absence of complaints from any of the dozens of other vending machine manufacturers. (The only items of interest to the companies that had contacted the treasury department were diameter, weight and thickness.)

Telegrams went out to Hobbs and Fraser, and a meeting was scheduled for Friday, February 14 in secretary MacVeagh's office. Hobbs stated he was bringing a lawyer with him and Fraser asked permission to do the same. Eames MacVeagh, who had been told of the Hobbs Company situation by his father, sent a wire:[463]

> Awfully sorry to learn of the opposition to the new nickel. Hope you will be able to put it through, no matter what compromises may be necessary as I feel anything would be better than the old one, and that the bending [sic – vending] machine may not be permanently effective against counterfeits.
> Eames MacVeagh
> 9:53am

Meanwhile, Edward Henson had been busy talking with business associates in Philadelphia. He managed to get the Rudolph Wurlitzer Co., and H. O. Wilbur & Sons, Inc. (chocolate candy manufacturers) to write letters of support to the treasury, but neither company would state they objected to the designs. Fraser contacted Daniel French and solicited letters of support from members of the Commission of Fine Arts. Notable among other letters was one from artist Kenyon Cox, who had just completed designs for the reverse of U.S. paper currency. Secretary MacVeagh had previously written to Cox: "Allow me to write…of the admiration for your design for the back of our notes…Your design is a completion of the delightful promise of your first sketch."[464]

Cox wrote on February 13:[465]

> Will you pardon the liberty I take in addressing you on what is no business of mine except as it is of interested to every citizen and, especially, to everyone interested in matters of art?

---

[463] *US Mint*, NARA-CP, op. cit., file 305310. Telegram dated February 10, 1913 to Franklin MacVeagh from Eames.
[464] *MacVeagh*, LoC. op. cit., box 16. Letter dated February 1, 1913 to Kenyon Cox from MacVeagh.
[465] *MacVeagh*, LoC. op. cit., box 16. Letter dated February 13, 1913 to MacVeagh from Cox.

Mr. Frazer [sic] has shown me this evening his designs for the new nickel and the alterations that have been attempted to fit it to the requirements of a machine for the protection of the nickel-in-the-slot men. The first thing that struck me was that the alterations were ruinous to his designs, and that it is hard on him to bring in this requirement after his design has been accepted and the dies made.

But there is a much larger question involved than that of the rights or wrongs of Mr. Fraser, or touching the fate of this particular design. The great question is whether the people of the United States have a right to a beautiful coinage or whether their right must forever be subordinated to those of the makers of a particular machine. I can understand and admit that the desire for beauty must give way to the convenience of all the handlers of coins – that is of the whole people. I can admit the milled edge and the low relief which will not interfere with stacking. But I understand that Mr. Fraser had met all these requirements and that it is now the naked question whether the government must, now and hereafter, make its coins to fit this machine or whether the machine must be made to fit the coins.

We have now perhaps the ugliest silver coinage in the world. A large part of its ugliness is in the very things which these makers of machines demand – the perfectly flat background with an open space all around, and the flat circle, a quarter of an inch in diameter, in the middle. The coins can, undoubtedly, be improved even with these features, but they can never be made really beautiful with them. Any design whatever would be largely spoiled by the insistence on these requirements.

If these requirements were necessary to prevent counterfeiting I could regretfully accept them, but I should not want to design the coins. I should feel, as I did about the fronts of the paper currency, that all any artist could do under such conditions would be to mitigate the necessary ugliness, and I should prefer to leave the job to someone else. But the requirements seem to be necessary only because certain people want to dispense with salesmen and certain other people want to avoid redesigning their machine. Are these interests sufficiently great to control the actions of the government and to forbid any real reform in our hideous coinage?

I have ventured to hope that we are on sufficiently friendly terms for me to speak frankly and as warmly as I feel; and I have been so delighted with your treatment of me and my design, that I want to bespeak consideration for other artists and for the artistic attitude in general. If I have been indiscreet pray pardon me, and believe me,

Yours very respectfully,
Kenyon Cox

At the Philadelphia Mint, Charles Barber hurriedly adapted the #1 model design by removing the lettering and date from a hub. He used this to impress a new pair of working dies that were slightly larger than normal in diameter. He then recut the legends and date, and retouched the figures by hand so the finished coin would resemble the version Hobbs was demanding. Four specimens were struck on February 13 and one was sent to MacVeagh the day of the final conference.

A Decision At Last

With secretary MacVeagh conducting the meeting much as if it were a legal hearing, a collection of lawyers, business people and artists presented their arguments for and against the new design. The letter of opinion issued by secretary MacVeagh on February 15 explains the meeting and its outcome to director Roberts:[466]

---

[466] *US Mint*, NARA-CP op. cit., file 305310. Letter dated February 15, 1913 to Roberts from MacVeagh.

The matters at issue with regard to the adjustment of the new nickel coin to the requirements of the ASTUMCO slot machine became clear after the hearings yesterday; at which, besides yourself, Mr. Barber of the Philadelphia Mint, Messrs. Hobbs and Carpenter of the Hobbs Manufacturing Company, and their attorneys Messrs. McKenney and Pritchard, Mr. Reith one of the inventors, Mr. Henson representing both inventors, Mr. Fraser, sculptor, and his attorney Mr. Hare, were present.

The conclusion I have arrived at is that it would not be judicious to make any further changes in the coin. The effort to make satisfactory changes has been continuous for more than two months; and it is evident to me that Mr. Fraser, to meet the requirements of the ASTUMCO people, has done everything he could do without sacrificing the essentials of his design. On the other hand, the requirements specified by the ASTUMCO representatives, to wit, a clear space between the rim and the rest of the design and a radical change in the cheek of the Indian are, in my judgment, impossible to concede without the practical abandonment of the artistic qualities of the design. This is not simply my opinion, but is the opinion of the sculptor, who has shown himself a man of great personal tolerance, and of various high authorities who have written me within a day or two.

But even these concessions the representatives of the slot machine were not able to assure us would be sufficient. They said frankly that the solution would still depend upon trials and tests after these changes had been made.

At the same time it was a fact that changes in the machine – in an effort to accommodate it to the new coin – had already been made; and I was impressed with the fact that the inventors were not at all at the end of their possibilities – so that a solution may be found in further changes in the machine rather than in the further changes in the coin.

Other slot machines would probably not be effected [sic] by a new coin as the ASTUMCO would be; and this would seem to be the reason why no other has been heard from. It was stated in the conference that seventy machines had been entered in competition at the Post Office Department, indicating a far larger number of slot machines than I had supposed existed. None, however, as I have said, of these machines has entered any objections to the new coin. The ASTUMCO machine alone makes any suggestions. And in this connection it is necessary to call attention to the fact that the ASTUMCO nickel slot machine is a new one, not yet much introduced – scarcely at all introduced. It still has its way to make; and it is still a question whether it will acquire a wide field. At least one of the large users has decided that this machine is, as yet, not at such a stage of perfection nor at such a price as would justify their using it. Altogether, therefore, the commercial interests involved in this case are not relatively important. They are but a very small fraction of the slot machine interests.

I am definitely impressed by the fact that the design as it now has become, under Mr. Fraser's efforts to adjust it, should stand.

It is fortunate that the commercial interests involved are relatively slight; for one must always be impressed in such as case by the claims of business. It is of course true that only the most serious business considerations should stand in the way of the improvement of the coinage; and this particular coin has great claims of its own because of its special quality. If we should stop new coinage – which is always allowed every twenty-five years – for any commercial obstacles less than imperative, we should have to abandon a worthy coinage altogether. This would be a most serious handicap to the art of the Nation; for scarcely any form of art is more influential than an artistic coin, where the coin is widely circulated.

You will please, therefore, proceed with the coinage of the new nickel.
Very sincerely yours,
Franklin MacVeagh

Before the hearing Roberts had spoken to the New York Telephone Company and been told they had examined Hobbs' device and "...had no interest in adopting it."[467] MacVeagh had also contacted the railway company and learned they were removing the test machines because of persistent failure. In corroboration of this, Fraser's attorney, Meredith Hare, wrote to MacVeagh on February 19 informing the secretary that the Hudson & Manhattan Railway Company, where Hobbs claimed the coin detector was enthusiastically received, had actually told Hobbs the machine was entirely unsatisfactory and ordered them removed. In an interesting twist of events, one of Hobbs' lawyers, Frederick D. McKenney, was a partner in the Washington law offices of Isaac Wayne MacVeagh – older brother of the secretary of the treasury.[468]

The Philadelphia Mint began production on February 18. By the next day, superintendent Landis reported they had minted $25,000 in buffalo nickels (500,000 coins) and would be putting twenty presses on the work by the 20th.[469] It appears they used the version tested on January 21. While production ramped up, director Roberts wrote to Hobbs and Henson informing them of the secretary's decision. Henson shot back an unpleasant letter stating in part:[470]

> ...Unfortunately, the Secretary would need to be a mechanical expert to enable him to understand....
> ...I know the Secretary thinks the design of the new coin is beautiful, but I failed to find among my friends, to a few of whom I have shown the coin, any that are of the Secretary's opinion. So far as the artist is concerned he is a faddist in his views. It seems to me such a pity that so much should be sacrificed that a coin of such doubtful artistic value should be issued.

Clarence Hobbs' office typewriter was active, too. His displeasure went directly to President Taft, who, with only two weeks remaining in his term had no interest in the matter, and sent the seven page protest to secretary MacVeagh. The letter is too long and repetitive to reprint here in its entirety, but it largely rehashed Hobbs' earlier objections to a new design. Most of his claims had been disproved during the hearing with MacVeagh, but the resourceful business owner came up with a couple of new variations:[471]

> 4 (a) It is not susceptible of mint finish, so called, but has a dull appearance similar to lead and for that reason may be more easily counterfeited.
> 4 (b) The roughened surface makes it particularly favorable for carrying dirt and disease germs from hand to hand.[472]
> 4 (c) The various inscriptions required by law are rendered so subordinate to the artistic design as to be in many cases almost illegible.
> 4 (d) ...the token of value will be worn away [after limited circulation] and the coin will cease to be a legal tender.

In the midst of his discourse, Hobbs made several useful points (discussed below). However, his letter, combined with a separate attack on the Buffalo nickel (titled *The Pro-*

---

[467] *US Mint*, NARA-CP, op. cit., file 305310. Memorandum dated March 18, 1913 to McAdoo from Roberts, p.3.
[468] *MacVeagh*; LoC. op. cit., box16. Letter dated February 21, 1913 to Franklin MacVeagh from Frederick D. McKenney. The lawyer suggests if the secretary had been involved earlier, a "practical" solution might have been possible. Isaac Wayne MacVeagh had been Attorney General during President Garfield's brief tenure, later ambassador to Italy, and held other special positions in Republican and Democratic administrations.
[469] *US Mint*, NARA-CP, op. cit., file 311716. Letter dated February 19, 1913 to Roberts from Norris.
[470] *US Mint*, NARA-CP, op. cit., file 308449 Letter dated February 19, 1913 to Roberts from Henson.
[471] *US Mint*, NARA-CP, op. cit., file 305310. Letter dated February 19, 1913 to Taft from Hobbs, p.3 (mint copy).
[472] This claim is similar to Henry Chapman's 1908 gripe about Bela Pratt's Indian head design half- and quarter-eagles.

posed Five Cent Coin. Reasons Why Same Should not be Adopted in its Present Condition) also sent to the President, generated only official silence.

Secretary MacVeagh sent a note to director Roberts commenting on Hobbs' correspondence:[473]

> Dear Mr. Roberts:
> I found at the White House the other day the enclosed letters from Clarence W. Hobbs to the President, enclosing an argument against the new nickel. I borrowed these papers in order that you might see how they (the Hobbs people) dealt with us after all the time and expense devoted to them on the assumption that they were really a growing concern.
> Please return these papers at your convenience.

MacVeagh also offered a private comment to Taft's secretary, Charles D. Hilles:[474]

> My dear Mr. Hilles:
> I have your letter of February 26, enclosing one from Clarence W. Hobbs. I had previously taken from the President a copy of the letter and also a copy of Hobbs' attack on the new nickel. I sent these to Mr. Roberts to encourage him in treating the next man who comes along with the same extraordinary patience and courtesy with which both he, Mr. Fraser, the sculptor, and I treated Hobbs. Hobbs caused us a delay of nearly three months in the issuing of this coin, and I finally had to decide the case against him for the reason that his demands could not be met. This was done a week or two ago in my office, where we had a full hearing. In return for this, Hobbs sends these delectable communications to the President.
> Every once in a while a public official is inclined to think, from his untoward experiences, that the only way to get the gratitude of the individuals who claim his time is to treat them with marked rudeness and discourtesy. Certainly Hobbs got all the time and attention out of this administration that any administration could afford to give to one manufacturing corporation.

The Buffalo nickel was now officially in production, and Hobbs Manufacturing Company would have to modify their devices if they wanted to compete for Post Office and private contracts.[475]

But Clarence Hobbs was not finished with his complaints. Each time a coinage bill passed one of the houses of Congress, Hobbs or his agent wrote to the mint. His letters usually began with a simple inquiry about availability of the new coins – just as would be expected from any coin collector. This was followed by complaints of the potential harm such a new coin would do to his coin detector business.[476]

Philadelphia Mint superintendent Landis was anxious to return to the accepted practice of annual destruction of old dies, and wrote to Roberts for permission to have the last of the Liberty five-cent coin dies destroyed:[477]

---

[473] *MacVeagh papers*, LoC. op. cit., box 7, lettercopy book, p.176. Letter dated February 27, 1913 to Roberts from MacVeagh.

[474] *US Mint*, NARA-CP, op. cit., file 305310. Letter dated February 28, 1913 to Hilles from MacVeagh. (Original in LoC *Taft papers*.)

[475] The degree of misrepresentation, deception and self-interest exhibited by Clarence Hobbs, Sr. is, to this writer, astounding for anyone engaged in respectable business. Only three years later, in August 1916, Hobbs was back at the mint. This time objecting to the new Winged Liberty dime by A. A. Weinman. His complaints were partially responsible for the abandonment of the first production design and a general perversion of the artist's work.

[476] *US Mint*, NARA-CP, op. cit., entry 235, vol. 411. Letter dated January 13, 1915 to Roberts from Hobbs (as *American Sales Machine Co.*).Acting director Dewey reassured Hobbs' agent, Mr. Fishback, that the mint would be sure to "…safeguard your interests."

[477] *US Mint*, NARA-CP, op. cit., entry 229, box 299. Letter dated February 24, 1913 to Roberts from Landis.

> Now that the new design five-cent nickel piece has been approved, would it not be well to destroy the dies and hubs of the 1912 design. The Engraver has on hand a lot of working dies made for this mint and those sent to San Francisco and returned. He also has in possession the pattern dies made in 1909 and 1910 for the five-cent piece with bust of Washington.
>
> If it is your opinion that these dies and hubs should be destroyed, I would thank you for authority to have this done.

Fraser and Roberts disagreed about payment for the extra work in dealing with the Hobbs complaints. On March 3, the last full day of the Taft administration, the mint finally agreed to pay the $2,500 commission, plus $666.15 for additional time and expenses from December 18, 1912 to February 14, 1913. The primary work of designing and issuing the new Buffalo nickel was now complete; however, more changes would be made within the next few months.

Chapter 9 – Most American of Coins

A Tiny Memorial

Fraser's nickel was a participant in more public ceremony than any of the other new designs issued from 1907 to 1921. The ceremony, however, was less about the nickel than about the design and its relationship to a public memorial proposed by department store magnate Rodman Wanamaker.[478]

The Buffalo nickel made its public debut during groundbreaking ceremonies for the National American Indian Memorial at Fort Wadsworth, on Staten Island, New York. There are no tours of this memorial and few have heard of it. On this spot once reserved for a grand memorial to Native Americans, there now stands the northern abutment of the Verrazano-Narrows bridge. The privately-funded project had been recognized by Congress in 1909, and groundbreaking took place on February 22, 1913, George Washington's birthday. The ceremony was described by historian Alan Trachtenberg in his article "Wanamaker Indians":[479]

> The national media, President Taft (in one of his last acts as President), his cabinet, various dignitaries, and thirty-three Western Native leaders, including Red Cloud (the son of the Ogalalla Lakota chief), White Man Runs Him (Crow), and Two Moons (Cheyenne, and one of Fraser's models for the nickel) among others. In a letter to the Office of Indian Affairs, Doctor Joseph Dixon, one of the monument's promoters, said "I cannot impress upon you the importance of having all the Indians invited bring...their entire paraphernalia. I want them to dress as though they were at a ceremonial or War Dance." It was important that the invited leaders conform to a very specific image of a natural and romantic Indian figure which, like Daniel Chester French's sculpture for the memorial, did not actually exist.[480]

---

[478] This is the same Wanamaker who funded the American art prize won by Fraser in 1898.
[479] Alan Trachtenberg, *Wanamaker Indians*; The Yale Review. April, 1998. pp.1-24 , excerpt.
[480] French was Chairman of the Commission of Fine Arts at this time.

After speeches by Dixon and Rodman Wanamaker, department store owner and backer of the project, President Taft addressed the crowd, proclaiming "...the erection of that monument will usher in the day which Thomas Jefferson said he would rejoice to see, when the Red Men truly become one people with us, enjoying all the rights and privileges as we do, and living in peace and harmony....[The Memorial] tells the story of the march of an empire and the progress of Christian civilization to the uttermost limits."[481]

With this, the President took a golden shovel and broke the earth. He was followed by Hollow Horn Bear (Yankton Sioux) who briefly addressed the crowd, and then joined the President in digging the ground with the thigh bone of a buffalo. Mountain Chief (Blackfeet) then lead the assembled Native group in a tribal "War Song." The United States flag was then raised to "The Indian's Requiem," a piece of "original Indian music" composed by Dr. Irving J. Morgan for use during lectures given by Dixon.

When the flag was fully raised, Morgan's song faded into a military rendition of the "Star Spangled Banner," which signified "the union of the first dwellers on the soil with the civilization of our day." Doctor George Frederick Kunz, President of the American Scenic and Historical Preservation Society, then presented a bronze plaque marking the site.[482] The President gave each of the chiefs a copy of James E. Fraser's new "Buffalo nickel," after which the crowd recessed to "Hail, Columbia!"[483] The groundbreaking ceremony was both a monument to the progress of Euro-American civilization, the empire which built the Wanamaker business, but also a somewhat hollow attempt to rectify the injustice of Native peoples. Perhaps the most significant event that day was the introduction and signing of the *Declaration of Allegiance*. The Declaration had been drafted by the several dozen tribal leaders in a hotel shortly before the ceremony, and dictated to Indian Commissioner Abbott. It fulfilled, if only in writing, one of Wanamaker and Dixon's chief goals, that "the sole desire has been to strengthen in the hearts of Red Men the feeling of allegiance and loyalty and friendship..." The Declaration read:

> *We, the representatives of the various Indian tribes, through our presence and the part we take in the dedication of this memorial do renew our allegiance to the glorious flag of the United States and of our hearts to our country's service. Through a conquered race, with our right hands extended in brotherly love and our left hands holding the peace pipe, we hereby bury all past ill feeling and proclaim abroad, to all the nations of the world, declare that henceforth and forever in all walks of life and every field of endeavor we shall be brothers, striving hand in hand...*

The Declaration, like the Memorial, was far more symbolic than it was real; there was never a promise of citizenship in the document, only an expressed hope. American Indians were handed, at the groundbreaking, their own eulogy and had their own requiem written for them. It may have made the most sense, for the tribal leaders in attendance, to nod their heads and tell the White audience what they so desired to hear. Red Cloud, speaking of his father, Red Cloud, who "has been a great fighter against the Indians, and against the white man, but he learned years ago to stop fighting..." and perhaps a peaceful if not invisible identity was the only means to maintain any sense of Native identity.

---

[481] *New York Times*, "Indians See Taft Handle the Spade," February 23, 1913, p.15.
[482] Here, George Kunz wears yet another of his many hats. Several of his letters to the mint are on this organization's stationery.
[483] *US Mint*, NARA-CP, op. cit. Letter dated February 19, 1913 to Roberts from Norris. Director Roberts received 40 of the new coins on February 20, 1913 and delivered them to the White House. Thirty-three were given to the chiefs and the balance to others in attendance. This is the legal release date of the coin although the first lot of 800,000 was sent to the Treasury on February 21. They were not released to banks until three days later. This seems like a paltry gift considering the large, ornate silver and bronze "peace" medals once given to tribal leaders.

The monument was never built – Dixon raised only $143 in donations – and after a generation, no one could locate the bronze plaque or recall why the monument was never built. The site was later appropriated for bridge abutments honoring an Italian explorer.[484]

With an impressive ceremony completed, the Indians must have thought the nickels were a special token made for the event and might have thought of the memorial with promise. But like most of the Great White Father's earlier promises to respect the Indians' customs and land, what the chiefs carried in their hands was all anyone had for them. Shorn of dignity and fundamental faith by paternalistic bureaucrats and dishonest Indian Agents, the new nickels bore no new promise to a disenfranchised people. Fraser, Frederic Sackrider Remington, Charles Marion Russell, Hermon MacNeil, A. Phimister Proctor and a herd of lesser craftsmen saw the Indian as a defeated anachronism, as close to extinction as the great plains bison. Something to be memorialized but not understood; honored only on terms of defeat.

George Kunz wrote to director Roberts thanking him for having the new nickels sent for the ceremony:[485]

> …The nickel 5¢ pieces were one of the features of the Indian Memorial, and no one more than the President, myself, and our Indian guests, could feel greater appreciation, nor express more marked approval of these novel and beautiful products of the Mint, than were felt and expressed when the bag of coins was opened and the pieces distributed.
> I wonder if it is possible to have either 100 or 200 more of them? The Art people are so much pleased with them that they want more. Two of the coins went to the new Art Exhibition, and two were placed on exhibition in the American Numismatic Society. I expect to be in Washington on Monday and Tuesday, and will try to visit you on Monday.

Out of 40 new nickels in the little velvet bag,[486] thirty-three went to the Indian chiefs present, two to an exhibition at the Metropolitan Museum of Art, and two to the American Numismatic Society. One coin was sent to Fraser by Kunz, who replied: "I want to thank you very much for sending me the new nickel. The event of the Indian Monument must have been very interesting indeed and it was very thoughtful of you to choose such an appropriate occasion to bring the coin before the public for the first time…."[487] The remaining two coins likely ended up in the pockets of President Taft and Rodman Wanamaker.

Public Commentary

Letters from banks inquiring about availability of the new coins and telephone and vending machine companies nervous about the prospects of a new coin, arrived at the mint in late February. The consistent reply of Roberts and MacVeagh was that the coins were of the same diameter, weight and thickness as the old design. This seemed to satisfy everyone

---

[484] The Verrazano Narrows bridge.
[485] *US Mint*, NARA-CP, op. cit., file 308449. Letter dated February 26, 1913 to Roberts from Kunz.
[486] Persistent myth is that there was a full bag of nickels - $100 or 2,000 coins – at the ceremony. However, when multiple sources are considered, it is obvious that the "bag of coins" Kunz mentions contained only the 40 pieces, $2.00, Roberts had supplied to the White House.
[487] *George F. Kunz papers*, American Museum of Natural History, Library Services Department, New York, NY. "Coinage" file. Letter (ND probably February 27, 1913) to Kunz from Fraser.

except Hobbs Manufacturing Company officials who believed the U.S. mint should change its coins to match their counterfeit detection mechanism.

As with every newly introduced coin design there were those who objected to the Buffalo nickel. An editorial in the *New York Times* of March 2, 1913 expressed the newspaper's opinion,[488]

> **The New Nickel**
>
> The new "nickel" is a striking example of what a coin intended for wide circulation as small change should not be. It bears on one side the too deeply stamped counterfeit presentment of a bison, on the other the head of an uncommonly unprepossessing Indian, and as art neither side is remarkable. The overcrowding of the small circles by large designs is a grave defect. The lettering is so small that it can only be deciphered by strong eyes in a bright light. The aim of the designer seems to have been to make an odd-looking thing, as unlike other coins as possible. It may be true that some of the first of these coins issued from the Sub-Treasury yesterday were sold in the streets for 10 or 15 cents each, but there will be no great eagerness to get them hereafter in preference to the old five-cent coins. The most conspicuous thing on a coin should be the mark of its value. The big V on the old nickel with the word "cents" plainly stamped below it exactly served the purpose. Strangers will often be at a loss to determine the value of the new coin. It may be said that we do not make coins with a view to service foreigners, but it is difficult to comprehend the idea that prevails in the Mint.
>
> The latest atrocities in coinage, until the new nickel appeared, were $20, $10, and $5 gold pieces. These are bad coins, in design and execution. Of course they have escaped much of the popular derision the new nickels will arouse, because there are not many gold pieces in circulation. The car-fare coin is always in use. It is to be hoped that the old nickels will be kept in circulation, and not crowded out by this new thing with deeply indented surfaces, which is not pleasing to look at while new and shiny, and will be an abomination when it is old and dull.

The *Times'* comments prompted coin collector Gardner Teall to send a letter in defense of the new nickel to the editor on March 3,[489]

> The Times editorial article on "The New Nickel" invites a defense of this coin. Contemporary record shows that nearly every new coin design produced by the United States Mint has evoked immediate and widespread criticism upon its appearance. The Lincoln penny still remains a cause for dispute of the first magnitude. However, the new nickel deserves to have a better fate than even sincere adverse opinion would have it meet. To suppose that the obvious in coinage has anything to do with the art displayed in this design is to start forth hand-in-hand with ignorance. Any change whatever from one prevailing before a new issue supersedes an old one, invariably finds many who are unprepared to accept it by reason of a public tendency to distrust departures from standards that appear to be established. The Times' article assumes the design of the new nickel to be "uncommonly unprepossessing." Immediately it strikes the writer that however unusual the portrait may seem to those used to the meaningless Indian head of past issues, the head appearing upon the new nickel is, as a matter of fact, nobly conceived, finely executed, and fraught with a dignity that is an accompaniment to true portraiture of the real Indian.

---

[488] *The New York Times*, "The New Nickel", March 2, 1913, p.C6.
[489] Gardner Teall, *The New York Times*, "The New Five-Cent Piece", March 5, 1913, p.16.

> In the placing of a true portrait of a real Indian upon a United States coin we have, at last, commemorated in a fitting way the noble Redman. Quite unlike the eager-visaged super in borrowed chieftain headdress (the type of the old one-cent piece) is this Indian of the new nickel, and though we may miss the insipid, fleshy female with wheat tucked in her chignon, who loaned some countenance to the old nickel, it will be a sentimental missing: one good for the soul. As to the buffalo on the reverse of the new nickel, we are right in commemorating him, for in many ways he stands as an equally noble symbol in our history's progress. It seems to me that the filling of spaces by the designer of the new nickel should not be considered in the light of crowding.
>
> The design is the most hopeful and satisfactory in coinage we have had. The coins of the ancient Greeks (such as the decadrachm of the Euainetus circa 410 B.C. – the art of the Ancient Greek coin designers never having been surpassed) should be studied by moderns for better understanding of what would constitute beautiful designing in the coins of today. A study of such Greek coins would also enable one to understand that the underlying principles of the Greek designs are practicable foundations for our own. The new nickel is a happy modification, technically, of the Greek die-cutter's way of working, a far happier one than appears in the designs of some of our current gold coins.
>
> The new nickel has been put to a wearing test (artificially but serviceably) which shows that the coin, even when worn down considerably by circulation, will still remain a very beautiful one, which fact should remove the criticism of pessimistic anticipation. The reverse of the old V type of nickel possesses virtues greatly over-estimated. We do not stop to turn one of these old nickels on its Liberty-headed face to examine the reverse inscription before accepting or tendering a five-cent piece. It is just as much a nickel...whether inscribed by small or large letters. Strangers will always be more or less at a loss to determine the value of any coins until they become used to them – the experience of foreign travel make this clear – but when strangers do get used to new coin types they pat little attention to inscriptions thereon. Types are what counts most in recognizing the various denominations and the "Buffalo and Indian-head" type of coin will surely be as easily recognized as the Liberty-head and V type of nickel.

The peripatetic Dr. George Kunz wrote to new treasury secretary William G. McAdoo on March 11 to counteract the negative remarks about Fraser's nickel:[490]

> Pardon my troubling you, a very busy man. However, as there have been many criticisms of the new five-cent piece on the part of those not competent, or not in a position to judge of its merits, I should be pleased to call your attention to certain circumstances in connection with the choosing of the design which I do not think have been very well understood.
>
> As one who can claim membership in the American Numismatic Society for twenty years, I am acquainted with the leading numismatists of the country and I have always had a strong interest in the fine Greek coinage. I have shown this coin to many of the leading artists of the city, and wish to express my opinion of it as one of the finest examples of art coinage that has ever come from the Philadelphia mint.
>
> The Indian head is very fine, distinctive, and true to type. It met with the approval of all the Indian chiefs that were present at the dedication ceremonies at Fort Wadsworth, Staten Island, at which I had the honor of handing them the first of the new coins. A specimen was [later] given to each of fifty or more of our leading artists and sculptors and every one of them was pleased with this typically American design of Indian and buffalo, our two greatest national emblems.

---

[490] *US Mint*, NARA-CP, op. cit., entry 229, box 299. Letter dated March 11, 1913 to McAdoo from Kunz.

> Both designs were modeled by James Earle Frazer [sic], and the late Augustus Saint-Gaudens told me personally that he considered him the greatest living sculptor. He has executed a portrait of Mr. Thomas A. Edison and one of the late E. H. Harriman, as well as many other prominent persons. He has enough work ahead to keep busy for the next six years.
>
> The coin stacks perfectly and is much more easily held in the hand than the old, flat-surfaced one. It very much resembles the ancient Greek coins in that the denomination of the coin is inconspicuous, a feature that has been unjustifiably criticized. This is an unnecessary feature, as nearly everybody will soon learn it. Few foreign coins give a denomination, even English coins being wanting in this respect.
>
> The new nickel was conceived mainly through the instrumentality of the director of the Mint, Mr. George E. Roberts, whom I have known for many years and who has been most conscientious in his work in regard to coinage.

Time has shown Fraser's design to be one of the most popular and enduring of any to appear on America's coins. It has been copied, imitated, used and reused to the point of triteness, yet a glance at one of the original nickels reveals the perfect balance of imagery and format created by one of the nation's best sculptors of the last century.

A Unity of Theme

Pairing of the American Bison and a Native American on the five-cent coin was, in Fraser's words, a "…perfect unity of theme. It has a pertinent historical significance, and is in line with the best tradition of coin design, where the purpose was to memorialize a nation or people."[491] Yet, it is unclear what meaning this theme held in Fraser's deeper thoughts or in the minds of contemporaries. Was it simply that Native Americans of the plains tribes and the bison had long coexisted, thus becoming dependent expressions of the American west? Or was it that both were shot, trapped, corralled and placed in captivity, hauled about for the amusement and entertainment of "civilized" city folk, and it was time to memorialize them before they vanished?

The juxtaposition of bison and Native American was not new in 1913. It was by then a cliché supported by popular song, invented western tails and renewed by dramatic cinematic adventures. Part of Fraser's genius was in placing the two in such intimate association that the connection could not be overlooked by anyone on the planet. Decades after production of the coin ceased, the buffalo nickel remained one of the most recognized icons of America. An illiterate resident of nearly any country can look at a worn, dateless specimen and immediately identify its origin.

---

[491] National Cowboy & Western Heritage Museum. Inscription accompanying the Buffalo nickel display.

Figure 42. Sculpted tableaux, **America,** *by John Bell (1811-1895) for the H. Doulton & Co., exhibit at the Philadelphia Centennial Exposition of 1876. It depicts the goddess America (top, center) wearing an Indian headdress and riding on a bison. She presides over a Native American and bison as two female figures (one hidden in this view) direct the onward course of America.* (Courtesy Library of Congress.)

Both tribal chief ($5 silver certificate of 1896 designed by G. F. C. Smillie) and bison ($10 United States note series 1901 designed by Charles R. Knight) had already graced circulating paper currency, although not on the same piece of money. The Native American is identified as Chief Ta-to-ka-in-yan-ka ("Running Antelope"), the bison is a composite of one from a group of stuffed specimens created by William T. Hornaday for the National Museum (now the Smithsonian Museum of Natural History) in 1889, and "Pablo" a bison in the National Zoological Park in Washington, DC.[492] Another original American had been portrayed in Bela Pratt's design for the 1908 half eagle and quarter eagle gold coins, although we have not the slightest hint of the model's name or tribe, or if a live model was used.[493]

---

[492] The bison on the $10 note was drawn in 1899 by artist Charles R. Knight using "Pablo" as the live model. At about the same time, Hornaday indicates that he was present when the glass front of the display case was removed so that a photo could be taken of the stuffed animals for use by the Bureau of Engraving and Printing. (See letter dated November 1915 to Lehigh Valley Railroad from Hornaday in *Bridges*.)

[493] An article by Gerry Muhl in *The Numismatist* in 1991 claims that Pratt's model was "Chief Thundercloud." This was based on material from Adele DeRosa of the Rochester Museum and Science Center, which has a "Pratt" correspondence

Figure 43. **Group of American Bisons in the National Museum,** *collected and mounted by William T. Hornaday.* **Right, White Shield,** *Chief of the Arikara photographed in 1908 by Edward F. Curtis.* (Courtesy Smithsonian Institution Archives; Library of Congress.)

Near the beginning of the twenty-first century, the connection between Native American and buffalo is more nostalgic than real. Some American tribes prosper through modern slot machines – not the kind Clarence Hobbs made – emptying the pockets of gamblers much as white traders purloined the wealth of many tribes. Others, less fortunate or further from major population centers, live in state-perpetuated poverty and alcoholism.

The American bison seems, for now, at balance with limited grazing land in major parks and preserves in the United States and Canada. Tourists can see the huge plains creatures in something close to a natural setting and urban zoos at last recognize the disservice to all of confining large animals to small cages.

The nickels Fraser struggled so long to design were abandoned in 1938 to a round of patriotic adoration begun with the Lincoln cent. They remained in common circulation until the early 1960s when a wave of popular coin collecting soon swept all but the most badly worn specimens from everyday use. Although the few that survive in commerce are dateless tokens, almost any child can still identify the buffalo and Indian as symbols of the long vanished American west.

Models for the Nickel – Obverse

It seems that nearly every new coin design generates some sort of controversy about the model who posed for the artist. Often this occurs because of a natural interest in the subject by the general public – a form of naughty notoriety akin to movie celebrities – also the genuine interest of artists in not making their figures literal portraits of paid staff. In some instances, such as Saint-Gaudens' mistress-model Davida, or the African-American Eugenia "Hettie" Anderson who posed as Liberty for the eagle and double eagle

---

folder containing a photo and obituary of Thundercloud. However, the file originated in 1920, three years after the sculptor's death, and contained nothing from Pratt, his heirs or anyone else naming Thundercloud as the model. The present author believes the name of any model for Pratt's design remains unknown.

coins, personal situations convinced family members to "adjust" the facts to suit their sensibilities.[494]

Bela Pratt avoided the problem by evidently using several photographs as guidance for his Indian head gold half eagle portrait. Victor Brenner's subject was one of hundreds of Lincolns sculpted from photographs and a death mask, and was supposed to be a literal portrait of the subject, thus mitigating the problem entirely.

Before the new Buffalo five-cent coins left the mint, there had been inquiries about the model for the Indian portrait. By the time the coins hit the pockets of streetcar riders the treasury had a box full of press and private requests for information. On October 11, 1913 director Roberts asked Fraser for the identity of the obverse model. Fraser replied two days later:[495]

> My dear Mr. Roberts:
> I have your letter asking whether or not the Indian head on the new nickel was a portrait or a type. It is a type rather than a portrait. Before the nickel was made I had done several portraits of Indians among these Iron Tail, Two Moons and one or two others, and probably got characteristics from those men in the head on the coin, but my purpose was not to make a portrait but a type.
> Hoping this answers your question adequately.
> I remain
> With best regards

With two of the possible Indian models identified, this should have taken care of the issue, however the same question continued to pester the mint and artist almost to the sculptor's death in 1953. Except for questions about his early sculpture, *End of the Trail*, the buffalo nickel generated more inquiries and newspaper coverage that any other work of art created by Fraser. The number and frequency of public inquiries resulted in the mint preparing a printed form letter to be sent in response to public correspondents. After explaining a little about the coin's history and the design, the form letter addressed the model:[496]

> In reply to an inquiry to Mr. Fraser's office concerning the model for the five-cent piece, his Secretary wrote as follows: "In Mr. Fraser's absence I can tell you briefly that the Indian is an idealized portrait and no individual can claim to be the prototype, although several seem to be doing so..."

Of particular interest is a never before published photograph probably taken in 1910 of Fraser sculpting a life-size bust of an Indian. The model, who resembles the portrait on the nickel, is sitting outside on a folded blanket on top of a table. Fraser stands a few feet away adjusting details of the sculpture. Both model and bust are in profile and it is clear that Fraser has made changes to the portrait when compared to the live model.

---

[494] See Burdette, *Renaissance of American Coinage 1905-1908* for more information about the models who posed for Saint-Gaudens' coin designs.
[495] *US Mint*, NARA-CP, op. cit., file 305310. Letter dated October 13, 1913 to Roberts from Fraser.
[496] *US Mint*, NARA-P, op. cit., entry 17, box 2, book 2. A single mimeographed sheet dating from after December 30, 1963 found in the back of a box of otherwise unrelated material. The Fraser quotation must date before his death in 1953, but the remaining content is probably contemporary with mid-1960s due to an internal reference to the Kennedy half dollar.

Figure 44. Photograph taken circa late 1910 of Fraser (left) sculpting portrait bust of a Native American. The man posing for the portrait is believed to be Sinte Maza (Iron Tail) who Fraser originally credited as being one of the models for the portrait on the nickel. (Courtesy of Smithsonian Archives of American Art, microfilm reel 490, frame 1441.)

The model in this photo appears to be either Ishiheo Nishes (Two Moons),[497] who was featured in the *101 Wild West Show*, or more likely, Sinte Maza (Iron Tail).[498] Two Moons made a comfortable living from performing in wild west shows. Being publicly identified with the new nickel only increased his notoriety. He was the cousin of "Two Moon," an actor who lived in Waterbury, Connecticut and is occasionally confused with his family member. Ishiheo Nishes died in 1917. Sinte Maza had been at the battle of the Little Bighorn, Dakota Territory on June 25, 1876, when Col. George Armstrong Custer led most of his command to their death. His profile seems to be the closest match for Fraser's portrait bust.

Examination of the photo shows that Fraser's portrait differs in several aspects from the model. The most obvious difference is in the sculpting of the chin and jaw, where Fraser has pulled the chin forward and added mass to the jaw. These characteristics are also evident in the nickel portrait, suggesting the change was deliberate, rather than a con-

---

[497] Cheyenne.

[498] Oglala Lakota. Not to be confused with Iron Hail (Wasu Maza), a Minneconjou Lakota, who also was at Little Big Horn and in 1890 at Wounded Knee. Iron Hail lived to be 99 and died in 1955. He was also known as "Dewey Beard" and by the nickname Fox Beard. Some biographies claim that Iron Hail was actually one of the models for Fraser. Considering Fraser's statement that several Indians modeled for him, this could also be true – he certainly "looks the part" in photographs. After nearly a century, there is little hope of sorting out the situation.

sequence of the appearance of a particular model. Overall the portrait bust resembles both the June 1912 model and the final portrait.

The other Native American whom Fraser said was part of the composite portrait was Ado-Ete (Big Tree).[499] Ado-Eete, a chief Kiowa warrior and cousin to Chief Set-T'ainte (Satanta, or "White Bear"), was born somewhere in the Kiowa domain at the time when pressures from expanding white population were threatening the tribe's traditional way of life. He was not publicly identified as one of the nickel models until several years after the nickel was released, by which time much of the novelty had worn off.[500]

Figure 45. Left to right: Sinte Maza (Iron Tail) photographed in about 1909, Ishiheo Nishes (Two Moons) photographed in 1907 and Ado-Eete (Big Tree) photographed in about 1900. (Courtesy Denver Public Library; by DeLacey W. Gill, Smithsonian National Anthropological Archives; by A. J. McDonald, Smithsonian National Anthropological Archives.)

Comparing the 1910 portrait bust with Fraser's later Indian heads from 1911 and 1912 reveals striking similarities in the eyes, lips, forehead and cheek; and differences in jaw, lower chin and hair braid. The comparison of finished coin and the models suggests the nickel portrait most resembles Sinte Maza, although it is clearly not his portrait.

Figure 46. Left to right: portrait bust of Native American circa 1910; electrotype for nickel, 1911; more refined electrotype for nickel, circa June 1912. (Left to right: Archives of American Art, American Numismatic Rarities, Lepczyk catalog.)

---

[499] Kiowa.
[500] Another man known as "John Big Tree" was an Onondaga and popular actor in Hollywood Western films. He was not a model for the nickel although he claimed that distinction sometime after Ado-Eete died in 1929.

In truth, none of the Native Americans mentioned by Fraser "posed" specifically for the new nickel. All had likely been models for Fraser at one time in the past, and all "sat" for the artist. But, by 1911 the sculptor had his raw material and created the portrait as a composite from previous studies.

Models for the Nickel – Reverse

The reverse of Fraser's new nickel was dominated by a side-view portrait of an American Bison, commonly called a buffalo. As a model, the sculptor selected an animal he identified as "Black Diamond," who lived at New York's Central Park Menagerie. Black Diamond was the offspring of a bull and cow donated to the menagerie by P. T. Barnum Circus Management Company and was born in 1893. The manager of the Central Park Menagerie, Bill Snyder, did all he could to maintain the animals in good condition although the zoo was small and had little space for large animals, such as buffalo, to graze or exercise. By 1911, when Fraser was completing his basic designs for the nickel, Black Diamond was eighteen years old and showing signs of deterioration.

Figure 47. Black Diamond photographed in about 1915 at the Central Park Menagerie. Note the relatively confined enclosure necessitated by the menagerie's small size. (Courtesy Bronx Zoo Library.)

But was Black Diamond really the buffalo Fraser sculpted? Some references state that Black Diamond lived at the New York Zoological Park (aka Bronx Zoo); however, custodial records do not mention Black Diamond. The sculptor appears to be the source of this confusion. In an article in the New York *Herald* published on January 27, 1913, Fraser commented that the "…animal model was a 'typical and shaggy specimen' which he found grazing in the New York Zoological Park." Later he wrote of the buffalo:[501]

> He was not a plains buffalo, but none other than Black Diamond, the contrariest animal in the Bronx Zoo. I stood for hours watching and catching his forms and mood in plastic clay. Black Diamond was less conscious of the honor being conferred on him than of the annoyance which he suffered from insistent gazing upon him. He refused point blank to permit me to get side views of him, and stubbornly showed his front face most of the time.

If Fraser was correct about the name of the bison he sketched, then he must have been mistaken about the animal's home. Despite Fraser's comments, William T. Hornaday, founder and director of the New York Zoological Park was unequivocal in his opinion.[502]

> The buffalo named "Black Diamond" was a Central Park animal, with which we have had nothing to do. I do not know how it came by its name; but I suppose the name was bestowed by Billy Snyder, the head keeper. If "Black Diamond" was as fine an animal as we are asked to believe, then I cannot understand why he should be sold to a butcher at a cut price.

Hornaday also commented about the bison on the nickel in a letter to Martin S. Garretson, Secretary of the American Bison Society:[503]

> Regarding the buffalo bull "Black Diamond," we have no information whatever. Judging by the character of the buffalo on the nickel, I should say from its dejected appearance that the animal was an inmate of some small menagerie and had lived all its life in a small enclosure. Its head droops as of it had lost all hope in the world, and even the sculptor was not able to raise it. I regard the bison on the nickel as a sad failure, considered as a work of art.

If one compares Black Diamond's photo with that of a plains specimen, it does seem that Fraser selected an animal that was well past its prime. It also appears likely that Black Diamond was the model, and that Fraser simply confused the two zoos.

Black Diamond's notoriety did not do much for the animal's future. By 1915 he was rheumatic and disabled from age and lack of exercise. The menagerie offered him for sale at auction on June 28, 1915, but there were no bidders. Zoo keeper Snyder then offered the buffalo for sale at $500, but again had no offers. Finally, the firm of August Silz, Inc., specialists in wild game meat, offered $300 and Snyder accepted. The money would help pay for a replacement bison, Siberian tiger and possibly an Indian leopard for display.[504]

---

[501] National Cowboy & Western Heritage Museum. Inscription accompanying the Buffalo nickel display. The Bronx Zoo was eleven miles from Fraser's studio while the Central Park Menagerie was about four miles away. Considering the distance and travel time, it seems reasonable that the sculptor worked at the Central Park Menagerie.
[502] *Bronx Zoo Library*, letter dated November 1915 to Lehigh Valley Railroad from Hornaday. The "cut rate price" was because the animal was old and not in prime condition. If it had died at the menagerie, it would have cost $25 to have the carcass hauled away and buried.
[503] *Bronx Zoo Library*, letter dated January 9, 1918 to Garretson from Hornaday.
[504] *New York Sun*, "Buffalo King on Block," June 28, 1915, and *Washington Post*, June 29, 1915. p.6.

Figure 48. American bison from the Wichita Wildlife preserve in Oklahoma. This animal is likely a descendent of bison shipped from the New York Zoological Park in 1907. Notice that the animal holds his head higher and more alertly than Back Diamond in his 1915 photo or as depicted on the nickel. (Photo of bison by James Ownby, copyright 2007 by James Ownby; nickel model image by Bill Fivaz.)

When the public learned Back Diamond had been sold to a meat packer for $300, several people, including banker Isaac Seligman, came forward with substantial offers. But, Silz refused all attempts to purchase the old buffalo although at least one offer exceeded one thousand dollars. One newspaper report indicated Silz thought he could get approximately $1,600 for the meat, mounted head and hide of the famous animal.[505]

In mid-November, Black Diamond was loaded on a truck, hauled off, and unceremoniously slaughtered. The dressed weight of his carcass was approximately 1,020 pounds. The meat sold for one dollar a pound or more to New York restaurants, hotels and gourmets.[506] His head was sent to New York taxidermist Fred Sauter for mounting, then displayed in the offices of Silz, Inc. The hide was made into a robe of which other examples commonly sold for about twenty-five dollars.[507]

Poor Black Diamond's saga does not end there. According to Buffalo nickel expert David W. Lange, "Around 1921 Silz sold his business to his former employee, Benjamin H. Mayer, and Mayer's partner, Morris Hoffman. Black Diamond was included in the sale provided that the trophy would remain on display. This it did until Hoffman & Mayer, Inc. closed in 1977, whereupon the head was relocated to the home of Mayer's daughter, Marjorie Mayer Curnen. It remains there to this day and has proved to be something of a local tourist attraction."[508]

Over the years, the Buffalo nickel remained one of the most enduring numismatic topics for the general public. As late as 1947 the coin's origin was central to a radio script broadcast on August 8 featuring James and Laura Fraser. The sculptor commented:[509]

> Well, when I was asked to do a nickel, I felt I wanted to do something totally American - a coin that could not be mistaken for any other country's coin. It occurred to me that the buffalo, as part of our western background, was 100% American, and that our North American Indian fitted into the picture perfectly.

---

[505] *New York Times*, "Zoo's Big Buffalo Sold to a Butcher," November 10, 1915. p.14.
[506] *New York Times*, "Zoo's Big Buffalo Sold to a Butcher," November 10, 1915. p.14.
[507] *Bronx Zoo Library*, American Bison Society scrapbooks. File titled "Black Diamond."
[508] *Lange*, The Complete Guide to Buffalo Nickels. p.28.
[509] *Fraser, James Earle; papers*, AAA. Microfilm reel 2548, frame 564. Typed radio script titled "Spotlight on Youth with Julie Haggeman," dated August 8, 1947, p.8.

> When I had finished the nickel, a controversy arose because of the fact that the locks for the turnstiles in the subways and slot machines that had just been invented, took only coins that were very flat, and my Buffalo Nickel was rugged and deep.
>
> Batteries of lawyers finally met with me in the office of the Secretary of the Treasury in Washington to try to do away with my design because they said the locks of the turnstiles and slot machines – their inventions – would be ruined.
>
> Finally I called to the attention of the Secretary of the Treasury that the Law on Coinage provided that three or four different designs of the same coin must be allowable and legal tender. Therefore to conform to this law, it became necessary that the locks in the turnstiles and slot machines be made to fit numerous designs. Then the locks were re-arranged. And the Buffalo nickel became legal tender.

After telling the story for 35 years, Fraser can probably be excused his minor inaccuracies and exaggerations.

Fraser's Coinage Legacy

Saint-Gaudens' influence on America modern coinage was clearly dominant until the middle of the twentieth century. His students, assistants and creative admirers dominated medallic and numismatic art long after their artistic style was considered passé. The master's premature death in 1907 opened the field to his younger assistants. While they professed homage to his ideals, the best of them struck out into more dynamic compositions and more American themes. James Fraser was probably the most successful of these in both economic and promotional aspects. His sculptures, while of the highest technical caliber, showed a gradual diminution of force and power as the years passed. Some of his latter work, although of monumental scale, such as the great winged horses flanking Memorial Bridge in Washington, DC, had begun to look like every other sculptor's work. To his wife and artistic equal, Laura Gardin Fraser, must go much of the credit for the later successes.

Beyond being a consummate self-promoter, James Fraser was deeply in tune with the American West. He knew its myths as well as it stark realities, and gained his greatest acclaim for depictions of simple, direct emotions expressed in solid form. The Buffalo nickel design is the most characteristically American coin ever issued by this nation. No other piece of circulating currency – coin or paper note – incorporates such clear symbols, articulated with direct, powerful sculpture. To accomplish this on any scale is a triumph; to accomplish it on a tiny disc only 21.2 mm in diameter is Jovian.

Fraser's work with the Mint Bureau did not end with the Buffalo nickel. During the next decades he advised, prodded and criticized commemorative and circulating coinage designs as a respected member of the Commission of Fine Arts and professional artist.[510]

The one aspect of coin design where Fraser might have made additional significant contribution was in helping his colleagues understand the best practical approach to having their designs coined. Commemorative designs were less of a problem than circulation designs – a commemorative was issued in limited quantities and did not have to fit all the needs of commerce such as stacking height and vending machine acceptance. Having learned how to get the best from his Buffalo nickel composition, Fraser seems not to have

---

[510] See Burdette, *Renaissance of American Coinage 1916-1921* for Fraser's role in production of the Peace dollar. See also Burdette, "Designer of Maine Centennial Commemorative Identified." *Coin World Magazine*, April 26 and May 2, 2003, for Fraser as a member of the Commission of Fine Arts.

provided his "secrets" to MacNeil or Weinman in 1916. Both these latter artists could likely have benefited from knowing of Fraser's use of electrotypes, and of having Medallic Art make the initial hubs. Using these strategies might have resulted in improved final designs and faster acceptance of their work. In 1921, work on the Peace dollar was so hurried that it is unlikely improvement in the process could have occurred.

Chapter 10 – Designs, Patterns & Proofs

Among designers of circulating U.S. coinage, James Fraser unmistakably recognized that he had to overcome several impediments to being awarded the design and seeing it successfully used on a coin. His approach to these differed from other artists and deserves examination in greater detail. The four primary obstacles were: competition, concept, design approval and implementation.

Following introduction of the Saint-Gaudens and Pratt gold coin designs in 1907 and 1908, there was increased interest by many professional and amateur artists in redesigning the silver and minor coins of the country. Innovative designs and production techniques used for the gold pieces convinced many that the mint was prepared to accept new, unconventional concepts for coinage. This heightened awareness for the possibility of new coin designs encouraged many to question the "sole source" commissions given to Bela Pratt and Augustus Saint-Gaudens. Assistant treasury secretary A. Piatt Andrew – the former mint director – was very influential with secretary MacVeagh. Andrew was also a proponent of open competitions and in early 1911 noted this preference to Eames MacVeagh, the secretary's son. "When I was in the Mint I was much interested in the plan of arranging for competition among medalists for an ideal set of coins." After an initial introduction to secretary MacVeagh and Andrew, Fraser's first task was to secure the coin design work for himself by eliminating the concept of an open competition.

Andrew's idea of open competition was circumvented by two strategies. The first, and most typical of Jim Fraser, was to be ingratiatingly intrusive:[511]

> The first step in the negotiations for the new nickel piece was taken by Assistant Secretary Andrew in 1911. As a result of his interest in the subject Mr. J. E. Fraser of New York, upon his own initiative, prepared several small wax models showing the Indian head and buffalo as they now appear on the coin, although in somewhat higher relief.

---

[511] *US Mint*, NARA-CP, op. cit., file 305310. Memorandum dated March 18, 1913 to Secretary of the Treasury William G. McAdoo from Director of the Mint George E. Roberts.

Fraser's initiative, charm and knowledge appealed to Andrew's artistic taste and personality as the sculptor pointed out the advantages of working with one, highly skilled artist, rather than being forced to take whatever a committee decided was best from hundreds of entries. According to Fraser, "Working with a competent man, there would be no doubt that a great many designs would be made; in fact, you would go on working till something of real merit was produced."[512] But the sculptor did not depend on charisma and logic alone to stifle competition. In addition to providing a commendatory letter from the late Saint-Gaudens, he went a step beyond what other artists might have done. "I am having some electro-plates made of the small sketches and I will send them to you when they are completed."[513] He took his wax or plaster sketches to Medallic Art Company where the Weil brothers made coin-sized reductions and electrotypes. This pushed the design from an artist's concept – something any artist could do – to a practical metal replica that Andrew, Roberts and MacVeagh could touch, admire and imagine as a real circulating coin. By stimulating the imagination and self-image of these key treasury officials, Fraser put himself above a mere competition. Secretary MacVeagh was so completely captivated by the little metal tokens that within a few months of meeting Fraser he wrote, "…it has been decided to have you present your ideas in the form of models of the same size as the legal coin."[514] This was not only a complete turn-around from Andrew's earlier comments, but indicates that MacVeagh accepted the electrotype tokens as substitutes for drawings, sketches, large models and pattern coins. More than anything else, Fraser's bison, Indian and Lincoln tokens had succeeded in removing not only possible competing individuals, but had abolished the *idea* of holding any type of competition. To keep the project moving forward Fraser offered his own enthusiasm:[515]

> Although I realize that no definite commission has been given me in regard to the designs for the new coins, I have become so much interested in the sketches that I have pushed them a little farther and now they are in the shape of electrotypes which I should like to submit for your consideration.

Free of competitors, Fraser could work unhindered with director Roberts and secretary MacVeagh on the concepts and subject. Much of this had occurred when the artist presented fully American images to Andrew and Roberts. Except for a peripheral head of Liberty, possibly intended for the silver coins, Fraser stuck to his original designs: Indian, bison, Lincoln. By presenting all three as if they were actual coins, Fraser limited officials to only those three subjects. Abe Lincoln's image ended up as a practical impossibility due to the need for legislation to replace Brenner's 1909 portrait. With just two intimately associated subjects remaining, officials had nothing to do but concentrate on an Indian/Bison nickel.

Formal acceptance of the nickel design revolved around making small changes in established portraits. Some of the surviving molds and electroshells, show different feather widths, or letter sizes. But, all of the changes were minor and some may have been accomplished solely to satisfy a lone commercial entity rather than for aesthetic improvement. Once MacVeagh and Roberts agreed to the placement of inscriptions, all Fraser had to do

---

[512] *US Mint*, NARA-CP, op. cit., file 305310. Letter dated July 20, 1911 to Andrew from Fraser.
[513] *Ibid.*
[514] *US Mint*, NARA-CP, op. cit., entry 235, vol. 387. Letter dated July 29, 1911 to Fraser from Roberts.
[515] *US Mint*, NARA-CP, op. cit., file 305310. Letter dated September 19, 1911 to MacVeagh from Fraser.

was scale small models into ones suitable for coinage use. To further ensure the final coin was as close as possible to his original work, Fraser had the reductions and hubs cut by Medallic Art under his supervision. This took all guesswork and excuses out of the hands of the Philadelphia Mint, and gave Fraser complete control of his product. Unfortunately, we don't know what the first die-struck sample coins looked like – it appears none were saved. Yet, it is unlikely that it differed much from the final 1912 models or the version put into circulation.[516] Changes demanded by Hobbs Manufacturing Co. were measured in thousandths of an inch, constituting little more than "noise" in the sculpted work.

Designs

Fraser's earliest designs for the Buffalo nickel were based on pencil drawings he made of bison at the New York Central Park Menagerie and his previous sculptural projects of Native Americans. Few of these drawings survive, although three surviving examples are shown below.

Figure 49. Drawings for reverse of the nickel, 1911. These are three of several compositions explored by the artist before settling on the familiar bison-on-mound version. Left, male bison in profile facing left, standing on the prairie, with head held in normal position. Front and back hooves approximately level with details suggestive of a grassy plain. Behind are mountains and rays. No denomination, date or other inscriptions. Center, bison on a nearly flat prairie with prominent hills and sunrise in background, head upward. Right, bison on flat, featureless ground, but with head lowered and hump more prominent. Below is the denomination 5 CENTS; above is the inscription E PLURIBUS UNUM both inscriptions in large bold lettering. (Courtesy James Earle Fraser and Laura Gardin Fraser Studio Collection, series 1, box 2, folder 7 [left, right] and series 2, box 4, folder 23 [center] National Cowboy & Western Heritage Museum, Oklahoma City, OK.)

After preparing several drawings and narrowing the design elements and overall composition, Fraser began making "sketches." These were small, circular models made of wax, plaster or clay with the design quickly cut into the material.[517] This gave Fraser a sense of relief and relative scale within the composition. It also allowed him to try variations on his ideas and to begin the process of adding detail critical to an effective coin or medal. A creative artist of Jim Fraser's caliber was not satisfied with a good likeness – that was assumed from the beginning. What he wanted was to convey the character, personality and nature of his subject. The Indian for the nickel represented not a specific person, but a

---

[516] Medallic Art made the first hubs in December 1912, presumably from the models dated 1912. If the initial pattern coins were dated 1912, back dated from January 7, 1913 when they were struck, there would have been considerable impetus to destroy all of the back-dated pieces before any could "leak" into public hands. Consider what a "1912 Buffalo nickel" would be worth in today's exaggerated numismatic marketplace.

[517] For simplicity, no distinction is made in the discussion between a relief model and a plaster mold from which relief models may be made by casting.

diverse culture, and as such he must possess and display these attributes while being recognized as a portrait. In making small sketch models – most were about three- or four-inches (76mm-101mm) in diameter, suitable for holding in one hand while scraping away plaster with a stylus – Fraser followed the lead of many other medallic sculptors, particularly his mentor Augustus Saint-Gaudens.[518]

Possibly the earliest plaster sketch model presents a Native American wearing the "traditional" ceremonial headdress, much as in Bela Pratt's 1908 half eagle design.

Figure 50. Native American with headdress by Fraser. Likely made during the first half of 1911 along with the larger-scale portrait, Lincoln and Liberty designs. This profile is similar to the final version, but has a more protruding chin and the eye is different. This is a plaster sketch model made from a mold. (Courtesy Wayne Wilcox.)

This initial sketch is a composite portrait of a Native American facing right. As expected of a sketch, the portrayal is as much a caricature as found on cigar or cornmeal packages than any real person. The profile is similar to that on 1911 pattern electrotypes, with the hair braid falling forward of the Indian's shoulder. The rim is narrow, irregular, and entirely omitted at the base of the bust. There is no date, the only inscription being UNITED STATES OF AMERICA, and the relief is low as would be expected from a design intended for coinage. There are at least two casts known of this design (Lepczyk lots #462, 463) and multiple versions may exist.

A similar portrait was used by A. Piatt Andrew as the emblem of his American Field Ambulance Service in 1915 in France. Andrew was a former mint director and assistant treasury secretary during most of the time the Buffalo nickel was being designed. He probably saw this early portrait and may have liked it well enough to imitate for his own use. However, this was an extremely popular and commonly encountered image at the time and its use may be nothing more than coincidence.

Among the other early sketch models from 1911 was likely a portrait without the headdress, although we have no plaster models of this version (see electrotypes, below). Acceptance of this, and the bison image, by treasury officials led to Fraser creating a series of small sketch models presenting variations on the portrait used on the coin. The figure, below, illustrates several of Fraser's plaster models or molds. Electrotypes of most models

---

[518] While working on the double eagle designs in 1906, Saint-Gaudens made more than 70 small plaster sketch models of his ideas, put them on display in his studio, and asked his assistants and visitors (Fraser among them) to indicate their preferences. Many of these pieces are preserved at the Saint-Gaudens National Historic Site in Cornish, NH.

are unknown. The approximate date of creation is included although this is speculative for all the design variations.

Produced spring/summer 1912

(Courtesy Heritage Auctions)

Similar to adopted design, but leftmost feather thin with angled end; third feather has rounded end. Braid ties touch rim. Field and portrait textured; note particularly the chin, cheek and neck. Considerable hair detail in upper center (compare to previous). Portrait leans more to right than other versions. Lettering and date small and thin.

Rim is wide and of irregular width. Greater distance between rim and design than on some other versions. Lepczyk lot #465.

Produced spring/summer 1912

(Courtesy Fred Weinberg)

Similar to previous with two eagle feathers in hair low and to back of head; tip of third feather shows behind neck. Feathers are tilted left more than on other versions; blanket or tunic across shoulder with strong suggestion of blanket folds. Chin lower and at more acute angle to neck than others.; cheek not sunken. Date "1912" in raised numerals on shoulder, larger digits than other versions. Inscription LIBERTY next to upper right rim in front of forehead. Braid ties touch rim. Field and portrait textured; note particularly the chin, cheek and neck. Designer's initials, JEF, below and slightly right of date.

Rim is narrow with slight irregularity between last feather and shoulder. Lepczyk lot #467.

Produced mid-1912/early 1913?

(Courtesy James Earle Fraser and Laura Gardin Fraser Studio Collection, series 1, box 2, folder 7, National Cowboy & Western Heritage Museum, Oklahoma City, OK.)

Similar to adopted design, but leftmost feather short with angled end; third feather is small and barely visible. Braid ties touch rim; blanket or tunic across shoulder with texture suggesting fabric. Chin more rounded than previous, cheek not sunken. Field and portrait lightly textured; note particularly the chin, cheek and neck. Considerable hair detail in upper center (compare to previous).

Rim is wide and of irregular width. Compass hole in center above braid. Greater distance between rim and design than on most other versions. Partial date "1912" or "1913" in raised numerals on shoulder, far from rim; last digit damaged with upper part clear, and lower portion suggesting a crooked "3."

Produced late 1912/early 1913

(Courtesy Fred Weinberg)

Similar to previous with two eagle feathers in hair low and to back of head, tip of third feather in full relief, sharply pointed and low, behind neck; feathers are wider than on other variations; blanket or tunic across shoulder blanket or tunic across shoulder with strong suggestion of blanket folds to left of date. Chin rounded neck nearly straight front and back, cheek somewhat sunken, neck short. Date "1913" in raised numerals on shoulder, close to rim; "3" has curved top. Inscription LIBERTY in thin, low relief letters next to upper right rim in front of forehead. Braid ties touch rim. Field and portrait lightly textured. No designer's initial.

Rim is narrow. Curved, thin "3" in date. Lepczyk lot #468

Bison Portrait – Produced mid-1912 ?

(Courtesy Heritage Auctions)

Male bison in profile facing left, standing on small mound or edge of hill, head lowered, texture to field suggestive of prairie grass. Bison's front and back hooves are approximately level. Below is denomination FIVE CENTS; above are inscriptions UNITED STATES OF AMERICA and E PLURIBUS UNUM. Lettering similar in scale to final design, but motto very small and barely readable. Legends separated from rim and bison very close to rim.

Incuse outline to back of animal; hump is smaller that on other versions with more space between design and rim above bison; tail lacks split; treatment of bison's coat more detailed than later. Word CENTS is uneven; hill or mound edge is steep and tuft of grass more prominent than on following. Overall more highly textured than later models.

May have been attempt to satisfy Hobbs Manufacturing Company.

Bison Portrait – Produced 1912

Male bison in profile facing left, standing on small mound or edge of hill, head lowered, hump is prominent; texture of field suggests prairie grass. Bison's front and back hooves are approximately level. There is less detail in the left front leg than on some previous versions. Below is denomination FIVE CENTS; above are inscriptions UNITED STATES OF AMERICA and E PLURIBUS UNUM. Lettering similar in scale to final design, with motto barely readable. Legends separated from rim and bison very close to rim.

This might be the final 1912-dated model of the pre-production buffalo nickel and may be the one used by Medallic Art Co to make hubs in December 1912. Slight differences exist between this version and the 1913-dated pattern, below, and the coin as issued for circulation.

(Courtesy James Earle Fraser and Laura Gardin Fraser Studio Collection, series 1, box 2, folder 7, National Cowboy & Western Heritage Museum, Oklahoma City, OK.)

There are twelve to fifteen obverse variations on the Indian design represented by electrotypes and small plaster models. Most appear to differ primarily in feather angle, width or detail, although other design elements fluctuate also. None of the models show the date they were made.

Role of Patterns

By 1905, changes in technology since the 1880s made the use of pattern coins almost obsolete. The greatest improvement had been in the availability of reducing lathes capable of cutting a complete, coin-size hub directly from a hard plaster model, bronze cast or copper galvano. The Philadelphia Mint's old Hill reducing lathe, in use since 1868, could do most of the cutting work on a hub, but considerable hand engraving and letter punching was still required to make a finished product. In November 1906, under pressure from President Roosevelt, the mint purchased a new electric Janvier reducing machine.[519] The Janvier could cut a complete coin-size hub from models up to 18-inches in diameter. It could also alter the relief of the hub without loosing detail, something the Hill lathe could not do.

With this new equipment, the mint engraving department was expected to turn out better quality hubs, faster than previously. Unfortunately, this was not the case. The government paid for equipment and installation, but the vendor provided only 1-1/2 days of setup and training on the Janvier. Within a month of installation, engraver Charles Barber was complaining about insufficient knowledge to operate the new reducing lathe, and asking for more training.[520] The request was fulfilled but the time actually used to cut hubs for the extremely high relief Saint-Gaudens experimental pieces of February 1907, and results indicate the mint engravers did not figure out how to consistently use the Janvier properly until the 1920s when John Sinnock succeeded George Morgan as engraver.[521]

---

[519] *US Mint*, NARA-P. op. cit., entry 4A, Box 2, "Supply Requisitions – Engraving Department, 1900-1906." Triplicate copy of a Mint purchase requisition dated November 3, 1906 signed by Charles Barber.
[520] *US Mint*, NARA-P. op. cit. Letter dated December 28, 1906 to Landis from Barber.
[521] One of the best examples of what could be done with the Janvier lathe is the 1918 Lincoln-Illinois commemorative half dollar. Engraver George Morgan prepared designs for both sides. John Sinnock, an associate engraver from 1917-

A pattern coin was only necessary when the director or secretary of the treasury wanted to hold a new coin design in his hands or roll it between the fingers before making a final decision. Most medal and coin designs were selected and modified based on plaster models, and hubs were cut directly from the approved models. There were exceptions, such as the MCMVII [1907] "Indian" head double eagle struck specifically for Saint-Gaudens to examine, 1909 motto-free cent, and 1909-10 pattern nickels. There were also experimental coins including the Saint-Gaudens extremely high relief double eagles and high relief, knife rim eagles also from 1907, and large diameter Buffalo nickels.[522]

A general question asked among coin collectors has been, "Why are there no pre-1913 pattern coins of the new design?" The conventional answer has been to point to the two types of 1913 pattern in the Smithsonian NNC, and say "These are all we know." Yet these examples post-date the final design almost as after-thoughts.

We now understand that patterns were made, but they were unconventional. Instead of being struck from dies at the Philadelphia Mint, they were little nickel-sized electrotype samples the artist made so secretary MacVeagh could see what the real coin would look like. Fraser's use of coin-size electroshells avoided the expense, time and potential confusion inherent in any artistic collaboration. By controlling all design and production processes including cutting the hubs, Fraser eliminated the need for mint-produced patterns. He produced his own coin patterns, to his specifications and on his schedule. Instead of taking many weeks for make a finished model, then waiting another month for the mint to cut hubs and dies, Fraser could produce his samples within a few days and show them to officials while ideas were still fresh. All that was left for engraver Barber to do was impress a set of experimental dies and strike some trial pieces on the director's order.[523] The little copper "nickels" Fraser had Medallic Art Company make satisfied Roberts and MacVeagh about the appearance and "heft" of the new design, and satisfied Barber about the design relief. The mint was probably equally pleased with this approach, since they did not have to cut hubs and dies, argue with the artist, or be accused of incompetence when the results were not what everyone expected.

The Buffalo nickel project was the only instance from 1907 to 1921 when mint staff were not accused of ineptitude in translating the artists designs into coin.

Electrotype Patterns

Electrotype pattern nickels are part of the steps Jim Fraser took toward a final coin design. After the design was accepted, Fraser appears to have treated these as studio clutter and made no effort to document or preserve them. A group of these pieces, along with small plaster molds and casts, turned up nearly half a century ago. They were the subject of considerable numismatic interest in the early 1980s, then slipped to near-obscurity. But

---

1919, made the hubs on the Janvier with very limited retouching of the hub and master die. These coins are among the best detailed of the early commemoratives. Compare with Weinman's 1916 half dollar or MacNeil's 1917 quarter for sharpness and fidelity. In this instance, the difference was that Sinnock had been trained to use the reducing lathe, Morgan had not. Sinnock returned as assistant engraver in 1922, then was appointed engraver on Morgan's death in 1925.

[522] The Philadelphia Mint also made "trial" coins to test a new design for mechanical suitability.

[523] In 1916 Barber and Morgan did the work from bronze casts of the artists' models. Quality and timeliness of the experimental dies suffered, resulting in further redesign of all three coins. It is speculated that had an outside company made the original hubs, the quality would have been better and the first 1916 designs might have been adopted without change. See Burdette, *Renaissance of American Coinage 1916-1921* for more details on the 1916 patterns.

electrotype patterns have now become of great interest as their purpose was better understood.

Fraser's next step, as has been mentioned elsewhere in the Buffalo nickel story, was unusual: he had reductions of some of the sketch models made by Medallic Art Company. These reductions, probably in hard wax or other cheap, easily cut material, were used to make coin-size "electroshells" or electrotypes (also called galvanos). The thin metal shell was filled with tin or type-metal to give it strength and sometimes painted or plated to simulate its final color. It was these small metal pieces that substituted for mint-struck pattern coins, and which are important in the final evolution of the Buffalo nickel design.

Once Fraser had captured the imagination of secretary MacVeagh and director Roberts by showing them what the Buffalo nickel would look like, he could then proceed to make more finished models that would eventually be used to cut reductions and coinage hubs. Engraver Barber and Fraser had discussed the making of reductions and hubs, and the artist was prepared to follow the mint engraver's suggestions. The two primary requirements for preparing useable coinage dies were relief low enough to permit producing the coins with only one blow of the press, and a diameter approximately five-times the diameter of the finished coin. Thus, for a coin 21.2mm in diameter, the plaster model should be approximately 101mm (4-inches) which is consistent with measurements of the design on most known plaster models for the nickel.

There are no records of how many design variations were tried, or the number of copies produced of each. A small group of plaster molds and electrotypes for the Buffalo nickel and other proposed designs appeared on the numismatic market in 1968, about two years after Laura Gardin Fraser died.[524] New York dealer Ray Freville of Reo Coins sold eleven of the electrotype pieces to Milton G. Cohen of Westwood, NJ. There appear to have been nineteen electrotype specimens in the original group. This included seven relating directly to the Buffalo nickel, two for the Lincoln cent, two for a 1915 commemorative quarter, one 1912 head of liberty, size of the quarter, two for the Grant memorial gold dollar and five not specified or duplicate. Mr. Cohen contacted *Coin World* magazine in 1972 who then sought expert advise from the Eric P. Newman Numismatic Education Society.[525] Some of the pieces were illustrated in advertisements for Numismatics Limited, a coin retailer located in Beverly Hills, CA,[526] and in a 1974 article by John W. Dunn titled "Design for a Dream Coin."[527]

The electrotypes were also included in a revised edition of Dr. J. Hewitt Judd's reference book on U.S. pattern coins edited by Abe Kosoff. Although a few other examples turned up in the Western Heritage Society Cowboy Hall of Fame collection of the James and Laura Fraser papers, little was known about the pieces. The first extensive publicity for either models or electrotypes occurred with the October 1980 sale of thirty plaster models

---

[524] The studio ephemera of sculptor Hermon MacNeil suffered a similar fate. Several years after his death, letters, drawings and other materials from his studio began appearing on the secondary market or were offered to numismatists and institutional collections. As recently as 2003 two high quality casts of MacNeil's 1916/17 quarter designs turned up at a New Jersey yard sale where they were purchased for a few dollars. It is presumed that much of the James and Laura Fraser and MacNeil material was recovered from "trash" thrown out of their studios after their death.
[525] Letter dated October 18, 1972 to James O. Johnson [editor of *Coin World* magazine] from Eric P. Newman. Courtesy Fred Weinberg.
[526] Numismatics Ltd., 9401 Wilshire Blvd, Suite 820, Beverly Hills, CA 90212. Advertisement dated May 2, 1975 illustrating and describing a 1912 Indian obverse and 1911 Lincoln obverse. Courtesy Fred Weinberg.
[527] John W. Dunn, "Design for a Dream Coin," *COINage*, August 1976, pp.46-49. Courtesy Fred Weinberg.

of coins, medals and statues by James and Laura Fraser conducted by Joseph Lepczyk.[528] Coordinated with the Lepczyk auction was a lengthy article in Coin World describing the models and concluding, "The exact provenance of the plasters being offered for sale is nebulous."[529] In June 1981 *COINage* published "The Numismatic Art of James Earle Fraser" by William S. Nawrocki which related the models and electrotypes to the career of Fraser and creation of the Buffalo nickel.[530] Six electrotypes were consigned to the Bowers and Ruddy Galleries, Inc. American Numismatic Association auction of 1981 and became the focus of a "Research Note" in the company's *Rare Coin Review* newsletter and price list.[531] The ANA catalog and preceding "Research Note" became the first attempt to provide a more rigorous description of the electrotypes and relate them to models from the Lepczyk sale. Over the past quarter century, a few models and electrotypes have appeared at auction or in dealer's price lists, but nothing more has been learned about the quantities or other varieties of these very interesting items. Unfortunately very little can be discerned about the sequence in which the models or electrotypes were made, so we have limited insight into Fraser's earliest concepts and the modifications made at the request of Clarence Hobbs and ASTUMCO.

The tables below illustrate major varieties of Fraser's electrotype patterns and attempt to place them in chronological order. Virtually all known pieces are of the obverse only. The reader is cautioned, however, that this list is neither complete nor necessarily in the correct order. Further, several electrotypes mentioned in Fraser's correspondence, and which should be readily identifiable, have not been located. Only specimens related directly to the Buffalo nickel are included. The Lincoln portrait proposed for use on the one-cent coin in 1911 and in 1952 is discussed in the chapters about Brenner's 1909 designs.[532]

Numismatists should exercise considerable caution in interpreting electrotype patterns. Unlike die-struck pieces, which are uniform in shape, weight and design, electrotypes show considerable variation from piece to piece. Although the artist may have used the same reduction for many electrotypes, the quick method of manufacture and temporary nature of the pieces produced specimens of highly variable quality. The artist may also have altered the model between batches of reductions. No measurement comparing one specimen with another can be considered completely reliable. No measurement of rim width or distance, or diameter or weight has significance because every piece will differ from the others. Additionally, some specimens may have been altered either by the artist, those working with him, or by later owners. We do not know how many examples of each variety were produced, but Fraser seems to have given them to interested parties without restriction.

Each item has been given an "E" number indicating experimental electrotype pattern for convenience; the numbers have no other purpose or significance. Obverse designs

---

[528] Public Auction and Mail Bid Sale (#36), October 23-24, 1980. Joseph Lepczyk, P. O. Box 751, East Lansing, MI 48823. Lots 461 to 490 inclusive. Lots 462-471 are positive casts and negative molds for the Buffalo nickel obverse and reverse. The coin models sold for $1,300 to $4,100 with most in the $2,100 range. The Lepczyk company is no longer in business and Mr. Lepczyk is deceased. On January 3, 2006 uniface Lincoln and Indian electrotypes were sold for more than $30,000 each by American Numismatic Rarities in "The Robert Michael Prescott Collection" lots 857 and 878.
[529] David T. Alexander, *Coin World*, "Fraser's plasters find collector marketplace," October 15, 1980, pp.81-90.
[530] William S. Naweocki, *COINage*, "The Numismatic Art of James Earle Fraser," June, 1981. p.32.
[531] Bowers & Ruddy Galleries, *Rare Coin Review* #38, "Extraordinary Set of Fraser Electro-trials to Appear in 1981 ANA Action," (May 1981), pp.24-25. Courtesy Fred Weinberg.
[532] The Liberty head was likely intended as a generic obverse design for the silver subsidiary coinage, which was a subject of current interest among sculptors, and not for either the nickel or a silver dollar.

are numbered E-1, E-2, E-3…, reverse designs are designated E-A, E-B, E-C….Where a design can be correlated to a primary source document or event, this is mentioned in the accompanying text. Repeated attempts to link specific designs to Fraser's letters and Mint Bureau documents have been unsuccessful and must await discovery of additional documents.

Indian Portrait – Electro #E-1
Obverse
Produced – Spring/Summer 1911
Photos are of electrotypes – no die struck examples

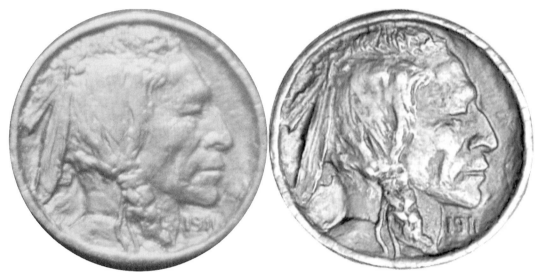

Composite portrait of Native American facing right; hair parted on right side and braided; two eagle feathers in hair low and to back of head, tip of third feather visible behind upper neck ; blanket or tunic across shoulder. Jaw rounded and in line with teeth; front of neck protrudes forward but not as sharply as previous. Portrait has a more finished appearance than previous. Date "1911" in raised numerals in field under chin. No inscription LIBERTY. Braid ties touch rim. Field and portrait textured; note particularly the chin, cheek and field behind neck. No designer's initial.

Rim is wide with slight irregularity between last feather and shoulder. The two photographs appear to be from different electrotype specimens; however, there may be multiple pieces made from the same model.

Contemporary comments:
JEF to APA: 7/20/1911. I am having some electro-plates made of the small sketches and I will send them to you when they are completed.

(Left, courtesy Fred Weinberg; right, courtesy American Numismatic Rarities.)

Indian Portrait – Electro #E-2
Obverse
Produced early 1912 ?
Photos are of an electrotype – no complete coins made

Composite portrait of Native American facing right; hair parted on right side and braided; two eagle feathers in hair low and to back of head, third feather behind neck; blanket or tunic across shoulder. Chin more rounded than previous, cheek not sunken. Date "1912" in raised numerals near rim, slanting to left, on shoulder. Inscription LIBERTY next to upper right rim in front of forehead. Leftmost feather wide with rounded end. Braid ties touch rim. Field and portrait textured; note particularly the chin, cheek and neck. Flat, almost featureless area at upper center. No designer's initial.

Rim is wide and uneven.

At least two specimens known: one is 20.1 mm in diameter and weighs 3.62 grams (55.9 grains), this appears to match Lepczyk lot #465.

Contemporary comments:
2/15/1913 Cox to FMacV: "...A large part of [the old design's] ugliness is in the very things which these makers of machines demand – the perfectly flat background with an open space all around, and the flat circle, a quarter of an inch in diameter, in the middle.

(Courtesy Fred Weinberg.)

Indian Portrait – Electro #E-3 (same model as E-2?)
Obverse
Produced early 1912 ?
Photos are of an electrotype – no complete coins made

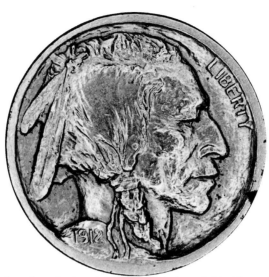

Composite portrait of Native American facing right; hair parted on right side and braided; two eagle feathers in hair low and to back of head, third feather behind neck; blanket or tunic across shoulder. Chin more rounded than previous, cheek not sunken. Date "1912" in thin, raised numerals near rim, slanting to left, on shoulder. Inscription LIBERTY next to upper right rim in front of forehead. Leftmost feather medium width with rounded end. Braid ties do not touch rim. Field and portrait textured; note particularly the chin, cheek and neck. Flat, almost featureless area at upper center. No designer's initial.

Rim is wide and uneven.

One specimen known in the National Cowboy & Western Heritage Museum. (This specimen and the one illustrated above it may be from the same model.)
Contemporary comments:
2/15/1913 Cox to FMacV: "…A large part of [the old design's] ugliness is in the very things which these makers of machines demand – the perfectly flat background with an open space all around, and the flat circle, a quarter of an inch in diameter, in the middle.

(Courtesy James Earle Fraser and Laura Gardin Fraser Studio Collection, series 1, box 2, folder 7, National Cowboy & Western Heritage Museum, Oklahoma City, OK.)

Bison Portrait – Electro #E-A
Reverse
Produced 1911 ?
Photo is of an electrotype

Male bison in profile facing left, standing on level portion of a small mound or edge of hill, head lowered, hump prominent, minor texture to field. Bison's front and back hooves are approximately level. Below is denomination FIVE CENTS; above are inscriptions UNITED STATES OF AMERICA and E PLURIBUS UNUM. Motto lettering is minute and unreadable. Legends and bison well separated from rim and from one another.

At least two specimens known: one is 21.1 mm in diameter and weighs 4.13 g (63.8 grains); specifications of the other are not known.

(Courtesy Fred Weinberg.)

U.S. Mint Patterns

Only occasionally do mint archives include memoranda disclosing the disposition of pattern and experimental coins. In the instance of the Buffalo nickel, several experimental and pattern pieces are discussed in a letter to director Roberts from Philadelphia Mint superintendent Landis dated March 3, 1913.[533] Other entries on the table below are from letters and memoranda where they are simply mentioned in the text, and not as the subject of the document.

Comment	Judd No.	Distributed			Returned		
		Quan.	To	Date	Quan.	To	Date
#1 Model. Possibly dated 1912	1st hubs. No initial	7	unknown	1/7/13	7?	Mint	1/17/13
#1 Model.	1/13/13 from 1st dies. No initial. J-1950	2	Mint Cabinet Collection	2/24/13	17 struck		
		6	Landis	2/24/13	6	Mint	2/28/13
		1	Fraser	2/24/13			
		1	President, to All Souls' Church, Washington (corner stone)	?			

---

[533] *US Mint,* NARA-CP, op. cit., file 311716. Letter dated March 3, 1913 to Roberts from Landis.

		3	Sec MacVeagh	2/24/13			
		1	lost	2/24/13			
		1	Robert Clark	2/24/13			
		1	Charles Barber	2/24/13			
		1	Albert Norris	2/24/13			
#2 Model. Unhardened dies	1/21/13 from Mint dies used for production. No initial.	1	Director Roberts	1/21/13			
		1	Fraser	2/5/13			
		1	Hobbs	2/5/13			
		1	Director Roberts	2/13/13			
		5	Landis	2/28/13	5	Mint	2/28/13
	Milling tests-A	20	Barber, others	1/22/13	20	Mint	1/22/13
	Milling tests-B	20	Barber, others	1/22/13	20	Mint	1/22/13
	Milling tests-C	20	Barber, others	1/22/13	20	Mint	1/22/13
Oversize planchets. Curved top '3'. Modified from #1 model.	2/13/13 larger diameter patterns. No Initial. J-1951	1	Sec MacVeagh	2/14/13	1	Mint	1914
	Lg Dia.	2	Mint Cabinet Collection	2/24/13			
	Lg Dia.	1	Landis	2/14/13	1	Mint	2/28/13

There is no mystery about why the mint struck several Buffalo nickels on large diameter planchets. Superintendent Landis stated on March 3, 1913:[534]

> …On February 13, 1913, four specimens of the new design 5-cent nickel piece were struck from dies with a diameter slightly greater than the standard. These dies were made in order to show the effect of a small space between the design and the border and with the intention, if it were thought desirable to have this space, of reducing the design so as to bring the coin to the standard diameter.

Using slightly oversize planchets should have allowed the mint to use extant hubs to make dies for the experiment. If the Hobbs Company had succeeded in their demands, the mint would have been ready to recut the hubs to a slightly smaller diameter. This would leave a gap between the border (rim) and the top of the design, satisfying Hobbs' demand at least on this one point.

Two of the four coins were melted: the one originally sent to secretary MacVeagh was evidently located by Roberts some time later; the coin held by Landis was evidently melted as soon as the regular issue reached circulation. The remaining two went to the mint coin cabinet (now Smithsonian Institution National Numismatic Collection) and reside there for the benefit of researchers and numismatists.

Engraver Barber often made pattern and trial coins with the reverse oriented "medal turn" rather than the conventional "coin turn." This was done with the Pratt gold coin patterns, and possibly the Lincoln cent patterns although none survive for examination. All Buffalo nickel patterns apparently have dies oriented "medal turn" which may be helpful in determining if a "new discovery" is genuine or a coin which has been cleverly altered.

---

[534] *US Mint*, NARA-CP, op. cit., file 311716. Letter dated March 3, 1913 to Roberts from Landis, p.2.

Five Cents – Model #1
Obverse 1, Reverse A
Struck January 7, 1913 (7 pieces – all destroyed)
Photos are of the plaster model – no pattern coins known

Composite portrait of Native American facing right; hair parted on right side and braided; two eagle feathers in hair low and to back of head, tip of third behind neck; blanket or tunic across shoulder; date "1912" in large, raised numerals on shoulder. Inscription LIBERTY next to upper right rim in front of forehead. Braid ties do not touch rim. Field and portrait textured; note particularly the chin, cheek and neck.

No designer's initial.

Rim is wide with slight irregularity between last feather and shoulder.

Male bison in profile facing left, standing on small mound or edge of hill, head lowered, field textured to suggest prairie grass. Below is denomination FIVE CENTS; above are inscriptions UNITED STATES OF AMERICA and E PLURIBUS UNUM. Lettering small and somewhat run together.

Rim narrower than on obverse and shows slight irregularity to left of hill.

Contemporary comments:
JEF: 8/26/1912. "I am ready to come to Washington with the models at once. Let me know when you want me."
JL: 12/31/1912. "As Mr. Fraser has expressed a desire to be present at the experimental striking of the new five-cent piece, I beg to inform you that we will be ready for this trial on Tuesday morning, January 7th. Will you kindly arrange for Mr. Fraser to be here at that time…"

This is the final 1912-dated model of the pre-production buffalo nickel and might be the one used by Medallic Art Co. to make hubs in December 1912. Slight differences exist between this version and the 1913-dated pattern, below, and the coin as issued for circulation. The author believes the patterns might have been dated 1912.

(Photo courtesy Bill Fivaz. Taken at the Philadelphia Mint, 1996.)

The Buffalo nickel design had been fully defined by August 1912, so there was little need to make extensive pattern or experimental pieces. Those made in early 1913 were intended to prove the striking characteristics of the new design, and to satisfy the demands of Clarence Hobbs and his business associates.

Five Cents – Model #2, J-1950
Obverse 2, Reverse B
Struck January 13, 1913 (17 pieces)

Composite portrait of Native American facing right; hair parted on right side and braided; two eagle feathers in hair low and to back of head, third feather behind neck; blanket or tunic across shoulder; date in raised numerals on shoulder; somewhat irregular with "3" too short. Braid ties touch rim. Inscription LIBERTY next to upper right rim in front of forehead. Light texture on chin and neck. No designer's initial.

Rim is wide and somewhat irregular.

Male bison in profile facing left, standing on small mound or edge of hill, head lowered, field textured to suggest prairie grass. Below is denomination FIVE CENTS; above are inscriptions UNITED STATES OF AMERICA and E PLURIBUS UNUM. Lettering small and somewhat run together particularly on motto; lettering matches #1 model reverse.

Rim narrower than on obverse and shows slight irregularity.

This is the best version of the pre-production buffalo nickel to survive and appears to have been made from unretouched dies; notice the highly textured fields on both sides. The numeral "3" has been added to the die and cut slightly smaller than the other digits. Lettering and other details consistent with the last 1912 model. Loss of detail and blurring are differences attributable to the reduction and hub cutting process. However, many details of hair braid on obverse and bison on reverse do not match those of the 1912 model.

(Photo Courtesy Smithsonian National Numismatic Collection, Douglas Mudd.)

Five Cents – Model #3 (recreation)
Obverse 3, Reverse C
Struck January 21, 1913 (9 pieces)

Composite portrait of Native American facing right; hair parted on right side and braided; two eagle feathers in hair low and to back of head; blanket or tunic across shoulder; date in raised numerals on shoulder; all digits of equal size and well formed. Braid ties do not touch rim but ends are indistinct. Inscription LIBERTY next to upper right rim in front of forehead. No designer's initial.

Male bison in profile facing left, standing on small mound or edge of hill, head lowered, field lightly textured to suggest prairie grass. Below is denomination FIVE CENTS; above are inscriptions UNITED STATES OF AMERICA and E PLURIBUS UNUM. Lettering small and somewhat run together particularly on the motto.

Rim is narrow and even.

Contemporary comments:
JL: 1/21/13. "The only change is in the border which has been made round and true"
CEB: 1/24/13. "One of the pieces was sent to the director…and eight pieces I am holding…31 blanks returned to the Superintendent."
JL: 1/24/13. "January 21st…nine…struck in the presence of…Barber, Norris, Hart, Fraser…and two representatives of the automatic vending machine."[Reith and Henson – RWB]
JL: 3/3/13. "…these are the dies which were afterward adopted and from which coins…are now being struck."

The image above is a recreation. No examples from this experimental group are known, although Landis' inventory lists four specimens as missing. Any specimens would probably be similar to the circulation design. Probably from copies of the #1 models which were altered by Fraser before new hubs were cut.

Note increased distance of lettering from the rim on both sides. Motto is still too small and barely legible. Both sides appear to be slightly smaller than model #1.

John Landis' letter of March 3, 1913 attempts to account for all pattern and experimental pieces made during the previous weeks. He had the following comments about the January 21 pattern pieces:[535]

---

[535] *US Mint,* NARA-CP, op. cit., file 311716. Letter dated March 3, 1913 to Roberts from Landis, p.1.

1	sent to the Bureau, January 21, 1913.
1	to the Designer, February 5, 1913.
1	to Mr. Hobbs, February 5, 1913.
1	sent to bureau, February 13, 1913.
	None of these four has been returned.
<u>5</u>	destroyed, February 28, 1913
9	Total

The mystery here is that descriptions of the dies indicate the original models were not accurately circular and that Barber corrected this. Without an example from this batch of patterns, it cannot be conclusively established that the #3 models matched circulation dies. However, Landis' letter of March 3 states this version was used to make circulation coins for 1913. The 1913 production coins do not have an irregular rim.

Five Cents – Judd-1951
Obverse 4, Reverse D
Struck February 13, 1913 (4 pieces). Hand engraved date and legends on dies.

Composite portrait of Native American facing right; hair parted on right side and braided; two eagle feathers in hair low and to back of head, tip of third behind neck; blanket or tunic across shoulder; date in raised numerals on shoulder, round-top "3"; somewhat irregular with thin, angular numerals. Inscription LIBERTY next to upper right rim in front of forehead; all letters recut into die and some show cutting of letter segments at varying depths in the die. No designer's initial.

Recutting of some details of portrait.

Planchet is 0.869-inches in diameter, although design is normal size. This produced a gap between rim and lettering/portrait consistent with the demands of Hobbs Manufacturing Company.

Male bison in profile facing left, standing on small mound or edge of hill, head lowered, field lightly textured to suggest prairie grass. Below is denomination FIVE CENTS with all letters recut in die; above are inscriptions UNITED STATES OF AMERICA and E PLURIBUS UNUM. Lettering small and somewhat run together, but sharply cut into the die. Many irregularities and overlaps of letter segments. E PLURIBUS UNUM is incomplete and more of a sloppy outline than true text.

Recutting of some details of bison. Hill has nearly vertical edge on left.

Rim similar to obverse and shows space between bison and rim. Notice incomplete right rear leg of animal.

Contemporary comments:
JL: 3/03/13. "…On February 13, 1913, four specimens of the new design 5-cent nickel piece were struck from dies with a diameter slightly greater than the standard. These dies were made in order to show the effect of a small space between the design and the border and with the intention, if it were thought desirable to have this space, of reducing the design so as to bring the coin to the standard diameter."

248

This experimental piece was made to show what the coin would look like if the Hobbs Company's request to make the design smaller and leave a prominent gap between design and rim were carried out. It appears Barber made a copy of the hub of J-1950, removed most of the lettering, then made a working die. New lettering and date were cut into the die by hand. Traces of the original lettering are visible in the inscriptions. It is not clear why this was done rather than simply impressing a slightly larger diameter die with the hub.

Note the sharp, stick-like character to lettering and frequent overlaps produced as each stroke of the graver cut to different depths in the die steel. The motto E PLURIBUS UNUM is little more than a confused outline and was obviously not re-engraved by Barber. Other lettering and the date show similar hand cutting of the characters. The observant collector will note that this is exactly the same style of hand engraving seen on some of the 1916 pattern half dollars, particularly in the obverse rays and reverse motto.

(Photos courtesy Smithsonian National Numismatic Collection, Douglas Mudd.)

Four specimens were struck February 13, 1913. Two were placed in the mint collection, one went to Secretary MacVeagh the day before he held a final conference about the nickel design, and one to superintendent John Landis.

Initial Production and Proofs

Mint officials recognized the potential for significant interest in the new nickel. Within two weeks of initial production for circulation, the Philadelphia Mint also struck 1,000 matte proof specimens for sale to collectors. As with the new gold designs and the Lincoln cent, it was felt the dies were too irregularly curved to permit the usual brilliant proofs. By sandblasting the dies prior to hardening (as was done on the Lincoln cent proofs), then striking the pieces on a medal press from new dies, the mint attempted to produce something distinctive for hobbyists. The edges of matte proof Buffalo nickels have a brilliant mirror-like surface which is different than that on circulating coins. For many collectors the result was less-than-convincing special coins. This left only the subsidiary silver coins available in brilliant proof version.

The following table shows dates of production for circulation and matte proof coins during 1913. The first circulation strike coins were made on February 18, 1913, and distributed by President Taft during ceremonies for groundbreaking of the American Indian Memorial, on Staten Island, New York February 22, 1913.

Mint	Type I		Type II		Matte Proof[536]
	Begin/End Dates	Production – Type I	Begin/End Dates	Production – Type II	
Philadelphia[537]	2/18 - 5/8	30,992,000	5/9 – 12/30	29,858,700	
	3/3 - 3/5	proofs			1,000
	3/20	proofs			300
	5/1	proofs			220
			5/26	proofs	250
			10/11	proofs	110
			11/18	proofs	285
			11/28	proofs	273
			12/24	proofs	196
San Francisco[538]	2/30 (?) - 4/19	2,105,000	?	1,209,000	N/A
Denver[539]	2/24 - 4/29	5,337,000	?	4,156,000	N/A
Totals		**38,434,000**		**35,223,700**	**Ty-I 1,520** **Ty-II 1,114**

Note: The *Medal and Proof Coins Book* indicates 1,114 Type-II proofs were made – 400 less than *The Guide Book of United States Coins* has traditionally stated at 1,514.

It can readily be seen from the above that type-I nickels were produced from mid-February to early May in Philadelphia, and during March and April at the other two mints. San Francisco Mint superintendent Frank Leach noted he had not seen any of the new coins in circulation although a "…great number of the new nickels…have been taken out

---

[536] *US Mint,* NARA-P, Record Group 104, entry 107F and 107G, *Medal and Proof Coins Book, 1906-1916.* Most entries are by assistant coiner Robert Clark. These are the total quantities accepted by the coiner; defective pieces are excluded.
[537] *US Mint,* NARA-CP, op. cit., file 311716. Letter dated February 18, 1913 to Roberts from Landis; and letter dated May 23, 1913 to Roberts from Albert A Norris, acting superintendent, Philadelphia mint.
[538] *US Mint,* NARA-CP, op. cit., file 312300. Letter dated May 26, 1913 to Roberts from Frank A. Leach, superintendent, San Francisco mint.
[539] *US Mint,* NARA-CP, op. cit., file 312278. Letter dated May 27, 1913 to Roberts from Frank M. Donovan, superintendent, Denver mint.

through banks and private individuals."[540] On orders from director Roberts, substantial portions of the initial production was held back after minting. San Francisco reported having 796,000 type-1 coins in storage on May 16, 1913. Denver held 2,316,319 as of May 27, and still had them sitting in the vaults on August 20. The Philadelphia Mint evidently delivered all their coins to sub-treasuries and banks soon after striking.

---

[540] *US Mint,* NARA-CP, op. cit., file 311716. Letter dated April 29, 1913 to Roberts from superintendent Leach.

Chapter 11 – Design Changes

Engraver Charles Barber expressed concern over the size of inscriptions and relative relief of the lettering on the new five-cent coin. His objections had been overruled by MacVeagh and the first coins were produced from the January 21 set of hubs touched up by Barber and approved by Fraser. The objections of Clarence Hobbs had wasted seven months of mint and Fraser's time, and by mid-January 1913 their complaints were more or less a dead issue. However, Hobbs had succeeded in giving the mint something it did not have before – quantitative information on the height of lettering.[541] In an acerbic letter to President Taft, Clarence Hobbs continued his complaints about the nickel design. Most of the arguments were self-serving, but he succeeded in identifying significant problems with the inscriptions before the coins were minted:[542]

> 4(d) The token of value upon the one side and the date line upon the other, in addition to being difficult to distinguish, is [sic] placed too close to the surface of the coin and are only .003 of an inch in depth, whereas the depth of these characters on the standard coin is .007. Consequently, when the coin has received 3/7 of the wear which the standard coin is capable of taking, the token of value will have been entirely worn away and the coin will cease to be a legal tender.

Hobbs was correct in identifying that the date and value did not have sufficient relief, or protection from wear. His prediction that these design elements would quickly be worn away in circulation proved correct. He also felt the legends were too small, and the mint examined the possibility of enlarging the word LIBERTY on the obverse.

---

[541] It seems odd that no one at the mint was able to make relief measurement from pattern and experimental coins produced during 1906 to 1921. The only quantitative measurements of design relief are those from Hobbs Manufacturing in 1913 and 1916. However, mint documents are filled with discussions of diameter to an accuracy of .0005 inch.
[542] *US Mint,* NARA-CP, op. cit., file 305310. Letter (excerpt) dated February 19, 1913 to President Taft from Hobbs.

Engraver Barber had been watching the new nickel dies carefully since production began in February. His department had to keep all three mints supplied with working dies, and after less than two weeks of production was finding that to be a difficult task:[543]

> ...I mentioned when in Washington that although we had made a few of the new nickel pieces, that the real test would come when we commenced regular coinage, well that test is certainly upon us.
>
> We find that we are getting only about one third the number of pieces per pair of dies that was produced by the old design,[544] consequently we are using three times the number of dies. This is taxing my department to the very limit, in fact I am only just able to supply the demand of the several Mints without their working overtime. I have had to call a halt on overtime in the coining room as I had not the dies to keep the presses running more than the regular working day. If I can only get a supply ahead then perhaps overtime might be considered, but while the dies are called for as fast as I can make them, there appears to be but small prospect of getting a stock in hand.
>
> I do not find any fault with the Coiners of this Mint or the other Mints. The difficulty is in the design and the shape of the die. In the first place the dies are so convex that if the feeders skip a feed the dies come together, this causes the loss of many dies, next the movement of the metal over the rough convex surface of the dies grinds small particles from the blank which remain in the low places of the die and fairly grinds all detail from the design, leaving a very poor, worn, faded out impression of both the Indian and the buffalo. This is the chief cause of the extreme demand for dies, as said before, when about one third of the regular production is obtained, the dies being worn smooth in some parts and in others too rough to be allowed to remain in the presses.
>
> If it was not the question of getting a large output in a short time, I certainly would suggest that fewer pieces per pair of dies be made and dies changed still more frequently, as I feel that a large proportion of our present coinage is not calculated to bring us any credit. My object in giving you this description of the condition of the nickel coinage is to account for my not having twenty or thirty pairs of dies to spare to send to Denver as you wrote Mr. Landis yesterday and which he showed me this morning. I cannot suggest any remedy, I only hope that after the rush and the demand becomes normal that fewer dies will be required and then perhaps some stock can be made which will relieve the pressure.
>
> One other cause for the destruction of the dies is brought about by the automatic feed or hopper. If a blank becomes fixed in the tube there is no one to notice or remedy this condition and in consequence the dies come together; formerly the attendant at the press saw the lodgment of a blank in the tube and dislodged it which allowed the blanks to fall in place and no damage was done.[545]

Barber's letter explains two of the most common reasons for retiring a die: excessive wear due to abrasion of particles from the blanks, and "clashing" of dies when they strike one another without a planchet between them. It also helps explain why 1913 Type-I nickels are usually found with sharp, well struck designs – the dies were changed frequently, before significant wear could occur. Lastly, Barber's comments explain why many Buffalo nickels appear to be weakly struck, yet have prominent legends.

---

[543] *US Mint,* NARA-CP, op. cit., entry 229, box 299. Letter dated March 11, 1913 to Roberts from Barber.

[544] In 1909 the Philadelphia Mint was averaging 164,943 nickels per obverse die and 162,551 per reverse die. (*US Mint,* NARA-CP, op. cit., entry 229, box 287. Memorandum dated January 11, 1910 by Rhine H. Freed to Landis, including maximum, minimum, and average number of pieces per denomination for obverse and reverse for 1909.)

[545] Automatic planchet feeding was one of the innovations introduced by director Andrew in February 1910. See Chapter 5 for more information.

Comments about die life are somewhat confusing. According to coiner Rhine Freed, in 1909 the average number of pieces struck from the obverse die of the old Liberty nickel was 164,943. In his letter, above, Barber claims they were striking only about one-third this number, or approximately 54,981 pieces, from new Buffalo nickel dies. However, in May 1913, he said that the average was 150,168 per pair of dies. Yet, problems seem to have continued into the next two years with multiple letters between Barber, the superintendent and the director exchanged concerning quality of both nickels and cents.

On October 2, 1914 Barber commented, "…The first few pieces from new dies are fairly good, but after that the coins, to my mind, are all unsatisfactory appearing more like worn coin than new."[546] A few days later he wrote, "…The dull and worn appearance of the San Francisco coin is due to the same cause. From the appearance of the coins, their dies were allowed to run much longer that the Philadelphia dies."[547] After finding a large number of defective nickels in the Philadelphia Mint's special assay delivery of nickels, acting director Dewey sternly commented, "…the means should be taken to improve the quality of the coins…The frequent blanking of the dies, and consequent blurring of the designs shown by your coins should not, however, be an excuse for increasing the cost of the coins."[548] To confuse matters further, by 1915 the coiner reported average obverse die life of just 42,332 pieces. This suggests that significant reduction in die life during the early weeks of Buffalo nickel production continued through the next calendar years, and might have resulted from problems related to both design and production equipment.

As with any new coin design, there were complaints and praise from the pubic and businesses. The most common complaint was that the new nickel was thicker or broader than the old Liberty pieces and stuck in vending machines and streetcar fare boxes. In response John Landis informed director Roberts, "…we have repeatedly examined the coins as to diameter and thickness and can find no difference between the new design and the old ones."[549]

Roberts had probably discounted much of Hobbs' letter to the President, but suggestions about the value and date wearing off, and the size of characters caused him to write to Fraser on March 30. In particular, his comment "…the token of value will be worn away [after limited circulation] and the coin will cease to be a legal tender," may have bothered the director. In his reply on April 1, Fraser stated:[550]

> I have your letter in reference to the five cent piece. Other sized letters can be made and I am ready to try them, but it strikes me that the five cents on the new nickel, although it is small, can be seen clearly and its meaning to a foreigner is much clearer than "one dime" on the ten cent piece and "V cents" on the old nickel.
>
> A coin is known by its <u>design</u> and when it is well known it is never questioned even when the inscription is entirely worn away. Not one person in ten thousand reads the inscription on a coin before paying it out.
>
> However if you wish it I will come to Washington and we can decide on what is to be done

After conferring with Roberts and then Barber in Philadelphia, Fraser approved enlarging the lettering of FIVE CENTS, and changing the ground from a hill or cliff edge, to

---

[546] *US Mint,* NARA-CP, op. cit., entry 246. Letter dated October 2, 1914 to Joyce from Barber. p.2. Quoted in full, below.
[547] *Ibid.*
[548] *US Mint,* NARA-CP, op. cit., entry 235, vol. 412. Letter dated January 18, 1915 to Joyce from Dewey.
[549] *US Mint,* NARA-CP, op. cit., entry 229, box 299. Letter dated March 11, 1913 to Roberts from Landis.
[550] *US Mint,* NARA-CP, op. cit., file 305310. Letter dated April 1, 1913 to Roberts from Fraser.

a nearly flat grassland to accommodate the extra height. The upper 2/3 of the design, from the bison's hooves upward, was not fundamentally altered. Below that, a recessed exergue was created and FIVE CENTS in larger letters was inserted. The upper border of this became the new ground upon which the animal stood. The rough field below and behind the buffalo, which Fraser had intended to represent the receding prairie, was smoothed. Barber also took the opportunity to strengthen the reverse legends. This produced the Type-II reverse which remained in use for the balance of the coin's life. By April 21 uniface trials of the new reverse had been struck and samples of old and new versions sent to director Roberts by Barber.[551]

> Please find enclosed two five cent nickel coins, one showing the change suggested and the other with no change, for comparison.
> If you think well of the alteration we could hold up the coinage for a short time while I make a new hub which would not take more than ten days, when we could go on with the coinage. As the demand for this coin appears to have abated I think it would cause no inconvenience.

Barber's letter, two die trials of the reverse designs, and a cover letter from Roberts were sent to Fraser on April 23. His response was a mixture of acceptance and concern that he had already spent too much time on the nickel. After taking a few lines to again express approval for Barber's work, Fraser concentrated on his own career:[552]

> Your letter of April 22nd last [sic – April 23rd] together with enclosure reached me in due course, and it seems to me that the nickel enclosed with the "Five Cents" made clearer is good and does not at all interfere with general design. I have also received your letter of April 23rd last in which you say the Secretary of the Treasury would like to have me come to Washington for a conference about the nickel piece and to telegraph when I can come. As the only change we have talked about in connection with the nickel piece is making the words "Five Cents" stronger, and as this has been done and can even be improved without my assistance, by straightening of letters, etc., I must assume that the conference will cover other matters.
> I have given the Secretary's request, sent through you, the most careful consideration and much as I should like to comply therewith and have the honor and pleasure of seeing the Secretary, I am forced to decline his kind invitation. I have matters here that require every hour of my time and thought. You do not tell me what, even as far as your information goes, the Secretary wishes to see me about, through of course I know from your two letters it is in some way connected with the new nickel.
> Looking back now I am aware, even more that I was just after the new nickel was approved finally and ordered struck, how much time and worry I spent on the controversies that arose in connection with the so-called coin-detecting machine people, and I should have only myself to blame if any further controversy whatsoever in connection with the nickel and involving me should arise. The fact is frankly that I am in the very midst of work, which I know to be vital to my career and cannot afford any interruption. Of course if the Secretary should be in town and should wish to consult me about anything, in which he thought I might be of use, I should feel it an honor to see him.
> PS: I enclose two reverse sides of nickel as requested.

---

[551] *US Mint*, NARA-CP, op. cit., file 305310. Letter dated April 21, 1913 to Roberts from Barber.
[552] *US Mint*, NARA-CP, op. cit., file 305310. Letter dated April 25, 1913 to Roberts from Fraser.

It is evident that Fraser had enough of the nickel. His previous requests for additional payment to cover part of the counterfeit detector work had been negotiated down to approximately half of what he felt was reasonable. He had read and re-read Hobbs complaints and was now hearing versions of them from Roberts. The new secretary, William G. McAdoo, wanted to discuss other changes in the coin, and would likely claim that the work had to be done without additional compensation. With profitable commissions lined up in his studio, Fraser had no interest in spending hours refining what he must have felt was already complete. The sculptor had also learned the difficult lesson of Saint-Gaudens: the mint was a sink hole of time and talent, consuming both in prodigious quantity then spitting out mediocre results.

Figure 51. **End of the Trail *(1894)* by James Earle Fraser as installed at the National Cowboy & Western Heritage Museum, Oklahoma City, OK.** (Courtesy National Cowboy & Western Heritage Museum, Oklahoma City, OK.)

The "…work…vital to my career…" Fraser mentioned was preparation of an 18-foot high plaster version of his sculpture *The End of the Trail* for exhibition at the 1915 Panama-Pacific Exposition in San Francisco. Given the time it took to enlarge a major work, make corrections and arrange for shipment, Fraser felt he had no time to devote to additional changes to the nickel. *The End of the Trail* was originally modeled in 1894, when Fraser was a teenager. The figure represented the fate of Native Americans as their lands were appropriated by white settlers. A small version was exhibited in the Paris Salon of 1898, where it received the John Wanamaker Prize from the American Artists Association, and the notice of Augustus Saint-Gaudens. The Panama-Pacific plaster version has survived into the 21st century, and is currently on exhibit at the National Cowboy & Western Heritage Museum in Oklahoma City, Oklahoma. The large version of Fraser's work won a gold medal in San Francisco and confirmed Fraser's position as a leading interpreter of the American West. Fraser ultimately recreated the work in bronze in numerous sizes, two of which were of monumental scale.

Roberts accepted Fraser's comments without reply, and forwarded the refusal to meet McAdoo to the secretary's office. The offer to meet Fraser may have been nothing more than a courtesy from the new secretary to the designer of the already-famous nickel, but the artist's letter effectively closed the door on any offers of future work from the mint.

Frank Leach, Superintendent of the San Francisco Mint, who was also a former mint director, offered his comments on the new reverse:[553]

> We received the new reverse dies for nickels, and note the change made in the lettering. I am sure that we will have better work and longer life of the dies. If the same change was made in the lettering of the obverse side, with the other made, would add fifty per cent to the life of the dies…

Permission was received from the assistant treasury secretary on May 23, 1913 to enlarge the obverse lettering "…especially the word 'Liberty'…"[554] but nothing was done. Additional suggestions for change were actively considered by the mint director and backed up with presumptions of increased die life or better striking quality. Taken together they could have substantially altered the appearance of the new nickel; however, the ideas were effectively squashed by an unexpected party – the engraver. On May 27 Barber wrote one of his long-winded essays to director Roberts in response to a letter on the 24th. Barber made several recommendations and discussed what would have to be done to "correct" the date problem and other matters:[555]

> The change suggested can of course be made, whether the life of the die will be increased "fifty per cent" is a correct statement is very doubtful, and only a trial will demonstrate.[556]
>
> It is an open question whether the life of the die is as important a matter as the quality of the coin and I quite agree with you that the dies are run too long and more dies should be used.
>
> There must always be a first and a last point of the die to give out and the question is, which is the more important, if the inscriptions remain good and the Indian head and buffalo are worn smooth it cannot be claimed as an improvement.
>
> The fact is the design is too large for the size of the coin and no thought has been taken of the necessary inscriptions. The coin has the appearance of having been made with the sole object of covering the whole space with an Indian head on one side and a buffalo on the other, the inscriptions being an after thought.
>
> To make the change it will be necessary to reduce the relief of the shoulder of the Indian as the date rests upon the shoulder, to increase the depth of the date without reducing the shoulder would make matters worse instead of better, it would surely require more pressure to get a perfect impression of the die. And that would make the life of the die shorter instead of longer.
>
> We now find that the date is the last place the metal fills and therefore to simply make the date deeper you will readily see would not be an improvement without as said before reducing the relief of the shoulder.
>
> Your directions were and you now repeat, that any change is not to be "radical", but must be so slight that it would be "scarcely noticeable to the public," may I say that any change we may make will be noticeable and that we find the coins are referred to by the public and designated according to the change, therefore, would it not be well before making any further change to consider in what way the coin can

---

[553] *US Mint,* NARA-CP, op. cit., entry 229, box 299. Letter dated May 16, 1913 to Roberts from superintendent Leach.
[554] *US Mint,* NARA-CP, op. cit., file 305310. Letter dated May 23, 1913 to Roberts from assistant secretary.
[555] *US Mint,* NARA-CP, op. cit., file 305310. Letter dated May 27, 1913 to Roberts from Barber.
[556] The quotation comes from Frank Leach's letter of May 16, 1913 to Roberts.

> be improved and make all changes at the same time whether they be radical or not.
>
> Mr. Clark has just handed me the following which does not bear out the statement [by Leach] that the change already made will make "longer the life of the dies."
>
> Last 12 pairs of dies before change, average per pair 150,168; 12 pairs since change, average per pair 109,389.
>
> Awaiting your further instructions.
>
> Respectfully,

The letter clearly explains why the date on the new nickel was not recessed, as would be done later on the Standing Liberty quarter. His analysis showed the obverse design would have to be reworked to lower relief of the Indian's shoulder if the mint were to also reduce the height of the date. This would have been a noticeable change in Fraser's design – not something particularly desirable to do. No mention is made of making the date incuse (as used on the imitative "Buffalo dollar" commemorative in issued in 2002), or of other possible alterations.

With Fraser having declined to consider further work on the nickel, and Barber telling the director that the desired changes would probably be immediately noticed by the public, the Buffalo nickel was left largely as-is. The problems of lettering size and relief of the value on the reverse were partially corrected when the Type-II reverse was adopted in May, 1913. But, improving relief of the date and other modifications would have to wait. A new hub was made in 1916, and minor changes were made to lettering and fields over the years, all of which escaped general notice.

Later Hub Changes

Mint files in the National Archives contain several letters and memoranda related to complaints about the visual appearance of the Saint-Gaudens, Pratt, Brenner and Fraser designs. All five were of a softer, less sharply defined character than previous coins and the public agreed with mint officials that the coins had a "worn out" or "blind" look to them. The situation was addressed in a series of letters by Charles Barber, Robert Clark and superintendent Adam Joyce to director Roberts in October 1914.

The first, from engraver Barber, responds to several coins sent to the Philadelphia Mint by director Roberts on October 1. These included sample cents and nickels from Denver, San Francisco and Philadelphia "…received regarding the poor execution of our minor coins…"[557] The letter is quoted in its entirety since portions deal with commonly encountered mint errors:[558]

> I have examined the one and five cent coins sent here by the Director of the Mint for an expression of opinion regarding the execution of the same, and beg to say, that in the case of the nickel five cent coin with the part of a circle cut in the edge is plainly a defective blank. The nickel coin with the defects on the field in front of the Indian head and under the chin was struck from a die that had been blanked in the press[559] and are parts of the design of the reverse die transferred to

---

[557] *US Mint,* NARA-CP, op. cit., entry 246. Letter dated October 6, 1914 to Roberts from Joyce.

[558] *US Mint,* NARA-CP, op. cit., entry 246. Letter dated October 2, 1914 to Joyce from Barber.

[559] He means the dies struck each other without a planchet between them; commonly called "clashed dies" by today's collectors of mint errors.

the obverse appearing on the coin. As soon as a die is blanked it should be removed from the press as good coin cannot be made from a defective die.

Regarding the general worn out appearance of both the one and five cent coin, I beg to say that the character of the work on both of these coins is such that they never do appear like new minted coins, they may be clean and bright, but the modeling is of the impressionist school and that is not and never was adapted to coinage, consequently a very small amount of coin is struck before what little detail there was in either coin is lost, and then it has the appearance of poor coinage. To make perfect sharp impressions from these dies it would be necessary to strike them like proof, that not being feasible with the large amount of minor coins required, I would advise a closer inspection of the coin and as soon as a die shows signs of wear, that it be removed and a new die [put in its] place instead. This I know will hamper the coinage and reduce the out put as it consumes time to set dies in the press, but if sharper impressions are demanded dies less worn must be used regardless of the result.

I have from the time that these coins were adopted called attention to the very obvious fact that neither was calculated for the purpose for which hey were intended, and I am still convinced that to make a perfect coinage with these dies is simply out of the question. The first few pieces from new dies are fairly good but after that the coins to my mind are all unsatisfactory appearing more like worn coin than new; this is the condition of the coins submitted, they are not the impressions of new dies, consequently have besides the defects mentioned the other defect namely, want of sharpness and clean cut distinctness that should appear in all coins which as said before come from the character of the design.

Philadelphia Mint coiner Robert Clark incorporated Barber's comments in a lengthy letter also sent to Joyce. He also included tables showing the weight of eighteen five-cent and nineteen one-cent pieces compared to the legal standards:[560]

…The three one cent coins vary as to sharpness and detail, one piece being much sharper than the other owing to the fact that it was struck from a new die, while the others were struck from a die that was in use for a short time. Great care is taken to produce perfect coinage, but an imperceptible fault develops into a noticeable one. When it is detected it is promptly corrected but between these two stages there may be coins with slight imperfections that escapes detection and gets into delivery. We guard against imperfections in coins to the extent that practical conditions will permit. As to the general worn out appearance of the coins, the character of the design is responsible for this. A small percentage of coin struck from new dies will look sharp and clear, but after running a short time the coins will loose a certain amount of detail and present a worn and dull appearance. They are bright and clean but lack the appearance of newly minted coins. If the same style lettering were used on both obverse and reverse sides the word "Liberty" and the date would show to better advantage. Under the present conditions in order to make every piece sharp and clear we would be compelled to substitute new dies at short intervals. That is not feasible where a coinage of upwards of 150,000,000 pieces is required during the year. If sharper impressions are insisted upon dies less worn must be used. This will reduce the output. We will however, in the future change the dies as soon as they show signs of wear. This will require many more dies. The dull and worn appearance of the San Francisco coin is due to the same cause. From the appearance of the coins their dies were allowed to run longer than the Philadelphia dies.

As to the range in weights of one and five cent pieces I find the five cent pieces within the legal tolerance. The question of the weight of individual pieces has never been raised, as long as all deliveries were within the tolerance….

---

[560] *US Mint,* NARA-CP, op. cit., entry 246. Letter dated October 5, 1914 to Joyce from Clark.

Clark refers to the Lincoln cent when he discusses the obverse legend and reverse lettering style. Minor coins contained no precious metal and the mints simply counted the coins placed in sacks and weighed the entire delivery in bulk. So long as the total weight was within tolerance, it was assumed the individual coins were satisfactory. This is similar to the mixing of light and heavy gold coins into lots that contained the correct weight of gold, even though individual pieces might be at the high- or low-end of legal weight tolerance.

By 1915 it was obvious that changes would have to be made in the Buffalo nickel if large scale production was maintained. An April 16, 1915 report from Philadelphia superintendent Adam Joyce to mint director Robert W. Woolley was indicative of the problem. During the first three months of 1915, the mint had struck 13,038,289 Buffalo nickels and used three hundred eight obverse dies and two hundred seventy-four reverse dies. The average obverse die life was 42,332 coins and the average reverse die life was 47,585 pieces.[561] A detailed list of dies used during that time shows a few producing over 100,000 pieces many others less than 10,000. One reverse die, #181, struck only nine hundred twenty pieces before being withdrawn. Where dies were pulled after striking only a few thousand pieces, the likely cause was mechanical failure of the planchet feeding mechanism which allowed dies to strike one another, and not problems with the design. However, when Buffalo nickel die life is compared with similar-sized foreign coins made at the mint – such as the Cuban five centavo and ten centavo pieces – the nickel dies were producing only about one-third the average number of coins.[562]

Figure 52. 1915 was the final year for which the original Buffalo nickel hubs were used. Compare with the carefully revised version used beginning in 1916, below. (Courtesy American Numismatic Rarities.)

At Barber's suggestion, director Woolley ordered new hubs made of the Buffalo nickel. Although cut from the same models as in 1913, this time Barber did considerable retouching of the hubs and master dies. Modern collectors treat the 1916 version as an improvement on the original, although the changes are really those Barber and others suggested in 1913. Over the next decade incremental improvements were made to the design. The most noticeable was a gradual flattening of the obverse field. By 1936 the fields were nearly flat which allowed the mint to polish dies and strike brilliant proof specimens for collectors in 1936 and 1937.

---

[561] Compare with 1909 nickels averaging 164,943 coins per obverse and 162,551 per reverse die. (See note, above.)
[562] *US Mint,* NARA-CP, op. cit., entry 246. Letter dated April 16, 1915 to Director from Joyce.

Figure 53. Significant changes in detail were made to the buffalo nickel for 1916. Not only was the word LIBERTY *sharpened and given greater height, but much of the Indian's hair and braid were re-engraved. On the reverse the bison's coat was strengthened and some of the roughness removed.* (Courtesy American Numismatic Rarities.)

The trend toward placing the portrait of historical persons on circulating coins, begun in 1909 with the Lincoln cent, continued in 1938 with introduction of the Jefferson nickel, and the last Buffalo nickels left the Denver mint in the summer of that year.

Of all circulating coins subject to redesign between 1907 and 1921 the Buffalo nickel has become the most loved and identified by the general public. It is a common coin of uncommon artistry; a bit of pocket change everyone from child to tycoon might have once owned. Weinman's dime, issued in October 1916, was more praised when first issued. The artistic herald of Saint-Gaudens' MCMVII double eagle found its home largely in the hands of counting clerks and wealthy pockets. Brenner's Lincoln cent fit every pocket but was small, quickly spent and devoid of "heft." It was Fraser's nostalgic American composition, silvery when new, that was handled, looked on, tendered and accepted a hundred million times a day.[563]

James E. Fraser was already well known when he designed the nickel. During a long career he was never without commissions, often having several underway simultaneously, and many others awaiting his attention. As possibly the most recognized of Augustus Saint-Gaudens' assistants, Fraser upheld the Master's ideals in his own designs and of artists he influenced. Fraser's most significant role in American numismatics was as sculptor member of the Commission of Fine Arts (1919-1924) under Charles Moore's skillful chairmanship, and as unofficial advisor for many years after his term expired. He, and wife Laura, influenced nearly every commemorative coin produced from 1919 to 1928. He also was deeply involved in the Peace dollar competition of late 1921, at one point acting as surrogate for mint director Baker.

Without Fraser's talent, numismatics would be the poorer for the loss of his personal creativity. Without his tenacity and ideals, we could have lost a generation of meaningful medallic art. By influencing designs for coins, medals and related art forms, James E. Fraser helped America conclude its renaissance of numismatic art.

---

[563] Nearly ninety years after the Buffalo nickel's introduction, the U.S. Mint produced a dollar-sized, 0.900 fine silver imitation as a collectible, and to raise money for the Museum of the American Indian in Washington, DC. The workmanship was solid, commercial quality die sinking without a trace of Fraser's immediacy and strength.

Chapter 12 – Panama-Pacific International Exposition

An exposition to mark the opening of the Panama Canal was proposed in 1904, the same year the United States received the concession to build the canal, by Rueben Hale, a prominent San Francisco merchant. Hale convinced other members of the Merchant's Association that, as the major west coast port for canal traffic, the city should hold a large exhibition. In addition to celebrating the opening of the canal, the exposition would also commemorate the 400th anniversary of Francesco deBalboa's discovery of the Pacific Ocean.

A bill introduced in U.S. Congress to provide $5,000,000 in startup money failed. Not long after, the 1906 earthquake and fire put all plans on hold. While the city was still recovering from the fire, the Pacific Exposition Company was formed to raise money to finance the proposed international exposition. The rebuilding of San Francisco seemed to stimulate fundraising for the exposition and some individual pledges exceeded $250,000. The company was financed by the wealthiest and most powerful men in California.[564] The exposition was seen by San Francisco businesses as a unique opportunity to "...draw the attention of the world to San Francisco"[565] and promote it as a "playground of America" for tourists.[566] With approximately $5 million raised from pledges, the state of California created a taxpayer-funded matching grant to help with initial expenses.

The exposition company's first challenge was getting official sanction for holding the event in far-western San Francisco rather than competing cities. New Orleans emerged as the primary competitor. There was considerable advertising and lobbying of Congress,

---
[564] Robert W. Rydell, *All the World's a Fair: Visions of Empire at American International Expositions, 1876-1916*. University of Chicago Press, 1984. p.214.
[565] Burton Benedict, *The Anthropology of World's Fairs: San Francisco's Panama Pacific International Exposition of 1915*. Scolar Press, 1983. p.67.
[566] *Benedict*. p.72.

with San Francisco promoting its mild climate (versus New Orleans' hot and humid summer weather), its racial homogeneity and nationwide interest in the city's recovery from the earthquake and fire. But the winning strategy proved to be the exposition company's willingness to give up federal funding if Congress approved their proposal.[567] It soon became obvious that New Orleans would not be awarded the event. President Taft made the final selection early in 1911, then presided over a groundbreaking ceremony on October 14 of the same year.

Figure 54. Postcard produced by the San Francisco Panama-Pacific Exposition committee asks citizens to encourage their Congressmen to vote for the San Francisco location. (Courtesy Library of Congress.)

The Exposition

After settling on a site for the exposition, the committee faced the challenge of unifying the visual appearance of buildings. Opening day was scheduled for February 20, 1915 with the exposition running only until December 4. George W. Kelham was chosen as chief architect of the exposition and, working with the architectural council, created a unifying design for the buildings and exhibits. The plan followed neoclassical and beaux arts dictates to produce impressive public structures that satisfied the functional requirements of exhibitors and complimented the bayside setting and San Francisco's rebirth.

Painter and designer Jules Guerin used a specially blended mixture of plant fiber and gypsum plaster (called "staff") colored to imitate travertine marble, which the ancient Romans had used as facing material on many buildings. The plaster was applied to the wooden frames of most buildings, freestanding walls and even some of the statues to create a unified color and texture. Guerin also used specific accent colors to identify architectural and decorative details.

---

[567] *Benedict.* p.81.

Figure 55. Typical of exposition buildings was Festival Hall the venue for concerts and ballet performances. (Photo by U. H. Berney courtesy San Francisco Memories, Inc., San Francisco, CA.)

At its opening, the exposition had a significant impact on the country. Railroads operated special excursion trains at reduced fares from the East Coast and central states. The exposition became far more than the local or regional event that some had anticipated, although all management was handled by area business people. Displays came from across the country and even the Liberty Bell was shipped from Independence Hall in Philadelphia to the exposition. The display soon became a favorite spot for celebrities and ordinary folk to have their photograph taken. While war raged in Europe, protagonists found resources to join the San Francisco celebration.

The fair featured a Ford Motor Company assembly line set up in the Palace of Transportation. It operated for three hours every afternoon and produced one car every 10 minutes. During the exposition 4,400 cars were manufactured nearly all of which were sold to California drivers.[568] There was also a reproduction of the Panama Canal covering five acres. Visitors listened to narration about the canal over a telephone as they rode through the model on a floating platform.

Many prominent visitors came to the exposition including President Woodrow Wilson, Theodore Roosevelt, Luther Burbank, Buffalo Bill Cody, Charlie Chaplin, Thomas Edison, D. W. Griffith, Al Jolson, Maria Montessori, Barney Oldfield, Henry Ford, Eddie Rickenbacker, William Saroyan and Helen Keller. Composer Camille Saint-Saens, Franklin D. Roosevelt, Phoebe Hearst, Mabel Normand and actor Fatty Arbuckle walked the exhibit grounds. Bandmaster John Philip Sousa brought his world famous band to the exposition and performed there for nine weeks.[569]

Several not-yet-famous people attended the exposition or sold adventurous activities to visitors. During the exposition, a pilot named Allan H. Loughead and his brother Malcolm took visitors on flights around the Bay Area in their hydro-aeroplane. For ten dol-

---

[568] Some of these purchasers may still be trying to find their way home through freeway traffic jams.

[569] Most of the prominent people who attended were reimbursed for their travel and accommodations. For example, Franklin Roosevelt was reimbursed $366.65 for travel and lodging from March 16 to April 10, 1915 (NARA-CP, RG-56, entry 43, "Account of Frank N. Bauskett, Special Disbursing Agent, National Exhibition Commission" account #17, voucher #106.)

lars each, passengers could get a panoramic view of the exhibition and surrounding Golden Gate area. The brothers soon became tired of visitors mispronouncing their Scot-Irish name "Log-head," and when Malcolm opened a brake manufacturing company in Detroit, he changed the spelling to the phonetic "Lockheed." Allan later founded a company still well known in aerospace and defense circles using the same phonetic spelling.[570]

Sculpture at the Exposition

Sculpture was used throughout the exposition to ornament and accentuate the architecture. Most of the sculptors who would later design circulating and commemorative coins for the United States during the 1920s and 1930s participated in the exposition. Alexander Stirling Calder was the chief of sculpture, and directed a large number of skilled craftsmen who prepared the more routine decorative plaster details. More than fifteen hundred works, including fountains, columns, friezes, statues, heroic tableaux and other relief art, were commissioned from the country's best sculptors. Given the vast quantity it is not surprising that much of the work was mediocre, yet the exposition committee was able to award a medal of distinction to virtually every artist who participated. Long lists of award winners were published in major city newspapers, and local papers ran feature articles about the success of hometown artists.

A clear winner with both the general public and artists attending the exposition was James Fraser's *End of the Trail* originally sculpted in 1894. Final preparation of a monumental version (shown below, at the exposition) was one of the factors that prevented Fraser from making further modifications to the Buffalo nickel in 1913. The sculpture was mounted on a high pedestal in a prominent location at the exposition. The fair visitors standing near the base give an idea of the size of Fraser's sculpture.

---

[570] Allan Loughead began work as an airplane mechanic in 1910, and soon earned his pilot's credentials. This was still in the days of "barnstorming" and becoming a pilot amounted to taking off and landing in one piece, more or less. In 1912 he and his brother, Malcolm, settled in San Francisco where they though they could make money charging people $10 for airplane rides over the picturesque Golden Gate and bay. With $4,000 borrowed from a local taxi cab company, they built a two-seater airboat and formed the Alco Hydro-Aeroplane Company. The venture failed and the brothers spent the next two years raising money – even panning for gold – to get the aircraft back from the taxi company. They succeeded just in time for the Panama-Pacific International Exposition, and the large crowds resulted in many visitors willing to pay for an exciting airboat ride and high altitude view of the exposition. With their profits the bothers formed the Loughead Aircraft Manufacturing Company in 1916, and moved operations to Santa Barbara.

Like its predecessor company, by 1921 Loughead Aircraft had failed and Malcolm quit the aircraft business. While Allan sold California real estate, Malcolm moved to Detroit and opened the Lockheed Hydraulic Brake Company which manufactured automobile and truck brakes of his own design. The company name was spelled phonetically because Malcolm had grown tired of hearing his name mispronounced "Log-head." In 1926 the aviation bug again bit Allan and he and draughtsman/engineer Jack Northrop borrowed money to open the Lockheed Aircraft Corporation. They used the same spelling as Malcolm's company in an attempt to connect the aircraft company with the successful Detroit brake company.

Figure 56. Fraser's **End of the Trail** *on the exposition's Avenue of Palms (left). Compare the man on the far left with the sculpture to grasp the scale of the work. Right, artist Alexander Stirling Calder works on his sculpture* **Star.** (Courtesy Library of Congress.)

The numismatic highlight of the event was production and sale of four commemorative coins and a souvenir medal. Three coins – dollar, quarter eagle and quintuple eagle – were in gold and the fourth was a silver half dollar. The fifty dollar coin was also authorized in two versions, one was octagonal in homage to the first quintuple eagles issued by the private California minters and the United States Assay Office of Gold; the second was round and supposedly based on the 1877 $50 gold patterns. The medal was struck at the exposition as part of the U.S. Mint's demonstration booth. Distribution at the exposition was entrusted to Farran Zerbe, numismatic promoter and known for his traveling exhibit "Money of the World." He was employed by the exposition company with the title of *Manager of the Department of Official Coins and Medals* and set up displays in the Liberal Arts Building.

Enabling legislation limited production to 25,000 gold dollars, 10,000 quarter eagles, 3,000 quintuple eagles (both varieties combined) and 200,000 half dollars. The Legislation authorized production of the coins on the exhibition ground, but after a legal opinion from the treasury's solicitor that coins could only be struck within a mint, all coins were actually produced at the San Francisco Mint. Only souvenir medals were made as part of the Mint Bureau's display in the Mines Building. Although Zerbe claimed that distribution was successful, thousands of pieces remained unsold when the exposition closed, many others tarnished while in storage during the exposition. Additional specimens were offered for sale for several months after the exposition closed. Large quantities of remaining coins and medals were melted.[571]

In addition to souvenir medals and coins, and the mint's on-site exhibit, a major effort was made by the Bureau of Engraving and Printing to promote the Panama-Pacific

---

[571] See Bowers: *Commemorative Coins of the United States: A Complete Encyclopedia*, for a more extensive treatment of sale and distribution of the coins.

Exposition by creating a series of four special postage stamps. These were issued in 1913 and various postal envelopes and covers were available during the fair.

Figure 57. Panama-Pacific commemorative postage stamps issued in 1913. L-R, one-cent "Balboa" printed in green, two cents "Panama Canal" printed in carmine, five cents "Golden Gate" printed in blue, and ten cents "Discovery of San Francisco Bay" printed in orange. (Courtesy Smithsonian National Postal Museum.)

The exposition committee encouraged the production of hundreds of trinkets, tokens and knickknacks in an attempt to make everything associated with the exposition a "collectible." Season tickets were personalized with photos of the purchaser.

Figure 58. Examples of PPIE season tickets including photos of the purchasers. (NARA.)

By the time the last visitor left the exposition, nearly 18 million people had passed though entrance turnstiles. The exposition generated sufficient profit to build the San Francisco Civic Auditorium, and an additional $1 million surplus.

Origin of the Commemorative Concept

The last major numismatic event of the 1909-1915 period was production of a set of coins to commemorate the Panama-Pacific International Exposition held in San Francisco, California during 1915. These special coins made no claim to being circulation tender, but were intended to produce revenue for the exposition organizing committee. As the first commemorative coins produced in a mint other than Philadelphia, they presented special logistical problems for Mint Bureau officials. They also served as prelude to redesign of the circulating subsidiary silver coins which would occur in 1916, and became a transition between the long-term directorship of George E. Roberts and the sixteen month tenure of Robert W. Woolley. This group of four denominations (five different designs) was also impetus for extensive commemorative coin programs that would carry through the 1920s until temporarily halted by opposition from President Hoover. The tentative beginnings of commemorative designs, starting with issues for the Columbian Exposition of 1892-93, Washington-Lafayette silver dollar of 1900, and Lewis and Clark gold dollars of 1903, now prepared to overflow Congressional hoppers with proposed commemorative coins – all for good and noble causes, at least according to the sponsors and promoters.

The Panama-Pacific designs also included the last substantive creative expression of Philadelphia Mint Engraver Charles Barber on American coinage.[572] Although Barber is credited with the obverse of the 1916-1917 McKinley gold dollar, that piece is devoid of artistic creativity and vitality. But, in early 1915, Barber's Panama-Pacific half dollar and quarter eagle were the clear equal of designs by outside artists.

Mint Bureau Preparations

Anticipating passage of a PPIE commemorative coin bill in 1914, mint director Roberts approached treasury secretary McAdoo and assistant secretary Malburn with a plan to keep the mint in control of designs and production. He would first obtain from the Commission of Fine Arts a list of America artists capable of preparing suitable coin and award medal designs. Then he wanted to contact some of them to determine their interest in a commission for a specific coin or medal and the suitability of compensation.[573]

Roberts' initial contact with the artists gave them time to experiment with the commemorative designs and devise preliminary compositions well before the bill actually became law. It appears that Aitken used the advance notice wisely and produced drawings that required only limited modification to finally win McAdoo's approval. Keck, Longman and Manship, however, do not appear to have been contacted until the bill was passed. All ended up with sketches that displeased McAdoo and Malburn, and resulted in the latter two artists' work being rejected.

Key to bringing the entire project to completion was the work of acting director Frederick P. Dewey, PhD. He filled the void created when Roberts resigned in November 1914 and served with good judgment and enthusiasm until Robert W. Woolley took office as director. He also supervised plans for the mint's exhibit at the PPIE and organized shipment of equipment. By the time Woolley was at his desk in March 1915, the difficult part of preparing commemorative designs was over and only die production remained. Dewey was "rewarded" by being shipped to Philadelphia to become Assayer and also supervise the annual settlement.

It was Dewey who suggested that mint engravers Charles Barber and George Morgan prepare drawings for all of the commemorative coins in parallel with the outside artists. According to his reasoning, this gave the mint a "fall back" position in case one or

---

[572] Coin collectors often abbreviate the name to "Pan-Pac." In its time the exposition's nickname was usually "PPIE" or "P-PIE."
[573] This is similar to the plan director Woolley followed in late 1915 when planning for the new subsidiary silver coin designs.

more of the artists failed to produce an acceptable design. This provided necessary flexibility to a very time-constrained process. It also showed secretary McAdoo that all the designers – government and private – were capable of similarly good and poor designs.

Legislation Passed

In late 1913 and through the first half of 1914 the mint's emphasis had been on preparing an exhibit of minting equipment and on-site production of a small souvenir medal. On June 3, Representative Julius Kahn of California introduced H.R. 16902 providing for the production of gold and silver coins commemorating the Panama-Pacific International Exposition. This was done at the request of the exposition company although it is unclear if Farran Zerbe was involved in the bill's preparation. The $50 "slug" had long been recognized as emblematic of California gold, and the other denominations were simply attempts to appeal to the pocketbooks of a range of souvenir buyers. A copy of the bill was sent to mint director Roberts who reviewed the bill's provisions, then contacted the Commission of Fine Arts requesting time on the agenda at the next meeting.[574] Roberts quickly prepared a memorandum for secretary McAdoo explaining the situation and asking permission to attend the Commission meeting:[575]

> Two bills are now pending in the Senate providing for the issue of souvenir coins. One of these, pressed by the Panama Pacific Exposition Company, provides for three denominations of gold coins and one denomination of silver coins. The other bill, introduced by Senator Root at the insistence of the American Committee upon the Celebration of One Hundred Years of Peace, contemplates the issue of twenty-five cent pieces with one side devoted to the opening of the Canal and the other to the celebration of One Hundred years of Peace.
>
> Both of these bills provide that the Secretary of the Treasury shall prepare designs for the proposed coins, and an appropriation is carried for that purpose.
>
> Although neither of these bills has become law, it seems to be not impossible that one, and perhaps both, will pass, and in that event there will be scant time in which to obtain the designs, prepare the dies, and do the coinage within the time contemplated by the bill. The coins, if authorized, should be ready for delivery early in 1915.
>
> Unless the Secretary desires to deal with the matter personally, or has other plans, I would suggest that the services of the Fine Arts Commission be enlisted in obtaining the designs. I think it would be well to have the advice of the Commission as to whether it will be best fro the Secretary to commission several artists of his own selection to prepare the designs, or to invite a considerable number of artists to submit designs in competition. It would also be well to have the opinion of the Commission as to the compensation that should be paid for the designs. I am bringing the matter up at this time because the Fine Arts Commission is in session today and will not meet again for several months. If the Secretary wishes to call in the aid of this Commission I think the matter should be laid before that body today. If the Secretary has no other plans, and approves of so doing, I will attend a session of the Commission today and confer with that body on the subject, obtaining its views as to the best method of dealing with the artists and arranging for further conferences upon the subject later.

---

[574] *US Mint,* NARA-CP, op. cit., entry 229, box 302. Letter dated July 21, 1914 to Roberts from William W. Harts, Secretary of the Commission.
[575] *US Mint,* NARA-CP, op. cit., entry 229, box 302. Memorandum dated July 24, 1914 to McAdoo from Roberts.

McAdoo approved and Roberts attended the commission meeting on July 24. Since the bills had not been adopted there was little to be done except provide Roberts with the names of several suitable artists and information on expenses.[576]

> The Commission of Fine Arts acknowledge receipt of your memorandum of July twenty-forth carrying the endorsement of the Secretary of the Treasury.
>
> You state that bills are now pending in the Senate providing for the issue of souvenir coins and that these bill contemplate an award-medal, a souvenir medal, and four different coins, one of which may require alternate designs. You have asked this Commission to recommend to you certain artists skilled in medal work for the executions of these designs.
>
> After consideration, this Commission make the following recommendations: For the award medal, Mr. A. A. Weinman, 441 West 21st Street, New York City; for the souvenir medal Mr. John Gelert, 11 East 14th Street, New York City; for the coins, Mr. Robert I. Aitken, 510 Park Avenue, New York City, – Miss Evelyn B. Longman, 11East 14th Street, New York City, – Mr. Paul H. Manship, 27 Lexington Avenue, New York City, – and Mr. Charles Keck, 148 West 36th Street, New York City.
>
> In the event that satisfactory arrangements can not be made with any one or more of the artists named, the Commission suggest as alternates: Mr. John Flanagan, 1931 Broadway, New York City, – Mr. Augustus Lukeman, 145 West 55th Street, New York City, – Sherry E. Fry, 1931 Broadway, New York City, – Miss Janet Scudder, 141 East 19th Street, New York City, – and Bela L. Pratt, Museum of Fine Arts, Boston, Massachusetts.
>
> The Commission further recommend that the amount anticipated to be available for the preparation of the designs be divided as follows: for each of the medals, one thousand dollars; for the coin requiring an alternate design, nine hundred dollars; for each of the other coins, seven hundred dollars.
>
> The Commission understand from your letter that the legislation for these medals and coins has not yet been effected, and that you are anticipating the passage of certain bills so that you may be prepared to expedite the work and to have the medals and coins ready at the opening of the Panama-Pacific International Exposition.

Roberts reported results of his meeting to McAdoo and suggested that the artists be contacted and their interest in a possible commission determined.[577]

> I went before the Commission of Fine Arts last Friday and presented the situation that will exist in case one or more of the bills authorizing souvenir coins are passed. Opinion was expressed and concurred in by the entire Commission that in view of the limited amount of time that could be allowed for the preparation of designs, it would be better to divide the work among selected artists at a stipulated remuneration for each piece. I coincide in this opinion.
>
> I am submitting herewith a letter from the Commission in which it gives a first and alternative list of artists with the recommendation that one medal or coin be allotted to each artist, and proposes a division of the fund carried by the bill for this purpose.
>
> Although neither of the bills has passed Congress it is so important that the artists who are to perform the work, in case the coins are authorized, shall have adequate time for thought over the designs that it seems to me well to take the subject up with the first list of artists in a tentative way, tell them what is pending, and ask whether they will be open to engagement in the event to coins are authorized. By so doing they will have the subject in mind and if disposed to accept the commis-

---

[576] *US Mint,* NARA-CP, op. cit., entry 229, box 302. Letter dated July 27, 1914 to Roberts from Harts.
[577] *US Mint,* NARA-CP, op. cit., entry 229, box 302. Memorandum dated July 29, 1914 to McAdoo from Roberts.

> sion will be ready to go ahead more promptly. I should, of course, also suggest that this correspondence be treated as confidential. I beg to inquire whether this suggestion has your approval? The justification lies in the fact that the time for having designs made and dies executed is becoming very short.

Roberts waited until early September to contact some of the artists and apparently received a mixed reaction. Robert Aitken seemed genuinely pleased to accept a design commission, if offered:

> In answer to your letter of the eleventh instant asking if I would be in a position to undertake to make the designs for one of the souvenir coins that may be issued in commemoration of the Panama-Pacific International Exposition. Permit me to state that I would consider myself honored if commissioned to prepare such designs.

Adolph Weinman declined due to the press of work already in his studio and the short amount of time until the opening of the exposition.[578] Manship, Longman, Keck and Gelert were not contacted, although none of Robert's correspondence indicates why they were omitted. The correspondence with Weinman was particularly helpful to Roberts who asked the sculptor for aid in better understanding what might need to be done.[579]

> Your letter of the 14th instant is at hand. I am sorry you are not so situated as to take on the task of making the award medal, for I remember your satisfactory work upon the medal for the Louisiana Purchase Exposition. Will you allow me to draw a little information from you as the most direct source from which it can be obtained? I have the impression that more than one award medal was made, but that the designs were changed only in part. At the time of writing to you the other day I was thinking of only one set of obverse and reverse designs. Please let me know just how many designs were necessary, as very likely the same plan will be used again. Also, would you mind telling me what you were paid for making those designs?

Weinman provided an explanation of how the Louisiana Purchase medals were designed, noting differences in shape and materials, and confided that he received $4,000 for all the medals and that another artist, who previously failed to complete the work, was paid $1,000.

Roberts sent a follow-up letter to Aitken. It was his hope that the artist would begin preparing design sketches well before the legislation was passed. He could not issue official design commissions because there was neither money nor enabling legislation. He had to trust Aitken to begin on his own, and that he would trust the mint to follow through on its promises. The letter to Aitken reads:[580]

> I am in receipt of your letter of the 12th instant and note with satisfaction that you would be glad to undertake to prepare designs for one of the souvenir coins that may be used in commemoration of the Panama Pacific Exposition.
> As stated in my former letter the bill providing for these coins has passed the Senate and been favorably recommended by the Coinage Committee of the House, but has not yet come up for action in this body. Until it passes both houses, of course, no definite arrangement can be concluded, but it has been thought well to take up the matter in a tentative way in order that the artists invited to submit

---

[578] *US Mint,* NARA-CP, op. cit., entry 229, box 302. Letter dated September 14, 1914 to Roberts from Weinman.
[579] *US Mint,* NARA-CP, op. cit., entry 235, vol. 405. Letter dated September 16, 1914 to Weinman from Roberts.
[580] *US Mint,* NARA-CP, op. cit., entry 235, vol. 405. Letter dated September 15, 1914 to Aitken from Roberts.

designs might have some notice of what was pending. The Secretary of the Treasury does not contemplate inviting competitive designs, but proposes to assign each of the coins to a selected artist, reserving the right, however, to disapprove and decline to accept or pay for the designs submitted if they fail to satisfy his judgment. He proposes to invite you to prepare the designs for the $50 gold piece which, as you see by the bill, is to be in two forms, one octagonal and similar to the California slugs issued in the early 50s. If you are not familiar with these pieces you can probably see them at the rooms of the American Numismatic Society in New York city.

This is perhaps all that can be said or done in the matter at the present time. The pending bill has been amended by the House committee to provide that the coins shall be ready for delivery by the opening of the Exposition, which is in February next. The time is already short for preparing designs, making the dies and doing the coinage, and you are not asked to undertake any work upon it prior to the passage of the bill, it will be very important that the work be taken up immediately after the passage of the Bill, and sketches submitted as soon as possible.

Roberts also went "off list" and contacted James Fraser (designer of the 1913 Buffalo nickel), who replied that he was willing to "make some designs for a medal…if the amount of money...does not include the expenses of the die making and striking."[581]

Of the three artists maintaining contact with Roberts, Aitken was apparently the most interested in the work. On November 13 he wrote asking for advice about the conditions of the commission, although the bill had not yet passed Congress. He did not mention his active negotiations with Adolph Miller, Chairman of the Government Exhibition Board, about designing the souvenir medal:[582]

…I write to state that the time left for this work is becoming very short.

Therefore if advice concerning the conditions under which this work is to be done could be given me at this time, it would do much to facilitate the actual working out of the designs, in case these coins are to be issued.

I am willing to take up this work at this time, at my own risk, in order not to be rushed in this important undertaking.

The facts that I should like to be informed upon are the following:
Just how much liberty would be permitted in the conception of these designs;
How does the Secretary of the Treasury intend furnishing the ideas or motives of the designs? If so, could not these ideas or suggestions be given now as well as the necessary lettering, etc.?

I have deferred writing you, because I felt that by now the House would have taken action upon the bill. But as they haven't (to my knowledge) I trust you will pardon the liberty I now take in asking that if possible this information be sent me.

Unknown to Aitken, director Roberts had sent his resignation, effective November 15, to secretary McAdoo. He also prepared a memorandum for assistant secretary Malburn discussing the commemorative coin project:

The bill providing for several souvenir coins and for the award and souvenir medals of the Panama Pacific Exposition has passed the Senate and is pending in the House. In view of the importance of getting an early start upon the designs as soon as the bill has become law. I suggested to the Secretary the advisability of opening tentative negotiations with several artists with a view to having them prepared to execute the designs speedily, as soon as authority was given. The whole

---

[581] *US Mint,* NARA-CP, op. cit., entry 229, box 302. Letter dated September 23, 1914 to Roberts from Fraser. Fraser prepared a design for a quarter but it was never submitted to the mint.
[582] *US Mint,* NARA-CP, op. cit., entry 229, box 302. Letter dated November 13, 1914 to Roberts from Aitken.

matter was laid before the Fine Arts Commission for its advice, and a letter received which was laid before the Secretary giving a list of competent artists and suggesting that each of the souvenir coins be assigned to an artist and a commission given for its execution. Acting upon this suggestion I wrote to Mr. Robert Aitken of New York City, asking him if he would accept a commission for the $50 piece, and received a reply that he would be glad to do so. I also addressed a letter to Mr. James E. Fraser, asking him if he would accept a commission for the award medal, and received reply indicating that he would do so. Although no commission has been given to either of these gentlemen, I consider that the Bureau is in a way, committed to them in case the act is passed by the Congress. I also had an accidental conversation with Mr. Paul Manship, an artist in New York City, about the other designs, and he expressed a desire to do the 50 cent piece. As our conversation was entirely accidental and informal I do not consider that there is any serious obligation in this instance, although I regard Mr. Manship as qualified for the task, and his name is included in the list submitted by the Fine Arts Commission. All of the correspondence relative to these negotiations is in the files and I suggest that you look it over before doing anything about the designs.

With Roberts heading to Chicago for a banking job, McAdoo appointed Frederick P. Dewey, PhD acting director of the mint. Based on experience at mint headquarters and knowledge of events, the appointment probably should have gone to Mary O'Reilly, however the treasury secretary was not yet ready to have a woman running the mint for an extended period of time.

Little was done by the mint regarding the commemorative designs until January 6, 1915 when Dewey advised Malburn that the Panama-Pacific Exposition bill had passed the House and was in a conference committee to resolve differences with the Senate version. Dewey also commented:[583]

> ...if the bill passes it will undoubtedly be impossible to have the designs and dies prepared in time for delivery not later than the day of the opening of the exposition. It is [Miss O'Reilly's] judgment that we should anticipate the passage of the bill and get the work started immediately.

Commemorative Coin Design

Everything changed on January 13, 1915. The Panama Pacific Exposition bill passed Congress and awaited President Wilson's signature. The law authorized production of up to:

25,000 gold dollars;
10,000 quarter eagles;
3,000 quintuple eagles, equally divided between round and hexagonal;
200,000 silver half dollars.

Gold coins were to be produced in the San Francisco Mint. Half dollars, however, could be struck either in the mint or at the mint's exhibit space during the exposition. Halves could also be melted so that the display could be kept operating, provided no more than 200,000 pieces were sold.

Dewey hastily arranged a meeting in New York with artists Aitken, Keck, Longman and Manship on January 14. During the conference Dewey outlined the basic requirements for the new coins, he also discussed the extremely aggressive schedule – one

---
[583] *US Mint,* NARA-CP, op. cit., entry 229, box 302. Memorandum dated January 6, 1915 to Malburn from Dewey.

which made no allowance for re-working designs. The next day Dewey wrote to the artists altering the inscription requirements slightly. "…It will be necessary to limit the designs for the exposition coins to a slight extent. They should contain the words "Panama Pacific Exposition, San Francisco," "United States of America," "1915" and should give the value of the coin in each case. There is no restriction as to the location of these various statements on the coin."[584] This was apparently the first time Keck, Longman and Manship had been officially contacted about the designs, and director Robert's decision not to contact them the previous September would now create problems for the artists. Dewey's memorandum to assistant secretary Malburn reads in part:[585]

> …I consulted the four artists named and made tentative arrangements for them to prepare the designs for the Panama-Pacific coins at $600 each for the original designs and $200 additional for the second $50 gold piece, each artist will submit sketches in a few days after the order is placed with them, and on the acceptance of the sketches will prepare a model from which the dies can be made. This will take some time, and it will probably be two weeks after the receipt of the order before the first model will be ready, and three weeks before the last one will be received. After the model is received it will be necessary to have the master dies made, and then the working dies. It will be absolutely impossible to comply with the terms of the bill requiring the delivery of the coins on the opening day of the Exposition February 20.
>
> The bill contemplates that the dies will be made at the Philadelphia Mint. There will be five sets of master dies. Their preparation at the Philadelphia Mint would require several months time. If we could have the master dies made outside, much time would be saved. This would be an expenditure of about $1,000. This sum would be a serious tax on the contingent fund of the Mint. I would suggest that in the interest of hastening the coinage, the Exposition authorities be requested to assume the cost of making the master dies outside the Philadelphia Mint.

Events moved quickly. The bill was signed on January 16 and just two days later Robert Aitken sent Dewey a note inquiring about the correct diameter for the $50 coin:[586]

> Last Saturday I visited the Numismatic Society and obtained a catalog of an exhibition of United States coins held in 1914, among the reproductions it contains I note that the fifty dollar coins, that were circular in form, are quite different in size. See enclosure. In case that I am to execute the new designs, it would be well that the diameter of this new coin be decided upon at an early date, as it will, in a way, control the design of the slug [the octagonal version – RWB], if one model is to be used in any way for both coins.

Accompanying the letter was a separate sheet with circles drawn representing the U.S. mint's 1877 $50 pattern coin – 2-inches in diameter; Kellogg & Co. $50 of 1855 – 1-9/16 inches in diameter; and Wass, Molitor & Co. 1855 – 1-1/2 inches in diameter. Dewey replied on January 21 stating:[587]

> I have given yours of the 18th instant regarding the size of the $50 gold piece careful consideration. In view of the fact that there has been so much variation in the size of this piece already made, I would suggest that you design the octagonal

---

[584] *US Mint,* NARA-CP, op. cit., entry 235, vol. 411. Letter dated January 15, 1915 to Longman from Dewey. Similar letters sent to the other three artists.
[585] *US Mint,* NARA-CP, op. cit., entry 229, box 302. Memorandum dated January 15, 1915 to Malburn from Dewey.
[586] *US Mint,* NARA-CP, op. cit., entry 229, box 302. Letter dated January 18, 1915 to Dewey from Aitken.
[587] *US Mint,* NARA-CP, op. cit., entry 235, vol. 411. Letter dated January 21, 1915 to Aitken from Dewey.

piece to follow the size of the original, and then arrange to round coin for the size best adapted to utilize the octagonal design. As our pattern piece, No. 1348 of the catalog, is two inches in diameter the round piece might be larger than the octagonal if more suitable.

The same day Aitken wrote his letter about the $50 coin's diameter, he notified the treasury department that hubs for the exhibition souvenir medal had been delivered to the Philadelphia Mint.[588] A few days later engraver Charles Barber complained that the relief of the hubs was excessive and they could not be struck on a coining press.[589] But, after making some tests, superintendent Adam Joyce said "…it has been demonstrated that the design of the medal can be brought up on the press…"[590]

It wasn't until January 21 that Dewey received official permission to award coin design commissions to the four artists:[591]

> …You are hereby authorized to make the following awards for the preparation of deigns:
>
> $50 gold coin – Mr. Robert Aitken;
> $2.50 gold coin – Mrs. Evelyn B. Longman;
> $1.00 gold coin – Mr. Charles Keck;
> $0.50 silver coin – Mr. Paul H. Manship.

Dewey immediately sent letters to the four artists offering them commissions to design specific coins and giving details for each. His letter to Evelyn Longman was typical:[592]

> In accordance with my recent conversation with you in New York, you are hereby authorized and requested to proceed with the preparation of the design for the new gold Quarter Eagle to be issued in commemoration of the Panama-Pacific Exposition at San Francisco. The compensation for the design is to be $600 with the express understanding that you will use all possible haste in preparing the design; that within a few days of the receipt of this letter you will submit sketches of one or more designs and on acceptance of the sketch you will proceed to perfect it and prepare a model from which the master dies for coinage purposes may be prepared. It is hoped that the model may be ready within three weeks from the acceptance of the sketch.
>
> The design must conform to the ordinary requirements of coining operations. The diameter and thickness will be the same as the present Quarter Eagle, and the coins must stack smoothly. The design must allow easy clearance of the dies.
>
> It is necessary that the designs contain the following words: "Panama Pacific Exposition San Francisco," "United States of America," "1915," "In God We Trust," and an unmistakable statement of the value of the coin. Please note that the religious motto has been added to the requirements given you previously. There is no restriction as to the location of these words.
>
> Please forward a formal acceptance of this commission.

The second paragraph of Charles Keck's letter reads:

> The design must conform to the ordinary requirements of coining operations. The coin will be 9/16-inch in diameter and correspond to the Louisiana Purchase

---

[588] *US Mint,* NARA-CP, op. cit., entry 229, box 302. Letter dated January 18, 1915 to Aitken from Dewey.
[589] *US Mint,* NARA-CP, op. cit., entry 229, box 302. Letter dated January 23, 1915 to Dewey from Joyce.
[590] *US Mint,* NARA-CP, op. cit., entry 229, box 302. Letter dated January 28, 1915 to Dewey from Joyce.
[591] *US Mint,* NARA-CP, op. cit., entry 229, box 302. Letter dated January 21, 1915 to Dewey from Malburn.
[592] *US Mint,* NARA-CP, op. cit., entry 229, box 302. Letter dated January 21, 1915 to Longman from Dewey.

and Lewis and Clark souvenir dollars, and the coins must stack smoothly. The design must allow easy clearance of the dies.

Dewey also recognized that it took time to make reductions and hubs from the artist's models, so he and Adam Joyce insisted that the artists deliver bronze casts that were four times the diameter of the finished coin. These provisions avoided the potential of damaged or broken plaster models and allowed the Philadelphia Mint engraving staff to cut hubs directly from the bronze casts.[593] To further expedite production of coins, he contacted Medallic Art Company in New York:[594]

> Owing to the shortness of the time available it may be necessary to have the master dies for the new exposition coinage made outside the mint. I would therefore ask you to state how soon after the artist's model is supplied you could forward the master dies to the Mint, and to state your price for making the dies for one coin. There will be five of the coins and would you reduce the price per coin if you were to do all of them?

Always ready to accept additional work, co-owner Felix Weil replied the next day:

> In answer to you favor of Jan. 22nd we beg to state that the price for making a master hub from which the dies are made will be Two Hundred dollars, per coin, that is the obverse and reverse; if we are to make the five we will reduce the price Fifty dollars on the total, making the five obverses and five reverses, for the sum of Nine Hundred and Fifty dollars. As to time, we will require about 8 to 10 days upon receipt of the models, to furnish the complete coin hubs; for the five coins, about 3 weeks.

Although the other artists replied to Dewey's commission offer with short letters of acceptance, Robert Aitken accompanied his acceptance with a design for the octagonal and round $50 coins. Obviously, Aitken had put the time since Roberts' visit to good use:[595]

> Enclosed please to find sketches for the obverse and reverse of the new Fifty-Dollar piece. They are so arranged as to show the application of the circular form to the octagonal.
> By way of an explanation of my design, permit me to state that in order to express in my design the fact that this coin is struck to commemorate the Panama-Pacific Exposition, and as the exposition stands for all that wisdom and industry have produced, I have used as the central motive of the obverse, the head of the virgin goddess Minerva. She is the goddess of wisdom, of skill, of contemplation, of spinning and of weaving, of horticulture and agriculture. Moreover she figures prominently upon the seal of the State of California. This head will make a beautiful pattern in the circle and the use of the dolphins on the octagonal coin do much to add to its charm, as well as express the uninterrupted water route made possible by the canal.
> Upon the reverse I use the owl, the bird sacred to Minerva, also the symbol of wisdom, perched upon a branch of western pine, behind which is seen the web of the spider, suggesting Industry.
> With these simple symbols, all full of beauty in themselves, I feel that I have expressed the larger meaning of the exposition, its appeal to the intellect.

---

[593] *US Mint,* NARA-CP, op. cit., entry 229, box 302. Letter dated January 18, 1915 to Dewey from Joyce.
[594] *US Mint,* NARA-CP, op. cit., entry 235, vol. 411. Letter dated January 21, 1915 to Medallic Art Co. from Dewey.
[595] *US Mint,* NARA-CP, op. cit., entry 229, box 302. Letter dated January 23, 1915 to Dewey from Aitken. The letter is accompanied by two four inch square sketches each having two leaves of paper. Clips on the left side, act as hinges. With the paper leaves closed (flat) the hexagonal design including dolphins is visible. With the top leaf lifted, one sees only the round coin design.

> I trust these designs will meet with the approval of the Secretary of the Treasury.

The next day Aitken offered several modifications to his designs including placing the inscriptions closer to the rim and using Roman numerals for the date. "As these designs will not be used in any other year, there will be no need to change the year as we must on other coins."[596]

Figure 59. Sketches of Robert Aiken first design for the $50 gold coin. Secretary McAdoo requested relatively minor changes to the composition before the coins were struck. (NARA.)

Dewey sent the artists letters and telephoned them pushing to have sketches immediately. Had he or Roberts contacted Longman, Manship and Keck the previous September, the others might have been better prepared. Manship wrote on January 27:[597]

> I am enclosing [for] you the design of the Panama Pacific Exposition half dollar.
> After working upon them in a larger size, of which I enclose a tracing, I made reductions to the actual size to present to you for your inspection. As soon as I hear from you I shall be pleased to devote my undivided attention to the execution of the model, which will be five times the actual size, for the die maker.
> I hope that you will like the indications that I send you.

Evelyn Longman also sent her sketches the same day:[598]

> I send you under separate cover a sketch of a design for the two and a half dollar gold piece. In this the aim has been, first of all to make a good coin. To attain this end in a coin of such small dimension, the symbols and details should be simple, used in the simplest manner and large enough to be deciphered easily; for this reason the head only of the eagle is shown on the side symbolic of the Nation. The denomination of the coin has been placed in the field with it so that its value may

---

[596] *US Mint,* NARA-CP, op. cit., entry 229, box 302. Letter dated January 24, 1915 to Dewey from Aitken.
[597] *US Mint,* NARA-CP, op. cit., entry 229, box 302. Letter dated January 27, 1915 to Dewey from Manship.
[598] *US Mint,* NARA-CP, op. cit., entry 229, box 302. Letter dated January 27, 1915 to Dewey from Longman.

be easily noted at a glance. The dollar sign universally used in the United States has been used in preference to the letter D. On the reverse, a cluster of fruit is shown symbolic of California, the greatest fruit growing state in the Union, and in a larger sense symbolic of the general fruition and achievement of the Panama-Pacific Exposition. The lettering on both sides is large enough to be easily read.

PS: The modeling is to be very flat so as to keep within the rim in stacking.

By January 29 acting director Dewey had all four designs in his office. He forwarded them to secretary McAdoo, who sent them to the Commission of Fine Arts for their opinion. Dewey also notified the artists of the progress. Three days later, Daniel C. French, chairman of the commission wrote to assistant secretary Malburn "…We beg to advise the approval and adoption of all the designs submitted…."[599]

Although the commission approved all four designs, Malburn and McAdoo held contrary opinions. Malburn commented in a memorandum:[600]

…Personally, I do not care for any of the designs except the $1.00. Unless you wish to reject the designs, I suggest that Dr. Dewey be authorized to take them to Philadelphia for an expert opinion as to whether they are suitable for coins.

McAdoo added his comments to the same memorandum:

They are all poor, I think. Ask Philadelphia about them and let our own people submit some designs.

The secretary's comments caused Malburn to send the designs to the Philadelphia Mint where engraver Charles Barber and coiner Robert Clark offered their suggestions. It also resulted in Barber being told to make sketches for all four coins. Thus, the artists and mint now were working in parallel and to some extent against one another.

Clark raised several practical difficulties the most significant of which was the diameter of the $50 piece:[601]

In planning a design for the fifty dollar octagonal gold piece to be made at the San Francisco Mint…I wish to impress upon you the necessity of bearing in mind these two fundamental facts.

Primarily, let the size of the coin be no greater than one and a half inches across the center, with the modern coinage relief, otherwise the dies must be adjusted in a hydraulic press, which is not part of the San Francisco Mint's equipment. Then again have the artist hold down his relief and not strive for the intense bold effect seen on good medals. A coin of this size requires an intense blow to bring into prominence clearly the finer details, and even then the greatest care on the part of the coining department, backed by long experience and skill, must be exercised. As there are to be so few of these pieces struck, the examination on the part of the public will be close and critical. It would seem that if there is any question as to whether the San Francisco Mint could turn out perfect pieces of this denomination, the task better be turned over to the parent mint, whose facilities and equipment enable them to meet all reasonable demands.

…The submitted sketches for the proposed coins appear in a general way to be satisfactory for coinage, if the suggestions mentioned above are observed.

---

[599] *US Mint,* NARA-CP, op. cit., entry 229, box 302. Letter dated February 1, 1915 to Malburn from French.
[600] *US Mint,* NARA-CP, op. cit., entry 229, box 302. Memorandum dated February 2, 1915 to McAdoo from Malburn. McAdoo's comment is in manuscript.
[601] *US Mint,* NARA-CP, op. cit., entry 229, box 302. Letter dated February 4, 1915 to Joyce from Clark.

Engraver Charles Barber supported Clark's suggestions about the maximum diameter of the $50, and also had specific comments about each denomination:[602]

[Fifty Dollar Coins Design]
If the diameter in the extreme of both the octagonal and round does not exceed one and a half inches with the relief kept down to what is known to modern coin relief, I am of opinion that it could be struck upon a coining press, any larger diameter would have to be made as a medal upon the hydraulic press. The date should not appear in both Roman and Arabic numerals, one date is sufficient.

Fifty Cent Design
If the model is made as shown in reduced and simplified design and is kept down to coin relief (modern coinage) I see no difficulty in the coinage.

Two and Half Dollar Coin Design
I think it would improve the design to place the inscription UNITED STATES OF AMERICA in upper half of design and IN GOD WE TRUST in lower.
I would suggest that the lettering in these inscriptions be slightly reduced in size and placed nearer the border.

One Dollar Gold Design
In making a working model it would be well to remember that the coin is only about half an inch in diameter and that the volume of metal is extremely small therefore, the relief must also be extremely low.
When the design is accepted I would suggest that the working model be furnished in bronze from which we can make the reductions [hubs]; the model should not be more than six diameters of any proposed coin.

Acting director Dewey prepared a memorandum for assistant secretary Malburn discussing the conference in Philadelphia:[603]

In accordance with the Secretary's instruction reaching me on the 3rd I had a conference in Philadelphia yesterday with the Superintendent, Engraver and Superintendent of Coining Department, regarding the proposed designs for the exposition coins.

With the exception of the $50 piece there was no practical objection found to the designs except the very general one that the relief must be kept low, and adjusted to the thickness of the coin.

The Engraver will begin by submitting sketches for a half dollar in a few days, the others to be taken up in order as follows: $1.00, $2.50, $50. May I suggest that, without definitely rejecting the present set of designs, the various artists might be requested to submit further designs. Their commissions read "you will submit sketches of one or more designs."

Outside the design itself the execution of the $50 piece is a problem depending somewhat upon the interpretation and fulfillment of the terms of the act authorizing this coinage. The act says that half the $50 pieces must be similar to the ones of 1851, and that the coinage shall be executed at the San Francisco Mint. If the new pieces are to approach the size of the old ones the San Francisco Mint has no press sufficiently powerful to strike them. If they are to be struck at San Francisco they must be considerably reduced in size from the 1851 model.

Considering that this will be a unique coin commanding much interest and attention, it seems to me that they might approach the size of the 1851 piece, and if possible, they should be struck at the Philadelphia Mint.

The next day, assistant secretary Malburn sent two short memoranda to McAdoo. The first discussed his meeting at the Philadelphia Mint and stated:[604]

---

[602] *US Mint,* NARA-CP, op. cit., entry 229, box 302. Letter dated February 4, 1915 to Joyce from Barber.
[603] *US Mint,* NARA-CP, op. cit., entry 229, box 302. Memorandum dated February 5, 1915 to Malburn from Dewey.

> ...the Engraver will submit sketches for the four coins.
> I have prepared letters to the Artists who made the rejected designs, asking them to submit other designs. It will expedite the matter if we can have these artists working at the same time that the Engraver is, and the selection of the better designs can be made when they are all in.

In the second, Malburn reminded McAdoo that the bill required coins to be struck in San Francisco. Considered together with comments by Clark and Barber about the $50 coin it was clear that a medal press would have to be sent to the west coast mint.[605] This was contrary to the advice of superintendent Joyce and acting director Dewey, but it was the only way to comply with the law. In addition to formalities, there was the political reality that the Wilson administration did not want to inadvertently offend either the residents of California or the west coast. To ignore the explicit instructions of the commemorative coin act, and strike any of the coins in Philadelphia would have raised howls of complaint from the western states. In spite of grumbling from the Philadelphia Mint, McAdoo approved sending a medal press to California.[606] The press was shipped to San Francisco on March 22 via the *Atchison, Topeka and Santa Fe Railway* for the sum of $385.22 which was paid from the San Francisco Mint's contingent fund.[607]

To the artists, terse, uninformative rejection notices, as if McAdoo did not want their participation, went out by mail on February 5:[608]

> The design submitted by you for the $1.00 gold piece to be coined at the United States Mint at San Francisco, in commemoration of the Panama-Pacific International Exposition, has been disapproved, and I request you, therefore, to submit another design.

By now there was no hope of delivering coins for the February 20 opening of the exposition. Yet, no one seemed concerned that the designs had not been selected. Critical time was wasted as the artists wrote back asking for comments on their first designs. Since the rejection came directly from McAdoo, he was the only one who could explain his objections. Evelyn Longman wrote on February 8:[609]

> Your letter of Feb 5th has just been received. Will you kindly inform me whether both sides of the design for the Quarter Eagle submitted by me were disapproved? It will help me greatly in making a new design if I may also now just what criticisms were made.

McAdoo's stilted reply must have been of limited help to the artist as she tried to prepare a design that would please the secretary:[610]

> ...The $2.50 gold coin is very small, and your design, on account of the details, would be very ineffective. The fruit is symbolical of some parts of California, but

---
[604] *US Mint,* NARA-CP, op. cit., entry 229, box 302. Memorandum dated February 5, 1915 to McAdoo from Malburn.
[605] *Ibid.*
[606] *US Mint,* NARA-CP, op. cit., entry 229, box 302. Memorandum dated February 5, 1915 to McAdoo from Malburn. Manuscript approval initialed by McAdoo.
[607] *US Mint,* NARA-CP, op. cit., entry 235, vol. 412. Memorandum dated October 5, 1915 to F. W. H. Shanahan, San Francisco Mint superintendent from Fred Chaffin, acting director.
[608] *US Mint,* NARA-CP, op. cit., entry 229, box 302. Letter dated February 5, 1915 to Keck from McAdoo. The other letters were identical except for the coin denomination. All were initialed by Malburn and Dewey.
[609] *US Mint,* NARA-CP, op. cit., entry 229, box 302. Letter dated February 8, 1915 to McAdoo from Longman.
[610] *US Mint,* NARA-CP, op. cit., entry 229, box 302. Letter dated February 12, 1915 to Longman from McAdoo.

hardly of San Francisco or of any feature of the Panama-Pacific Exposition. The head of the eagle is, to my mind, unattractive, and the amount of the coin is ineffectively placed.

Longman set to work and by the 19th had four new designs for the secretary's consideration:[611]

> In response to your favor of February 12th, I send herewith six sketches for the two and a half dollar gold piece. These have been made in the actual size, as I believe this will aid you in judging the ultimate result. It is to be understood that these are unfinished and intended only to convey the general idea and arrangement.
>
> Numbers 1 and 2 show a reduction of the original drawing submitted by me, which I send for comparison with the new ones.
>
> Number 3 represents one of the courts of the Panama-Pacific exposition with the Golden Gate in the distance. (As you doubtless know, the general scheme of the San Francisco Fair is a system of courts opening on the bay.)
>
> Number 4 is a grizzly bear, an emblem occurring on the State Seal of California.
>
> Number 5 shown one of the great trees of California, the model being the "Grizzly Giant," the oldest and largest tree in the Mariposa Grove.
>
> Number 6 shows the national bird; but for a small coin I much prefer the head alone.
>
> Trusting that some of these designs will meet with your approval, I am....

It was not until several months later that Dewey wrote in response to an inquiry from Farran Zerbe:[612]

> Replying to your inquiry of the 6th instant I beg to say that several sketches of design for the $2.50 gold piece were submitted by Miss Evelyn B. Longman of New York, but none were acceptable. Miss Longman visited Washington for the purpose of consulting the Department in regard to further sketches, was taken ill while in this city, and was not able to take up the work of submitting sketches until much beyond the time which could be afforded to her, and the Engraver of the Mint was directed to submit sketches.

The comment about Longman being taken ill while in Washington seems odd and might have been an excuse for some other difficulty in completing the commission.

Paul Manship also requested information about why his design was rejected:[613]

> ...I am proceeding according to your request with the making of a new design. It would greatly facilitate the work if you would inform me of your criticisms of my former effort, as I could then avoid the same mistakes.

The next day he sent additional sketches, commenting "I trust that amongst these you may find an appropriate expression for the subject."[614]

If Longman found McAdoo's comments about her design of limited help, the criticism Manship received was even more nebulous:[615]

---

[611] *US Mint,* NARA-CP, op. cit., entry 229, box 302. Letter dated February 19, 1915 to McAdoo from Longman.
[612] *US Mint,* NARA-CP, op. cit., entry 235, vol. 411. Letter dated May 14, 1915 to Zerbe from Dewey.
[613] *US Mint,* NARA-CP, op. cit., entry 229, box 302. Letter dated February 10, 1915 to McAdoo from Manship.
[614] *US Mint,* NARA-CP, op. cit., entry 229, box 302. Letter dated February 11, 1915 to McAdoo from Manship.
[615] *US Mint,* NARA-CP, op. cit., entry 229, box 302. Letter dated February 12, 1915 to Manship from McAdoo.

> ...I do not know that I can point out the specific features of your design that are objectionable, but I feel that there is a general lack of appropriateness in the design for the purpose for which it is intended.

It was obvious that McAdoo simply did not like Manship's design, but it is difficult to understand why assistance from the Commission of Fine Arts was not requested. It may be that McAdoo preferred to avoid using outside artists, with the simplest way to do this being to reject their designs. The same day Manship's work was rejected, McAdoo was shown half dollar designs by mint engraver Charles Barber:[616]

> I transmit herewith two sets of photographs of the design of a fifty cent silver coin for the San Francisco Exposition proposed by the Engraver at the Philadelphia Mint.
> In submitting these designs for a fifty cent coin it should be understood that they are only to convey the idea or intention of the thought as expressed in material, there being no effort at finish or detail. For example, there are no features on the figure of Columbia; the inscriptions are only hurriedly cut in the plaster. If carried to a finish, all detail will be given due consideration. For instance, the letters will be after the best examples of Roman, and the whole design made as artistic as it can be.
> It remains to consider the treatment of the edge of the coin. It has been suggested to indent E PLURIBUS UNUM on the edge. I would suggest indenting SAN FRANCISCO, CAL. as this statement does not appear elsewhere on the coin.

Barber had prepared obverse and reverse designs for the secretary's consideration. Rather than pencil drawings, as the artists had submitted, Barber sculpted plaster sketch models which better conveyed the effect of a coin than a flat drawing.

Figure 60. Obverse and reverse designs for the Panama Pacific half dollar by Charles Barber as first submitted. (NARA.)

Acting director Dewey apparently expected a quick decision by secretary McAdoo when he wrote to Joyce on the 13th:

> I delivered Mr. Barber's designs for the San Francisco half-dollar to the Assistant Secretary immediately upon my return to Washington, and was in hopes to

---

[616] *US Mint,* NARA-CP, op. cit., entry 229, box 302. Memorandum dated February 12, 1915 to Malburn from Dewey. We don't know if these were seen before or after the letter was sent to Manship.

have a decision in the matter before this. As, however, the Secretary has not yet notified me of his decision I would suggest that you urge upon Mr. Barber that he proceed at once and as rapidly as possible with the design for the $1.00 gold piece.

From the context of Dewey's letter it appears he had already decided that Manship's design was out of the running and it would be a simple matter to select Barber's work. But as so often seemed to happen at the mint, no one bothered talking with the artist; Manship was left wondering what to do next:[617]

On the 11th ultimo, in compliance with your request, I mailed you four additional sketches for the half-dollar piece to be coined in commemoration of the Panama-Pacific International Exposition at San Francisco. In view of the fact that I have had no acknowledgement, to date, of your receipt of these, and as I realize that an immediate beginning must be made upon the work in order to complete it in time to secure the anticipated results, I draw the subject to your attention, trusting that you will inform me of your final decision in the premises.

At the same time, will you not kindly return to me, with your commands, the sketches recently sent you, and very greatly oblige.

Assistant secretary Malburn passed the letter to McAdoo along with the sketches, Barber's half dollar designs and his own recommendation:[618]

I hand you herewith Manship's first sketch for Panama-Pacific half dollar, which has been disapproved. I also hand you his second sketches, which have not yet been passed upon, and the design made at the Philadelphia Mint for the same coin.

The Mint design seems to me to be so far ahead of Manship's, and as his second design is no improvement on the first, but is, on the contrary, in my opinion, even less suitable, I recommend, in view of the fact that the Exposition is already open, and that haste is essential, that Mr. Manship's second design be rejected and that the Mint be instructed to proceed at once to prepare the dies for the coins.

The same day, Dewey gave orders for the Philadelphia Mint to prepare dies of the new commemorative half dollar:[619]

I am returning herewith photograph of Mr. Barber's design for the Exposition half dollar. The design marked No. 1 [obverse – RWB] appears to be satisfactory to the Secretary but as yet has not been finally accepted. In regard to the design marked No. 2 the Secretary does not like the introduction of the dolphin in this manner. It is suggested, first, to leave it out altogether. If, however, you think that would leave too large a blank space on the coin I would thank you to sketch in some other detail for this space and submit the amended design for the approval of the secretary. I would also thank you to submit an amended design with this space left blank.

Barber quickly prepared modified versions of the reverse by replacing the dolphins with oak and olive branches. He also supplied a version with no ornamentation next to the shield.

---

[617] *US Mint,* NARA-CP, op. cit., entry 229, box 302. Letter dated March 2, 1915 to McAdoo from Manship.
[618] *US Mint,* NARA-CP, op. cit., entry 229, box 302. Memorandum dated March 3, 1915 to McAdoo from Malburn.
[619] *US Mint,* NARA-CP, op. cit., entry 229, box 302. Letter dated March 3, 1915 to Joyce from Dewey.

Figure 61. Modified reverse designs for the half dollar. The design on the right was accepted by secretary McAdoo. The design at the left is the same model that originally had dolphins on it. Barber scratched off the aquatic mammals to create a version with plain fields, left, as McAdoo suggested. (NARA.)

Versions of Barber's reverse design date from at least 1892 when he prepared a nondescript edition with skinny eagle for the Columbian Exposition half dollar. This was recycled in 1906 as a proposed revision of the Philippine coinage begun in 1903. Apparently the dolphins were new for 1915.

Figure 62. Charles Barber's drawings for reverse of 1893 Columbian Exposition half dollar and 1906 revised Philippine coinage.[620] (NARA.)

A rejection letter was sent to Paul Manship on March 5. Again, McAdoo could give no specific reasons for his disapproval of the designs, only that they were not appropriate:[621]

> In response to yours of the 2nd regarding the four additional sketches for the San Francisco half dollar piece which you have submitted, I regret very much to say that no one of the designs is satisfactory. They do not seem to me altogether appropriate to the coin and the conditions of its issue. As the time is already short,

---

[620] *US Mint,* NARA-CP, op. cit., entry 331, box 1 (left) and entry 229, box 250 (right).
[621] *US Mint,* NARA-CP, op. cit., entry 229, box 302. Letter dated March 5, 1915 to Manship from McAdoo. A more direct draft dated March 4 appears to contain editing by both Malburn and McAdoo.

> I cannot wait for other designs and am therefore obliged to finally rejected yours and to have the Philadelphia Mint proceed with the design.
> The sketches are returned herewith.

Manship did not go away quietly. On March 10 he sent a bill for $150.00 to the mint for "...3 days time employed in composing and sketching design for proposed half-dollar...as per instructions of Mr. Dewey, at $50.00 per diem."[622] This elicited an extended discussion within the mint about paying Manship for his time when the commission implied payment was to be made only after acceptance. The new mint director, Robert Woolley, felt that artist should be paid $100 for his efforts, while McAdoo and Malburn wanted to pay nothing. After obtaining a legal opinion, Woolley came around to McAdoo's view and noted: "There seems to be no precedent for compensating Mr. Paul Manship for time spent in preparing his rejected design...I find that director Roberts invariably made it plain to those he commissioned...that they were to receive no pay should said designs be rejected."[623] Although Roberts had never issued a commission to Manship or discussed it individually with him in a formal manner, as he had done with Aitken and Fraser, the payment request was rejected and the matter closed.

While Longman and Manship were struggling to obtain information from treasury authorities, Robert Aitken took his rejection letter direct to Col. William Harts at the Commission of Fine Arts. Charles Keck also complained and Col. Harts visited secretary McAdoo on February 11 to find out why the secretary had rejected the $1 and $50 coin designs.[624]

> ...I present herewith my principal objections to those designs.
> The design for the $50 gold piece was appropriate enough in the Greek coin from which it is evidently copied. The head of Pallas, and the owl, sacred to her, conveyed some meaning on that coin, but none, so far as I can see, in the present instance, except as the head of Pallas may be identified with that of our own Goddess of Liberty. The spider-web is not accepted now a days as the symbol of industry, if that was the artistic meaning, but the contrary; and the miniature dolphins floating in the air in front of Minerva's face seen very inappropriate. So too does the legend "In God We Trust – 1915" on the rim of Minerva's shield.
> The design of the $1 gold piece is better. While the head of Poseidon is good, it takes up too much room, and the trident and hand are awkwardly placed. The $1 coin is so very small, that to make the letters sufficiently large to be decipherable, any decoration such as a hand, must necessarily be very small. I am also not sure that some more appropriate head than that of Poseidon cannot be found for a coin for this Exposition.

Clearly, had treasury and mint officials contacted the commission and discussed their concerns, the commission might have been able to resolve any problems, and the mint could have stayed with the original artists.

---

[622] *US Mint,* NARA-CP, op. cit., entry 229, box 302. Letter dated March 10, 1915 to Dewey from Manship.
[623] *US Mint,* NARA-CP, op. cit., entry 229, box 302. Memorandum dated March 19, 1915 to Malburn from Woolley.
[624] *US Mint,* NARA-CP, op. cit., entry 229, box 302. Letter dated February 12, 1915 to Harts from McAdoo. "Pallas" refers to Pallas Athena, the Greek goddess equivalent to the Roman Minerva. "Neptune" is the ocean god's name typed in the letter, but this has been crossed out and replaced by Poseidon, the equivalent in the Greek pantheon.

Charles Keck also replied to the rejection letter. He had expected to have more information from the mint about his designs, but hearing nothing wrote on February 16:[625]

> ...I started to make other designs, but as there was nothing in your letter to indicate just what the difficulty was, I feel that I am working somewhat in the dark.
> Would you therefore be so kind as to indicate just what your criticism is so that I will not make the same mistake. By way of making my design clear, will you permit me to state, that on account of the smallness of the coin and amount of lettering to go on it, I am obliged to use the simplest forms, hence on the one side I have used the two dolphins to indicate the union of the two oceans, while on the other side the head of Neptune, to indicate the triumph of navigation. I have put the lettering on one side in order to make the head as large as possible.

In reply Malburn copied the information sent to the commission and forwarded it to the artist two days later. Keck was clearly interested in the commission and within a few days had prepared plaster sketch models and had them photographed:[626]

> In accordance with your instructions I have restudied the design for the one dollar gold coin and am sending to you in this enclosure photographs of four different compositions. The photographs have been reduced to nine sixteenths of an inch, the size of the gold dollar.
> The upper left hand coin represents Balboa, the upper right hand coin represents labor crowned with the laurels of victory to indicate the successful completion of the Panama Canal and Exposition; the lower left represents Poseidon indicating the triumph of navigation; the lower right hand is a restudy of my original submission to you. The reverse side of the coin is, I take it, satisfactory as your criticism did not include that side.
> In all the designs submitted I have taken pains to follow your suggestion for having the letters as large as possible, if fact the letters shown are slightly larger in actual size than those on our present sliver quarter dollar, and the heads are as large as the head on our present ten cent piece.
> The sketches from which the photograph was made are not finished works and to this is to be ascribed the slight irregularity of outline.
> If you desire to see the plaster models from which the photograph was made kindly advise me and I will send them to you.

Keck now followed Barber's footsteps in showing his designs as photos of three dimensional models rather than flat drawings. Considering the remark about Barber's plaster half dollar design being "so far ahead of" Manship's pencil drawings, this approach may have benefited Keck more than he realized.

---

[625] *US Mint,* NARA-CP, op. cit., entry 229, box 302. Letter dated February 16, 1915 to McAdoo from Keck.
[626] *US Mint,* NARA-CP, op. cit., entry 229, box 302. Letter dated February 23, 1915 to McAdoo from Keck. The small photos are still in the NARA correspondence files, however they have faded to the point were the image is almost completely obscured. The original negatives are preserved in the Smithsonian Archives of American Art.

Figure 63. Preliminary designs for the gold dollar by Charles Keck. (Top left to bottom right) Balboa, canal worker, Poseidon, and Poseidon with curled beard. The canal worker design was adopted after removal of the laurel leaves from his cap. Note that to the left of Poseidon's trident (lower right) the motto E Pluribus Unum appears to have been scratched off the model. (Courtesy Charles Keck papers, Smithsonian Archives of American Art.)

The designs were interesting enough for Dewey to offer useful comments to the artist:[627]

> ...Both Balboa and Labor head have much to commend them, but the location of Balboa's name is not satisfactory. Would it be feasible to place it elsewhere without injury to the general design?
> Again, while the head of Labor is much admired, yet there is nothing sufficiently characteristic of labor about it to show what it is. One has to be told what it represents. Could you increase the labor characteristics of the design without too much change in the general conditions?

Barber was hard at work on the three remaining designs plus models for the half dollar. On February 27 acting director Dewey called the Philadelphia Mint to learn of the mint's progress. Superintendent Joyce told him, "Mr. Barber states that he has a design for the San Francisco gold dollar underway and expects to have it photographed about the middle of next week and will send a copy down as soon as received."[628] The photos arrived the next week. Unlike the mint's half dollar design, of which the sketched obverse was at least graceful, Barber's gold dollar was simply ugly.

---

[627] *US Mint*, NARA-CP, op. cit., entry 235, vol. 411. Letter dated March 1, 1915 to Keck from Dewey.
[628] *US Mint*, NARA-CP, op. cit., entry 229, box 302. Letter dated February 27, 1915 to Woolley from acting superintendent Albert Norris.

Figure 64. Gold dollar design proposed by Philadelphia Mint engraver Charles Barber, February 1915. (NARA)

An official description accompanying the photos explained the designs:[629]

Obverse:
Shield of the United States surmounted by CORNUCOPIA containing fruit and flowers emblematic of abundance, also the product of CALIFORNIA, beneath the shield, olive branches emblematic of peace, the whole surrounded by the inscription "UNITED STATES OF AMERICA – ONE DOLLAR"

Reverse:
In the center a Beehive emblematic of industry, to the right a torch represents light, knowledge, to the left a CADUCEUS emblematic of Commerce, beneath laurel, emblematic of victory, the result of industry, Knowledge and Commerce surrounded by the inscription "PANAMA PACIFIC EXPOSITION - CAL. 1915"

It was going to be up to secretary McAdoo to select the best design for the tiny dollar coin. While he was considering the designs, Barber was ordered to "proceed with the sketch of the fifty dollar gold piece as rapidly as possible, giving no attention to the $2.50 for the present."[630]

Robert Aitken also had received a copy of McAdoo's criticism of his designs and must have been somewhat irritated by the secretary's insinuation that his design was a mere copy of an ancient coin. He not only defended his work but challenged the secretary to come up with a better idea:[631]

> On behalf of the designs submitted by me for the new Fifty Dollar gold piece, I feel it my duty to say, that they were not designed in haste, but were the result of the slow elimination of ideas. I have been working upon these designs since Mr. Roberts first wrote me last September.
> Being aware that these coins are destined to find their way into the Numismatic collections of the world, and appreciating that the thought expressed upon them should be reduced to its simplest form, I have taken from the seal of California the head of Minerva, the goddess of all that an Exposition means, the display of intellectual accomplishment. You will remember that she was adopted as the feature of the seal because of the analogy of her birth and that of California into statehood.

---

[629] *US Mint*, NARA-CP, op. cit., entry 229, box 302. Letter dated circa March 2, 1915 to Woolley from Joyce.
[630] *US Mint*, NARA-CP, op. cit., entry 235, vol. 412. Letter dated March 3, 1915 to Joyce from Dewey.
[631] *US Mint*, NARA-CP, op. cit., entry 229, box 302. Letter dated February 18, 1915 to McAdoo from Aitken. Note that Aitken had been working on the medal and coin designs since the pervious summer, unlike the other artists.

> I state these facts, not that I wish to induce you to accept the designs, but because I realize how little a pencil sketch suggests the ultimate beauty of the coin, which depends upon its modeling.
> Any changes that you might care to suggest, the rearrangement of the inscription or the elimination of any detail, can be worked out in the model. Or, should you have an idea better suited to a new design, it will be most welcome.
> I await your further instruction.

Aitken attached a gold foil copy of the California State seal to illustrate his authority for relating Minerva to California. Conspicuously absent was any offer to make a new design entirely on his own. The artist set to work making a plaster model of this design and on March 4 Aitken telegraphed McAdoo to request an appointment for Saturday March 6. Dewey wired approval for the meeting and also asked Charles Keck to come to the secretary's office the same day.

The two artists met separately with McAdoo, Malburn and Dewey and discussed changes to the designs. Keck was to modify the workingman's cap and remove the laurel leaves from the head of Labor to give it more "workman like" character; the reverse with dolphins was approved without change. Aitken had to remove the spider web, rearrange the dolphins on the octagonal format, and use only the Roman numeral date. By the afternoon of March 6, McAdoo had approved the gold dollar and $50 coins. Dewey wrote to the Philadelphia Mint the following Monday:[632]

> I beg to advise you that the Secretary of the Treasury has accepted the design submitted by Mr. Aitken for the $50 gold piece, and that of Mr. Keck for the $1.00 gold piece. Will you please request Mr. Barber to submit a design for the $2.50 gold piece as soon as possible.
> Mr. Barber's altered designs for the $0.50 silver piece are before the Secretary and you will be advised immediately when the Bureau is informed by him which are definitely accepted.

By Wednesday the half dollar designs were approved and Barber was ordered to make minor alterations and proceed with the work after final approval by Dewey.

Only the quarter eagle gold piece awaited final acceptance. Barber sent photos of his plaster sketch models to Washington on March 16 along with a description of the design. Since only eight days elapsed between the time Barber was told to stop work on his version of the $50 coin, and the date on which he sent photos of the $2.50 coin to Woolley's office, it is possible that Barber simply re-lettered his $50 design to suit the smaller gold coin. With the engraving department under considerable pressure to produce working dies, it is likely the engraver adopted any expediency available to him.

The quarter eagle designs met with an overwhelmingly positive reception at the treasury department:[633]

> Mr. Malburn, like myself, is enthusiastic over Mr. Barber's design for the $2.50 gold piece, and we believe that Secretary McAdoo will think as we do. Just as soon as it is possible to do so, which may be some day next week, I will have the photographs submitted to him, and provided he approves, will authorize you to go ahead with the manufacture of the dies. From my talk with Mr. Barber I gather that this arrangement will enable us to furnish the working dies to the San Francisco Mint at a much earlier date that would otherwise have been possible.

---

[632] *US Mint*, NARA-CP, op. cit., entry 235, vol. 412. Letter dated March 8, 1915 to Joyce from Dewey.
[633] *US Mint*, NARA-CP, op. cit., entry 235, vol. 412. Letter dated March 19, 1915 to Joyce from Dewey.

Producing the Coins

Events now turned from design to production. With the half dollar and quarter eagle being prepared by the Philadelphia Mint, the engraving department would have followed its usual procedures in preparing hubs and dies. Although it has usually been stated that the mint made reductions either directly from plaster models or first made a galvano (or electroplate shell), this may not have been the case. Some of the Saint-Gaudens and Pratt hubs were prepared from bronze casts of the models. Robert Aitken also commented that he had to have bronze casts made of his $50 coin models so the mint could cut hubs.[634] Aitken contacted director Woolley on March 13 to ask whether his models should be sent to the mint or Medallic Art Co. for reductions and hubs:[635]

> …The then acting Director of the Mint, Mr. Dewey, said that he would inform me as to whether I should deliver these models to the Medallic Art Company to have hubs or dies made, or that they should be delivered to the Mint at Philadelphia. This information has not reached me yet.
> Will you please be so kind as to give this matter your attention.
> Permit me to state that in all cases regarding the recent coins, the hubs have been made here in New York by the Medallic Art Co. By this means the designers of the coins have been in a position to make further study and refinements upon the designs, for the reason that a reduced wax pattern is made by this company, from the models before the die or hub is made. This gives the sculptor the opportunity of seeing his model reduced to the actual size of the coin, so that if any change of detail is necessary, it can be made.

Aitken exaggerated when he said that all recent hubs had previously been made in New York. The only occasions when hubs had been made outside the Philadelphia Mint were in 1909 and 1912–13. Victor Brenner had his first set of hubs made by Medallic Art Co. in March 1909, but the mint altered his design and made its own hubs for the coins released to circulation. In December 1912 Medallic Art made hubs for Jim Fraser's Buffalo nickel, then made a second pair in late January 1913. It is unclear if the mint used either of these for production dies.[636]

Director Woolley met with Aitken and Keck at the U.S. Assay Office in New York on March 18 to discuss production of the coins with the artists. During the meeting it was decided to have hubs for both coins cut at the mint.[637] However, the next day Woolley decided that gold dollar hubs could be cut by Medallic Art Co. after "…Mr. Ira Bennett, the Washington representative of the Panama-Pacific Exposition Company…commission[ed] the Medallic Art Company…to make the dies at the price of $200 quoted in their letter of January 22, 1915, to Mr. F. P. Dewey, acting director of the mint. I know this arrangement will be very satisfactory to you inasmuch as you can be in constant touch with the work."[638]

The $50 Panama-Pacific coin models were taken to the Philadelphia Mint on April 3, but Aitken was told they would have to be shipped back to New York so that bronze

---

[634] *US Mint*, NARA-CP, op. cit., entry 229, box 302. Letter dated April 7, 1915 to Woolley from Aitken.
[635] *US Mint*, NARA-CP, op. cit., entry 229, box 302. Letter dated March 13, 1915 to Woolley from Aitken.
[636] Henri Weil, co-owner of Medallic Art Co. cut the Saint-Gaudens double eagle hubs in January 1907 while using the Philadelphia Mint's new Janvier lathe, but this was before Medallic Art Co. was organized and would not have been known to Aitken.
[637] *US Mint*, NARA-CP, op. cit., entry 235, vol. 411. Letter dated March 17, 1915 to Aitken from Woolley.
[638] *US Mint*, NARA-CP, op. cit., entry 235, vol. 411. Letter dated March 19, 1915 to Keck from Woolley.

casts could be made. The sculptor decided to take the models back with him and had casts made at this own expense. "One set of casts have been made, but I did not consider them successful, so have ordered others. I think they will be ready for delivery within the next five days."[639] A second set of casts were made and they, too, were unsatisfactory. It was ten days before casts Aitken approved reached the mint,[640] but problems persisted:[641]

> ...The casts for the fifty dollar piece were received yesterday. They were not at all satisfactory and therefore in order to expedite the work of the engraver, I am obliged to go to New York today to see Mr. Aitken with regard to them, authority for which trip I will ask you to provide on your return from the West.

It was April 26 when satisfactory $50 coin casts were received at the Philadelphia Mint. Aitken said that a previous set was damaged when one of the casts was broken in transit.[642]

While Aitken was struggling to finish his models and provide usable casts to the mint, Charles Keck had sent his work to Medallic Art Co. on March 26. A minor discrepancy in the diameter of the coin created little delay and on April 5 the diminutive $1 gold coin hubs arrived at the Philadelphia Mint.[643] By April 21, three months after passage of enabling legislation, the first sample of the Panama-Pacific Exposition gold dollar commemorative coin was shipped to director Woolley's office.[644]

> As per your request by phone today, I beg to enclose herewith for the Secretary a sample in bronze of the one dollar Panama-Pacific Exposition gold piece. I would thank you to return this at the convenience of the Secretary.

Like all early dies, these did not have the distinctive "S" mint mark which would be added later. The bronze sample was approved and returned to Philadelphia on April 22. Working dies (absent the "S") were shipped to San Francisco the same day, completing Charles Keck's coin design work for the exposition.[645]

Missing Mintmark

Mint director Robert Woolley was in San Francisco when the first shipment of six-pairs of one dollar commemorative coins dies arrived on April 27. On inspection of the dies, the coiner discovered that they lacked the "S" mintmark normally applied to all dies used at the western mint. Woolley sent a telegram to Philadelphia the evening of April 29:[646]

> Mint mark of San Francisco Mint omitted from dies for one dollar gold piece. Is this an oversight or was it done intentionally? Please see that dies for other coins are properly marked unless there is good reason for not doing so.

Superintendent Joyce replied at 8:24 the next morning:[647]

---

[639] *US Mint*, NARA-CP, op. cit., entry 229, box 302. Letter dated April 7, 1915 to Woolley from Aitken.
[640] *US Mint*, NARA-CP, op. cit., entry 229, box 302. Letter dated April 17, 1915 to Woolley from Aitken.
[641] *US Mint*, NARA-CP, op. cit., entry 229, box 302. Letter dated April 20, 1915 to Woolley from Aitken.
[642] *US Mint*, NARA-CP, op. cit., entry 229, box 302. Letter dated April 26, 1915 to Woolley from Joyce.
[643] *US Mint*, NARA-CP, op. cit., entry 229, box 302. Letter dated April 5, 1915 to Woolley from Joyce.
[644] *US Mint*, NARA-CP, op. cit., entry 229, box 302. Letter dated April 21, 1915 to Woolley from Joyce.
[645] *US Mint*, NARA-CP, op. cit., entry 229, box 302. Letter dated April 22, 1915 to Woolley from Joyce.
[646] *US Mint*, NARA-CP, op. cit., entry 229, box 302. Telegram dated April 29, 1915 to Joyce from Woolley.
[647] *US Mint*, NARA-CP, op. cit., entry 229, box 302. Telegram dated April 30, 1915 to Woolley from Joyce.

> Mint mark omitted intentionally as entire Panama Pacific coinage is done at San Francisco. Half dollar dies forwarded today without mark. Shall mark be placed on fifty and two & a half dollar gold dies?

Woolley wired back the same day:[648]

> Make new sets of dies for dollar gold pieces and fifty cent silver piece containing San Francisco mint mark and forward at earliest possible moment. Also place San Francisco mint mark on fifty dollar and two and half dollar pieces. Presumption of those ignorant of special act governing this coinage would be that coins were struck at Philadelphia. Dies received and in transit will be returned.

Joyce had understood that no mint mark was necessary since all of the coins were, by law, to be struck only at the San Francisco Mint. However, Woolley pointed out that unless one were familiar with the legislation, the presumption would be that absence of a mintmark indicated production at Philadelphia. The director explained further in a letter to Joyce:[649]

> ...I regret that you omitted the mint mark of the San Francisco Mint from the dies for the Exposition coins. Had you consulted me, I should have told you to put them on, because the numismatists and the public generally, in the absence of this mark, would conclude that they were struck at the Philadelphia; also because the people of the far west, who use gold and silver money to the exclusion of paper, are very proud of this Mint and would be justified in regarding the omission of the mark as an intentional slight. I realize that this phase of the matter did not occur to you....

The half dollar dies were still at the Philadelphia express agent's office and Joyce was able to retrieve the package before it left the city. After having the mintmark added, these were reshipped on May 3 along with three pair of mint marked gold dollar dies. The original dollar dies without mintmark were returned to Philadelphia.[650] No other dies without the "S" mintmark left the Philadelphia Mint.

Failure to add the mintmark was an understandable lapse by Barber and the engraving department. Fortunately San Francisco Superintendent Shanahan and Woolley had noticed the error before coins were released to the exposition company for public sale. Residents of California were extremely proud of their mint and of its role in sustaining the city of San Francisco after the earthquake and fire of 1906. Omission of the "S" mintmark would have raised howls of protest from all parts of the west and could have led to issuance of the coin at both Philadelphia and San Francisco. The extent of local pride is evident in an article from the San Francisco *Examiner* of June 16, 1915. Accompanying a large photo of the first-strike ceremony for the $50 gold coin, is an effusive article describing the first dozen coins struck by local celebrities.

Delivery of Dies

The table below lists the shipment and delivery of coinage dies to the San Francisco Mint for the Panama-Pacific International Exposition. Available documents may not cover all shipments.

---

[648] *US Mint*, NARA-CP, op. cit., entry 229, box 302. Telegram dated April 30, 1915 to Joyce from Woolley.
[649] *US Mint*, NARA-CP, op. cit., entry 229, box 302. Letter dated April 30, 1915 to Joyce from Woolley.
[650] *US Mint*, NARA-CP, op. cit., entry 229, box 302. Letter dated May 4, 1915 to Woolley from Joyce.

Denomination	Shipped (Philadelphia) Quantity	Date	Received (San Francisco) Quantity	Date	Comment
$1 hubs	1 pair	4/4/15	1 pair	4/5/15	From Medallic Art Co. to Philadelphia Mint.
$1	6 pairs	4/22/15	6 pairs	4/27/15	Plus collar and planchet cutting tools. One rev die badly cracked. No "S" mint mark.
50¢	5 pairs	4/30/15			No "S" mint mark. Recalled from Philadelphia express office.
50¢	5 pairs	5/4/15	5 pairs	5/8/15	Mint mark "S" added.
$1	3 pairs	5/3/15	3 pairs	5/8/15	With mint mark.
$50 round	3 pairs	5/14/15	3 pairs	5/20/15	With mint mark. One obverse die badly cracked.
$50 octagonal	3 pairs	5/14/15	3 pairs	5/20/15	With mintmark. Plus collars and planchet cutting tools.
$2.50	3 pairs	5/27/15	3 pairs	6/3/15	
$1	6 reverse	6/2/15	6 reverse	6/8/15	Requested 5/29/15.
50¢	4 pairs	6/11/15	4 pairs	6/17/15	Six pair requested 6/2/15.
50¢	1 pair	6/19/15	1 pair	6/24/15	
$50 round	3 obverse	6/30/15	3 obverse	7/6/15	
$50 octagonal	2 obverse	6/30/15	2 obverse	7/6/15	
$1	5 obverse	6/30/15	5 obverse	7/6/15	
$1	10 reverse	6/30/15	10 reverse	7/6/15	
Medal	3 pairs	8/3/15	?	?	Second shipment of dies for Aitken's souvenir medal struck at the mint exhibit.

The following table lists Panama-Pacific commemorative coins by delivery date and samples reserved for the Annual Assay Commission.[651] Silver half dollars were not included in the assay reservation because they were authorized to be melted and restruck as necessary. Note that delivery date is not necessarily the date coins were struck.

Delivery date	Denomination	Quantity Struck	Assay Quantity	Quantity Melted	Net Mintage
May 28, 1915	Gold dollar	4,000	4	n/a	n/a
May 28, 1915	Half dollar	12,000	0	n/a	n/a
June 7, 1915	Half dollar	48,000	0	n/a	n/a
June 22, 1915	$50 Octagonal	609	1	n/a	n/a
June 22, 1915	$2.50 gold	4,000	4	n/a	n/a
June 22, 1915	Gold dollar	1,500	2	n/a	n/a

---

[651] *US Mint*, NARA-CP, op. cit., entry 273. Daily production from January 11, 1911 through June 30, 1915. Also minutes of the Annual Assay Commission for 1916.

Delivery date	Denomination	Quantity Struck	Assay Quantity	Quantity Melted	Net Mintage
June 23, 1915	$2.50 gold	3,000	3	n/a	n/a
June 24, 1915	$2.50 gold	3,017	4	n/a	n/a
July 9, 1915	Gold Dollar	?	10	n/a	n/a
July 10, 1915	$50 Round	?	1	n/a	n/a
July 16, 1915	Gold dollar	?	10	n/a	n/a
July 28, 1915	$50 Round	?	1	n/a	n/a
August 4, 1915	$50 Round	?	2	n/a	n/a
August 4, 1915	$50 Octagonal	?	1	n/a	n/a
August 5, 1915	$50 Octagonal	?	1	n/a	n/a
Totals	Half dollar	60,000	0	32,866	27,134
	Gold dollar	25,026	26	10,026	15,000
	Quarter eagle	10,011	11	3,266	6,745
	$50 Octagonal	1,503	3	864	639
	$50 Round	1,504	4	1,027	477

Destruction of unsold coins was approved on October 27, 1916. This included 28,786 halves plus unspecified gold coins held by Zerbe. Members of the 1916 Assay Commission asked permission to purchase some of the commemorative coins at face value, as had been customary for normal circulation coins. In this instance, director Woolley denied permission and the assay pieces were melted.

Souvenir Medal

A commemorative (or souvenir) medal was also part of the PPIE coin legislation, but had actually been planned several months before Representative Kahn submitted his proposal to Congress. Contrary to the coin situation, the medal was commissioned, designed and dies produced with little difficulty. Credit for this success rests equally with the Government Exhibition Board and sculptor Robert Aitken. The board gave the artist clear instructions, a good idea of what it wanted from the creative standpoint, and then let the work be done. For his part, Aitken made a straight forward proposal to the board, told them clearly what he could do, and then made sure that all details of design, hub cutting and delivery were taken care of. All substantive work on the medal was completed before the PPIE legislation passed Congress in January 1915.

Medal designing began with a suggestion on March 21, 1914 by James L. Wilmeth, Treasury Department Representative PPIE, Government Exhibition Board, Department of Interior, to Mint Director George Roberts:[652]

> This Department has under contemplation the scheme of operating and disposing of the output of the presses of the Mint and the Bureau of Engraving and Printing at the coming exposition at San Francisco, and such being the case, it is necessary that some study be given to the design of the medal and engraving which will be stricken from said presses.
> The following ideas have been suggested for consideration in connection with the medal to be struck from the coining press of the Mint Bureau.

---

[652] *US Mint*, NARA-CP, op. cit., entry 229, box 302. Letter dated March 21, 1914 to Roberts from James L. Wilmeth, Treasury Department Representative PPIE, Government Exhibition Board, Department of Interior.

A medal showing on the obverse side Old Neptune rising up from the sea and smiting the Isthmus with a sword, thus dividing the two Continents. On the reverse side a likeness of Colonel George W. Goethals, the Army Officer in charge of the construction of the Canal.

A medal showing one of the foregoing views on one side, and on the other a view of the Golden Gate, San Francisco.

A medal showing one of the foregoing views and some scene characteristic of San Francisco, or its harbor.

A medal showing one of the foregoing views and some likeness of the Canal, or Catun Locks.

It is not known by this office whether any one of the foregoing ideas could be utilized in medal work, and it would be appreciated if you would refer the matter to the coin designer of the Philadelphia Mint for his views and comments thereon.

An estimate should be secured from the Mint showing the cost of making two dies and such duplicates of the same as may be required from time to time as those in service become worn and unfit for further use. If there is to be any charge for designing the medals, this should be also stated. If the pig metal is to be melted and rolled at the exposition, some approximation should be given as to the number of blanks which can be manufactured daily, and ideas as to the cost thereof. It is understood that at previous expositions it has been found necessary to dip the medals in a gold solution, and if you can furnish any information as to the cost of this work, this also would help the Department in planning the work.

Unless the Mint operatives can perform this work in the Treasury space, it would probably facilitate operations if we could secure the names of some exhibitors in this line of work at San Francisco who will show plating processes in one of the exhibit buildings.

The letter was sent to Philadelphia Mint Superintendent John Landis where it was given to the engraver for a response to the design and technical questions. Barber's reply of March 31 indicates something very simple, such as portrayal of a government building, would be cheap to make and sell well to the masses:[653]

Replying to the inquiry of Mr. James L. Wilmeth, Chief Clerk and Representative, Treasury Department, regarding certain designs suggested for a souvenir medal to be struck in the Government Exhibit at San Francisco, I beg to say that I do not consider any of the described designs as suitable for the purpose for the following reasons.

First: As the medal is to be struck as a coin with one operation of the press, the relief must be the same as a coin, which is extremely low, and being low should be simple, otherwise it becomes confused and indistinct. The design with Neptune rising from the sea and smiting the Isthmus and a portrait of Colonel Goethals for the other side would not permit of the low simple treatment desirable for a cheap medal. The other designs are all pictorial in character and should have light and shade to develop the design. Pictorial subjects do not lend themselves to medallic treatment especially as the prime motive, landscape may occupy a minor place as an accessory but as already stated a pictorial design and in low relief and all one color would mean nothing in a cheap medal.

I beg to suggest that as these medals are to be sold to the public, that a simply showy design that will attract the eye of the masses and at the same time have some connection with the Mint exhibit would appear to be desirable. I would therefore suggest, that a view of the government building with appropriate inscription for one side, with the Shield of the United States decorated for the other would make a design that could be more suitable for the purpose. In this connection I beg to

---

[653] *US Mint*, NARA-CP, op. cit., entry 229, box 302. Letter dated March 31, 1914 to Landis from Barber.

say that of all expositions that I have any knowledge of, more medals were sold at Chicago than any other, and the design was the government building on one side and an inscription on the other.

In regard to the blanks or planchets, I do not approve of their being made at the Mint exhibit; this was tried at St. Louis and to the best of my knowledge was a failure, the planchets being eventually purchased. The Mint buys the metal for all medals because it is better prepared, the blanks can be purchased all ready for striking and no doubt there will be some exhibitor doing gilding who will gladly undertake the gilding as was the case in St. Louis at a cost of about four cents each. Blanks the diameter of the Double Eagle have been most used at Expositions and have been purchased for $20.00 per thousand. I cannot state the price today.

Evidently Wilmeth and his colleagues on the government board weren't prepared to settle for "..a view of the government building…" and a simple shield. They wanted to see what their original design suggestion would look like, and Barber was instructed to make a drawing. About two weeks later, acting superintendent Albert Norris forwarded the drawing to director Roberts:[654]

I beg to submit a design for reverse of medal to be struck at the Panama-Pacific Exposition 1915 at the Government exhibit. The design represents Neptune smiting the Isthmus with his trident as suggested in letter of Mr. Wilmeth Representing the Treasury Department.

Figure 65. Charles Barber's sketch of a proposed PPIE souvenir medal based on a written design description submitted by the Government Exposition Board in March 1914. The side featuring Neptune (obverse, on the left) may have been the predecessor of Barber's $2.50 gold commemorative design accepted the following year. (NARA.)[655]

Barber's sketch is not what would be expected from an artist who thought a building looked good on a cheap medal. The reverse portrait of Goethals certainly stays close to the persistently awful work seen on cheap souvenir medals sold to the masses. The obverse, however, shows lively Neptune riding on a Hippocampus and using his trident to divide the Isthmus of Panama. It is not only a reasonably well-balanced composition, but the Neptune side bears a resemblance to the final obverse for the $2.50 gold piece (see below). There was promise of something more than commonplace in this design.

The attitude of engraver Barber and the Philadelphia Mint seemed more cooperative and additional information was provided for Wilmeth on April 22:[656]

---

[654] *US Mint*, NARA-CP, op. cit., entry 229, box 302. Letter dated April 13, 1914 to Landis from Barber.
[655] *Treasury*, NARA-CP, record group 56, entry 664, box 4. Obverse and reverse pencil drawings on card stock. No date.
[656] *US Mint*, NARA-CP, op. cit., entry 229, box 302. Letter dated April 22, 1914 to Landis from Barber.

> When I submitted a sketch for the medal to be struck in the Exposition at San Francisco I did not state any cost for the original dies and hubs, neither did I give the cost of duplicate dies as I was under the impression from the letters recently received from the Director that he had come to the conclusion that under the Act of January 29th, 1874 all this character of work should be done at the Mint and as he says in regard to the dies and cutters we are making for the badge for National Match for Military Schools we were to "sink the cost of dies." At the exposition held in Seattle, the Director decided that no charge was to be made for the dies used in striking the souvenir medal. If the cost of dies is required I can furnish an estimate as soon as the design is settled.
>
> I cannot judge how many pieces per pair of dies should be made until the design is approved and then only if certain blanks are used. The blanks made at the exhibit may be entirely different from any we have had any experience with, in that case it will be an experiment that can be settled only by trial. At the recent exhibit in New York I learn that three pairs of dies were used and 15,000 pieces were made, that I think is about the limit of dies in any exposition that I have knowledge of.

A few days later acting superintendent Norris advised, "…I beg to inform you that the engraver reports that it would be well to allow three months for the preparation of master dies and hubs, the cost of which would [be] $500. The working dies would be $25 per pair."[657]

As part of the cost estimate for the mint's exhibit, Clifford Hewitt, who was in charge of exhibit planning, noted that the melting, rolling, cutting and minting equipment for the demonstrations would produce approximately 3,750 medals per day.[658]

> I think 3,750 finished medals per day will, in all probability, supply the demand, but that is governed largely by crowds.
>
> …I believe the machinery should be in operation all the time, turning out blanks to demonstrate to the public the processes in coinage. There is practically no added expense, as the metal can be melted over and over running the exhibit on the above plan.
>
> …At the St. Louis Exposition the contract price for gold plating the medals was five cents each; at the New York Electric Exposition the price paid was 3-1/2-cents each. I think it would be desirable to make medals of different finishes: the plain alloy, gold finish, oxidized and sand blast. We made medals of the above finishes at the St. Louis Exposition and found a large sale for them.

Evidently, this is where mint officials obtained their expectation for the quantity of medals that could be sold during the exposition. The "…3,750 finished medals per day…" figure mentioned by Hewitt does not appear in later correspondence. However, Hewitt was in the mint's booth every day during the exposition and he must have communicated his expectations to Treasury Department special agent Charles A. Harbaugh.

On June 4, 1914 Representative Julius Kahn (D-California) introduced HR 16902 which provided for the coinage of one silver and three gold commemorative coins for the Panama-Pacific International Exposition, plus a souvenir medal and an award medal. A copy found its way to director Roberts on June 17 and the director, on learning that the California Congressional delegation was determined to have the bill passed, arranged to

---

[657] *US Mint*, NARA-CP, op. cit., entry 229, box 302. Letter dated April 28, 1914 to Roberts from Norris.
[658] *US Mint*, NARA-CP, op. cit., entry 229, box 302. Letter dated April 29, 1914 to Landis from Clifford Hewitt, Foreman of Machinists, Philadelphia Mint.

consult with the Commission of Fine Arts at its July meeting.[659] Representative Khan's bill and the Commission's discussion of potential coin and medal designers evidently ended consideration of anyone at the Mint Bureau designing the medal.

But the medal design did not go into suspended animation. Adolph C. Miller, Chairman of the Government Exhibition Board for the Panama-Pacific International Exposition, still wanted a souvenir medal to sell at the exposition. Noting the terms of Rep. Kahn's bill, and after meeting with mint director Roberts in early September, sculptor Robert Aitken contacted the government board offering to design the much-desired medal. Aitken was one of the more self-promoting of the era's best sculptors and frequently tried to avoid design competitions if he felt he could get the work on his own.

After Roberts' September visit, Aitken began work on several designs for possible use by the PPIE. Of the artists contacted by the mint, he is the only one who seems to have spent significant time working on designs well before the authorizing act was signed.

In late November Miller and Aitken exchanged letters of agreement for design of the souvenir medal:[660]

> In accordance with our agreement made in your offices on the sixteenth inst., permit me to state that I will make designs for the obverse and reverse of the commemorative medal, to be made by the Government presses at the San Francisco exposition, and deliver plaster models of same to you for the sum of $1,000 (one Thousand dollars). This sum to be payment in full for all work done by me in the preparation, and delivery of the plaster models to you.

Miller acknowledged the agreement two days later:[661]

> I hereby accept your proposal, dated November 25, 1914, to make designs for the obverse and reverse of the commemorative medal…

Wilmeth had remained involved in the negotiations and Miller turned to him for advice on the advisability of having reductions and hubs made by an outside company, not the Philadelphia Mint. Aitken was fully aware of the mint's poor reputation for translating artist's work into coins and medals and wanted Henri Weil at Medallic Art Company to make the necessary hubs:[662]

> I send you attached hereto a note from Mr. Robert Aitken with regard to the advisability of the construction of "hubs" or "mother dies" to be used in connection with the production of the commemorative medal. The principle object of this, I take it, is to ensure a faithful reproduction of the artist's design on the lines intended by him, to avoid the sharp definition of outline which is usual and desirable in ingots intended for circulation as money.
> I shall be glad to have your views upon this matter.

Having Medallic Art make the hubs would cost an extra $200, yet there is no hint that this was objectionable. Wilmeth wanted to have the dies finished quickly and to the satisfaction of the artist:[663]

---

[659] *US Mint*, NARA-CP, op. cit., entry 229, box 302. Letter dated June 17, 1914 to Roberts from Thomas W. Hardwick, Chairman of the House Committee on Coinage Weights and Measures.
[660] *Treasury*, NARA-CP, op. cit., entry 664, box 1. Letter dated November 25, 1914 to Adolph C. Miller, Chairman of Government Exhibition Board, PPIE from Aitken.
[661] *Treasury*, NARA-CP, op. cit., entry 664, box 1. Letter dated November 27, 1914 to Aitken from Miller.
[662] *Treasury*, NARA-CP, op. cit., entry 664, box 1. Letter dated December 14, 1914 to Wilmeth from Miller.
[663] *Treasury*, NARA-CP, op. cit., entry 664, box 1. Letter dated December 14, 1914 to Miller from Wilmeth.

> I am returning herewith the letter of Mr. Robert Aitken with regard to the construction of "hubs" to be used in connection with the production of the commemorative medal for the Panama-Pacific International Exposition.
>
> I think Mr. Aitken's views are correct, and in my judgment it would be entirely proper to authorize him to proceed as outlined in his letter. At the time of Mr. Aitken's visit he thought it would require only a week's time to produce the hubs. I trust this can be done so that we may have the design for the Mint people at the earliest practical date. The time is short at best and we should like to get to work on the dies at the very earliest moment.
>
> As I recall, it was our understanding that the cost of the design and the production of the dies was to be paid from funds received from the Exposition Company. The total expenses of the plate printer, including travel, per diem and assistant, will be $3,450. This design and dies will be $1,200 additional, making a total of $4,650.
>
> It would be appreciated if the payment to Mr. Aitken for his design and the dies, amounting to $1,200, could be temporarily taken up by the Government Exhibition Board pending the consummation of the deal with the Exposition Company as to the sale of medals, etc., the amount to be reimbursed out of the first funds paid by the Exposition Company. I am making this suggestion for the reason that the allotment for the Treasury Department is encumbered with practically all it will stand.

As his final contribution to the medal design project, Aitken made sure that the hubs were delivered personally to the Philadelphia Mint so there would be no delay. While he could have relied on Medallic Art to ship the hubs to the mint, his personal touch of taking the hubs from New York to Philadelphia at his own time and expense was typical of his approach toward the commission:[664]

> In my proposal dated November 25, 1914, you will note that it stated that upon delivery of the finished designs for the Commemorative Medal, in plaster, to you, that the work as far as I am concerned was finished.
>
> In view of the fact that the hubs were to be made here in New York, I have delivered the finished plaster models to the Medallic Art Company, who are at work upon the hubs.
>
> Feeling as I do, that my part of the work is finished I take the liberty of enclosing my bill.
>
> It is my intention however to deliver the hubs, as soon as they are ready, to the Philadelphia Mint, in person. My interest in the Medal is such that I feel it important that I take the hubs to the Mint myself.

On January 14 Superintendent Adam Joyce told Miller the hubs had arrived:[665]

> I beg to advise you that I have this day received from Mr. Aitken, of New York, the steel reductions for the models for the souvenir medal of the exposition.

With approval of the bill authorizing medals and coins for the PPIE, and inclusion of payment for the artists' work coming just after the hubs were delivered, Miller took the time to reassure Aitken that payment would not be significantly delayed. He also took a moment to thank the sculptor not only for the quality of his design, but for the way in which he handled the entire commission:[666]

---

[664] *Treasury*, NARA-CP, op. cit., entry 664, box 1. Letter dated January 5, 1915 to Miller from Aitken.

[665] *Treasury*, NARA-CP, op. cit., entry 664, box 1. Letter dated January 14, 1915 to Miller from Adam Joyce, Superintendent of the Philadelphia Mint.

[666] *Treasury*, NARA-CP, op. cit., entry 664, box 1. Letter dated January 18, 1915 to Aitken from Miller.

> I am glad to hear that the work has progressed to the point where the hubs have been delivered to the Philadelphia Mint. The bill for your design, and that of the Medallic Art Co. for the two hubs, have been turned over to the Treasury Department, inasmuch as under an Act recently approved by the President, that Department has been given authority to get designs both for the Commemorative Medal and the souvenir coins. This, however, will not affect you except to involve a slight delay in settlement of your account.
>
> I want to thank you for the business-like promptness you have shown in handling this matter. You already know what I, and all others who have seen it, think of your design.

Robert Aitken's souvenir medal was to be the only product of the U.S. Mint available to exhibition visitors until May of 1915. The trouble-free commission and production could have been an example for the coin designs, but circumstances operated against the coins. Sales of medals during the early weeks of the fair should also have given Farran Zerbe new ideas on how to market the mint and BEP products he sold. Yet, he seems not to have learned from events and continued his very limited and uninspired sales efforts.

Farran Zerbe – Marketing Coins and Medals

Initially, the Treasury Department planned to turn over sale of its products to a concessionaire. Bids were solicited and the proposal from Charles S. Muir & Company of Washington, DC was accepted on March 7, 1914. Their bid of $9,710 to sell engravings and souvenir medals produced by the Mint and BEP exhibits was more than $3,000 greater than the next highest bid.[667] For their money, the company acquired exclusive rights to sell these and other souvenirs at the exposition. The company had to pay its expenses plus the cost of materials from the profit on sales. This had been done at other expositions and was preferred by treasury officials over other options.

But by March 19, the Government Exhibit Board and its chairman Adolph C. Miller had decided they wanted to retain sales rights. According to a letter from Muir to congressman David J. Lewis:[668]

> ...Mr. Wilmeth, [Treasury Department representative], said the principle reason was that inasmuch as my bid was so high, the Board knew that I was figuring on a profit and that they concluded that the Government might have not only the amount I agreed to pay, but my profit as well.

Muir also contacted Maryland Senator Blair Lee and others who all supported award of the concession to Muir based on his bid having been accepted. At the suggestion of assistant treasury secretary Charles S. Hamlin, Muir made a counter offer:[669]

> ...it being thought advisable for the Treasury Department to operate the concession itself, and as the best results can only be obtained by having someone experienced in this line of work to take charge of the business incident to the sale of the medals and engravings, I would like to make a proposition to run the concession for the Treasury Department on an equitable profit-sharing basis, and ask that this proposal be considered favorably not only in view of the fact of my having

---

[667] *Treasury*, NARA-CP, op. cit., entry 664, box 2. Bid summary sheet dated March 7, 1914.
[668] *Treasury*, NARA-CP, op. cit., entry 664, box 2. Letter dated March 19, 1914 to Hon. David J. Lewis from Charles S. Muir.
[669] *Treasury*, NARA-CP, op. cit., entry 664, box 2. Letter dated March 30, 1914 to Wilmeth from Muir. p.1.

been interested in similar work at three different expositions, but also for the reason that I was the highest bidder of the concession.

Muir's offer was to pay $5,500 cash plus twenty-five percent of revenue to the treasury. But this did not deter Miller, who pushed ahead with the idea of the Government handling medal and engraving sales, and also proposed several possible designs for the medal. (See the section on design of the souvenir medal, above.) On October 24 Miller contacted the treasury representative's office, stating that the Government Exhibition Board was going to offer the medal and engraving concession to the exposition company. In exchange, the exposition would pay $5,500 plus furnish utilities (gas, electricity, water) at no charge.[670] Available documents give no explanation for why this arrangement was better for the government than either of Muir's offers.

Passage of the commemorative coins and medal act further confused matters and the Government Exposition Board turned over concession rights to the exposition company. Instead of a cash payment plus all utilities, the exposition company agreed to pay for the coin and medal designs ($5,000), the cost of metal, ink and other materials and one-half of the utilities. The total value was probably not greater than Muir's original bid, and likely much less than the treasury would have received if it had accepted Muir's $5,500 cash plus 25% of sales. As a consolation, Muir was given a similar concession at the San Diego Exposition at a reduced rate to avoid a messy public argument.[671]

With opening day only weeks away, the exposition company had no time to entertain bids and was not really interested in competition. The company wanted to maximize revenue and hired flamboyant self-promoter Farran Zerbe to sell the medals, engravings and other items. As a private organization, they could award contracts to whomever they preferred. This was the case with Farran Zerbe and the *Department of Official Coins and Medals*. Zerbe made a convincing case to Theodore Hardee, Chief, Department of Liberal Arts, and board members that his *Money of the World Exhibit* would attract visitors to the fair and attention to the concession booth, thus increasing sales. With this in mind, the exposition company hired him as a temporary employee to manage all official coin and medal sales. He was to sell the souvenir coins, medals, engravings, printed silk items such as handkerchiefs and scarves, and assorted knickknacks from his exhibit space. All of the profits went to the exposition company.

Mint Exhibit

The Treasury Department had five major exhibits at the fair: Bureau of the Mint, Bureau of Engraving and Printing, Public Health Service (disease prevention and control), Coast Guard (lifesaving demonstrations), and Office of the Supervising Architect (government buildings and designs). For coin and medal collectors, the two areas of greatest interest were the Mint and BEP, and it was their products Zerbe was hired to sell.

The mint had a large space of 2,979 square feet in the Mines and Metallurgy Building. In this space they demonstrated the processes involved in coining money. The display included a melting furnace capable of producing a temperature up to 2,000 degrees F. (far left in photo, below), molds, rolling mill, strip cutter, upsetting machine, coin dryer, a two-

---

[670] *Treasury*, NARA-CP, op. cit., entry 664, box 2. Memorandum dated October 24, 1914 to Asst. Sec. Thompson from S. H. Marks acting for Wilmeth. p.4.
[671] *Treasury*, NARA-CP, op. cit., entry 664, box 3. Multiple documents in correspondence folder "M."

sided coin reviewing machine, an automatic weighing machine and electrolytic refining equipment. Central to the display were two presses. One was a modern electrically driven Uhlhorn-type 150 ton coinage press on which mint employees were planning to strike bronze souvenir medals. The other item was an old screw press dating from 1797 shipped to the exposition so visitors could compare old and new technology.

Figure 66. Bureau of the Mint exhibit at the exposition. The display was supposed to demonstrate the steps in producing coins. Souvenir medals were struck on the coinage press (center). The exhibit could operate only a few hours per day because Farran Zerbe was unable to sell medals as quickly as they were produced. (Courtesy American Numismatic Association.)

The mint's space also included large cases (against wall underneath the triangular pediments) showing a collection of national medals, rolled coin strip, punched strip, and sample ingots of gold and silver as used by the mints and assay offices. To avoid problems of theft, Clifford Hewitt, who was in charge of the exhibit, had imitation ingots and strip cast in copper and lead, then plated with silver or gold. Instead of $50,000 in precious metal on display, the plating amounted to only $170.[672] The Uhlhorn press could strike ninety medals per minute and it was these that Zerbe proposed to sell to visitors.[673]

The Bureau of Engraving and Printing was allotted a much smaller space of only 748 square feet. Their demonstration consisted of a motorized plate press on which BEP employees printed portraits of the President and vice president, the American eagle, treasury building, White House, a battleship and other designs. Staff explained the process for producing currency, bonds, stamps and other government obligations. These paper prints, as well as some made on silk, were also sold by Zerbe's concession. All arrangements, physical and financial, seemed fine on paper. With the Treasury Department still primary supplier to Zerbe's concession, everyone felt confident of good results.

---

[672] *Treasury*, NARA-CP, op. cit., entry 664, box 4. Letter dated June 11, 1914 to Wilmeth from Hewitt.
[673] *Treasury*, NARA-CP, op. cit., entry 664, box 4. Memorandum to Assistant Treasury Secretary William Malburn from Wilmeth. pp.1-3.

Money of the World

Farran Zerbe's exhibit was titled "Zerbe's Unique Money of the World." It had a prominent space in the centrally located Liberal Arts Building. His advertising flyers often called the display the Department of Coins and Medals or sometimes the Coin and Medal Department. The first snag in sales of mint and BEP products came when it was realized

Figure 67. Sales booth for coins, medals and engravings, and display of "Zerbe's Unique Money of the World" operated by Farran Zerbe who was an employee of the exposition company. (Courtesy American Numismatic Association.)

that none of the coins would be ready for opening of the exposition. Only the souvenir medal, designed by Robert Aitken, had usable dies ready and could be struck as planned. While they were very artistic and well designed, the plain bronze version sold for just 25-cents, gold plated it cost 50-cents and a .900-fine silver version cost $1.00. A lot of medals would have to be sold to pay Zerbe's salary and expenses. The first delivery of bronze medals arrived on February 19, just one day before the exhibition opened.[674] Several hundred engravings were delivered on the 22nd and Zerbe finally had something to sell.[675] With initial fair attendance somewhat sparse, Zerbe was missing the "jewels" of his product offering. Engraved prints sold little better than the medals.[676] In an attempt to boost sales, "…Zerbe took it upon himself to have one of his sales ladies on duty yesterday (Sunday) in our Mint Exhibit."[677] The Special Agent overseeing Treasury Department exhibits did not like the idea of selling medals on Sunday, the only day during which the treasury exhibits were closed. "I notified him (Zerbe) this morning that I would not tolerate

---

[674] *Treasury*, NARA-CP, op. cit., entry 664, box 4. Medal delivery order No. 1 dated February 19, 1915 from exhibition comptroller Rodney Durkee to treasury special argent H. P. Huddelson.
[675] *Treasury*, NARA-CP, op. cit., entry 664, box 4. Engraving delivery order No. 1 dated February 22, 1915 from exhibition comptroller Rodney Durkee to treasury special argent H. P. Huddelson.
[676] *Treasury*, NARA-CP, op. cit., entry 664, box 6. Price list distributed by Zerbe on or before June 24, 1915. p2.
[677] *Treasury*, NARA-CP, op. cit., entry 664, box 6. Daily report dated April 12, 1915 to Wilmeth from Harbaugh.

Sunday sales. He was very angry about it."[678] However, permission was eventually granted and ten days later Zerbe added a second sales woman to the Mint exhibit.[679]

By May, attendance was looking better and the exposition company boasted of making a $2,000 profit every day. Treasury officials, however, attributed this more to creative accounting than to actual paying customers. When the Mint Bureau requested reimbursement for $800 paid to Robert Aitken for his gold $50 designs, exposition officials had to plead poverty saying that "…the Exposition Co. is somewhat pressed for ready funds at this time…"[680] and asked for an extension.

Zerbe contacted the mint director's office on April 26 asking for information on when the coins would be available and for descriptions of the designs. Acting director Dewey replied on May 1:[681]

> In reply to yours of the 26th ultimo I beg to inform you that the working dies for the $1.00 and $0.50 exposition coins have already been forwarded to the San Francisco Mint, and the rest of them will follow as soon as they can be prepared at the Philadelphia Mint. For information as to when you may expect the coin you are advised to consult the San Francisco Mint authorities who have the matter directly in charge.
>
> Much of the work in the preparation of the designs was carried out over the telephone, and verbally, so that we have no really complete description of the artists thoughts and conceptions in preparing these designs. I think it would be far preferable for you to address the artists directly in order to get a full and complete statement from each one of them on these matters. The designers and their addresses are as follows:
>
> $50.00   Mr. Robert Aitken, 147 Columbus Avenue, New York.
> $1.00   Mr. Charles Keck, 40 West 10th Street, New York.
> $2.50 and $0.50   Mr. Charles Barber, U. S. Mint, Philadelphia
>
> It would not be feasible at this time to forward the designer's models from which the master dies are being made.

What Dewey did not realize was that dies originally shipped did not have the "S" mint mark and had been recalled to Philadelphia. Zerbe wrote again on May 6 asking if a woman sculptor had been considered for the $2.50 design, and again if he could have the original plaster models of all the designs for display.[682] Dewey's reply the following week gave Zerbe the information he requested. Director Woolley eventually approved sending the souvenir medal plaster models to Zerbe, but not the coin models.[683]

> Replying to your inquiry of the 6th instant I beg to say that several sketches of design for the $2.50 gold piece were submitted by Miss Evelyn B. Longman of New York, but none were acceptable. Miss Longman visited Washington for the purpose of consulting the Department in regard to further sketches, was taken ill while in this city, and was not able to take up the work of submitting sketches until much beyond the time which could be afforded to her, and the Engraver of the Mint was directed to submit sketches.

---

[678] *Treasury*, NARA-CP, op. cit., entry 664, box 6. Daily report dated April 12, 1915 to Wilmeth from Harbaugh.
[679] *Treasury*, NARA-CP, op. cit., entry 664, box 6. Daily report dated April 21, 1915 to Wilmeth from Harbaugh. Wilmeth granted permission for Sunday sales beginning May 25.
[680] *Treasury*, NARA-CP, op. cit., entry 664, box 6. Letter dated June 9, 1915 to Wilmeth from Harbaugh.
[681] *US Mint*, NARA-CP, op. cit., entry 235, vol. 411. Letter dated May 1, 1915 to Zerbe from Dewey.
[682] *US Mint*, NARA-CP, op. cit., entry 229, box 302. Letter dated May 6, 1915 to Dewey from Zerbe.
[683] *US Mint*, NARA-CP, op. cit., entry 235, vol. 411. Letter dated May 14, 1915 to Zerbe from Dewey.

> The Director of the Mint, who has been out of the city for several weeks, will be at his desk tomorrow, when the matter of lending the models to the exposition will be submitted to him.

Working dies for the half dollar and gold dollar with the "S" mint mark arrived in San Francisco on May 8 and coins were soon available. The first batches included 4,000 gold dollars and 12,000 commemorative halves,[684]

With good spring weather and a reduction in train fares during May, attendance surged and many days were described as having "large crowds." Yet the crowds were not buying from Zerbe's Coins and Medal Department. The booth was relatively small and sat in the middle of the Liberal Arts place – a structure encompassing more than five acres of floor space. The Philadelphia Mint display was supposed to operate all day striking souvenir medals. But sales were so poor than medals had to be melted so there would be material on which to demonstrate mint operations. The Philadelphia Mint was also supplying gold plated and silver versions as well as extra bronze medals. Delivery orders though May 30 show that Zerbe was selling approximately 1,000 bronze medals, 120 silver medals and 250 engravings per week.[685] But, the mint exhibit could produce more than 18,000 medals per week.[686] Thousands had to be melted to provide metal to keep the exhibit running. More than 13,000 had accumulated in storage at the mint's exhibit space waiting to be sold.[687] Several thousand bronze medals tarnished or discolored in the Pacific climate and had to be replaced. The treasury's special agent, Charles A. Harbaugh, thought the situation was largely the fault of Zerbe and the exposition company whom he called "engineers…not businessmen."[688]

Sales problems reached the boiling point on June 3 when Harbaugh met with Zerbe. His letter of the next day states in part:[689]

> The other day I wrote you relative to the possibility of shutting down our mint exhibit owing to the lack of a supply of metal.
> Mr. Zerbe called me up yesterday and stated that an order was on the way directing us to re-melt medals now on hand, whenever necessary to keep things going.
> This man, Zerbe, is an unsatisfactory chap to deal with. He gives you the feeling that he suspects you will not give him a square deal, and at the same time you have the feeling that he wants to "put something over" on you.
> I can see that the whole trouble (in the matter of keeping our exhibit running a reasonable number of hours daily) is due to an utter lack of selling ideas on the part of the Exposition people, alias Zerbe. These medals are sold at only two places – in our exhibit and at a booth Zerbe has over in Liberal Arts bldg. I told Zerbe yesterday he ought to have them on sale in fifty booths on the grounds. He replied that they didn't want to employ so many salespeople. I suggested that they

---

[684] *US Mint*, NARA-CP, op. cit., entry 273, vol. 1. Ledger of daily coinage from January 1, 1911 through June 30, 1915. Quantities for half dollars and gold dollars were entered for May 28, 1915. This is the first production entry for PPIE coins.
[685] *Treasury*, NARA-CP, op. cit., entry 664, box 4. Letter dated November 20, 1915 to Zerbe from Harbaugh.
[686] Weekly revenue would have been approximately $225 which would barely cover the expense of product, sales people, and other expenses. With average attendance of 470,000 per week, sales should have been more than five times what Zerbe was able to achieve.
[687] *Treasury*, NARA-CP, op. cit., entry 664, box 4. Letter dated May 29, 1915 to PPIE president Charles C. Moore from Harbaugh.
[688] *Treasury*, NARA-CP, op. cit., entry 664, box 6. Letter dated June 18, 1915 to Wilmeth from Harbaugh.
[689] *Treasury*, NARA-CP, op. cit., entry 664, box 6. Letter dated June 4, 1915 to Wilmeth from Harbaugh.

> be sold on commission, thereby obviating salaries. He said they didn't propose to give commissions.
>
> You see, they are afraid the dimes will get away from them, and so fail to connect with the dollars. These medals should be on sale not only at the Exposition, but at numerous places downtown. If the selling end were properly handled I feel sure we could have two meltings daily, and present to the public every process they are required to pass through. As it is, we must nurse the operations along, giving only a part of them.
>
> To show you how shortsighted they are on sales, I will refer to a talk I had with one of their women here in our booth. She recalls an instance where a man came along and wanted to purchase 1,000 bronze medals in a single lot on condition that he be given a reasonable discount. This they absolutely refused to do, and so missed the sale, evidently preferring to make a thousand sales at full price [25-cents]. In another such case the prospective purchaser wanted to buy 500 medals.
>
> When I try to convince Zerbe that something is wrong with his end of it, he tries to tell me how much better this coining proposition has been handled at former expositions, and criticizes our operations here. He says we ought to operate for shorter periods, and proceed with the various processes slower. As a matter of fact our operations are as brief as they can be and present any demonstration at all, and as for speed, the machines are run as slowly as possible. There is no getting around it – the whole trouble rests with the salesmanship end of it. I feel we did the right thing to pass the metal purchases to them [the Exposition Company]; the responsibility for curtailing our operations is now theirs…
>
> …If the Expo. Co. had a man in charge of their end of it who understood the value of publicity and selling, and if they would give him proper latitude as to methods of pushing the medals, I think we would have no reason for complaint.
>
> PS: I find from a computation of costs that the bronze medals cost the Expo. Co. 0.87 of a cent each [$0.0087]. And yet they cannot afford to discount on large sales or give a commission. These medals are sold at 25-cents each.

The problems caused by poor medal sales continued and on June 9 Special Agent Harbaugh met with Dr. Frederick Skiff, the exposition company's Director General, to discuss payment of $800 owed the mint for the $50 gold coin designs. Farran Zerbe's name came up and Harbaugh was referred to Rodney Durkee, "…who it seems has charge of Zerbe and his outfit…"[690]

> I went directly to Mr. Durkee's office and threshed out the business with him. He told me he was so busy he had to entrust the details of his work to others. He himself isn't satisfied with Zerbe, and said he did not hire him. I took the opportunity to tell him how Zerbe has missed some big orders because he would not give a small discount, and stated that I thought he ought to have the medals on sale all over the grounds as well as downtown on a commission. He seemed to think well of the idea, and I think something will come of it.
>
> …Dr. Skiff told me to run our exhibit only two hours daily for the present: from 11 to 12 a.m., and from 2 to 3, or 3 to 4 in the afternoon. Will try this and see how it goes.

With the door open to exposition management, Harbaugh sent another letter on June 10. This time it was about the commemorative coins.[691]

---

[690] *Treasury*, NARA-CP, op. cit., entry 664, box 6. Letter dated June 9, 1915 to Wilmeth from Harbaugh.
[691] *Treasury*, NARA-CP, op. cit., entry 664, box 6. Letter dated June 10, 1915 to Durkee from Harbaugh.

> I desire to bring to your attention a matter affecting the sale of the souvenir one dollar coin and the 50-cent piece, now being offered the public by your agent, Mr. Zerbe.
>
> These coins…are sold only from Mr. Zerbe's booth in the Liberal Arts Building. It appears that prospective purchasers, stopping at the booth, are in some cases skeptical as to the genuineness of these coins, and decline to purchase them. This is brought out by inquiries made at our Mint exhibit. Visitors to this exhibit have expressed this skepticism, and asked whether these coins are on sale here. They seem to think their sale from our space would be a guarantee that they are what they are represented to be at Mr. Zerbe's booth.
>
> The foregoing raises the question why these coins have not also been placed on sale in our Mint exhibit, as it is presumed to be the desire of your company to dispose of as many of these coins as possible.

A skeptical buying public can be easily understood. Like other fairs and expositions, the Panama-Pacific International Exposition attracted many souvenir makers. Visitors were offered dozens of different medals, tokens and imitations of California $50 gold pieces. Imitations of small California, Yukon, Washington and other fantasy "gold pieces" abounded. The average person had little to ensure they were buying a genuine coin at Zerbe's booth and not some base metal replica. However, the U.S. Mint "made" money and could be trusted to sell only the real thing.

June 15 brought an impressive ceremony to strike the first fifty-dollar gold pieces on a medal press. Attended by upwards of sixty San Francisco area dignitaries, the date marked the first time that Zerbe had a full complement of coins and medals available to sell.[692]

(San Francisco Examiner - June 16, 1915)[693]

First of $50 Coins Struck at S.F. Mint
Superintendent Shanahan Works Levers. Initial "Slug" to Commemorate Exposition Goes to C.C. Moore
Other Noted Citizens Handle Levers; 3,000 Pieces to be Struck; Price is $100 Cash

> In the San Francisco Mint yesterday the coining of the Exposition memorial $50 gold pieces was begun. The coins are the highest in value ever struck off under the authority of the United States or any other government. Each one is to be sold for twice its nominal value as a coin of the realm, the $50 premium in each coin going into the treasury of the Exposition.
>
> Superintendent T. W. H. Shanahan of the local mint coined the first $50 gold piece, operating the levers on a machine weighing fourteen tons, sent to San Francisco especially for the Exposition coinage. At the conclusion of the work of striking off 3,000 $50 gold pieces, it will be returned to the Philadelphia Mint.
>
> **In Form of Old "Slug."**
>
> A piece of gold bullion cast in the form of this old California "$50 slug" but smooth, was placed between the dies. Shanahan pressed a lever and the dies came slowly together. For several seconds, to a thin, shrill crunching sound, heard faintly above the panting of the big motor, the indicator passed number after number recording the tons of pressure exerted. As a pressure of 480,000 pounds was reached the motor automatically struck work, the dies parted and the first $50 coin

---

[692] *Treasury*, NARA-CP, op. cit., entry 664, box 6. Daily report dated June 15, 1915 to Wilmeth from Harbaugh.
[693] *US Mint*, NARA-CP, op. cit., entry 229, box 302. Newspaper clipping from the San Francisco Examiner (ND, June 16, 1915) date derived from text and record date of event.

of the United States stood revealed. Shanahan lifted it from the steel bed and presented it to President Charles C. Moore.

"It means pride and profit to us," said Moore. "Don't forget that double 'P' – pride and profit. There is pride for us in the minting of this coin by the government in commemoration of the Panama-Pacific International Exposition, and profit in the premium to be paid. Numismatists will seek these coins with zeal."

May Make Own Coins.

Announcement was made that those wishing to purchase the $50 pieces might operate the machine, after the first ten coins were struck off, and reserve the coin they made themselves. Exception was made of the twenty-fourth and twenty-ninth coins to be minted. These had been asked for by Colonel George Goethals, builder of the Panama Canal, who wanted them as presents for his two sons aged 24 and 29 years.

In presenting the first $50 gold piece to President Moore, Superintendent Shanahan said:

"In commemoration of the Panama Pacific International Exposition, and pursuant to the act of Congress approved January 16, 1915, I am about to strike the first fifty dollar coin ever issued under authority of the laws of the United States. The issue is limited to three thousand pieces, one-half octagonal, one-half round. The design is:

"OBVERSE: Minerva, the goddess of wisdom, handicrafts, inventions, arts and sciences – UNITED STATES OF AMERICA – $50.00 MCMXV. In field: IN GOD WE TRUST.

"REVERSE: The owl, sacred to Minerva, the symbol of wisdom, perched upon a branch of Western pine. PANAMA-PACIFIC EXPOSITION, SAN FRANCISCO. In the field: E PLURIBUS UNUM. The designer's initials, R. A. The San Francisco mint mark, the letter 'S.'

"The dolphins occupying the angles of the octagonal coin and encircling the central field suggest the uninterrupted water route made possible by the Panama Canal.

"It is said that the motives used in these designs were selected by the sculptor, Robert Aitken, because of their simple dignity and far-reaching significance, as well as their decorative pattern.

"The coin should be of particular interest to all Californians, as the sentiment involved relates not only to commemorating the greatest of world expositions, but also brings to mind the historic fifty dollar slug of pioneer days.

"In passing and approving the act providing for this coinage, the Congress and the President have given a rare and exclusive tribute to California and the exposition."

Moore Coins Second One.

The second of the $50 pieces was coined by President Moore, the third by Captain Carlos Miranda of the Argentine training ship *Presidente Saramento*, now at this port. Julius Kahn, author of the act providing for the special coinage, operated the levers as the fourth piece was struck. United States Circuit Judge W. W. Morrow became a coiner to stamp the fifth. Shanahan then called upon Mrs. Lovell White, who coined the sixth. The seventh was coined by Mayor James Rolph, Jr. and the eighth by United States District Judge William C. Van Fleet. He remarked that it was the first money he had ever really made. Mrs. James L. Tucker served as coiner in striking off the ninth, and the tenth was coined by United States District Judge Maurice T. Dooling.

The first ten coins will be certified by Robert W. Woolley, Director of the Mint at Washington, and [Superintendent] Shanahan. The next ninety will be certified by the local [Superintendent] alone.

Tevis Coins Eleventh.

William S. Tevis, who presented to the Mint a pair of dies with which the old California "slugs" were struck in the early '50s, coined the eleventh of the new $50 pieces. Mrs. Frederick P. Dewey, wife of the Acting Director of the Mint at Washington, struck off the twelfth.

Greeted by laughing warnings from many friends, Postmaster Charles W. Fay stepped forward and coined the thirteenth.

Aside from the 3,000 $50 pieces, the local Mint will coin special exposition half dollars, gold dollars and $2.50 gold pieces.

The following table summarizes initial strikes of the $50 octagonal coins and their purchasers. There is no record of purchasers after the first thirteen pieces were struck. Presumably, these were the only people who came forward with cash in hand during the ceremony. After the event, employees of the coining department produced additional octagonal pieces through June 22 for a total of six hundred eight,[694] plus one piece reserved for the Assay Commission.[695]

Coin Number	Person Striking
No. 1	T. W. H. Shanahan, Superintendent of the San Francisco Mint. The coin was presented to Charles Caldwell Moore who accepted it on behalf of the Exposition Company.
No. 2	Charles C. Moore, President of the Exposition Company. Personal purchase.
No. 3	Captain Carlos Miranda of the Argentine brig *Presidente Saramento*.
No. 4	Congressman Julius Kahn, sponsor of the commemorative coin and medal legislation.
No. 5	W.W. Morrow, U. S. Circuit Court judge
No. 6	Mrs. Lovell White, Vice President of the Women's Board
No. 7	James Rolph, Jr. , Mayor of San Francisco
No. 8	W. C. Van Fleet, U. S. District judge
No. 9	Mrs. James L. Tucker
No. 10	M. T. Dooling, U. S. District judge
No. 11	William S. Tevis
No. 12	Mrs. Frederick P. Dewey, wife of the Acting Director of the Mint
No. 13	Charles W. Fay, Postmaster of San Francisco
No. 24	Struck by mint staff and reserved for Col. George W. Goethals, who was not present.
No. 29	Struck by mint staff and reserved for Col. George W. Goethals, who was not present.

Octagonal specimens were struck first because of their connection with the U. S. Assay Office of Gold issues in 1851, and their obvious novelty value. Round versions of the large gold coin were not made until July marking the earliest that complete sets of all varieties were available for delivery.

---

[694] *US Mint*, NARA-CP, op. cit., entry 273, vol. 1. Ledger of daily coinage from January 1, 1911 through June 30, 1915. Six hundred nine octagonal $50 coins were struck prior to June 30. The ledger lists them all under the date of June 22, which is likely the date the last pieces were struck.

[695] *US Mint*, NARA-CP, op. cit., entry 7 (NN3-104-03-002), Assay Commission files 1911-1931. The 1916 report shows that one octagonal $50 coin was reserved from the delivery of June 22, 1915. The next entry for $50 pieces is July 10 when one round example is listed.

The conversations between Durkee, Skiff and Harbaugh evidently encouraged Zerbe to make some changes:[696]

> ...I certainly expressed myself very pointedly in the interviews. I can see that what I said bore fruit, for the $1 and 50-cent coins are now being sold from the Mint booth, and they are going "like hot cakes." Orders are being taken, also, for the $50 coin.
> Zerbe told me that the medals would be placed on sale at a larger number of places.

Unfortunately, by June 24 Zerbe had stopped selling gold coins at the mint's exhibit although no reason was given.[697]

> Good attendance. Zerbe has discontinued selling six souvenir gold dollars from our exhibit, although his circulars and printed envelopes advertise such. Sells them six for $10 from booth in Liberal Arts. Sales being lost through this, as persons wishing to purchase six for $10 from our exhibit in some instances will not try to find Zerbe's booth in Liberal Arts.

Letters and daily reports do not indicate why gold dollar sales were stopped but tension continued between Zerbe and the treasury's representative. So few medals were being sold that the mint employees still had to re-melt and strike medals many times to keep their demonstration running at minimum. Repeated handling of the alloy made the pieces brittle and Zerbe complained about having to supply another 7,000 ounces of copper to correct the problem. Even the sales women became an irritant with Harbaugh complaining: "Requested Zerbe to transfer one of his saleswomen.... She was constantly sticking her nose into our business... Another woman was assigned to...sell medals and souvenir engravings."[698]

Over the balance of the exposition's run, it does not appear that medal and coin sales improved. The relationship between the treasury department and Farran Zerbe fared no better. With nearly six hundred thirty-five acres of exhibits, Zerbe's little booth could not offer the kind of public exposure necessary to sell large quantities of medals and souvenir coins. Not long before the fair closed, Zerbe requested some of the materials from the mint's booth for use in his educational exhibit, but was turned down.[699] Likewise, his request for the souvenir medal dies was denied because, "… if he got the dies, he would no doubt coin the medals hereafter on a large scale, and I doubt the legality of this procedure, after the fair has closed…"[700] Finally, he tried to order 1,400 extra engravings just two weeks before the exhibition closed. Harbaugh, clearly not willing to trust Zerbe's motives, refused to supply the items.[701]

Zerbe's saleswomen continued selling medals up to the very last moment, and he reported selling 10,000 (at 10-cents each) to exhibitors and workmen as they dismantled displays. There were also glimmers of cooperation such as Zerbe's gift of "…five hundred

---

[696] *Treasury*, NARA-CP, op. cit., entry 664, box 6. Daily report dated June 18, 1915 to Wilmeth from Harbaugh.
[697] *Treasury*, NARA-CP, op. cit., entry 664, box 6. Daily report dated June 24, 1915 to Wilmeth from Harbaugh.
[698] *Treasury*, NARA-CP, op. cit., entry 664, box 6. Daily report dated July 23, 1915 to Wilmeth from Harbaugh.
[699] *Treasury*, NARA-CP, op. cit., entry 664, box 7. Letter dated November 20, 1915 to Wilmeth from Zerbe. Reply of same date.
[700] *Treasury*, NARA-CP, op. cit., entry 664, box 7. Letter dated December 15, 1915 to Wilmeth from J. H. Marks, Special Agent.
[701] *Treasury*, NARA-CP, op. cit., entry 664, box 4. Letter dated November 20, 1915 to Zerbe from Harbaugh. The treasury department did not want Zerbe selling mint or BEP items after the fair closed.

souvenir medals and fifty sets of souvenir engravings" to the treasury's representative. Total cost of Zerbe's generosity was about $10.00, but at least he made the gesture. The mint and treasury staff dismantling the exhibit "...used part...as bribes to get courtesies extended in the way of getting quick shipment of boxes to our spaces. The way the men go for them one would imagine they were $20 gold pieces."[702]

Locking the Gates

The exhibition's gates closed for the final time on December 4 at which point almost 18 million people had paid to attend. Farran Zerbe saw no need to stop selling his wares and moved his operation to the service building to fulfill mail orders. In March 1916, Superintendent Shanahan notified Charles C. Moore of the Exhibition Company that his mint still held $89,750 in gold and $14,393 in silver coins (28,786 half dollars). Moore asked that the coins be melted[703] and Zerbe added that this was necessary to protect the people who had purchased the coins at a premium.[704] Superintendent Shanahan was finally empowered on October 16, 1916 to melt the commemorative coins remaining in his mint and to accept any unsold pieces from Zerbe for destruction.[705]

The Panama-Pacific International Exposition turned a profit of more than $1 million and was considered one of the most successful large exhibitions of its time. Although other great exhibitions were to be held, no others promoted American plastic arts and sculpture as did the PPIE. The medals and coins were, also, among the best designs created for any exposition. Sales, however, were disappointing with every aspect under Zerbe's control producing less than expected results. Medal sales did not exceed 42,000 of all varieties, which is barely four times the number of gold dollars sold. The reasons for poor sales seem to have been twofold. First, the exposition company and their employee, Zerbe, insisted on selling the coins, medals and prints primarily at Zerbe's booth. Despite numerous suggestions by treasury staff that medals and prints should be placed on sale at many locations and sold on commission, the exposition company refused to budge. Given the huge scale of the exposition grounds, it is unlikely that anyone went far out of their way to locate Zerbe's booth just to buy a medal. These souvenirs competed with dozens of private medals sold throughout the fair, and if the official medal was not conveniently available in every building, many others were available for purchase.

Explaining poor coin sales is a little more complicated. These four coins were the only commemorative coins issued for the exposition and were legal tender. It is understandable that they would not be farmed out to other exposition retailers on commission. But Zerbe's display space, consisting of hundreds of coin-shaped objects mounted in neat rows, tended to make the special coins merge into the general "coin clutter" of his booth. No amount of signage or flyers could rescue the commemoratives from a plethora of similar-looking items. Although expensive, the coins were well within the budget of exposition attendees, many of whom saved for this once-in-a-lifetime experience and spared no expense on enjoying the event. In addition to inadequate display, the coins suffered from public skepticism as to their legitimacy. Zerbe had no credentials to prove that these were

---

[702] *Treasury*, NARA-CP, op. cit., entry 664, box 7. Letter dated December 15, 1915 to Wilmeth from Marks. p.3.
[703] *US Mint*, NARA-CP, op. cit., entry 229, box 302. Letter dated April 13, 1916 to Shanahan from Moore.
[704] *US Mint*, NARA-CP, op. cit., entry 229, box 302. Letter dated October 2, 1916 to McAdoo from Zerbe.
[705] *US Mint*, NARA-CP, op. cit., entry 229, box 302. Letter dated October 16, 1916 to Shanahan from mint director von Engelken. See *Bowers* for additional information of Zerbe's post-exhibition sales efforts.

real coins produced by the U. S. Mint. At an event where large numbers of coin-like imitation $50 slugs, medals and other trinkets competed for attention, potential coin buyers had to first convince themselves that these were genuine coins. Harbaugh's comment about the gold dollars "selling like hotcakes" when sold at the mint display suggests that, as with the medals, Zerbe's marketing plan was defective. Had the coins been sold at both Zerbe's booth and the mint display – where buyers could feel confident they were receiving genuine coins – it is reasonable to speculate that the entire issue might have been sold. Had Zerbe and the exposition company followed the advice of treasury special agent Harbaugh, it is probable results would have been much better for all concerned.

Silver Half Dollar Design – Charles E. Barber

Design of the half dollar had originally been assigned to Paul Manship. With secretary McAdoo completely opposed to any of Manship's designs, Barber's alternate was selected for use. The obverse, as shown below and on the coin, is one of the mint engraver's best allegorical compositions for a coin. The figure of Columbia, scattering flower petals in welcome to the sunrise through the Golden Gate, is derived from his earlier medallic work, particularly for the annual assay medals. The cherub behind her holds a cornucopia overflowing with flower petals to symbolize the abundance brought to all by the Panama Canal. This is an adaptation of the reverse of the 1908 Atlantic Fleet medal.

The reverse is less creative, featuring a typical eagle-on-shield with olive and laurel branches. Barber's original version, with two dolphins symbolizing the Atlantic and Pacific oceans, was more interesting that the final composition. But secretary McAdoo either did not understand the allegory, did not care for it, or simply did not like aquatic mammals on coins.[706] To adapt the design to the secretary's liking, he scraped off the dolphins, made a cast copy, and then added large oak and olive branches. The balance of the reverse design remained much the same, although it was irrelevant to the commemorative theme of the coin.

Figure 68. Charles Barber's obverse and reverse sketch models for the Panama-Pacific half dollar. (NARA.)

---

[706] McAdoo might also have felt there were too many dolphins on the Panama-Pacific coins. They appeared on initial designs for everything except the quarter eagle. In August 1916, the secretary readily approved use of two dolphins on Hermon MacNeil's revised Standing Liberty quarter obverse, so he evidently thought dolphins were appropriate for circulation coins.

As produced for sale to exposition visitors, the half dollar (at least the obverse) was a remarkably good design produced under unusual conditions of haste.

The designer of the coin has never been conclusively established. Nearly all published sources credit Barber with the obverse and assistant engraver George Morgan with the reverse. However, in correspondence to coin dealer David M. Bullowa, acting director Mary O'Reilly said:[707]

> …As stated in our former letter, the records of this Bureau and those of the Mint at Philadelphia, indicate that Mr. Charles E. Barber was the designer of both sides of the Panama-Pacific fifty-cent piece. We have no way of establishing any fact to the contrary.

Just three months later O'Reilly forwarded this statement from the Philadelphia Mint:[708]

> "I wish to say that I have gone through very carefully the correspondence of this office covering the years 1913, 1914 and 1915, and I can find no reference to the designing of the Panama-Pacific half dollar and quarter eagle.
>
> "In my opinion, Mr. Barber and Mr. Morgan collaborated in the designing and modeling of these two coins, but not as Mr. Bullowa suggests: that one took one side and one took the other, as Mr. Morgan's technique of handling the details is very obvious on both sides of both coins. The conception of the designs may have been Mr. Barber's and he may possibly have worked on the models or on the master dies, but Mr. Morgan's technique is unmistakable.
>
> "As these two coins were the product of the Engraving Department, it would naturally follow that the designs would be submitted by the head of that department, namely Mr. Barber. In developing the original designs, preliminary sketches on paper on through the development of the sculptured models, I am quite certain that Mr. Barber and Mr. Morgan would confer frequently.
>
> "No mistake could be made, in my opinion, in crediting both men with the execution of these two coins. I am certain that this is correct."

Figure 69. Final design for the half dollar as struck at the San Francisco Mint in 1915. (Courtesy American Numismatic Rarities.)

---

[707] *US Mint*, NARA-CP, op. cit., entry 104-83-0037, "Case Files on Commemorative Coins." Letter dated March 7, 1936 to David M. Bullowa, 10 West 86th Street, New York, NY from O'Reilly.
[708] *US Mint*, NARA-CP, op. cit., entry 104-83-0039, "Case Files on Commemorative Coins." Letter dated June 16, 1936 to Bullowa from O'Reilly. Person from Philadelphia Mint being quoted is not mentioned.

The official description, as provided by Mary O'Reilly, reads:[709]

> OBVERSE – Columbia scattering fruits and flowers, attendant with cornucopia or horn of plenty, to signify the boundless resources of the West. Background, Golden Gate illuminated by the rays of the setting sun, with the inscription PANAMA-PACIFIC EXPOSITION – 1915.
>
> REVERSE – Shield of the United States surmounted by American eagle and supported on the one side by a branch of oak, emblem of strength, and on the other side by the olive branch of peace. The inscriptions are UNITED STATES OF AMERICA, with the value of the coin and motto IN GOD WE TRUST.

The half dollar reverse is similar to earlier designs by Barber including the reverse of the Philippine coins issued in 1903, a proposed revision of that design in 1906, and an 1893 Columbian Exposition half dollar (see above). From available correspondence and drawings it is likely that the reverse design was Barber's and that Morgan prepared part or all of the model. A similar situation may have applied to the obverse as well.

Gold Dollar Design – Charles Keck

Charles Keck's gold dollar design follows closely his canal worker sketch first submitted to the mint (see above). The primary changes were removal of the laurel leaves from the worker's cap, change in the shape of the hat, and refinement of the lettering. Together, these seem to have increased the "labor characteristics of the design" satisfying Dewey and his treasury department superiors. Evidently, the portrait's "labor-ness" was not clear to many viewers, and it was repeatedly mistaken for a baseball player.

The reverse was largely as originally submitted, although the elongated dolphins are more fanciful than anatomically true.

Figure 70. Final design for the gold dollar as struck by the San Francsico Mint. The coin is only 9/16-inch in diameter. Compare with the model of the worker, above. (Courtesy American Numismatic Rarities.)

Keck was forced to squeeze a great deal of lettering into the coin's tiny diameter, and the design suffers from crowding of text, particularly on the reverse.

Gold Quarter Eagle Design – Charles E. Barber

Sculptor Evelyn Longman was initially engaged to prepare designs for the gold quarter eagle. Secretary McAdoo rejected all of her sketches and, after the artist became ill

---

[709] *US Mint*, NARA-CP, op. cit., entry 104-83-0039, "Case Files on Commemorative Coins." Letter dated March 5, 1936 to Bonnie Bakken, 185 Pick Avenue, Villa Park, IL from O'Reilly.

during a trip to Washington, DC, the mint fell back on designs prepared by engraver Charles Barber.

This composition, along with the half dollar obverse, are the mint engraver's best coinage design work. An ancient Greek Hippocampus cavorting in the newly joined oceans seems both a balance to Aitken's static Minerva and Owl, and a statement of the excitement nearly everyone felt about the benefits of the isthmus canal. It is amazing that Barber could have produced such dreadfully stuffy work as the 1909/10 Washington nickel, then come up with this very appropriate and successful commemorative design; although one could wish for more detail in Columbia's face.

Figure 71. Gold quarter eagle design by Charles Barber. This obverse and that of the companion half dollar are the engraver's best coinage designs of his long career. (Courtesy American Numismatic Rarities.)

Considering the speed with which Barber produced the quarter eagle design, it is possible this was derived from his 1914 PPIE medal sketch, or that it was originally intended for the fifty dollar gold coin. The presumption is that when secretary McAdoo accepted Aitken's modified designs, Barber simply altered his work to suit the remaining coin.

The reverse emulates one of those designed by George Morgan as variations on an 1877 half dollar reverse. The defiant eagle stands on a closed scroll inscribed E PLURIBUS UNUM, all of which is supported on an ornamental standard similar to that used for Roman Legionary emblems. As on Barber's half dollar reverse, the design has no connection with the exposition being commemorated.

Barber's description reads:[710]

> The design for the obverse of the Quarter Eagle shows a figure of Columbia representing the United States, seated on the mythical sea horse riding through the waters of the canal which joins ocean to ocean.
> Columbia, by means of the caduceus, emblem of commerce, offers this new trade highway to the nations of the world.
> The reverse represents the Ame3rican Eagle resting on a standard bearing the motto "E. Pluribus Unum."

---

[710] *US Mint*, NARA-P, op. cit., entry 660, box 120, folder. Letter dated September 2, 1915 to Joyce from Barber.

Gold Quintuple Eagle & Souvenir Medal Designs – Robert I. Aitken

Gold coins with a face value of $50 had been proposed on several occasions during the 19th century. In 1877 two pattern pieces were struck to illustrate the concept, but were rejected as impractical for circulating coinage. The exposition coin legislation envisioned an octagonal $50 coin similar to pieces struck by the United States Assay Office of Gold in 1851. Although not a U.S. mint product, the large coins were closely identified with California and the San Francisco area. Robert Aitken's Panama-Pacific quintuple eagle (known as a "half union" in 1877) became the only coin of this denomination issued by a United States mint facility.[711]

Figure 72. Robert Aitken's first sketches for the $50 coin. The crooked line on the obverse is the edge of a corrective overlay. The sketch is made in two overlapping sections that allow the viewer to switch between hexagonal and round formats. (NARA.)

Aitken was one of the most meticulous sculptors of his era. He was known as a shrewd negotiator and an artist willing to put in the "advance time" necessary to ensure his clients were fully satisfied with the results. He and Jim Fraser were likely the most competitive of New York sculptors from 1910 to 1925.

Aitken's design was consistent with others adopted for the exposition; however, it does not have the freedom and sense of motion conveyed by either of Barber's compositions. The work is consistent with a static adaptation of ideas from the California state seal and stands in stark contract to the sculptor's souvenir medal and John Flanagan's award medal. The $50 coins may be the result of an outstanding artist having too much advance notice of the commission and simply preparing something suitable, but not outstanding.

The final production version seems to lose whatever character the sketches promised. Poor Minerva (Athena in the Greek pantheon) has a protruding jaw and a strange pucker to her lips, while the owl looks more confused than wise.

---

[711] Gold bullion pieces of this denomination were issued by the mint beginning in 1986 using a poor imitation of Saint-Gaudens' 1907 double eagle design. These are approximately the diameter and weight of pre-1934 $20 coins, and are considered non-circulating legal tender pieces.

Figure 73. Hexagonal and round versions of the $50, or quintuple eagle, gold coin. Compare with the design sketch, above. (Courtesy American Numismatic Rarities.)

Souvenir Medal Description

Unknown to director Roberts, Aitken had been contacted by James L. Wilmeth of the treasury department's Government Exhibit Board, and offered a contract to design a souvenir medal to be struck at the treasury department's PPIE exhibit. Although Wilmeth had preliminary contact with the Mint Bureau, (Charles Barber made a sample "…simple showy design that will attract the eye of the masses…") this was dropped when Aitken agreed to a $1,000 commission for the medal design.[712] This souvenir medal was later incorporated in Representative Kahn's PPIE coin legislation, but Aitken retained the design commission. This was completed in January 1915 and medals were struck by the Philadelphia Mint and on the exhibition site. There is no mintmark on the medal.

---

[712] *US Mint*, NARA-CP, op. cit., entry 229, box 302. Letter dated March 21, 1914 to Roberts from Wilmeth.

Figure 74. Panama-Pacific International Exposition souvenir or commemorative medal by Robert Aitken. These were struck at the U.S. Mint's exhibit and sold for the exposition company by Farran Zerbe.

The artist supplied the following description of his exposition souvenir medal:[713]

> This commemorative medal is to be struck by the government presses on the exhibition ground as a demonstration of the minting process and also as a souvenir.
>
> The obverse shows a winged Mercury, the messenger of heaven, the first of inventors, the furtherer of industry and of commerce, opening the locks of the canal through which passes the *Argo*, symbol of navigation. Upon her canvas the setting sun is reflected as she sails for the west.
>
> The quotation, "On! Sail on!" from Josquin Millers' poem to Columbus, is used as a suggestion of the uninterrupted voyage made possible by the canal. There is also the inscription "To commemorate the opening of the Panama Canal, MCMXV."[714]
>
> Upon the reverse is shown the central motif, the Earth, around which is entwined two female forms suggesting the two hemispheres, holding in their hands cornucopias typifying abundance, these are so arranged in the design as to become one, the idea being that the canal brings together the worth of the world.
>
> Below these flying forms is shown the sea gull, the bird of the canal zone. The inscription upon this side reads "The Panama-Pacific International Exposition, San Francisco, California, MCMXV.

Award Medal – John F. Flanagan

An award medal and a souvenir medal were included in the PPIE legislation in addition to the four coins. As explained above, Robert Aitken ended up with the souvenir medal commission as well as the $50 gold coin. The award medal commission would, under normal conditions, have been given to one of the artists on the Commission of Fine Arts' preferred list. The delay in proposing legislation and its late passage on January 16, 1915 caused the exposition company to take matters into their own hands, as explained by Adolph Miller, Chairman of the Government Exhibit Board.[715]

> I have your letter of January 19th asking my view of the desirability of accepting the design prepared by Mr. John Flanagan, sculptor, of New York, at the insistence

---

[713] *US Mint*, NARA-CP, op. cit., entry 229, box 302. Undated (probably January 18-30, 1915) description by Aitken.

[714] Note that the canal opened on August 15, 1914 (MCMXIV), not in 1915 (MCMXV) as indicated on the medal.

[715] *US Mint*, NARA-CP, op. cit., entry 229, box 302. Letter dated January 21, 1915 to Malburn from Adolph C. Miller, Chairman of the Government Exhibit Board.

of the Panama-Pacific International Exposition Company, for an award medal. The matter is not one that comes within the lines of my official responsibility as Chairman of the Government Exhibit Board and I assume, therefore, that you merely wish an expression of my opinion.

I do not feel competent, with my present knowledge, to express an opinion. Mr. Flanagan is not known to be in any way and if the responsibility were mine I should have to make some inquiries. The design that was prepared at the insistence of the Government Exhibit Board for the commemorative medal which is to be struck by the Bureau of the Mint, was prepared by Mr. Robert Aitken, a well known sculptor, formerly of California and now of New York, and I satisfied myself before entering into negotiations with Mr. Aitken that he was the most competent person in sight for the design.

Pressure from the exposition company was sufficient to cause assistant secretary Malburn to decide to award the medal commission to John Flanagan, as had already been done by the exposition. Unfortunately, Flanagan had to settle for $1,000 from the government instead of $1,500 the exposition company had promised. After losing $500 in the deal, Flanagan was probably less than pleased with the outcome.[716]

...you are hereby authorized to make the following award for the preparation of a design of award medal, this authorization being additional to those mentioned in department letter to you of the 21st instant:

Design of award medal to Mr. John Flanagan,
New York, N. Y., compensation $1,000.

Mr. Flanagan was orally advised that the compensation would be $700 if his award was accepted, but inasmuch as he had been previously requested by the Exposition Company to prepare the designs for which he was to receive from them the sum of $1,500, and further because it is found that the appropriation is sufficient to permit of the payment of $1,000, the award is made at the latter named figure. Please advise Mr. Flanagan to this effect, and request him to submit a duplicate photograph of his design for the files of the Fine Arts Commission, in accordance with their request.

Figure 75. 1915 Panama Pacific Exposition award medal by John Flanagan. The obverse inscription reads: "Divine Disiuncta, Iunxit Homo" ([That which was] divinely separated, [has been] joined by man).

---

[716] *US Mint*, NARA-CP, op. cit., entry 229, box 302. Letter dated January 26, 1915 to Flanagan from Malburn.

During 1915 2,500 silver award medals were struck, and in 1916 an additional 2,000 were minted for a total of 4,500 pieces. Some of these were gold plated for first place awards.[717]

Patterns and Proofs

The short time available for design and production of the exposition coins virtually eliminated the luxury of pattern or experimental coins. There were no variations of the designs once hubs were cut. Unlike the problems with design relief encountered in 1907, neither the mint nor Medallic Art Co. seem to have had any difficulty making successful production dies. Granted, the coins were to be made in very limited quantities, so minor problems could be ignored and the presses worked at maximum pressure if needed.[718]

Correspondence indicates that uniface trial pieces were struck in lead (probably of all designs) and at least one specimen of the $1 in bronze. An interesting letter from Philadelphia Mint superintendent Adam Joyce notes that gold trial pieces were made of the $50 coins (both versions) and asks permission to strike examples of the other designs:[719]

> I have on hand a specimen of each of the two varieties of the special fifty dollar gold coin for the San Francisco Exposition struck at this mint in trying the dies. If there is no legal objection I beg to be authorized to retain these two coins and place them in the Cabinet of this mint, in accordance with Article 15, Section 11 of the amended regulations approved June 4, 1910.
>
> I would also request authority to strike and retain for placing in the Cabinet copies of the other special coins for the San Francisco exposition before sending the dies to the San Francisco Mint.

Joyce's request was approved on May 19.[720] The reference book *United States Pattern Coin, Experimental and Trial Pieces* by J. Hewitt Judd (8th edition) lists several pattern and experimental pieces for the dollar and half dollar. All of the pieces listed are from dies that omit the "S" mintmark. Only one pair of uniface trial pieces, one dollar J-A1915-1 and J-A1915-2 in bronzed white metal, come anywhere close to matching extant historical descriptions. Two specimens of the half dollar struck in gold (J-1960) were made on cut down double eagle coins and were probably prepared solely for private gain. The two other half dollar pattern varieties, J-1961 in silver and J-1962 in copper, could have been made as legitimate trial strikes as mentioned by Adam Joyce, above. Dollar coins struck in gold and of the correct weight could also be trial pieces, however examples in silver or from planchets of incorrect weight were likely also struck for personal gain. Lastly, the $50 octagonal (J-1971) and round (J-1973), both in silver and without mintmark, are inconsistent with both the date of the order to add the mintmark, and the gold trial pieces mentioned by Joyce. Absent further corroboration these, too, must be considered unauthorized specimens. J-A1915-3, a uniface copper impression is consistent with known mint procedures in testing dies.

---

[717] *US Mint*, NARA-P, op. cit., entry 107D. Medal department summary table of dates and quantities struck at back of volume.

[718] We have no official documents indicating the striking pressure used for any of the four commemorative coins. The San Francisco *Examiner* article concerning the first-strike ceremony, indicates that the $50 piece required 240 tons per square inch of pressure to produce a complete coin. Since other mint documents indicate that 150 tons is the maximum coinage dies of that era could withstand, the newspaper may have been exaggerating.

[719] *US Mint*, NARA-CP, op. cit., entry 229, box 302. Letter dated May 18, 1915 to Woolley from Joyce.

[720] *US Mint*, NARA-P, op. cit., entry 660, box 120, folder 2. Letter dated May 19, 1915 to Joyce from Woolley.

The half dollar and dollar patterns mentioned above could have been made either before or after the order to add the mintmark. However, they would have had little novelty value if they were the same as the normal coins. It is the author's speculation that all of the half dollar and dollar pieces in off-metals and of non-standard weight were made after director Woolley issued his order on April 30, 1915. Therefore, the only legitimate trial or experiential pieces would be those in a) the correct alloy and weight; b) bronze; c) uniface lead; d) uniface bronze or brass. Examples could be from dies without the mintmark or with the "S" mintmark, however coins with the mintmark would be nearly identical to production pieces and probably not traceable.

Comment	Judd / Pollock No.	Distributed			Returned		
		Quan.	To	Date	Quan.	To	Date
$1 No "S" mintmark	None	1	Director, Secretary, Assistant Secretary	4/21/15	1	Mint	4/22/15
50¢ obverse lead	None	1	Director	After 4/21/15	1	Mint	5/19/15
50¢ reverse lead	None	1	Director	After 4/21/15	1	Mint	5/19/15
$50 round gold	None	1	Mint Collection	5/18/15			
$50 octagonal gold	None	1	Mint Collection	5/18/15			

Epilog and Ephemera

Agitation for new subsidiary silver coin designs increased in intensity after release of the Buffalo nickel. By 1914 we find Victor Brenner submitting unsolicited silver coin designs, and being told "At present the Secretary of the Treasury is so completely occupied with various matters…that it is impracticable to consider the matter."[721]

It appears that assistant treasury secretary William P. Malburn was the first to bring the subsidiary silver coins to McAdoo's attention in a January 18, 1915 memorandum:[722]

> From the accompanying memorandum of the Acting Director of the Mint you will observe that the present silver half dollar, quarter and dime were changed in 1892, and a new design may, therefore, be adopted in 1917 (corrected to 1916). This can be done any time in the year, and therefore, if you desire, a design may be made and coinage commenced on January 2 of that year.

Malburn had also obtained a legal opinion indicating that it was the year the design was adopted, not year of first issuance, that was important. McAdoo's only comment was to add, "Let the mint submit designs before we try anybody else," to the original memorandum. Much of the mint's energy in early 1915 was focused on preparing designs for the Panama-Pacific International Exposition and meeting the very tight deadlines imposed by Congress. Considerable time was also required to produce new hubs for the Lincoln cent and Buffalo nickel. It may have been this flurry of creative activity that prompted acting director Dewey's memorandum and Malburn's letter. However the process began, changing the circulating silver coins could wait until the commemoratives were safely completed and a new director was in office.

---

[721] *US Mint*, NARA-CP, Record group 104, entry 235, vol. 405. Letter dated October 14, 1914 to Brenner from Roberts. The sculptor had contacted the director about designing the silver coins as early as April 3, 1913. He submitted unsolicited designs in February 1914, which were returned to Brenner on June 7, 1916 after the artist learned of the MacNeil and Weinman designs.

[722] *US Mint*, NARA-CP, op. cit., entry 229, box 303. Memorandum dated January 18, 1915 to McAdoo from Malburn.

On June 2, 1915 an "Authorization for Work" form was issued to the engraving department, which authorized work on "New Design for U. S. Coin."[723] The new Mint Director, Robert Woolley, may have seen the opportunity for both political and practical advantage with new designs. Knowing that a national competition was both impractical and likely to fail (as in 1891), and having had success with commissioning sculptors of proven ability to design the previous coins, the mint director devised a limited competition for the three coin designs. Woolley felt that with the change in design there should also be a change in concept, so that each of the three silver coins could have a distinctive design.

The burst of creative enlightenment begun by Saint-Gaudens and reignited by Jim Fraser and the PPIE commemoratives was now ready for its greatest test – silver subsidiary coinage and eventually the silver dollar.

1913 Liberty Nickel

The well-publicized 1913 Liberty nickel is linked to the Buffalo design by a group of coins purchased in 1942 by Burdette G. Johnson and Eric P. Newman from the estate of Colonel H. R. Green. Five 1913 Liberty nickels, one Type-I Buffalo pattern without Fraser's initial, one type-I buffalo with initial, and one Type-II Buffalo struck in bronze, were housed in a custom-made case with acetate covered slots for the eight coins. The coins were purchased together in the case, but it is not known if that is how they left the mint.

Circumstantial evidence suggests the 1913 Liberty coins were made during the last weeks of 1912 or early 1913. As normal operating procedure Barber and Morgan would have made Liberty nickel obverse dies dated 1913 during the fourth quarter of 1912 in order to be ready for production on January 2, 1913. With the Buffalo nickel not being officially accepted until December 18, 1912, it is very likely that several production dies were made and kept with the engraver's stock of dies. A few trial pieces could have been made from the dies, although there was little to "test" since the design had been in use since 1883.

We know that Liberty nickel dies existed at least until February 24, 1913:[724]

> Now that the new design five-cent nickel piece has been approved, would it not be well to destroy the dies and hubs of the 1912 design. The Engraver has on hand a lot of working dies made for this mint and those sent to San Francisco and returned...
> If it is your opinion that these dies and hubs should be destroyed, I would thank you for authority to have this done.

Realistically, it appears that someone at the Philadelphia Mint took one of the 1913-dated Liberty die sets and made a few examples using whatever planchets were available. The inconsistent quality of the pieces implies a hasty operation, and certainly not die trials. A medal press could have been used to strike a small number of pieces – production presses had automatic planchet feeders and required a "run-up" to production speed.

A former mint employee, Samuel W. Brown, was the first to display the coins at the 1920 ANA annual convention. We don't know when Brown was hired by the mint, but

---

[723] *US Mint*, NARA-P, op. cit., entry 4A, box 2, Jan–Dec, 1915. Job order number 8310. A search of other historical documents has produced no specific record of the decision.
[724] *US Mint*, NARA-CP, op. cit., entry 229, box 299. Letter dated February 24, 1913 to Roberts from Landis.

by 1906 he held the position of an assistant to the curator of the mint collection had been recommended for a salary increase.[725]

> ...Mr. Brown now receives one thousand dollars a year, whereas Mr. Meek, also an Assistant in the same room, receives a larger amount. Mr. Brown is quite as capable and efficient as Mr. Meek and I respectfully recommend that the two men be placed on the same basis as regards salary, Mr. Brown thereby receiving an increase.

Superintendent John Landis had this to add in support of the increase:[726]

> ...Samuel W. Brown, Assistant Curator...passed a very creditable examination for the position of Curator and Mr. Comparette tells me he is undoubtedly his most efficient assistant, that he leaves him practically in charge of the room during his (Mr. Comparette's) absence.
> Mr. Brown receives a lower salary than those occupying similar positions of importance and I would therefore submit for your approval an increase in his compensation from $1,000 to $1,200 per annum.

The only negative comments about Brown came from director Andrew in January 1910. The director was upset about the poor quality of gloves that had been accepted by Brown, who was by now the storekeeper, and shipped to San Francisco. Apparently, Andrew blamed Brown for the problems and wrote:[727]

> ...considering the quality of the gloves accepted by your storekeeper and sent to the Mint at San Francisco the inferiority of which is patent to anyone as per sample returned to this Bureau from San Francisco, I would call to your attention the importance of selecting someone more competent to fill the position of Storekeeper than Samuel W. Brown, the present incumbent.

He was a clerk-storekeeper at the mint in 1912, but resigned on November 24, 1913 "...to go into business for himself."[728] The resignation notice is interesting in that Landis wrote directly to the secretary, and received a response from assistant secretary John S. Williams – not director Roberts. This seems an unusual procedure for a routine matter involving a clerk-storekeeper.

The true story of the 1913 Liberty nickels will have to await the location of letters and other documents mentioning the coins.

T. Louis Comparette – A Friend at Court

Modern auction catalogs and coin guide books are filled with references to certain high-profile collectors having obtained choice or rare coins from the Philadelphia Mint. Usually these ascribe the acquisition to some supposed "under-the-table" deal by one of the mint's principal officers – an accusatory finger is often pointed toward engravers Barber or Morgan. Persistent insinuation is that a collector or dealer obtained some choice piece by payment of money beyond face value of the piece. There are several well documented instances of Morgan doing work for, or providing unusual specimens to collectors.

---

[725] *US Mint*, NARA-CP, op. cit., entry 229, box 244. Letter dated May 12, 1906 to Landis from Comparette.
[726] *US Mint*, NARA-CP, op. cit., entry 229, box 244. Letter dated May 21, 1906 to Roberts from Landis.
[727] *US Mint*, NARA-CP, op. cit., entry 235, vol. 385, p.97. Letter dated January 27, 1910 to Landis from Andrew.
[728] *US Mint*, NARA-CP, op. cit., entry 359. Letter dated November 20, 1913 to Secretary of the Treasury (McAdoo) from Landis.

There are also clear references to Barber (and probably Morgan) doing private commission work while employed by the mint. These seem to have been open secrets at the time, as verified by the existence of signed receipts on mint stationery – something not to be expected from one dealing in unauthorized goods.

After examining thousands of documents from the 1905-1921 period, it is evident that many unofficial transactions were probably not made by the engravers or senior treasury staff. In 1907-08 the mint director and assistant treasury secretary distributed the gold Saint-Gaudens experimental and limited production coins under instructions from President Roosevelt. However, that and the Treasurer's hoard of gold are the only instances which can be confirmed. With the exception of direct sales from the mint's cash window, one man seems to have been responsible for much of the distribution. The same person may also have inadvertently created the so-called "Zerbe proof" silver dollars of 1921. This person was Dr. Thomas Louis Comparette, curator of the Philadelphia Mint Cabinet of Coins and Medals from 1905 to 1922.

Throughout much of his tenure, Comparette played a consistently advisory role. He did not make decisions but often provided advice (sometimes accurate, sometimes not), and "insider" comment on the coins and designs produced during this time period. He had a wide network of dealer and collector friends with whom he was in regular communication by letter, telephone and personal visit. As curator he had a trusted position with the mint and could work directly with outside individuals, unlike that of any other employee. He had access to new coinage at the time it was first produced. He knew when a new issue was about to be made and how to obtain a few specimens for the mint collection and his associates. He occasionally entered the production room and selected coins from the day's work or had them struck for him. Also unique among numismatists, he had access to coins submitted for the annual Assay Commission – the "pyx" coins from each mint. These last are of particular interest because they were often the first pieces struck from a new pair of dies. They were sometimes caught on a cloth by the press superintendent, put directly into a small cloth sack, sealed, and sent to the Philadelphia Mint for use the following year.[729]

Dr. Comparette had a special interest in the Joseph P. Mitchelson collection maintained by the Connecticut State Library. Mitchelson and Comparette had been good friends for many years until the former's death in 1911. Mitchelson, who was a tobacco merchant, bequeathed his coin and paper money to Connecticut with the stipulation that it would be placed on public display and new coins added each year as they were issued by the U.S. mint. In the autumn of that year Comparette was "loaned" by the mint to the State of Connecticut for several weeks so he could prepare an inventory and advise the Library on how to manage and protect the collection.

George S. Godard, Librarian of Connecticut, was responsible for updating the Joseph P. Mitchelson collection[730] Comparette and Godard became friends and their mutual

---

[729] The Assay Commission was a ceremonial body. Specimens intended for the Assay Commission' use may have been selected for appearance. They were supposed to look nice so laymen on the Commission would be impressed with the quality. The real work of determining compliance with legal specifications used "special assay" coins. These were selected from each batch of metal and sent to Philadelphia or Washington for the purpose of assaying production coins on a continuing basis.

[730] Joseph Mitchelson of Tariffville, Connecticut and T. Louis Comparette were good friends. When Mitchelson died in 1911 he bequeathed his large coin collection to the Connecticut State Library. Included was a stipulation that the collection should be kept up to date. The U.S. Mint permitted Comparette to go to Connecticut and inventory the collection which then came into the custody of George Godard, Librarian of the State of Connecticut. Godard took a continuing interest in the collection and corresponded with Comparette regarding new issues and varieties. Comparette and Godard

interest in the collection's historical value encouraged Comparette to continue supplying coins to the Connecticut State Library. Within their correspondence there are several references to pyx coins as well as other unusual situations. In 1914 the curator commented,

> Would you like to secure the gold coins of the D. and S. mints for 1913? If so, I can get them for you from the Pix [sic – pyx] coins.... I have had some specimens laid aside. If you should desire them, very well; if not, no special trouble will be caused for then they will be thrown into circulation.[731]

In 1917 he made a similar comment,

> No old-type half dollars were made at any of the mints last year; but I am told that San Francisco made some of the old-type dimes. If that information is correct they will appear in the picks [sic – pyx] at the meeting of the Assay Commission next month, and I shall see to it that you secure specimens.[732]

Again in 1920 he provided elusive San Francisco eagles (126,500 struck, most melted),[733]

> Here are two eagles struck at the San Francisco mint in 1920. With some difficulty I was able to secure four specimens from the pyx, of which I send you these, one for your collection, the other for Sen. Hall....

It is likely that access to the pyx coins was normal for the mint collection curator and the examples above are simply ones where the activity is mentioned.

The mint's coin collection was one of its most popular public attractions and the "poor stepchild" of the Mint Bureau. Rare coins were displayed in large oak cases around the inner wall of the rotunda in the Philadelphia Mint building, and in a large hexagonal center display. Similar displays of coins, artifacts, and other objects of cultural interest were popular attractions in every city. At the mint, visitors could view strange and unusual coins and medals, and see coins being struck on the production floor. As a souvenir of their visit, they could purchase small medals, booklets, or for $1.00 obtain Louis Comparette's 1913-14 catalog of the collection. Revenue went directly to the general fund and was not reinvested in the collection.[734]

Comparette had an annual budget of only $500 for purchasing coins and medals for the collection. From this small sum he had to buy proof specimens and other pieces from the mint's cashier the same as any coin collector might. He was required to request sample coins for the mint Collection every year: there was no automatic accession policy. The Assay Commission (or pyx) coins were a handy source of branch mint specimens; however cents and nickels were not included. After 1907, Comparette's task became more compli-

---

were friendly enough that Comparette sometimes included confidential information in his letters, and Godard would in turn occasionally complain about various local political issues.

[731] *Connecticut State Library*, record group 12, box 77, folder "Mitchelson-Comparette." Letter dated February 28, 1914 to George S. Godard, State Librarian from T. Louis Comparette. Only a portion of the coins reserved for the Assay Commission were actually used during tests. The remainders were placed into circulation. The term "pyx" is often spelled phonetically in Comparette's letters. This occurred because he dictated them to a secretary who did not know the special meaning of the word "pyx" and occasionally substituted "pix" or "picks."

[732] *CSL*, op. cit. Letter dated January 12, 1917 to Godard from Comparette.

[733] *CSL*, op. cit. Letter dated March 1, 1921 to Godard from Comparette.

[734] Until 1908, the *per diem* employees who acted as guides produced and sold medals to visitors. The profits were split amongst the guides as a supplement to their wages. Director Leach curtailed most of this activity, and Director Andrew prohibited all sales of private booklets and medals.

cated because he had to write to Denver and San Francisco reminding them to save coins for the mint collection. We've already seen how the windfall of gold coins hoarded by treasurer McClung was used to expand the collection's buying power in 1912 and 1913. He also used his outside connections to encourage donations, and occasionally traded duplicates with collectors. If this seems a little "unsavory" to modern collectors it will be useful to recall that the mint collection was carried on treasury accounts at face value. In theory, it could have been used just like any other reserve of coin or currency to reduce debt on some short-term services account.[735]

Special access and "insider deals" at the mint were common accusations hurled at anyone who seemed to be able to obtain coins more easily than others. At times, Comparette admitted to "insider trading" as in the following exchange of letters regarding McKinley gold dollars. However, nothing suggests the curator accepted any form of payment except for the face value of coins and postage. Available letters also imply the number of historical or museum collections benefiting from the curator's attention was very small. From Comparette:[736]

> I shall see to it you and Mr. Hall secure specimens of the McKinley Memorial Gold Dollar. They are not sold here, but by the Association whose Headquarters are in Youngstown, Ohio. The sale of them has also been arranged through several banks. For a long time it was supposed that they were not obtainable here at the mint at all; but now I believe that I can secure specimens. I shall look after the matter as soon as possible.

From Godard:[737]

> In a former note you mentioned something about the McKinley Memorial Gold Dollar as first minted being unsatisfactory. I hope you can arrange for us to have a specimen of this first "unsatisfactory" issue as well as the revised.

From Comparette:[738]

> Inclosed [sic] please find two sets of the McKinley Memorial Gold Dollar, dated 1916 and 1917 respectively. One set is for the Library and the other for Sen. Hall.
> You secure these at their face value, but no statement to that effect is to be made public, and privately only with caution. For all specimens are supposed to be sold for account of the McKinley Memorial Association. These specimens were procured before delivery.

From Godard:[739]

> I can assure you we appreciate getting the 1916 and 1917 McKinley Memorial Gold Dollar. Without someone near the throne I am sure some of us would not get as near to it as we now believe ourselves to be.[740]
> I appreciate the desirability of keeping inside information still inside.[741]

As additional commemoratives were issued Comparette took an active role in securing specimens for the Mitchelson collection and probably others.[742]

---

[735] Director Andrew ordered all hubs and dies for pattern coins destroyed in May, 1910. He could nearly as easily have ordered every piece in the mint collection melted and cast into bars.
[736] *CSL*, op. cit. Letter dated February 13, 1917 to Godard from Comparette.
[737] *CSL*, op. cit. Letter dated February 14, 1917 to Comparette from Godard.
[738] *CSL*, op. cit. Letter dated March 5, 1917 to Godard from Comparette.
[739] *CSL*, op. cit. Letter dated March 8, 1917 to Comparette from Godard.
[740] *CSL*, op. cit. Letter dated March 12, 1917 to Comparette from Godard.
[741] *CSL*, op. cit. Letter dated March 12, 1917 to Comparette from Godard.

> Herewith inclosed are two specimens of the Illinois State special half dollars, struck at this mint…This is a short-circuit way for these coins to reach you, as they are supposed to be sold only by the Illinois State Centennial Commissioners, and at $1.00 each; so just keep them in reserve 'till sometime after they have been on sale out there, or about two or three weeks.

Maine Centennial and Pilgrim Tercentenary halves also entered the Connecticut collection by the "back alley," avoiding the sponsoring committee's stipulations and fees. Godard wrote:[743]

> Your good letter of the 23rd inst. with the accompanying Maine Centennial half dollar, received, for which please accept our best thanks….we are looking forward to the Pilgrim Tercentenary Half-dollar, which I assume will be another work of art.

To which Comparette replied when he sent the Pilgrim coins:[744]

> The enclosed need no explanation. I regret that you have not received them from here sooner. But the fact is that I have never been able to secure them, as there was an inhibition on getting them out. That still is in force, but at last I found a back alley. Of course the matter is again confidential. Quite possibly both you and Senator Hall have secured specimens from the Commissioners but these extra pieces will not come amiss. I might add also that I could have secured specimens two or three weeks ago, but they were not in perfect condition. They had run the regular course of the presses and besides were from old or considerably used dies, and so not so perfect to begin with and then more or less scratched. These two specimens are the first from new dies and were taken off the presses without allowing them to strike others or falling down the usual way.
> One of them is for Sen. Hall. I have no doubt but that you will see him soon and can hand it to him, if you will be so kind.

The Grant Memorial gold dollars and silver half dollars presented an interesting situation. The sponsoring committee dreamt up a scheme to force collectors to buy a substantial number of half dollars in order to purchase the highly prized gold dollar. Comparette explains in an April, 1922 letter:[745]

> Herewith I am sending you two varieties each of the Grant Memorial gold dollar and half-dollar…For these you need remit only face value…
> You may have found out that the Commission is trying to push the sale of the Grant Memorial coins in a rather peculiar manner. To secure a gold dollar one must also take 15 silver half-dollars, and since there are two varieties of the gold pieces (as also two of the half-dollar) one must purchase 30 half-dollars in order to secure the two varieties, or make a total investment of $36.50. The measure will probably defeat its purpose. A one-and-two plan might have worked out well.
> P.S.: To save your eyes: the two varieties of the Grant coins are distinguished by the presence of a star above name GRANT on some of them.

For $3.00 the Connecticut State Library had acquired coins that would have cost twelve times as much if purchased through the issuing committee.

---

[742] *CSL*, op. cit. Letter dated August 28, 1918 to Godard from Comparette.
[743] *CSL*, op. cit. Letter dated September 30, 1920 to Comparette from Godard.
[744] *CSL*, op. cit. Letter dated December 7, 1920 to Godard from Comparette.
[745] *CSL*, op. cit. Letter dated April 20, 1922 to Godard from Comparette.

Special arrangements also extended to coins struck for circulation but intended for other purposes by the treasury department, such as the 1920 and 1921 double eagles. Here we find Comparette openly stating his actions were "irregular:"[746]

> Herewith I am sending you a [1920] Twenty Dollar gold piece, just struck. It is for the Reserve Funds and not to be issued for general circulation, and the securing of the specimens for others than the government collection is probably irregular, so please do not let the fact become public knowledge. For others will demand specimens as soon as they learn that a few ~~have them~~ are out.

Six months later Comparette gently reminded his friend, George Godard, that the Mitchelson collection had gotten a good "deal" on the double eagle transaction:[747]

> By the way, you and the Senator were lucky in re the 1920 Double-eagles. But very few of them got out. All the rest are under seal along with the reserve funds, and the repeated efforts of scores to secure specimens have so far proved unavailing. I have been trying to get a specimen for the American Society in New York, but in vain. Dealers have offered as high as $30 for a specimen. I have an urgent commission now to get one at $25, but it is useless to try it. Sometime, undoubtedly, they will be obtainable, but nobody now can surmise when. Perhaps the next Secretary of the Treasury will find a way to be accommodating and release a bag of them for the hungry collectors.

The 1921 double eagles proved to be more difficult to obtain as indicated by this exchange of letters, first from Comparette on December 15, 1921:[748]

> Some [1921] double eagles are being struck here at the mint. Do you wish one? Also some Two Colono gold pieces have been struck here for Costa Rica. They are about the size of a gold dollar. Have you secured specimens?

Godard replied the next day:[749]

> We both, too, desire to have specimens of the double eagles and of the two Colono gold pieces now being struck for Costa Rica.

In return Comparette advised on December 22:[750]

> ...up till now I have not been able to secure the Double eagles. I confidently expect to succeed, however, though it may not be until the last days of the year. By that time I may be able to include some of the Peace dollars, now in course of preparation.

Then, finally, success:[751]

> By express I am sending you two Double Eagles, two <u>Dos Colones</u> gold pieces, and four Peace dollars.

---

[746] *CSL*, op. cit. Letter dated May 5, 1920 to Godard from Comparette.
[747] *CSL*, op. cit. Letter dated December 7, 1920 to Godard from Comparette.
[748] *CSL*, op. cit. Letter dated December 15, 1921 to Godard from Comparette.
[749] *CSL*, op. cit. Letter dated December 16, 1921 to Comparette from Godard. "We" includes Connecticut State Senator Henry Hall.
[750] *CSL*, op. cit. Letter dated December 22, 1921 to Godard from Comparette.
[751] *CSL*, op. cit. Letter dated January 3, 1922 to Godard from Comparette.

The 1920 $20 coins were eventually released into circulation; however the 1921 pieces were retained in treasury vaults as Reserve Funds until they were melted during the mid-1930s. The 1921 double eagle remains one of the great rarities of the Saint-Gaudens series.

1921 also brought the first production of standard silver dollars since late 1904. Production began in late February at Philadelphia and within a few days Comparette advised he was attempting to secure some for the Mitchelson Collection:[752]

> We are coining silver dollars here now and I have tried, but in vain, to secure specimens for you and the Senator. They are not to be given out, at least not now.

Nothing happened for nearly two months, then on May 7 the new "Morgan dollars" were suddenly available. Comparette wrote with obvious pleasure,[753]

> Here are two fine silver dollars, among the firstlings from a new die. They are almost as fine as proofs.
> They were released only yesterday, so that you will be among the first to secure specimens, but it will not be long till everyone has or will have had a specimen; then the usual knocking at the clumsy cartwheels will be resumed.

Godard was not expecting the coins and wanted more,[754]

> Glad to get your good letter of the 7th inst. enclosing the two fine silver dollars, 1921. They came like lightening from a clear sky. I will see that Senator Hall gets one of them. I wish you would send two more if you will, for we need two in our collection, and I would like one for myself. I am enclosing herewith check for $5.00 covering these issues.

Comparette sent an additional three coins although he implies that some were not as nicely struck or free of marks as others. He also suggested a new design be selected for the dollar coins, although he was probably not aware of work by the American Numismatic Association and Commission of Fine Arts on this subject:[755]

> I am enclosing the dollars you requested, three instead of two…
> Some of these you will find to be fine specimens from fresh dies, almost as fine as the old-time proofs.
> I think we should start a concerted movement to have a new design made for the Dollar. It looks as if the coinage might be very extensive before the end comes.

A year after sending the second batch of 1921 Morgan dollars to Godard, Comparette shipped several newly struck examples. He called these "semi-proofs" and stated they were struck on a medal press just like the old-time proofs had been:[756]

> It has just now occurred to me that you and also Mr. Hall, then living, secured fine specimens of the 1921 standard silver dollars. They were perfect specimens, caught by hand from a new die, and thus were unmarred by striking against other coins, as nearly all are.
> Those pieces without a doubt entirely satisfy both collections, so that neither is apt to be interested in the "semi-proofs" I send you. While these are much finer

---

[752] *CSL*, op. cit. Letter dated March 7, 1921 to Godard from Comparette.
[753] *CSL*, op. cit. Letter dated May 7, 1921 to Godard from Comparette.
[754] *CSL*, op. cit. Letter dated May 10, 1921 to Comparette from Godard.
[755] *CSL*, op. cit. Letter dated May 14, 1921 to Godard from Comparette.
[756] *CSL*, op. cit. Letter dated May 15, 1922 to Godard from Comparette.

> specimens and struck on a medal press, yet they are not in strict sense of the word proofs, though not a whit inferior.
>
> Should this be your feeling in the matter do not hesitate to return the coins. I took a notion, rather suddenly, to send the coins, one of them coming into my hands just as I was preparing to dispatch the others. Had I reflected more about it I should probably not have included them.
>
> All this is little more than to say that you and Mrs. Hall must not feel any delicacy about returning these or anything else I may in future send you.

As always, Godard appreciated the consideration of his friend and sent a check to cover the Morgan dollars and other coins:[757]

> I am enclosing herewith check for $10 covering the Grant [gold dollars and halves] and other items. We were very glad to get the "proof" 1921 regular dollar, which you were thoughtful enough to send to us and Mrs. Hall.

Comparette's "almost as fine as proofs" Morgan dollars presently in the Mitchelson Collection have an uncanny resemblance to so-called "Zerbe proofs." These are high quality 1921 circulation strike Morgan dollars which appear similar to modern proof-like specimens. The standard story is that they were made at the insistence of collector dealer Farran Zerbe as a consolation prize when the mint used the old Morgan design instead of a new peace design suggested by Zerbe the previous year.[758] This conjecture, however ignores the active Congressional, ANA, and Commission of Fine Arts work toward producing a peace dollar. A Congressional resolution was introduced on May 7 with the support of director Baker and mint staff.

An alternate scenario is that Comparette objected to the weakly struck and scratched dollars available from press bins. He asked the coiner to notify him when new dies were installed on one of the normal presses. When this occurred, Comparette rushed to the press room floor with a cloth (or towel) in hand and caught several of the first coins from new dies as they were ejected from the press. (He would not have caught them in his bare hands because newly struck coins are hot.) The curator may have done this several times in order to have a supply of pristine new dollar coins for collectors wanting a nice specimen of the new coin.[759]

The second group of 1921 Morgan dollars, delivered nearly a year later, closely match descriptions of so-called Chapman proofs. These are supposed to be proof dollars struck at the request of Philadelphia numismatist Henry Chapman. They are of higher quality than Zerbe proofs and more closely resemble proof dollars made in 1904 and earlier. Comparette described them as, "semi-proofs" and "…much finer specimens…struck on a medal press, yet they are not in strict sense of the word proofs, though not a whit inferior." We do not know what he meant by not strictly proofs: possibly only the dies were polished and not the planchets. Again, the Mitchelson collection examples appear to be the same as Chapman proofs including having a square rim indicative of being struck on a medal press.

---

[757] *CSL*, op. cit. Letter dated June 7, 1922 to Comparette from Godard. State Senator Henry Hall had died suddenly in February 1921. His widow asked Comparette to continue sending coins to keep her late husband's collection up to date. Successive letters show little interest by Mrs. Hall in the collection and it is likely that Hall's coins were purchased by Godard.

[758] To further confuse matters, various promoters claim the Zerbe proofs were from the Philadelphia and/or San Francisco Mints – what happened to Denver? Also, there is no documentation for any special coin struck for Zerbe.

[759] This is consistent with Comparette's selecting the best looking pieces available for the mint collection and to send to Godard.

A very interesting item in the Americana auction sale of January 15-17, 2002 by Stack's, Inc. of New York sheds additional light on these 1921 "semi-proofs."[760]

> **George T. Morgan Letters and Receipt for Proof Morgan Dollars and Bechtler Proof Restrikes, 1921-1922.** Average Extremely Fine. These three handwritten letters and one U.S. Mint Payment Receipt shed light on some of the most obscure American coinage rarities...The Proof 1921 Morgan Dollars which collectors have long called "Chapman Proofs" are revealed in these pages as specifically made for famed Philadelphia coin dealer Henry Chapman through U.S. Mint Chief Engraver George T. Morgan. Apparently setting the stage for this transaction is Morgan's calligraphic letter of March 26, drawing attention to "...quite a large payment in Life Insurance I must meet on April 2nd can you let me have check about that time." On April 1, 1921, Morgan acknowledges receipt of $25 "from Mr. Henry Chapman." A hand-written receipt of June 11, 1922 records the cost of "3 gold Chinese Medals $93.22... 4 Silver Chinese Medals, $4.00 [apparently pattern Chinese silver Dollars], *10 Proof Silver Dollars 1921, $10.00,* Balance due on Chinese Medal dies, $50.00."

Available documents give no insight into why these "semi-proofs" were struck or if they were made at Chapman's request. Godard's coins were sent almost a month before the date on the Morgan receipt, which casts doubt on the coins having been struck specifically for Chapman. The receipt noted above shows Morgan receiving only face value for any of the coins, so any additional payment would have been off-record.

Special services for public collections from the Philadelphia Mint ceased on Dr. Comparette's sudden death in June 1922. Within months the mint was closed to visitors due to an attempted robbery at the Denver facility. No successor was appointed and by the next summer the mint collection, begun by Adam Eckfeldt a century before, was transferred to the Smithsonian in Washington, DC.[761] It appears no accounting was ever attempted of the mint collection's records, and Comparette's office papers and personal letters were discarded. Whatever insights his files may have contained were lost forever.

---

[760] Stack's *Americana* auction sale. January 15-17, 2002, lot 475.
[761] The collection was supposed to be transferred in its entirety. Unfortunately, only the coins, medals, paper currency and related items actually made it to Washington. Virtually none of the models, galvanos, casts, hubs and dies also entrusted to Comparette's stewardship left the Philadelphia Mint. It is presumed they remain there to this day.

Appendix

Biographies

Abram Piatt Andrew

Abram Piatt Andrew (February 12, 1873 – June 3, 1936), economist and Congressman, was born in La Porte, Indiana, the older of two children and only son of Abram Piatt and Helen Merrell Andrew. His grandfather, Abraham Piatt Andrew, had been one of the founders of La Porte, where he and a brother operated a store and owned the first steam sawmill in the county. Andrew's father, Abram Piatt Andrew, Sr., was commander of the 21st Indiana battery in the Civil War, and was a man of wide influence. In 1869 Abram Sr., joined Abraham Andrew in founding a bank in which he remained active for sixty years.

Young Abram went to Lawrenceville School (New Jersey) and then to Princeton, where he took part in debating and was class valedictorian. After graduation in 1893, he enrolled as a graduate student at Harvard, spending two years also at the universities of Halle, Berlin, and Paris (1897-99), and received his Ph.D. from Harvard in 1900. The same year he was made instructor in the department of economics at Harvard University and three years later he became assistant professor of economics, a position he occupied until appointed Mint Director in 1909. While at Harvard he served as assistant editor of the *Quarterly Journal of Economics*. He was also a member of the athletic committee, and was particularly active in the affairs of the Cercle Français, an organization devoted to the propagation of interest in French literature. Through this association he was honored in 1906 by the minister of public instruction in France with the title of "Officier d'Académie." Among students on whom his teaching made a lasting impression was Franklin D. Roosevelt.

Piatt Andrew predicted the panic of 1907 in an article published in the New York *Journal of Commerce* on January 1, 1907. In 1908, when the National Monetary Commission was organized to devise a plan of permanent relief from the kinds of financial collapse that had afflicted the United States in the past, Andrew was engaged to assist the commission in its research. During two years' leave of absence from Harvard University, he visited London, Berlin, Paris and other important financial centers of Europe to collect information concerning foreign banking systems. Upon his return he edited the commission's publications, which comprise more than twenty volumes and constitute the most comprehensive library dealing with the world's banking that had been published to that date. He also had a large share in framing the bill and report of the National Monetary Commission. Along with George M. Reynolds, Henry P. Davison, Paul M. Warburg, and Frank A. Vanderlip, he became one of the inner core of advisers in the drafting of the "Aldrich Plan."

In August 1909, President Taft appointed him Director of the Mint, and during his brief administration the organization of the mints and assay offices was radically overhauled. The number of employees reduced by several hundred, thereby accomplishing an annual saving of more than $100,000. Andrew's tenure as mint director is nearly unknown to most coin collectors. He is credited with introducing improved operating procedures and innovations, such as automatic feeding of blanks into coin presses and automatic weighing of gold and silver coins. He also supported production of a catalog of the Philadelphia Mint Cabinet of Coins, and use of a hoard of Treasury Department gold to benefit the collection. He also shares responsibility with Eames MacVeagh for bringing the talents of James Fraser into the Mint Bureau.

Unfortunately, he was also responsible for the largest destruction of historical pattern coin hubs and dies in the history of the mint – an act of senseless ruin unequaled by any director before or since. He also was the instigator of legal action and harassment of pattern and experimental piece collectors. As mint director and later assistant secretary, Andrew's immediate influence on American coinage was considerable. Yet, within two years most of his administrative changes were abandoned and his long term impact was largely negative.

In June of 1910 he became first assistant secretary of the treasury, resigning in July, 1912. On submitting his resignation to President Taft, he complained that the department had been hampered by the idiosyncrasies and incapacity for decision of secretary Franklin MacVeagh. During the period 1910–1912 he was also treasurer of the American Red Cross Association.

His defeat for the Republican Congressional nomination in 1912 and the outbreak of war in 1914 turned Andrew's interest in other directions. Andrew was one of the first Americans to take an active part in World War I. He traveled to France in December 1914, where he secured from the French Army authorization for American volunteer ambulance units to serve with the French divisions at the front. With American volunteers as drivers, and with cars purchased from American donations, he built up an organization known as the American Field Ambulance Service. Before any American troops had arrived in France, it had thirty-four ambulance sections and twelve *camion sections* serving with French troops in France and in the Balkans. This organization took part in every great battle in which French troops were engaged in 1915, 1916 and 1917. Staffed by more than 2,400 young Americans, it formed the largest organized representation which the United States had on the battle front during the first three years of the war.

After entry of the United States into the war, Andrew turned over his organization to the American Army and was commissioned Major, and subsequently Lieutenant-Colonel. His period of service with the French and American armies covered more than four and a half years. He was decorated by the French Army with the Croix de Guerre, and the Legion of Honor, and by the United States with the Distinguished Service Medal.

After World War I, Andrew helped to found the American Legion and later became vice-commander for Massachusetts, where he maintained his home. Turning back to politics, he was elected to the House of Representatives in the fall of 1921 to fill a vacancy and served continuously in the next seven Congresses (1923-36). He was a delegate to the 1924 and 1928 Republican National Conventions. Andrew was independent in his thinking and not afraid to express his views. He urged the reduction of World War I debts and the repeal of prohibition (1930), opposed the soldier's bonus in 1932 because of the treasury's large deficit, and was an enthusiastic supporter of a large and efficient navy. Princeton University gave him an honorary A.M. in 1923 and later made him a trustee.

Andrew's writings covered many phases of financial questions. Among those which attracted wide attention were his arraignment of the policies of secretary Shaw in his articles "The Treasury and the Banks under Secretary Shaw and The United States Treasury and the Money Market," issued at the time of the retirement of the former secretary of the treasury in 1907, both of which were pleas for an absolute divorce of the treasury from "the Street." Several of his studies concern the currency questions of foreign countries, notably "Currency Problems of the Last Decade in British India" in the *Quarterly Journal of Economics* for August 1901, and "The End of the Mexican Dollar" in the same journal in May, 1904. Other articles treat of different aspects of panics, such as "The Influence of the Crops Upon Business, Hoarding in the Panic of 1907" and "Substitutes for Cash in the Crisis of 1907," the latter describing more than 200 substitutes for money used at that time. He kept a personal collection of the illegal monetary substitutes. The collection was donated to the American Numismatic Society by his sister, Helen Patch, in 1950. He has contributed articles upon other economic subjects to the *Yale Review*, the *North American Review*, the *Review of Reviews*, and other publications.

Andrew never married. He maintained a long-standing relationship with Henry Sleeper who lived on a nearby estate, and he was also a favorite of painter Cecilia Beaux another Gloucester resident. In the spring of 1936 he went home to Gloucester, Mass., to recuperate from influenza and died there, of cerebral thrombosis, in June. In accordance with his will, services were held jointly by a Catholic priest, a Baptist minister, and a Jewish rabbi. After cremation his ashes were scattered by airplane over his estate.

Sources:
Donald L. Kemmerer, "Abram Piatt Andrew." *Dictionary of American Biography, Supplements 1-2: To 1940.* American Council of Learned Societies, 1944-1958. Reproduced in History Resource Center. Farmington Hills, MI: Gale Group. Modified and updated by Roger W. Burdette.
Andrew Gray, "The American Field Service." American Heritage magazine, December 1974.
J. P. Dunn, *Indiana and Indianans* (1919), III, 1374-76;
Princeton Univ. *Bric-...-Brac,* 1894 and 1895;
Daniel R. Fusfeld, *The Economic Thought of Franklin D. Roosevelt* (1956);
Nathaniel W. Stephenson, *Nelson W. Aldrich* (1930);
A. P. Andrew, "For Love of France," *Outlook,* Dec. 27, 1916 (with portr.);
"Memorial Addresses," 75 Cong., 1 Sess., *House Doc.,* No. 347 (with portr.);
Who Was Who in America, vol. I (1942);
N. Y. Times, Oct. 28, 1935, June 3, 1936;
N. Y. Herald Tribune, June 3 and 4, 1936;
information from Mass. Dept. of Vital Statistics;
Information from National Archives and Records Administration, record groups 56 and 104.
"Biographical Sketch," taken from the *National Cyclopedia of American Biography,* and modified by Andrew's sister, Helen Patch, revised by Roger Burdette.

Victor David Brenner

Victor David Brenner (June 12, 1871 – April 5, 1924) – sculptor and medalist – was born in Siauliai (Shavely), Lithuania, then part of Russia, on June 12, 1871. His father was a metal worker who also did engraving and seal carving. As a teenager he refused to be apprenticed and instead practiced seal cutting and engraving along side his father. At sixteen, he left home and took up the trade of jewelry engraver and sculptor in several eastern Russian cities. According to an article in the 1920 *Numismatist*, undercover officers of the Tsar's secret police commissioned him to duplicate an official seal belonging to a high government officer. He was arrested and convicted of counterfeiting, but while awaiting a train to Siberian exile, friends helped him escape prison. At only nineteen, his talent was such that soon after arriving in New York City aboard the steamer *Gellert* on May 17, 1890, he found work – repairing watches.

He studied at the Cooper Union, National Academy of Design and later the Art Student's League while working in a small watch shop on the east side of New York. His earliest known medallic work dates from 1891 and shows a remarkable fluidity of line for a young sculptor without significant formal training. A chance encounter with Mrs. Felix Warburg lead to a subsidy that allowed him to study in France. From 1898 to 1901, Brenner studied with Louis Oscar Roty (1846-1911), Alexandre Charpentier and, at the Academie Julian, he studied with Peuch, Verlet, and Dubois in Paris. He was sufficiently successful during the 1890s that he was able to bring his mother, a sister, Miriam, and two brothers, Morris and Samuel, to the United States. He joined the American Numismatic and Antiquarian Society in 1894.

Parisian training and perfection of his technique quickly moved Brenner to the forefront of American medalists. He joined the National Sculpture Society and New York Architectural League in 1902, and later the National Arts Club. A short period back in France in 1904 to study with Roty and to help establish his brother, Michael, as a sculptor in Paris, was followed by his permanent return to the United States in 1906 when he joined the American Numismatic Association. In August 1907 he was one of two sculptors (the other being Daniel Chester French) whom President Roosevelt threatened to bring into the Philadelphia Mint to help supervise production of the Saint-Gaudens' design gold coins.

Brenner frequently exhibited his work and awards were abundant. He received a bronze medal at the 1900 Paris Exposition and an honorable mention at the Paris Salon; a bronze medal at the 1901 Panama-American Exposition in Buffalo, NY; a silver medal at the 1904 Louisiana Purchase Exposition in St. Louis, MO; a gold medal at the 1910 Universal Exposition in Brussels, Belgium; a silver medal at the 1915 Panama-Pacific International Exposition in San Francisco, CA. In 1922 he was awarded the J. Sanford Saltus silver medal from the American Numismatic Society for achievement in medallic art and exhibited at the National Sculpture Society, and the Museum of Fine Arts, Boston.

Some of his many portrait plaques include: James Abbott McNeill Whistler; Carl Schurz; Collis P. Huntington; Fridtjof Nansen; J. Sanford Saltus; Washington Irving; George Washington; John Paul Jones; and Abraham Lincoln. He did work for the Metropolitan Museum of Art in New York City; the Art Institute of Chicago; the Paris Mint; the Luxembourg in Paris; the Museum of Fine Arts in Boston, MA; the New York Historical Society; and Clark University in Worcester, MA. A catalog of Brenner's medallic creations has more than 120 entries dating from 1891 through 1923.

Brenner's creations are represented in the collections of the Whistler House Museum of Art in Lowell, MA; the San Diego Museum of Art in San Diego, CA; the Walters Art Gallery in Baltimore, MD; the University of Michigan in Ann Arbor, MI; the University of Notre Dame in Notre Dame, IN; Harvard University in Cambridge, MA; the Baltimore Museum of Art in Baltimore, MD; the Maryland Historical Society in Baltimore, MD; the New York Public Library in New York City; the Brooklyn Borough Hall in Brooklyn, NY; the City of Pittsburg in PA; the Yale University Art Gallery in New Haven, CT; the City of New York on Long Island; and the New York Historical Society in New York City.

Victor Brenner was one of a very few American artists who specialized in medals and other small bas relief works. He left only one well-regarded large scale work, an ornamental fountain titled *Song to Nature (Zeus and Persephone)*, located in Schenley Park, Pittsburgh, PA. Although he is well known to collectors of U.S. coins as designer of the Lincoln cent, his artistic reputation faded quickly following his death.

Brenner died from lung cancer in New York City on April 5, 1924.

Sources:
Glen B. Smedley, "The Works of Victor David Brenner – A Descriptive Listing," *The Numismatist* (reprint), 1983.
Who Was Who in American Art, vol. I, page 75; Davenport's Art Reference 2001/2002, page 284; Fielding's 1986, page 99; Mallett's, page 52; Dealer's Choice Biographical Encyclopedia of American Painters... page 171; Whistler House Museum of Art files.
Peter Kostoulakos, ISA — Fine Art Consultant.
Samuel Auerhaim, "Recollections of Victor D. Brenner," *The Numismatist*, January 1959. pp.27-28.
Frank Passic, "Find A Numismatic Grave," *Numismatist*, October 2006. pp.40-47.

James Earle Fraser

James Earle Fraser (November 4, 1876 – October 11, 1953) was born in Winona, Minnesota. His father was Thomas Alexander and mother Caroline West Fraser. He had one sister, Pearl. His father was a mechanical engineer employed by the Chicago-Milwaukee Railroad. During construction of the railroad from Mason City, Iowa, into the Black Hills of South Dakota, the family moved to the Dakota Territory. During their first year in the territory, the Frasers lived in a railroad boxcar. Native Americans were frequent visitors to the Frasers' camp. At night, James Fraser recalled, "We were surrounded by packs of wolves. Their mournful howling caused my spine to tingle and impressed upon me the lonely vastness of the West." At the age of eight, James started carving things out of stone from a nearby quarry. His father wanted him to be an engineer, but he received such praise from railroad officials about his art that his father finally relented. At the age of 15, James was sent to study at the Art Institute of Chicago.

Before he was 17, a model of one of his most celebrated works was completed. His *End of The Trail* statue showing a weary Indian slumped down over his rack-ribbed horse has been copied (some say "pirated") around the world. It is often regarded as the best-known sculpture in America.

After graduating from the Art Institute of Chicago, Fraser traveled to France where he studied under the French sculptor Jean Alexander Falguiere, attended Ecole'des Beaux Arts, the Julian Academy, and the Colarossi. Young Fraser exhibited his model "End of the Trail" in Paris in 1898, which won him the $1,000 prize sponsored by the American Art

Association and Rodman Wannamaker. It also attracted the attention of the world renowned artist, August Saint-Gaudens, who asked him to become his assistant. This initial contact led to a strong friendship, and Fraser became Saint-Gaudens' disciple.

The artist's four years with Augustus Saint-Gaudens shaped his future. From The Saint he gained inspiration, developed techniques and working habits that were to dignify his contributions. Saint-Gaudens gave his young protégé an important break when he recommended that Fraser do the bust of President Theodore Roosevelt. The great artist complained that he was too ill to comply with the President's request that he do the portrait.

At their first meeting in the East Room of the White House, the President said, "You are a much younger man than I expected, Mr. Fraser. It goes to show how merit must find its level, doesn't it? It can't be kept down. I asked Saint-Gaudens for the man who could do the job, with perfect confidence in his choice. The fact that he sent you proves that you are the man."

When Fraser had the bust set up in clay, he returned to Washington for the final sittings. Many felt that Roosevelt would not be able to sit still long enough to pose. "The President posed for me faithfully for two weeks, morning and afternoon, in the East Room," he wrote, "and though he frequently had to receive cabinet members and to attend to business with other officials, often we had two hours of uninterrupted time together."

From this time throughout his life, James Earle Fraser was never without commissions. After Saint-Gaudens' death in 1907, the artist took up residency in New York and established a studio in picturesque MacDougal Alley in Greenwich Village. He was one of the first to make artistically fashionable what was once a block of famous old carriage houses of New York aristocrats. Among the group of artists and writers who came here, several were to grow into national prominence, principally, Robert Henri, Gertrude Vanderbilt Whitney, Daniel Chester French, Albin Polasek, Anthony de Francisci, George Deforest Brush, Ernest Lawson, James Huneker, and the poet Edwin Arlington Robinson. Beginning in 1906 through 1911, Fraser was instructor in sculpture at the Art Students' League in New York City.

Apart from many large-scale works, Fraser was known as a gifted designer of medals. These included medals to honor Saint-Gaudens; Thomas Edison; the E. H. Harriman Safety Medal; the Medal of Award by the Academy of Arts and Letters; the Award Medal of the American Institute of Graphic Arts; American Committee for Relief of Devastated France medal; Yale University Howland Memorial Medal; Theodore Roosevelt Memorial Association Medal of Honor; and the Melville Medal for the American Society of Mechanical Engineers. Fraser further distinguished his career by designing two important military medals; the Victory Medal of World War I and the Navy Cross.

To most coin collectors, Fraser is best known for his Buffalo nickel design (1913) and collaboration with his wife, Laura Gardin Fraser, on the Oregon Trail commemorative half dollar. As a member of the Commission of Fine Arts, Fraser was dedicated to promoting the highest standards of quality for U. S. coinage, and he had significant influence over the Peace dollar and designs of many commemorative coins.

Sources:
Excerpted from a brief biography by Dean Krakel, Managing Director of the National Cowboy & Western Heritage Museum, Oklahoma City, OK.
The Columbia Electronic Encyclopedia Copyright © 1994, 2000, 2001, 2002 Columbia University Press. Licensed from Columbia University Press.
The Columbia Encyclopedia, Sixth Edition. Copyright © 2001 Columbia University Press.

Infoplease® Dictionary Copyright © 1999, 2000, 2001, 2002 Family Education Network.
Random House Webster's Unabridged Dictionary Copyright © 1991 by Random House, Inc. and in digital format as contained in Random House's Dictionary Database Copyright © 1997.
Archives of American Art, James Fraser papers.

Franklin MacVeagh

Franklin MacVeagh (November 22, 1837 – July 6, 1934) secretary of the treasury, third son and seventh child of Maj. John and Margaret Lincoln MacVeagh and younger brother of Isaac Wayne MacVeagh, was born near Phoenixville, Chester County, Pa. His mother was a distant cousin of Abraham Lincoln; his father, a prosperous farmer, hotel-keeper and local politician, was a great-great-grandson of Edmund MacVeagh, a native of Ireland, who was in Philadelphia about 1689.

Franklin graduated from Yale College in 1862. He spent the next two years in New York studying law at Columbia University, from which he received the degree of LL.B. in 1864, and reading in the office of Judge John Worth Edmonds. After practicing for a short time he was forced by ill health to seek rest. In 1866 he went to Chicago, where he became a member of a wholesale grocery firm. As he later explained, he abandoned the law to enter business for two reasons: "…first, to lead a life of pecuniary ease; and second, to have done with ill health" (*The Twenty Years' Record of the Yale Class of 1862*). He was soon able to buy out his partners' interests. The business survived the difficult periods of the panic of 1873 and the Chicago fire and became one of the largest of its kind in the Middle West. It was operated on the principle that with a proper selection of subordinates the continuous presence of the owner was not required.

MacVeagh traveled widely, spending long vacation periods in Europe, where he indulged his hobby of studying architecture. He was deeply interested in civic reform. After the great fire of 1874 he was one of the organizers and the first president of the Citizens' Association of Chicago, which successfully promoted the complete non-political reorganization of the fire department, the substitution of a strong and responsible city government for a hodgepodge of bureaus, and the enlargement of the water supply. He was actively connected with the Civil Service Reform League of Chicago and its vice-president, 1884-85; president of the Chicago Bureau of Charities, 1896-1904; and a trustee of the University of Chicago, 1901-13. Always inclined to non-partisanship, he left the Republican party in 1884 and was the Democratic candidate for United States senator ten years later; in 1896 he joined with other Democrats in opposing William Jennings Bryan's free silver policy, later drifting back to the Republican party; in 1928, however, he supported Alfred E. Smith for the presidency.

During the entire administration of President Taft, 1909–1913, MacVeagh was Secretary of the Treasury. He had had no real banking experience, though he had been a director of the Commercial National Bank of Chicago for twenty-nine years. He contributed little toward solving the problem of currency reform, leaving it to the national monetary commission. He supported recommendations for the creation of a central banking system for the rather naïve reason that it would prevent future panics. Nor was he influential in the tariff controversy, though he is sometimes credited with having suggested President Taft's policy of piecemeal revision downward. What he did contribute to the administration was a businesslike management of the treasury department and a spark of progressiveness in an otherwise conservative cabinet.

The customs service was rehabilitated following the report of a Congressional investigating committee which exposed fraud in the importation of sugar during preceding administrations. Antiquated regulations requiring payments to the treasury to be made in certain kinds of currency were modified for the convenience of the public. Other reorganizations were effected to promote efficiency and economy. MacVeagh tried to obtain a systematic compilation of the pension rolls and provision for the retirement of overage employees. He chafed under the existing appropriation methods, which gave the executive no real power in budget making. In his relations with the conservative leaders of Congress he was more independent than most of his predecessors. As Taft is said to have remarked, he was "…a little tinged with insurgent doctrines." Against Taft's wishes he supported the candidacy of Senator Albert J. Beveridge for reelection in 1910. Throughout the presidential campaign of 1912, however, he loyally supported Taft against Theodore Roosevelt.

At the time of his administration MacVeagh was described as being short in stature, slender, white-haired, blue-eyed, and always well groomed. He was married on Oct. 2, 1866, to Emily Eames of Chicago. One son, Eames MacVeagh, survived him; four other children died in infancy or early childhood. His death was caused by myocarditis and pneumonia, and he was buried in Graceland Cemetery, Chicago.

A number of articles and addresses by him were published, among them "A Program of Municipal Reform" (*American Journal of Sociology,* March 1896); "Departmental Economy" (*Independent,* Dec. 22, 1910); "Civil Service Pensions" (*Annals of the American Academy of Political and Social Science,* July 1911); "Banking and Currency Reform" (*Journal of Political Economy,* December 1911); "President Taft and the Roosevelt Policies" (*Outlook,* May 18, 1912).

Sources:
Edward Conrad Smith, "Franklin MacVeagh." *Dictionary of American Biography, Supplements 1-2: To 1940.* American Council of Learned Societies, 1944-1958. Reproduced in History Resource Center. Farmington Hills, MI: Gale Group.
Who's Who in America, 1932-33; *N. Y. Times,* July 7, 1934;
A. W. Butt, *Taft and Roosevelt, the Intimate Letters of Archie Butt* (2 vols., 1930);
The Twenty Years' Record of the Yale Class of 1862 (1884); Yale Univ., *Obit. Record of Grads.* (1935);
Paul Gilbert and C. L. Bryson, *Chicago and Its Makers* (1929);
H. F. Pringle, *The Life and Times of Wm. Howard Taft* (2 vols., 1939);
The Commercial and Financial Chronicle, 1909-13, *passim;*
Current Literature, Feb. 1911;
Annual Report of the Secretary of the Treasury on the State of the Finances for the years 1909-12;
Chicago News, July 7, 10, 1934;
Chicago Tribune, July 7, 1934.

Bibliography

U.S. mint records for the period 1909-1915 are incomplete condition: many items present in the archives in 1961 cannot be located. Fortunately, the General Services Administration microfilmed several hundred documents relating to the Buffalo nickel in 1961. This microfilm (#T620) forms the backbone of virtually all research efforts on this coin. Part of the material concerning the Lincoln cent was consolidated into one file at the National Archives, however it is obvious that much material is missing.

Alexander, David T., ed., Thomas K. DeLorey technical ed. *Coin World Comprehensive Catalog & Encyclopedia of United States Coins*. World Almanac imprint of Pharos Books. New York. 1990.

American Bison Society, scrapbooks. Bronx Zoo Library. Wildlife Conservation Society Archives.

American Numismatic Association. ANA Research Library, 818 N Cascade Ave., Colorado Springs, CO 80903.
Various extracts from The Numismatist and American Journal of Numismatics.

American Numismatic Society. New York, NY.

Anderson, B. Wyle. "The Economic Prophesies of George Evan Roberts." *Annals of Iowa 1976*, Volume 43, No. 5, pp.362-370.

Andrew, Abram Piatt, (Jr.); papers. Archive of the personal papers and letters of A. Piatt Andrew, Jr. Privately held. Referenced as [*Andrew*].

Annual Reports of the Director of the Mint, 1908-1915. Annual volumes with most data reported by fiscal year. United States Government Printing Office.

Ashbrook, William Albert. *A Line A Day for Forty Odd Years; the Diaries of William A. Ashbrook*. Johnstown, Ohio, 1939. Ashland University Archives, Ashland, OH 44805. Microfilm, 1 reel. Personal diaries of Congressman Ashbrook privately printed. [*Ashbrook*]

Beaux, Cecilia; papers. Archives of American Art, Smithsonian Institution, 7500 9th Street, NW, Suite 2200, Washington DC 20560.

Benedict, Burton. *The Anthropology of World's Fairs: San Francisco's Panama Pacific International Exposition of 1915*. Scholar Press, Berkeley, CA 1983

Bowers, Q. David. *Commemorative Coins of the United States: A Complete Encyclopedia*. Bowers and Merena Galleries, Inc., Wolfeboro, NH: 1991.

Breen, Walter H. *Walter Breen's Complete Encyclopedia of U.S. and Colonial Coins*. F.C.I. Press/Doubleday, New York: 1988.

Bridges, William. *Gathering of Animals: an Unconventional History of the New York Zoological Park Society*. New York Zoological Society, Harper: 1974.

Brown, Dee. *Bury My Heart At Wounded Knee: An Indian History of the American West*. Holt, Reinhardt & Winston; New York:1971.

Burdette, Roger W. *Renaissance of American Coinage 1916-1921*. Seneca Mill Press LLC. September 2005.

— *Renaissance of American Coinage 1905-1908*. Seneca Mill Press LLC. May 2006.

— "Designer of Maine Centennial Commemorative Identified," *Coin World Magazine*, April 26 and May 2, 2003.

— *Examination and Report on Proof One-Cent Coins Minted 1909–1916*, Version 1.0. Whitman Publishing LLC. June 26, 2006. Private analysis.

Central Files, Office of the Director of the Mint. National Archives and Records Administration, College Park, MD. Record Group 104, entry UD, box 81, folder 1.

Commission of Fine Arts. National Archives and Records Administration (NARA-DC), Washington, DC. Record Group 66. [*CFA. NARA-DC*]

Comparette, Thomas Louis, ed. *Catalogue of Coins, Tokens and Medals In the Numismatic Collection of the Mint of the United States at Philadelphia, PA*. Third edition. Government Printing Office, Washington, DC: 1914.

Cortelyou, George B.; papers. Library of Congress, Manuscript Division. Washington, DC. [*Cortelyou*]

Daily Coinage January 1, 1911 to June 30, 1915. National Archives and Records Administration, College Park, MD. Record Group 104, entry 273.

Dalton, Kathleen. *Theodore Roosevelt: A Strenuous Life*. Alfred Knopf, New York. 2002.

Department of the Treasury, United States Mint, 809 Ninth Street, NW Washington DC. Ms. Maria Goodwin, historian.

Elmhirst, Dorothy Whitney Straight; papers. Division of Rare and Manuscript Collections, collection #3725, box 2, folder 20. Kroch Library, Cornell University Library. Ithaca, NY

Failor, Michael M. and Eleonora Hayden, *Medals of the United States Mint Issued for Public Sale*. Department of the Treasury, U.S. Government Printing Office. Revised: 1972.

Free Library of Philadelphia, The. Print and Picture Collection, 1901 Vine Street, Philadelphia, PA 19103-1198.

Gray, Andrew. "The American Field Service." *American Heritage Magazine*, December 1974.

Hayden, E. Parker and Andrew L. Gray, eds. *Beauport Chronicle: The Letters of Henry Davis Sleeper to Abram Piatt Andrew, Jr. 1906-1915*. Historic New England, Boston. 2005.

Heckscher, August. *Woodrow Wilson*. Charles Scribner's Sons, New York, 1991.

Kohler, Sue A. *The Commission of Fine Arts: A Brief History 1910 – 1995*. The Commission of Fine Arts, The National Building Museum, Suite 312, 441 F Street, NW, Washington, DC 20001: 1995.

Korbley, Charles A; papers. Indiana University, Lilly Library, Manuscripts Department.

Kunz, George F.; papers. American Museum of Natural History, Library Services Department, New York, NY. "Coinage" file.

Judd, J. Hewitt. *United States Pattern, Experimental and Trial Pieces*. 3rd Edition. Whitman Publishing Company: 1965.

— *United States Pattern Coin, Experimental and Trial Pieces*. 8th Edition. Q. David Bowers, ed. Whitman Publishing Company: 2003.

Lange, David W. *The Complete Guide to Buffalo Nickels*. Third edition. DLRC Press, LLC. Virginia Beach, VA: 2006.

— *The Complete Guide to Lincoln Cents*. Bowers and Merena Galleries, Inc, Wolfeboro, NH: 1996; 1999.

Leach, Frank A. *Recollections of a Newspaper Man – A Record of Life and Events in California*. Samuel Levinson pub., San Francisco, California. 1917. Reprinted by Beekman Publishers, New York: 1974. Reprinted by Bowers and Merena Galleries, Inc., 1982.
Interesting account of life in California in the late nineteenth century. The final chapter reviews the author's work as mint director. A useful resource although it includes many errors and personal distortions particularly involving the Mint Bureau.

MacVeagh Franklin, papers. Library of Congress, Manuscript Division. Washington, DC. Referenced as *MacVeagh; LOC*.
Secretary of the Treasury Franklin MacVeagh's papers include five folders of material on the Bureau of Engraving and Printing (including material on washing paper currency which carries through to William G. McAdoo's papers) but none on the U. S. Mint. Most of his press copy books from 1909 to 1912 are not in the LOC collection; some may be stored in NARA RG-56 but have not been indexed.

Moore, Charles; papers. Archives of American Art, Smithsonian Institution, 7500 9th Street, NW, Suite 2200, Washington DC 20560. Microfilm reels 1887 – 1889.

Moore, Charles; papers (1901-1940). University of Michigan Bentley Library. Ann Arbor Michigan.

Morison, Etling E. ed, John H. Blum, Alfred D. Chandler. *The Letters of Theodore Roosevelt*. Harvard University Press, Cambridge, Massachusetts: 1952.

Morris, Edmund. *The Rise of Theodore Roosevelt*. Coward, McCann & Geoghegan, New York: 1979.

— *Theodore Rex*. Random House, Inc., New York: 2001.

Museum of San Francisco, 945 Taraval Street, San Francisco, CA 94116.

National City Bank. *In Memory of George Evan Roberts 1857-1948*. New York, NY: 1948. Booklet, 26p.

National Cowboy & Western Heritage Museum, Oklahoma City, OK. *James Earle Fraser and Laura Gardin Fraser Studio Collection*.

Philadelphia City Archives, The. Suite 150, 3101 Market Street, Philadelphia, Pennsylvania 19104.

Pollock, Andrew W. III. *United States Patterns and Related Issues*. Bowers and Merena Galleries, Inc, Wolfeboro, NH: 1994.

Raymond, Wayte, ed. "United States Proof Coins." *The Coin Collector's Journal*, January/February 1950. pp.3-11.

Reichenberger, Jeffrey M., *Charter Legacy: Numismatic Chronicle from the Diaries of William A. Ashbrook, 1905 – 1920*. Unpublished manuscript, 2007.

Roosevelt, Theodore; papers. Library of Congress, Manuscript Division. Washington, DC. Referenced as *Roosevelt: LOC*.

Roosevelt, Theodore; papers. Harvard University Library, Manuscript Collection. Boston, MA. Referenced as; *Roosevelt: Harvard*.

Roberts, George Evan; papers. Iowa Historical Society. Manuscript and special collections.

Rydell, Robert W. *All the World's a Fair: Visions of Empire at American International Expositions, 1876-1916*. The University of Chicago Press, Chicago, IL. 1984.

Saint-Gaudens, Augustus; papers. Dartmouth College, Rauner Special Collections manuscript. Referenced as *Dartmouth: box no.; folder no.*
Letters and personal papers of Augustus Saint-Gaudens and member of this family. Portions missing due to destruction in 1904 studio fire. Many letters to and from Theodore Roosevelt are duplicated in the *Theodore Roosevelt papers* in the Library of Congress collection. Includes original drawings of coin designs.

Saint-Gaudens, Augustus; papers. Library of Congress, Manuscript Division. Washington, DC. Referenced as *Dartmouth: reel no.; frame no.*
Microfilm copy of the Dartmouth collection.

San Francisco Memories. 4104 24th Street #575, San Francisco, CA 94114

Seymour, James W. D., ed. *Friends of France, 1914-1917*. Houghton Mifflin Company, The Riverside Press Cambridge, Massachusetts: 1920.

Sleeper, Henry Davis. *Beauport Chronicle: The Intimate Letters of Henry Davis Sleeper to Abram Piatt Andrew, Jr*. E. Parker Hayden and Andrew Gray, ed. Society for Preservation of New England Antiquities: 1991.

Smithsonian Institution, Museum of American History, National Numismatic Collection, Washington, DC. Richard Doty, PhD, Curator of Numismatics.
Examination of pattern coins, models and related materials 1909-1915. Photos of the coins provided by Douglas Mudd, National Numismatic Collection.

Statistical Tables for the Annual Report, 1915-1924. National Archives and Records Administration, College Park, MD. Record Group 104, entry 253, box 1, folder 1.

Swiatek, Anthony and Walter Breen. *Silver and Gold Commemorative Coins*. New York: Arco publishing Co., Inc. 1981.

Taft, William Howard, papers. Library of Congress, Manuscript Division. Washington, DC. *Referenced as* [*Taft, LOC*].
Taft kept meticulous, well organized files on thousands of subjects. The Mint-related files are very sparse and contain little of relevance to the current work. The bulk of his papers reveal only one letter sent by the President to Fraser: a form letter inviting Fraser to participate in the Rostron medal competition. There are no letters to Brenner. Taft's secretary generally passed letters relating to coinage directly to secretary MacVeagh.

Taxay, Don, ed. *The Comprehensive Catalog and Encyclopedia of United States Coins*. Scott publishing Co. New York: 1971.

— *The U.S. Mint and Coinage*. Arco Publishing Co. Inc., New York: 1966.

— *An Illustrated History of U. S. Commemorative Coinage*. Arco Publishing Co. Inc., New York: 1967.

Todd, Frank Morton. *The Story of the Exposition, San Francisco – Panama Pacific International Exposition, 1915*. G.P. Putnam's Sons: New York. 1921.

United States Mint. National Archives and Records Administration, Philadelphia, PA, Washington, DC, College Park MD, San Bruno, CA.

Vermeule, Cornelius C. *Numismatic Art in America – Aesthetics of the United States Coinage*. Belknap Press of Harvard University Press, Cambridge, MA: 1971.

Weinman, Adolph A., papers. Smithsonian Institution Archives of American Art. Referenced as *Weinman; AAA*.
Microfilm plus 10 boxes of manuscript and photos from Weinman's albums.

Wels, Susan. "Spheres of Influence: The Role of Women at the Chicago World's Columbian Exposition of 1893 and the San Francisco Panama Pacific International Exposition of 1915." San Francisco State University, 1997.

Wexler, John., Ron Pope, Kevin Flynn. *The Authoritative Reference on Buffalo Nickels*. Second Edition. Zyrus Press, Inc. Irvine, CA. 2007.

Wexler, John and Kevin Flynn. *The Authoritative Reference on Lincoln Cents*. KCK Press, PO Box 538, Rancocas, NJ. 1996.

Wheatley, Todd. "The Panama Canal Service Medal – The 'Junk' Medal." *The Medal Collector*, November 1983.

Index

Act of 1873. 17
Act of 1890. 17
Acton, Thomas. 104.
Adams-Woodin pattern book. 111-112.
Ado-Ete. 221.
Aitken, Robert I. 161; PPIE coin 267, 270-276, 284, 287-290, 303, 307, 314-316; PPIE medal 269, 274, 292-293, 297-299, 302, 316-318.
American Numismatic Association (ANA). 21, 65, 147, 322, 330, 339; auction 236.
American Numismatic Society (ANS). 50, 70, 167, 213, 215, 271, 340.
Anderson, Giles R. 77-78, 83-86.
Anderson, Harriet (Hettie) Engenia. 218
Andrew, Abram Piatt, Jr. 81-83, 88, 91.
Ashbrook, William. 57, 137-138, 146-148, 150-152.
Arabic numerals. 96, 278.
Assay Commission. 99, 101, 110, 147, 205, 292-293, 308, 324-325.
Atlantic fleet medal. 26, 311.

Bailey, Robert C. 152-153, 176.
Barber, Charles E. 17, 21, 23-26, 45, 87, 322-334; cent 36-37, 39-40, 42-43, 48-49; avoids association w/cent 44-45; blacksmith 162; Buffalo nickel 163-171, 183, 194-198, 200-201, 203-204, 206, 235, 246-248, 251-257; Janvier lathe 234; medal turn patterns 76-77; metallurgical tests 134, 138-139, 144; pattern definition 99; pattern cents 74-79; pattern hubs 104-111, list 112-131; proof cents 77; PPIE 267, 274-279; 281-283, 286-288, 291, 294-295, 311-316; PPIE medal 295-296, 303; removes cent initials 54-64, 74-75; stella 131; supports Brenner 43-44, 46-47.

Barnum Circus Management. 222.
Belden, Bauman L. 104.
Berger, Anthony. 30-31.
Big Tree. see Ado-Ete.
Bigelow, William Sturgis. 16, 20-21, 44, 56, 162.
Black Diamond. 222-224.
Bombay Mint. 142.
Brand, Virgil M. 62-63 78, 86-87.
Brandt Cashier Co. 62-63, 180.
Brenner, Victor D. 18, 219, 237, 257, 260, 289; Barber's objections 41, 43-44, 46-47, 60; bio 336-337; Canal medal 23-24; cancer 70; cent designs 25-27, 29-39, 48-49, 62; copies French coins 31-33, 36-37; half dollar 35; hubs 43-48; initials 40, 42, 55-57, 60-61, 65-67, 74-75, 81; Lincoln photo 30-31; pattern cents 73-77; proof cents 77-81; sculpture 70; subsidiary silver coins 34, 69, 70.
Brinton, Jasper Yates. 104.
Buffalo nickel. Native American models 218-222; bison 222-225.
Buckley, Matthew J. 198.
Bulkley, Robert J. 137, 139-140, 142, 174, 178.
Bureau of Engraving and Printing (BEP). 93, 175, 181, 265, 293, 299-302, 309.
Butts, Archibald. 190

Calder, Sterling. 265-266.
Calder, William M. 156.
Carpenter. C. U. 191, 196, 201-202, 207.
Carpenter, Frederick (Fred) W. 83, 86.
Carpenter, Virginia. 91.
cent. 9, 10, 97, 163, 168-169, 174, 215, 237, 259-260; alloy experiments 134-138, 142; approval 50, 59; Bren-

ner's name on 38-42, 74-75; design competition 24-27; design cost 35; die radius 41; final reverse 38; French coin copied 32, 37; initials added 75; Lincoln's hair 29-30; matte proofs 76-77, 249; old designs 16-17; patterns destroyed 1909 73, #1, 74, #2, 76, #3, 76, lead 73, medal-turn 76-77, 242; Saint-Gaudens' designs 19-20; vending machine use 133, 182-183, 185, 197, 200.
Chapman, Henry. 100, 111, 155-158, 208, 330-331.
"Chapman proofs." 330-332.
Chapman, S. H. 44, 100.
coinage renaissance. 10, 13, 206.
Colombia. 22.
Columbia. figure of 36, 39, 281, 311, 313-314.
Commission of Fine Arts. 162, 329, 331, 335; nickel 170, 186-189, 192, 205, 225, 260; PPIE 267-269, 277, 281, 284, 296, 317.
Compagnie Universelle du Canal Interoceanique. 22-23.
Comparette, Thomas Louis. 108, 139, 149, Treasurer's gold coins 155-159; coins to Mitchelson collection 323-331.
Conkling, Roscoe. 104.
Connecticut. 55, 57, 83.
Connecticut State Library. *See Mitchelson Collection.*
correspondence handling, mint. 82.
Cortelyou, George B. 23, 36, 74, 81, 164.
Cox, Kenyon. 148, 161, 188-189, 205, 239.

Denver Mint. 52, 90, 326, 331; cents 68-69; nickels 195, 248-249, 252, 257, 260.
Department of Official Coins and Medals. 265, 299-300, 302, 304.
design competition. 1891 17; cent 25; nickel 166, 170-172, 175; Rostron medal, 189..
Dewey, Frederick P. 158, 253, 267, 272-282, 284, 286, 288-289, 303, 308, 313, 321.
double eagle. 13, 15, 17, 20, 22, 46, 56-57, 60-61, 79, 85, 87, 93, 105, 110, 112, 128-130, 163, 167, 218, 234, 260, 295; J-1773 pattern 130-131; in Treasurer's hoard 146-147, 156-157; PPIE blanks 319; pyx 328-329.
Durkee, Rodney. 305, 309.

E Pluribus Unum. on Buffalo nickel 173, 229, 232-233, 240, 242, 244, 246-247; on cent 32, 37; PPIE 281, 286, 307, 314; on Washington five cent 95-96.
eagles. Remaining from treasurer destroyed 159.
Edwards, John H. 99, 147-148.
Einstein, Edwin. 104.
Elder, Thomas L. 100, 103, 110-111, 157
Ellison-McCartney, William G. 104, 135.
End of the Trail. 219, 255, 264-265, 333.
experimental pieces. *See patterns.*

Farmers and Mechanics' National Bank of Philadelphia. 97.
Federal Reserve note. 161.
fin. *defect* 163.
flying eagle cent. 16
Ford Motor Company. 176-177, 263.

four dollar stella. 104; designs 119, 123.
Fraser, James E. 18, 148, 169, 208, 210, 251; Belgian coin design 168; bio 337-338; coinage legacy 225-226; Commission of Fine Arts 186-188, 205; design approach 166, 168-175, 161-163, 216, 227-228; design changes 253-257, 260; electrotypes 234-241; Hobbs interference 183-185, 190-193, 195-197, 199-205; Kenyon Cox letter 206-207; Lincoln cent design 70-71, 98, 169, 173, 188; meets Andrew 164-165; mint support 64, 162, 194; mint to pay for electros 170; nickel designs 229-233; nickel design accepted 194; nickel introduced 211-212; PPIE 271-272, 284, 315, 322; praises Barber 197-198, 254; President Taft 188-189; Rostron medal 189.
Freed, Rhine H. 106, 112, 253.
French, Daniel C. 170, 186-187, 189, 192, 200, 205, 211, 277, 334, 339.

Gilbert, Cass. 186-187.
Gilded Age. 15, 18.
Gobrecht, Christian. 113.
Godard, George S. 324, 326-331.
Goethals, George. 22, 294-295, 307-308.
Goloid dollar. 98, 204, 110.
Government Exhibition Board.
Great White Fleet. *see Atlantic Fleet.*
Griffin (Special Agent). 103.
Guerin, Jules. 263.

half cent. 137-138, 141-142.
Hall, Henry. 326-328, 329, 330-331.
Hagen, Mark. 112.
Hamlin, Charles S. 299
Harbaugh, Charles A. 296, 304-305, 309-311.
Hardwick, Thomas W. 297.
Hart, Samuel E. 194, 197, 200-201, 244.
Haseltine, John. 100-104, 108-111.
Haverty, John B. 104.
Hayes, Rutherford B. 104, 110.
Hering, Henry. 18, 94, 166.
Hewitt, Clifford. 296, 301.
Hill reducing lathe. 233.
Hornaday, William T. 217-218, 227.
Huddelson, H. P. 302.

Idler, William. 101, 103.
In God We Trust. 16, added to Lincoln cent 49-52, 59, 76; on Washington nickel 96-97; omitted from Buffalo nickel 170; on pattern hubs 114, 116-118, 125; Coinage Act of 1912 138; on PPIE 274, 278, 284, 307, 313.
Iron Hail. *see Wasu Maza.*
Iron Tail. *see Sinte Maza.*
Ishiheo Nishes. 220-221.
Isthmian Canal Commission. 22-23.

Janvier reducing lathe. 23, 45, 64, 75, 163, 233-234.

Kahn, Julius. 268, 293, 296-297, 307-308, 316.

Keck, Charles. 18, 267, 269-270, 272-274, 276, 284-286, 288-290, 303, 313.
Kelham, George W. 262.
Kellogg & Co. 273.
Kelly, Margaret Valentine. 82, 90, 174.
Kopp, Arthur William. 147-148, 150-151.
Korbley, Charles A. 139-140.
Kunz, George F. 212-213, 215.

Lambert, Albert Leslie. 90, 92.
Leach, Edwin R. 23.
Leach, Frank A. 21, 26, 29-30, 32, 35-37, 39, 42-45, 48-50, 54-55, 61-62, 65, 81-82, 93, 99, 104, 144, 147; Buffalo nickel 161; cent patterns destroyed 73-74, 76; cent requests 49, 53; 81-82, 87; praise for Barber 22, 44; religious motto added 48-49; San Francisco superintendent 249, 256-257; visits Oakland CA 23, 67; Washington on coin 23, 26-27, 93-94, 97-98, 166.
Lee, Blair. 299.
Lewis, David J. 299.
Liberty Bell. 263.
Linderman, Henry R. 103-105, 110, 112.
Lincoln, Abraham. 15-16, 20, 24-25, 29-31, 989, 219, 337.
Lincoln half dollar. 20, 25, 33, 35-36.
Lincoln nickel. 21
Loeb, William. 21.
Lockheed Aircraft Co. 264
Longacre, James B. 17, 25, 52, 56, 113, 118, 127.
Longman, Evelyn. 189, 267, 269-270, 272-276, 279-280, 284, 303, 313.
Loughead, Alan H and Malcolm. 264.
Low, Lyman H. 53, 86-87, 100.

MacMonnies, Frederick William. 18.
Malburn, William P. 10, 267, 271-273, 277-279, 282, 284-285, 288, 318, 321.
Manning, James H. 101-103, 110-111.
Manship, Paul. 161, 267, 269-270, 272-274, 276, 280-285, 311.
Marion National Bank. 97.
McAdoo, William G. nickel 215, 255; PPIE 267-269, 271-272, 276-284, 287-288, 311, 313-314, 321,
McClung, Lee. Gold coins 147-148, 150-155, 326; role in Andrew resignation 175; Washington nickels 97.
McCulloch, J. C. 97.
McKinley gold dollar. 267, 326.
McKinley, William. 17, 164.
medal commissions. Mint staff doing 87-88.
Medallic Art Company. 83, 87-89, 200, 229, 276, 290.
Mehl, B. Max. 100, 111.
Miller, Adolph C. 271, 297-300, 317.
Miller, Josquin. 317
Millet, Francis (Frank) D. 19, 23-24, 189.
mint contingency fund. For mint collection 109; to buy back half unions 110.
missing mint mark, PPIE. 290-291.
Mitchelson, Joseph C., collection. 324-326, 328-330.

Moore, Charles. 260.
Moore, Charles C. 306-308, 310.
Morgan, George T. 26, 45, 56, 61, 75, 87, 91, 102, 105, 111-112, 114-119, 125-126, 130-131, 212, 234, 268, 313-315, 323-325.
Muir, Charles S. 299-300.

Napier weighing machine. 89
National Archives and Records Administration (NARA). 10; mint files split 83.
New Orleans. 57, 90, 261-262.
Norton, Charles D. 175; role in removal of initials from cent 50, 54-55, 58-61, 65, 67, 74.
Norton, Eliot. 31

O'Reilly, Mary M. 272, 312.
Oklahoma. 224, 255.

Pacific Exposition Company. 261-261, 265, 268, 289, 291, 298, 300, 302-305, 308, 310-311, 317-318.
Panama Canal. 21-22; medal 22-24; PPIE 261, 263, 307, 311, 317.
Panama-Pacific International Exposition (PPIE). 9, 17-19, 256, 263-268, 312; Barber-best designs by 269; coin delivery 281, 284, 291; coins 269-271, 274-276, 278, 281, 290; coin sales 308; design 282, 291; die delivery 294; Fraser-PPIE sculpture 256; legislation 270, 274; medal 295-300; souvenirs 308; stamps 265-266;
patterns. cent designs 73-77; destroyed by mint 112-121; electrotypes 233-240; nickel designs 240-247; legality 102-104, 108.
Peace dollar xiii, 75, 87, 138, 163, 185, 226, 260, 328, 331, 334.
pester the mint. 51, 73.
planchet experiments. 138-146.
planchet feeding, automatic. 90.
Pratt, Bela Lyon. 15-16, 18-22, 44, 50, 77, 83, 93-94, 161, 164, 217, 219, 227, 230, 242, 257, 289; design fee 29, 34-35, 163; initials on coin 56, 58-59, 61; PPIE 269.
Preston, Robert E. 23, 43-47, 53, 58-63, 82, 85, 109.
proof dollars, 1921. 330-332.
proofs. cent 77-79; nickel 248-249.
pyx. 157, 325-326.

railway strike. 92.
reducing lathe. 23,45,75,163,233.
reduction in force. 89-92
Ricketts Circus, medal. 88.
Rigg, Edward. 138-139, 142.
Roberts, George Evan. 69-70, 104, 109, 133; alloy experiments 134-135, 138-139, 147; Buffalo nickel108, 162, 164-171, 173-174, 179-181, 183184, 186-190, 192-196, 198-199, 203-106, 208-210, 213, 216, 219, 228, 235, 241-242, 250, 255, 267, Type II 253-254; nickel defects 252-253, 256-257; opinion of Lincoln cent 70-71, 98, 174; PPIE 267-271, 275-276, 284, 287, 293, 295-297, 316, 323; treasurer's gold 148-155; Washington nickel patterns saved 97-98.

Roman numerals. 276.
Roosevelt, Franklin D. 236, 333.
Roosevelt, Theodore. opinion of coinage 19, 15, 17-19, 42-43, 82, 163-164, 166, 189, 234; canal medal 22, 24-26, 94; cent 21,30-31, 35, 38, 40, 42; new designs 19-21, 93; pattern coin sale 99, 104, 110; PPIE 263.
Rostron, Arthur H. 189, 345.
Royal Mint, London. 104, 134-135, 138, 142, 146.

Saint-Gaudens, Augusta "Gussie." 18, 35.
Saint-Gaudens, Augustus Louis. ix-x, xiii-xiv, 15, 17-22, 30, 34-35, 38, 44-45, 47, 56-59, 61, 73, 78, 82, 85, 87, 93-94, 105, 110, 112, 128-131, 147-149, 156-157, 159, 162-163, 166-167, 169-170, 173, 185, 189, 215, 218, 225, 227-228, 230, 233-234, 255, 257, 260, 289, 322, 324, 329, 333-334, 339; cent 20.
San Francisco Mint. 81, 90, 256-258; cent 51-53, 56, 59, 68-69; Leach 23; nickel 195, 210, 248-249, 253; PPIE 9, 255, 261-263, 265-266, 272-274, 277, 283, 286, 288, 290-297, 303-304, 306, 312, 315, 317, 319, 322-323, 325-326, 339, $50 gold striking 306-308.
scrap metal. use 23.
Shaw, Leslie Mortier. 19-20, 164, 336.
silver subsidiary coins. 10, 17, 34, 54, 162, 236, 267, 321-322; French 32, proofs 248.
Silz, August. 224.
Sinte Maza. 220-221.
Snowden, Archibald Loudon. 100, 108-109, 110-111.
Snowden, James Ross. 99.
Sousa, John Phillip. 264
standing eagle. 22,123.
sunk relief. 15, 20, 23, 44, 94.

Taft, William Howard. Administration 15, 21,54-55, 81, 110, 164-165, 175-176, 189; Anderson complaint 83; approves cent 50, 59, 76; inauguration 42-43; Buffalo nickel 166, 188, 208-211, 213, 248, 251; PPIE site 262.
Teichman, Saul. 10.112.
terra incognito. 9.
three cent. 137-138, 140-141, 143-144, 146.
Thompson, J. Whittaker. 101-103, 110.
Thompson, W. U. 158.
Tiffany & Co. 88.
Two Moons. *see Ishiheo Niches.*

Uhlhorn coin press. 301

Walker, Stephen A. 103.
Wanamaker Prize. 255.
Wass, Molitor & Company. 273.
Washington Masonic Monument. 93.
Washington nickel. 26, 93-98, 106, 180, 314.
Wazu Maza. 218.
Weil, Henri. Deitsch Bros. 45, 87; competition complaint 83; nickel reductions 192-193, 228, 275; PPIE coins 297.
Weinman, Adolph A. 19, 66, 69, 161, 189, 226, 260; PPIE 270-271.
Weiss, Oscar K. 97.
Wilmeth, James L. 293, 295, 297, 299, 316.
Wilson, Woodrow. 176,189, 263, 272, 279.
Woodin, William H. 89, 97, 100, 105-112.
Woolley, Robert W. 70, 259, 267, 284, 288-291, 293, 303, 307, 311, 320, 332.
Works, John D. 146.

Zerbe, Farran. 65,89,324,330; mint practices 100, 109-111; PPIE 265, 268, 280, 293, 299-311; Treasury opinion of 304.
"Zerbe proofs." 325, 330-332.